BITTER FRUIT

BITTER FRUIT

The Politics of

Black-Korean

Conflict in

New York City

CLAIRE JEAN KIM

Yale University Press

New Haven / London

Published with assistance from the Kingsley Trust Association Publication Fund established by the Scroll and Key Society of Yale College.

Designed by Mary Valencia. Set in Palatino and Helvetica type by Keystone Typesetting, Inc.
Printed in the United States of America by Sheridan Books, Chelsea, Michigan.

Library of Congress Cataloging-in-Publication Data
Kim, Claire Jean.
    Bitter fruit : the politics of Black-Korean conflict in New York City / Clair Jean Kim.
        p. cm.
    Includes bibliographical references and index.
    ISBN 0-300-07406-9 (alk. paper)
    1. Afro-Americans—New York (State)—New York—Rela-tions with Korean Americans.   2. Afro-Americans—New York (State)—New York—Politics and government—20th century.   3. Black nationalism—New York (State)—New York.   4. Korean Americans—New York (State)—New York—Politics and government—20th century.   5. Afro-Americans—New York (State)—New York—Economic con-ditions—20th century.   6. Korean Americans—New York (State)—New York—Economic conditions—20th cen-tury.   7. New York (N.Y.)—Race relations.   8. New York (N.Y.)—Politics and government—1951–   .   I. Title.
    F128.9N4 K56 2000
    9747'.100496073—dc21   00-035174

A catalogue record for this book is available from the British Library.

10 9 8 7 6 5 4 3 2 1

To my parents:

Jeung A. Kim,

Young C. Kim,

and

Joseph A. Brackett

CONTENTS

ACKNOWLEDGMENTS

This book began as a dissertation written for the Department of Political Science at Yale University. I had the good fortune there to have three committee members who are inspirational scholars and teachers as well as terrific people: Adolph Reed Jr., James C. Scott, and Rogers M. Smith. Each of them has significantly influenced my work, my view of the world, and my way of being in the profession. I cannot repay these debts, but I do wish to acknowledge them here. I am also grateful to the other Yale faculty members who gave me encouragement and support while I was writing the dissertation, including Ian Shapiro, Douglas Rae, David Plotke, and Micaela di Leonardo. Roger Waldinger, Stephen Steinberg, and Frances Fox Piven also generously assisted me in thinking through the project at different points. My thanks, too, to Ira Katznelson, whose gentle but rigorous criticism compelled me to question my assumptions and think more clearly about my dissertation project.

I completed the dissertation and turned it into a book manuscript while teaching at University of California, Irvine. I am grateful to my colleagues at UCI for the support, advice, and encouragement they gave me during this process. Russell Dalton, chair of the Department of Politics and Society, and R. Bin Wong, director of the Asian American Studies Program, arranged time off from teaching for me, and Bernard Grofman and Karen Leonard read and critiqued the entire dissertation. Special thanks to Dorothy Solinger for her insightful comments on my work and for teaching me by example about professional integrity and achievement. Cheryl Larsson from Social Sciences Computing Services provided assistance with graphics and more. I would also like to thank John Covell at Yale University Press for his guidance and support.

By rights, my husband, Michael I. Katz, should be mentioned on the title page. Fortunately for me, he understands the arbitrariness of academic conventions. He is my most unforgiving critic, my biggest fan, my best friend, and a constant rebuke to my cynicism about human nature. He knows this book is as much his as it is mine.

My research was supported in part by grants from the American Association of University Women, the Institute for Intercultural Studies, and the Yale Department of Afro-American Studies.

A NOTE ON TERMINOLOGY

Throughout the book, I use the term "Black" inclusively, to refer to both African Americans and immigrants from Haiti and other Caribbean nations. Where the information is relevant, I specify particular national origin / ethnic groups within the Black community (for example, Haitians). I capitalize the word "Black" in my own writing but leave intact original materials that use the lower-case form. I often use the terms "Haitians" and "Koreans" rather than "Haitian Americans" and "Korean Americans" in order to emphasize the liminal political status of these recent immigrants and / or their self-identification with their countries of origin, although I do use the latter set of terms when referring to 1.5- or second-generation populations.

I know better than to try to suggest an authoritative definition of the phrase "Black nationalism." I use it in the most generic sense, to refer to a perspective that views Black people as an immanent nation living under White domination. (See Chapter 3 for further elaboration.) I typologize different varieties of "Black nationalism" only when these distinctions bear directly upon my analysis. Finally, I characterize the Black nationalist groups I am studying as "radical" insofar as they proffer a fundamental, sometimes even revolutionary, critique of racism in American society (as opposed to more "moderate" integrationists who are sanguine about the possibility of constructive reform within existing structures). I am aware that all of these terms are ambiguous and highly contested. My aim, therefore, is not to define them once and for all but merely to clarify how I am using them in this book.

I engaged in only minimal editing of the interviews excerpted throughout the text. I removed repetitive phrases and stray words but did not "clean up" the quotes to the degree that many authors do. As a result, the quotes are sometimes not as readable as they could be, but I believe that letting the interviewees speak in their own words as much as possible is more important than providing a perfectly easy read. I hope the reader will agree.

1

Exposing

Racial

Power

[It is] difficult to establish the significance of racism in a society whose self-presentation denies that significance.

Peter Fitzpatrick

Black-Korean conflict has become part of American urban mythology. Since the 1970s, conflicts between Korean immigrant merchants and Black customers and neighborhood residents in cities such as New York, Los Angeles, and Chicago have attracted growing media coverage. News magazine programs, local news broadcasts, newspapers, magazines—even talk shows like *Geraldo* and *Sally Jesse Raphael*—addressed this persistent form of "interminority" conflict throughout the 1980s. Black cultural productions, such as Spike Lee's movie *Do the Right Thing* and Ice Cube's rap piece "Black Korea," also spoke to the phenomenon. Then, of course, the Los Angeles rebellion of

1992 played a crucial role in etching Black-Korean conflict into American popular consciousness. As Blacks (and Latinos) engaged in looting and Korean merchants defended their stores with rifles, many observers identified Black-Korean conflict as the latest American urban conflagration.[1] One scholar referred to it as the "racial conflict of the moment" (Ikemoto 1993); another, "the new urban crisis" (Chang 1993).

The conventional wisdom about Black-Korean conflict is captured in the racial scapegoating story. Habitually put forward by journalists, the racial scapegoating story goes something like this. Shut out of the mainstream economy by historical discrimination and hit hard by recent global economic changes, urban-dwelling Blacks are frustrated and angry. Enter Korean immigrants, who open stores in poor Black neighborhoods and rapidly achieve economic success by virtue of their hard work and thriftiness. Resentful of these new immigrants' success, Blacks lash out at them, irrationally venting their accumulated frustrations on this proximate, vulnerable, and racially distinct target. Korean immigrants, who are responsible for neither America's sordid history of racial discrimination nor global economic changes, simply get caught in the wrong place at the wrong time. They find themselves, through no fault of their own, caught in the crossfire, watching their American Dream slip away.

Like every good story, this one has some truth to it. But it is seriously incomplete. Historical discrimination, economic competition, Black rage, immigrant dreams and prosperity—these are all genuine features of Black-Korean conflict. The problem is that the racial scapegoating story isolates these features and rips them out of the overall context of how *racial power* operates in contemporary America. Racial power refers to the racial status quo's systemic tendency toward self-reproduction.[2] It finds concrete expression in a wide variety of political, economic, social, and cultural processes that tend cumulatively to perpetuate White dominance over non-Whites. Putatively impersonal forces such as global restructuring and deindustrialization are in fact mediated by racial power so that Whites systematically accrue greater benefits from and suffer fewer burdens from these developments than do non-Whites. Black-Korean conflict, which appears in the racial scapegoating story as an irrational Black reaction to objective and inexorable processes, turns out to be, upon closer examination, the "bitter fruit" of deeply entrenched patterns of racial power in contemporary American society. Racial power shapes the structural setting for Black-Korean conflict, conditions the form and rhetoric of Black collective action that arises against Korean merchants within this setting, and determines how major opinionmakers interpret and respond to such action. Because it focuses only on select and decontextualized elements of this broader drama, the racial scapegoating story misses the forest for the trees. My aim in this book is to illuminate the forest: to expose racial power and render visible its pivotal role in generating, shaping, and managing Black-Korean conflict.

Black-Korean conflict has taken myriad forms. I have chosen to focus on the Red Apple Boycott of 1990, a retail boycott and picketing campaign led by Black nationalist, Haitian, and Caribbean activists against two Korean-owned produce stores in Flatbush, Brooklyn.[3] The boycott began after the Korean manager of the Family Red Apple store, Bong Ok Jang, allegedly beat a Haitian woman customer, Ghiselaine Felissaint, during an argument at the cash register.[4] Residents of the largely Haitian and Caribbean neighborhood of Flatbush gathered in front of the store to protest the alleged beating, prompting a Korean store employee to flee across the street to a second Korean-owned store, Church Fruits (which subsequently became a second target of the boycott). Over time, Black nationalist, Haitian, and Caribbean activists transformed this spontaneous gathering into a sustained, organized, purposive boycott and picketing campaign through which they highlighted the alleged beating of Felissaint as a symptom of the oppression of Black people in American society.[5] Significantly, the Red Apple Boycott was a social movement that constituted part of a larger Black Power movement that arose in New York City during the 1980s. The conflict provoked a powerful response from the Korean American community and institutions such as the judiciary, the City Council, and the mass media—all of whom pressured the newly elected Mayor David Dinkins, the city's first Black mayor, to condemn the boycotters. It was this concerted counteroffensive—more than the activities of the boycotters themselves—that transformed what had begun as a neighborhood scuffle into a major political crisis for the new Dinkins administration and a significant moment in New York City history.

Since the Red Apple Boycott was a sustained, organized, purposive collective action, it allows me to make the strongest possible case against the irrational outburst theory of the racial scapegoating story and in favor of my narrative about racial power and Black resistance.[6] I have deliberately chosen it as an extreme rather than representative case. As Jewel Bellush and Dick Netzer observe, "Many issues may be carried to extremes, or reduced to absurdity, in New York politics, but there are lessons to be learned in those extreme manifestations" (1990, 5). Dismayed by the mainstream media's condemnation of the Red Apple Boycott as racial scapegoating, Assemblyman Al Vann appeared on ABC's *Like It Is* on October 21, 1990, and urged the public to consider these questions: "Why are there brothers and sisters who are willing to invest that kind of time and energy to try to close down a store? What motivates them? What is the history in that?" To answer Vann's questions, we need to move beyond conventional wisdom to an investigation of how Black-Korean conflict takes place in a broader context of racial power and resistance. Along the way, we will learn something important about racial dynamics in contemporary American politics.

THROUGH A NARROW LENS: STUDIES OF BLACK-KOREAN CONFLICT

Scholarship on Black-Korean conflict is, on the whole, more nuanced and sophisticated than journalistic renditions of the racial scapegoating story. However, most scholars are not independent observers of racial conflict as much as they are active contributors to and borrowers from dominant racial discourses that circulate among the academy, officialdom, and the mainstream media (van Dijk 1993).[7] Thus it should not surprise us that the multidisciplinary literature on Black-Korean conflict tends to naturalize or cover up racial power through three interrelated practices: decontextualization, depoliticization, and delegitimation. The three practices are linked in the following way: the more one focuses on overt group behavior to the neglect of broader contextual forces, the less likely one is to grasp the political significance of that behavior and the more likely one is to condemn it as irrational or pathological.

Many works decontextualize Black-Korean conflict by narrowing their analytic lens to focus primarily on the overt, face-to-face behavior of the two groups. The very phrase "Black-Korean conflict" indeed invites and often reflects a superficial, dyadic focus. In these works, key contextual elements—features of the structural setting, economic forces, ongoing stereotypes and prejudices—are not so much ignored as they are taken as given, as departure points, rather than subjected to analysis themselves. Once isolated and decontextualized from the relevant context of racial power, Black collective actions against Korean merchants can indeed appear aggressive, senseless, and unfair. Pyong Gap Min (1996), for instance, presents the middleman economic formation as a given, and asks only how Blacks and Koreans act within this formation, rather than asking, say, how the middleman economic formation might itself have come about as a result of racial power.[8] In their work on Black-Korean conflict, Ivan Light et al. (1994) foreground ideational factors such as Black alienation and Black nationalist ideology, but because they fail to locate these with reference to historical patterns of White dominance, they end up reiterating the standard Black irrationality trope. Similarly, Heon Cheol Lee (1993) criticizes Black activists for racializing Black-Korean conflicts—as if American society were not itself already profoundly racialized![9] Because they see the immediate context for Black-Korean conflict as objectively given rather than as the product of racial power, these scholars invariably place responsibility for the conflict squarely on the shoulders of Black collective actors.

Once overt behaviors are taken out of their full generative context, they are easily dismissed as psychologically rather than politically driven.[10] Many academic works depoliticize Black-Korean conflict by failing to search out or ignoring evidence that Black collective action against Korean merchants is in fact explicitly directed toward the attainment of certain political goals. What these works suggest instead is that Black collective action is structurally and/or psychologically determined (Ong, Park, and Tong 1994; Jo 1992; Cheng and Espiritu 1989). The idea here is that certain structural conditions lead to mass psychological disruption, which leads inexorably to chaotic collective outbursts.[11] References to Black people's disturbed psychological states are commonplace in the literature on Black-Korean conflict: Pyong Gap Min (1996) talks about Black "hostility"; Lucie Cheng and Yen Le Espiritu (1989) mention Black "anger," "wrath," and "overt racial hostility." A few works acknowledge the presence of Black political leaders or activists but only to condemn them for exploiting mass discontent out of self-interest (Ong, Park, and Tong 1994) or facilitating the potentially genocidal "anger of the masses" (Light et al. 1994). In other words, these works depict Black activists as demagogues who exploit popular psychological disruption rather than as legitimate political leaders articulating an empowerment agenda to a dispossessed population. The problem with these works, as Jerome Skolnick says in another context, is not their examination of psychological aspects of the conflict per se (a perfectly valid endeavor) but their "substitution of a psychological analysis for a political one" (1969, 257). Denied political agency, Black collective actors appear as little more than water molecules that predictably come to a boil under certain specified conditions.[12]

In his 1996 book, Pyong Gap Min proffers a structural-psychological rather than political reading of Black-Korean conflict even though his own data seem to point in the other direction. Entitled *Caught in the Middle: Korean Communities in New York and Los Angeles,* Min's book reiterates the well-established middleman minority argument that Blacks vent their structurally induced frustrations on Korean middlemen because they constitute a proximate and vulnerable target.[13] Although Min briefly mentions Black national-ist ideology and the notion of community control in his discussion of the Red

Apple Boycott, he treats these as attitudinal or psychological factors that predispose Blacks toward "rejecting" or scapegoating Korean middlemen rather than as longstanding political beliefs that underwrite Black collective action against oppressive conditions. Indeed, Min discusses Black activists' explicit claims that they were not scapegoating Koreans during the Red Apple Boycott as a cover-up for their true psychological motives, and presents telephone survey data demonstrating Black misconceptions about Korean merchants' sources of capital as direct "evidence that the behavior and statements of Black boycott leaders unconsciously reflected their intent to scapegoat Koreans, despite their denial that this was the case" (1996, 101). This last move is troubling for several reasons: it assumes without proving a connection between certain popular misconceptions and overt behavior; it judges such behavior to be "scapegoating" based only on speculation about the actors' "unconscious" motives and despite the actors' claims to the contrary; and it conflates the views of Black boycott leaders with those of randomly selected Black respondents in a telephone survey. Min's commitment to a structural-psychological interpretation prevents him from noticing when and where his own data point toward a more political explanation of the Red Apple Boycott and Black-Korean conflict in general.

Once Black-Korean conflict is depicted as an essentially psychological phenomenon bereft of political significance, it is easily dismissed as irrational or pathological or even evil.[14] Decontextualized, depoliticized readings of Black-Korean conflict inevitably do the work of delegitimation as well. Having reduced Black collective action against Korean merchants to racial scapegoating or misdirected hostility, most scholars also condemn it, whether explicitly or implicitly.[15] In doing so, they appear to assume the existence of a universal, transhistorical calculus of right and wrong according to which truly objective evaluation is possible. Some scholars delegitimate Black collective action by characterizing it as essentially anti-Korean, anti-Asian, or otherwise racist, thereby undercutting the Black actors' claims that they are engaged in an antiracist struggle. It is telling that scholars cite rap artist Ice Cube's "Black Korea," which contains offensive slurs against Koreans, more often and more extensively than they do speeches by or interviews with Black activists involved in real-life conflicts with Korean merchants (Park 1996; Okihiro 1994). A related tendency involves locating Black-Korean conflict in the grand historical trajectory of anti-Asian activity in the United States, comparing it, for instance, to the exclusion of Chinese immigrants in 1882 or the wartime internment of Japanese Americans (Chang 1993).[16] This contextualizing move is troubling because it obscures that Blacks have also suffered racial oppression in the United States and that it was Whites who inflicted these experiences on both non-White groups. Scholars who make this move simply evoke one narrative of racial oppression (Asian American) to deny the legitimacy of the other (Black) instead of confronting the normative dilemmas raised by the convergence of the two. The ultimate delegitimating move practiced by some scholars is likening Black-Korean conflict to the Holocaust. Ivan Light et al. (1994), for instance, argue that the Black nationalism espoused by Black activists is an "anti-middleman" ideology that "legitimate[s] violence and destruction" of the kind seen during *Kristallnacht*. Once again, Blacks are likened to a powerful, persecuting majority and their own bitter experience of racial oppression is denied.

Assumptions about Black psychological disruption lead many scholars writing about Black-Korean conflict to make questionable methodological decisions. Starting off with the assumption that Black collective actors are behaving irrationally, these scholars seem to see little reason to investigate seriously the actors' perspective. Some scholars interview Koreans firsthand but rely on indirect sources of information about Black collective actors. Min (1996), for instance, conducts extensive personal interviews with Koreans but uses only secondary sources and a small random telephone survey to glean Black opinions. Other scholars do interview Blacks, but ignore the reality of intra-Black diversity in doing so. Moon Jo (1992), for example, presents the views of Black civic and church leaders as "Black" views on Black-Korean conflict, even though his interviewees are committed to resolving such conflict (and therefore obviously cannot speak for those promoting it). Most scholars writing on Black-Korean conflict find themselves trapped in this vicious circle between a priori judgments about a monolithic and disrupted Black state of mind and the failure to investigate rigorously what Black participants have to say about their own actions.

Through the practices of decontextualization, depoliticization, and delegitimation, most extant works on Black-Korean conflict end up recapitulating the racial scapegoating story, albeit with more sophistication and depth than are found in most journalistic renditions. By reducing purposive protests against racial oppression to irrational psychological outbursts, these works render invisible the role that racial power plays in generating, shaping, and managing Black-Korean conflict. There are a handful of works on Black-Korean conflict that avoid some or all of these pitfalls (Abelmann and Lie 1995; Yi 1993; Cho 1993; Ikemoto 1993). Emphasizing cultural, symbolic, and

discursive factors, these works do address the role of power and White dominance, albeit somewhat unsystematically. They provide a good start that I try
to build upon in this book.

THROUGH A WIDER LENS: RACIAL POWER, RACIAL ORDERING, AND RESISTANCE

How, then, do we expose racial power and render visible its connection to
Black-Korean conflict? Before moving on to the concept of racial power itself,
I propose that we take Michael Omi and Howard Winant's racial formation
framework (1994) as a starting point. This framework holds that "race" is not
a set of genetic or phenotypical characteristics but rather a socially constructed and contested concept.[17] The notion that race is a social construction
rather than a physical reality inhering in nature is a hard pill for many of us to
swallow. After all, most of us take for granted that some people are White,
Black, Asian, etc., and we are reasonably sure that we can, in most cases, tell
who is who. Yet scholars have shown that racial distinctions have not always
existed, that they were constructed during a particular historical epoch (starting with the conquest of America) to justify and reinforce a system of privilege for those of European descent (deemed "Whites"), and that they have
varied across time and place (Roediger 1991; Fields 1990). Omi and Winant's
work is one of the most influential elaborations of the social constructionist
approach to race.

Unlike most mainstream social science scholarship, which adopts an essentialist approach to race, Omi and Winant's racial formation theory thus
denaturalizes race. That is, it exposes racial categories and meanings as (all
too) human constructions that pervade the social, economic, political, and
cultural realms and function in all of these to maintain the dominance of
Whites over non-Whites. This is not to imply that race is an illusion or incon-
sequential—quite the contrary. As Winant reminds us, it is imperative that we
"recognize the salience a social construct can develop over half a millenium
or more of diffusion, or should I say enforcement, as a fundamental principle
of social organization and identity formation" (1994, 16).[18] What racial formation theory does is push us to look beyond what is superficially apparent; to
ask, for instance, not just why inequalities among racial groups exist, but how
these groups get reconstituted on a continuous basis as distinct "races" and
how this affects the ultimate distribution of goods. I take racial formation
theory as a theoretical departure point. Thus I start with the assumption that
racial categories and meanings are continuously being reproduced and challenged with profound social-structural implications. To develop the racial

formation framework further and enhance its applicability to Black-Korean conflict, I introduce a few supplemental concepts in this book.

The first and most important supplemental concept is that of racial power. If dominant racial categories and meanings are constantly contested, how is it that they persist in force over time, reliably shoring up White dominance? The cumulative and interactive political, economic, social, and cultural processes that jointly reproduce racial categories and distributions and perpetuate a system of White dominance are all manifestations of racial power.[19] We might think of racial power as the systemic tendency of the racial status quo to reproduce itself. Once racial categories and meanings get established as a way of classifying and constituting bodies in society, they tend to reproduce themselves and their consequences via various processes, and it is this systemic tendency that I am calling racial power. Although Omi and Winant do not discuss such a concept, it is consistent with their larger framework.

This notion of racial power owes more to Michel Foucault than to Robert Dahl. That is, I conceive of racial power not as something that an individual or group exercises directly and intentionally over another individual or group but rather as a systemic property, permeating, circulating throughout, and continuously constituting society. I do not use the phrase "White racial power" because it erroneously suggests that Whites possess and deliberately exercise racial power against others when in fact Whites, too, are constituted *qua* Whites by the operation of racial power. While Whites are undeniably the primary beneficiaries of racial power, they are also its subjects. As Foucault writes: "[Power is] something which circulates . . . It is never localized here or there, never in anybody's hands, never appropriated as a commodity or piece of wealth . . . [Individuals] are always in the position of simultaneously undergoing and exercising this power" (1986, 234). Sometimes, of course, Whites do conspire to dominate non-White groups, but the operation of racial power does not depend on such a conspiracy. Racial power is a systemic tendency that expresses itself through myriad processes, some of which involve intentional domination and some of which do not. Foucault's exhortation is on point here:

> Let us not, therefore, ask why certain people want to dominate, what they seek, what is their overall strategy. Let us ask, instead, how things work at the level of on-going subjugation, at the level of those continuous and uninterrupted processes which subject our bodies, govern our gestures, dictate our behaviours, etc. In other words . . . we should try to discover how it is that subjects are gradually, progressively, really and materially constituted

through a multiplicity of organisms, forces, energies, materials, desires, thoughts, etc. We should try to grasp subjection in its material instance as a constitution of subjects. (1986, 283)

Rather than asking how and why Whites conspire to dominate non-Whites, let us ask instead how racial power works via cumulative and interactive processes in the political, social, economic, and cultural realms to continuously reconstitute racial categories, meanings, and distributions in a way that maintains White dominance in American society.

The second supplemental concept I wish to introduce in this book is that of a *racial order*. My contention here is that racial power operates not only by reproducing racial categories and meanings per se but by reproducing them in the form of a distinct racial order. (I frequently use the verb form, *racial ordering*, to emphasize the dynamic and continuous nature of these reproductive processes.) Because Omi and Winant's racial formation framework presents racialization processes—or the processes by which people get defined and characterized as racial groups—as open-ended and highly variable, it does not give us the conceptual tools we need to grasp how relational and even mutually constitutive racialization processes can be. My notion of a racial order emphasizes that each group gets racialized or positioned relative to other groups.[20] I conceive of the American racial order not as a single-scale hierarchy (A over B over C) but as a field structured by at least two axes: that of superior/inferior and that of insider/foreigner. Blacks and Whites constitute the major anchors (bottom and top, respectively) of this order, and incoming immigrants and other groups get positioned relative to these two loci.[21] The racial order stands at the intersection of the discursive-ideational and social-structural realms: it is a discursively constructed, shared cognitive map that serves as a normative blueprint for who should get what in American society. We can think of racial power in the United States, then, as the American racial order's tendency toward self-reproduction. Although we can speak of a global racial order, I focus in this book on the American racial order and its local instantiation in New York City.

Let me lay out the book's argument in schematic form. Overall, I contend that racial power is the key to understanding why Black-Korean conflict occurs, why it looks the way it does, and why it gets resolved in the way that it does. More specifically, racial power (1) helps to generate Black-Korean conflict by reproducing a racial order that juxtaposes the two groups and renders conflict between them highly probable; (2) shapes the form of Black collective action against Korean merchants by defining both the ideational and physical parameters within which such action unfolds; and (3) manages Black resistance by delegitimating and even criminalizing it with reference to the dominant racial discourse.

Allow me to elaborate on these claims a bit. The differential positioning of Blacks and Asian Americans (including Korean immigrants) in the American racial order and their physical juxtaposition in the urban economy creates an immanent tendency for conflict between the two groups. When Black collective action against Korean merchants does arise, it does so as part of a longstanding tradition of Black resistance to racial oppression in the name of "community control." This tradition is conditioned by racial power in terms of its imagination (its proponents embrace the imposed racial category "Black" and reverse its meaning from negative to positive) as well as its protest forms and targets (its proponents directly address the spatial segregation imposed on Black urban populations and target "outsider" merchants, teachers, and landlords operating in Black areas). To clarify the historical embeddedness of this tradition of Black resistance, I introduce and explore the concept of *frame repertoires*—the final supplemental concept presented here (see Chapter 3). This concept builds on the notion of "framing" laid out by Snow, Benford, and colleagues in their influential writings on social movements (Snow and Benford 1992, 1988; Snow et al. 1986; Snow, Zurcher, and Eckland-Olson 1980).

Korean Americans, who most often respond to Black collective action by defending their position within the racial order against this challenge from below, can also be said to be responding to the parameters laid down by racial power. In this book, Korean immigrant merchants and their advocates are not innocent scapegoats, mysterious ciphers, or mere bystanders but historical agents actively negotiating the distinct opportunities and constraints presented within the American racial order. Finally, by generating and reinforcing a dominant racial discourse that I call "colorblind talk" (discussed in Chapter 2), racial power works to delegitimate and ultimately silence Black dissent. The quieting of Black collective action against Korean merchants ritualistically affirms the American racial order: Blacks are confirmed as the pathological underclass; Korean merchants as the hardworking model minority; Whites as neutral enforcers of colorblind justice. In American society, racial dissenters can indeed speak truth to power, but power garbles the message, rendering it harmless.

Most studies of Black-Korean conflict view the subject through a narrow lens, focusing on the dyadic, superficial aspects of the conflict and screening out the larger picture. The result is some version of the racial scapegoating argument, which holds that Korean merchants have found themselves in the wrong place at the wrong time, "caught in the middle" between Black and White antagonists and unfairly bearing the brunt of Black irrationality. As I have suggested above, the racial scapegoating argument misses the forest for the trees. In this book I aim to illuminate the forest—to widen our analytic lens to expose racial power and render visible its important connection to Black-Korean conflict. Once we apprehend the workings of racial power, we can see that Korean immigrants are not detached bystanders but rather are profoundly implicated in the American racial order from the moment they arrive in the United States—not because they wish to be but because each group's position is invariably defined in relation to those of other groups. We can see, too, that Black collective actors are not mindlessly lashing out at the nearest target but purposefully reacting to the existing parameters of oppression. Finally, we are compelled to dispense with simplistic judgments about who is innocent and who is blameworthy and forced to confront the acute normative dilemmas raised when two racially subordinated groups clash head-on in their respective struggles for empowerment.

BREAKING OUT OF THE VICIOUS CIRCLE

As I indicated above, many scholars writing on Black-Korean conflict get trapped in a vicious circle between a priori judgments about a monolithic and disrupted Black state of mind and the failure to investigate rigorously what Black participants have to say about their own actions. My primary methodological aim has been to break out of this circle and to investigate by means of intensive personal interviews the worldviews, beliefs, and opinions of *both* Black and Korean participants in the Red Apple Boycott. To my knowledge, I am the only scholar writing about Black-Korean conflict who has conducted interviews with the December 12th Movement, the Black activist group that led the Red Apple Boycott.[22] In addition, I conducted interviews with members of the Korean American community, and with others involved in the conflict. I quote frequently and at length from these interviews throughout the book so that the reader can, as much as possible, hear the voices of the participants.

In all, I conducted sixty-nine interviews (see "List of Interviewees"). I selected people who were directly involved in the Red Apple Boycott, either as proponents or opponents, as well as interested and / or expert observers. I also engaged in "snowball sampling" by contacting people named by prior interviewees. The final list included Black, Haitian, and Caribbean activists and boycott participants; Korean American merchant advocates; Korean American community leaders and activists; Black, Haitian, and Korean American clergy; representatives of Black and Korean American interest group organizations (such as the New York Urban League, Congress of Racial Equality, Korean Americans for Social Concern, etc.); Flatbush area residents; elected and appointed borough, city, and state officials; New York City Human Rights Commission staff; members of the Mayor's Committee investigating the boycott; journalists; lawyers; and scholars. All interviews were loosely structured and open-ended, with questions varying according to the interviewee. They were conducted in person (with two exceptions) and in English; they ranged from 45 to 120 minutes; and they were tape-recorded and fully transcribed (with a handful of exceptions).

Other major data sources included primary documents relating to the Red Apple Boycott (transcripts of public hearings, letters to elected officials, official reports, protest flyers, etc.); demographic and economic reports published by city agencies; newspaper articles (from mainstream, Black, and Korean American papers); television program transcripts, and secondary sources.[23]

CHAPTER OUTLINE

The discussion of the Red Apple Boycott stands at the center of this book, in Chapter 4. First, though, in Chapter 2, I examine how racial power generated the setting for Black-Korean conflict in New York City, and in Chapter 3, I explore the Black Power movement of which the Red Apple Boycott was a part. In Chapter 4, at last, I analyze the boycott as a social movement within this larger movement, with special attention to the mobilization of Haitian immigrants under the broad Black Power umbrella. In Chapter 5, I explore the Korean American community's response to the boycott, and in Chapter 6, I examine the efforts of the mainstream media, the courts, and public officials to delegitimate the boycott and compel Mayor David Dinkins's intervention in the conflict. In the conclusion I offer a few final thoughts on racial power and resistance in contemporary America.

2

Racial

Ordering

We are inserted in a comprehensively racialized social structure. Race becomes "common sense"—a way of comprehending, explaining, and acting in the world.

Michael Omi and Howard Winant

One reason racial power remains invisible to us is that we take its effects for granted. We tend to think of the forces that bring Blacks and Koreans into contact, for instance, as objective, inexorable, and unmediated by politics and power. Yet, as I suggested in Chapter 1, it is racial power—concretely expressed in the myriad political, economic, social, and cultural processes that reproduce the racial order—that shapes the terms upon which these two groups come face to face. In this chapter I examine the way in which racial ordering set the stage for the Red Apple Boycott in New York City. This is not as straightforward a task as it might appear. After all, Whites do not get together and conspire to perpetuate the racial order per se. Nor do they collectively decide to stack the deck by thwarting Black business ownership and facilitating Korean immigrant business ownership. Nevertheless, racial categories, meanings, and distributions are constantly reconstituted in American society, perpetuating the position of Whites at the apex of the racial order and those of non-White groups below. Again, my notion of a racial order emphasizes that groups get racialized both relatively to one another and differently from one another. It is because Blacks are relegated to the bottom of the racial order that they are less equipped to capitalize on small business opportunities, and it is because Korean immigrants are positioned somewhere above Blacks that they are more equipped to capitalize on the same. In the context of a racial order in which group fates are relative and intertwined, one group's incapacity becomes another's opportunity. Small business ownership thus becomes an index of group position in the racial order, and Korean-owned stores become visible symbols of racial inequalities.

I begin this chapter with a brief account of the historical origins of the American racial order, followed by a concise discussion of the dominant racial discourse that I call "colorblind talk." In the rest of the chapter I show how racial ordering in contemporary New York City set the stage for the Red Apple Boycott.

RACIAL ORDERING: A BRIEF HISTORY

If racial power refers to the racial order's systemic tendency to reproduce itself, how and when did this order first emerge in the United States? Most scholars writing in the social constructionist vein concur that Americans of European descent defined themselves as "White" in relation to successive racial "others" (American Indians, African slaves, Mexicans, Asian immigrants, etc.) whom they encountered beginning with the conquest of America. In my view, a distinct American ordering of racial groups was firmly established by the end of the nineteenth century, and it is this same order that continues to structure American society today, at the dawn of the twenty-first century.

Race in America has always been about who gets what. Prior to the conquest of America, Europeans had distinguished between Greeks and barbarians, and between Christians and heathens, but they had not yet developed the concept of race. It was only as they encountered or forcibly imported different groups of color whose labor they sought to exploit in the context of economic development in the New World that Americans of European descent began to construct a classification system in which different human "races" were identified, evaluated, and ranked. By the early 1800s ethnologists, craniologists, and other researchers were lending the imprimatur of science to such efforts (Gould 1996). The basic idea behind such classification was simple: the more evolved and higher-ranking the race, the more fit it was to hold various powers, rights, and privileges. Such classification was especially important in the justification of Southern slavery. As a separate and inferior race, the argument went, Black slaves did not deserve and could not handle the political, economic, and social privileges properly reserved for Whites.

Over time, Black and White came to clearly define the bottom and top poles of the American racial order, respectively, but where did Asian immigrants and their descendants fit in? Where were they located in the racial order? I argue elsewhere that Asian immigrants and their descendants, who were legally classified as "Mongolians" or "Asiatics," have been *racially triangulated* between Blacks and Whites, or located in the American racial order with reference to these two preestablished points, from the mid-1800s to the present (Kim 1999).[1] The image of a triangle is appropriate here because the American racial order is not a simple vertical hierarchy (A over B over C) but rather a field constructed on at least two dimensions or axes, that of superior / inferior and that of insider / foreigner. Asian immigrants and their descendants have been "triangulated" insofar as they have been racialized both as inferior to Whites and superior to Blacks (in between Black and White), and as permanently foreign and unassimilable (apart from Black and White).

Two types of White discursive practices have operated simultaneously to place and maintain Asian Americans in this distinctive position in the racial order: 1) processes of *relative valorization,* whereby Whites valorize Asian Americans relative to Blacks on cultural and / or racial grounds in a way that reinforces White dominance over both groups; and 2) processes of *civic ostracism,* whereby Whites construct Asian Americans as immutably foreign and unassimilable with Whites on cultural and / or racial grounds in a way that excludes Asian Americans from civic membership. These two sets of practices are linked both analytically (they both depend on an essentialized reading of Asian / Asian American "culture") and functionally (they operate jointly to maintain Asian Americans in this triangulated position).

By triangulating Asian Americans, White elites sought to have their cake and eat it, too.[2] Their explicit aim in the mid-1800s—expounded by countless politicians, journalists, and industrialists—was to secure an alternative to slave labor for the rapidly expanding capitalist economy of the West (hence the relative valorization) while forestalling the formation of another "degraded" non-White laboring caste that would make demands upon the polity (hence the civic ostracism). Just as the racial categories of Black and White helped to reconcile the institution of slavery with widespread democratic ideals (Fields 1990), so did the racial category of Mongolian / Asiatic help to reconcile the exploitation of Asian immigrant labor with these same ideals.

What does the American racial order of the mid-1800s have to do with the Red Apple Boycott of 1990? My contention here is that the American racial order—and, specifically, the racial triangulation of Asian Americans within that order—has persisted over time and remains relatively intact in the contemporary era. This is not to say that the racial order has remained untouched by the passage of a century and a half. In the 1800s, the racial order was codified in law: Whites, Blacks, and Asian Americans each possessed a distinctive legal status accompanied by certain privileges and / or exclusions. Since 1965, the racial order has lost the overt backing of law, which is now prima facie racially neutral or "colorblind." However, the racial order as a shared cognitive map classifying different groups with concrete distributional consequences has survived. Continuously regenerated through racial discourse, it is now embedded in the collective American psyche. Hence Korean immigrants even today are racialized as Asian Americans, valorized relative to Blacks, and ostracized from the body politic—all of which bears directly on Black-Korean conflict. The racial ordering that set the stage for the Red Apple Boycott in 1990 in New York City has deep historical roots.

COLORBLIND TALK

Before moving on to the contemporary racial order in New York City, I want to briefly discuss the dominant racial discourse of the post-1965 era. I have referred to this discourse above as "colorblind talk."[3] Like all forms of power, racial power depends on discourse for its operation. As Foucault writes: "Relations of power cannot themselves be established, consolidated nor implemented without the production, accumulation, circulation and functioning of a discourse. . . . We are subjected to the production of truth through power and we cannot exercise power except through the production of truth" (1986, 229–30). Yet how is it possible that racial ordering persists today when colorblind talk reigns supreme? How can groups be racialized and treated accordingly when overt references to racial differences are taboo? As it turns out, this is only an apparent paradox. Colorblind talk furthers racial power not through the direct articulation of racial differences but rather by obscuring the operation of racial power, protecting it from challenge, and permitting ongoing racialization via racially coded methods. In all of these ways, colorblind talk helps to maintain White dominance in an era of formal race neutrality.

Colorblind talk proffers a particular definition of race and racism, a particular reading of the American historical trajectory, and a normative ideal. It rests on an essentialist view of race as a morally arbitrary physical property; defines racism as overt, individual acts of prejudice that can be countered through education and antidiscrimination law; and suggests that America is moving inexorably toward the promised land of race-blindness. Note that colorblind talk's liberal-individualist thrust denies, by definitional fiat, the very possibility of systemic group dominance.[4] Further, its teleological reading of history and conflation of prescription and description (we should be colorblind . . . we are steadily moving toward colorblindness . . . we are very nearly colorblind!) suggest that the American Dilemma is nearly resolved.[5] Colorblind talk exerts a near hegemonic influence over the realms of the mainstream media, the academy, and officialdom. Consider the fact that most political debate between liberals and conservatives takes place entirely within the parameters of this discourse, or the fact that Martin Luther King, Jr., perhaps the most famous proponent of this discourse, remains the most quoted figure on racial matters to this day.

Colorblind talk, which was a progressive, reformist ideology when originally espoused by civil rights leaders, has become, in the post–civil rights era, a powerful tool for racial retrenchment (Gotanda 1991). An astute observer of the 1960s might have foreseen such a development. During the civil rights movement, Martin Luther King Jr. and his colleagues exhorted the nation to live up to the American creed by dismantling segregation and ushering in a new era of colorblindness. When the national government moved toward prima facie neutrality in law, policy, and rhetoric in the mid-1960s, it did so partly in response to political pressure generated by the civil rights movement, but also in an effort to undercut emergent radical movements in the Black, Chicano, American Indian, and Asian American communities. It took ominous race-based organizing and demand making to get government officials to start talking about colorblindness. White powerholders enshrined colorblind talk in part because it proved such an effective means of delegitimating Black nationalist groups like the Student Nonviolent (later National) Coordinating Committee, Congress of Racial Equality, and the Black Panther Party (Peller 1995), and their counterparts in other communities of color. From the moment of its appropriation by the state, in other words, colorblind talk became a dam holding back the tide of more radical racial change. It should not surprise us that colorblind talk is now the preferred weapon of conservatives seeking to roll back reforms in affirmative action, redistricting, and other areas.[6]

By distorting both the nature and extent of America's race problem, colorblind talk provides cover for the continued operation of racial power in the post-1965 era. We can think of it as a veil that hides the American racial order from view, protecting it from challenge. The most egregious efforts at racial classification are permissible within this discourse as long as they are racially coded, or expressed in cultural rather than explicitly racial terms. As Simon Cottle notes, "Language can sustain racialized meanings, even when publicly such may appear to be declined or disavowed. Discourses on 'race,' then, may not necessarily reference 'race' at all" (1992, 3). White opinion-makers no longer talk about the racial natures of the "Negro" and "Mongolian," but they do talk about the cultural values of the urban underclass and the model minority. No two tropes are more central to contemporary racial ordering than this pair of colorblind myths, which effectively classify Whites, Asian Americans, and Blacks without any mention of race at all.[7] Since these myths played an important role in the Red Apple Boycott, I will discuss them briefly here.

Introduced by journalists in the 1980s, the underclass trope was popularized by William Julius Wilson's *The Truly Disadvantaged: The Inner City, the Underclass, and Public Policy* (1987). Its proponents argue (with widely varying degrees of sophistication) that Black urban poverty is the result not of racism but of some combination of economic forces (economic restructuring, deindustrialization, disinvestment in the inner city, etc.) and social deviance (drug use, teenage pregnancy, crime, dependency on welfare, etc.). The underclass myth reflects colorblind talk (it is grounded on Wilson's claim about "the declining significance of race"), passes the test of colorblind talk (it blames Blacks for certain cultural/behavioral deficiencies without making claims about their racial natures), and reinforces colorblind talk (if Blacks are responsible for their own problems, then society is off the hook). Clothed in the legitimating language of science, the underclass myth continuously re-racializes Blacks (reconstructs them as a distinct racial group with certain negative characteristics), which serves to both perpetuate and justify their low status in American society.[8]

The model minority myth, which first emerged during the mid-1960s, was resurrected during the early 1980s just as the underclass myth was gaining ground (Osajima 1988). This makes sense when we consider that the two myths complement each other quite well. Like the underclass myth, the model minority myth reflects colorblind talk, passes its test, and reinforces it.

During the 1960s, journalists and scholars first reported on Asian American "success" stories as an explicit rebuke to Blacks involved in collective demand making of one kind or another. Thus the model minority myth, from the start, triangulated Asian Americans relative to Blacks and Whites, albeit in cultural rather than explicitly racial terms. It reprised both relative valorization and civic ostracism practices by presenting Asian Americans as culturally superior to Blacks and yet culturally distinct from Whites and detached from politics.[9] Since the 1980s, the model minority myth has worked as an effective foil to the underclass myth, demonstrating once again that groups are racialized relatively to yet differently from one another. Consider the two myths as mirror images: the underclass is lazy, undisciplined, lacking in family values, criminally inclined, unable to defer gratification, deviant, dependent, and prone to dropping out; the model minority is diligent, disciplined, possessed of strong family values, respectful of authority, thrifty, moral, self-sufficient, and committed to education. Whites—the unspoken overclass to the underclass and majority to the model minority—are factored out of the picture as if they were neutral, colorblind, wholly disinterested observers. The overall message here is that American society is open and fair, and that Asian Americans succeed because they have the right cultural values, while Blacks fail because they do not. As we shall see, these two colorblind myths not only helped to reproduce the racial order within which the Red Apple Boycott occurred but also governed the mainstream public's interpretation of this event.

LOCAL ORDERING: BLACKS IN NEW YORK CITY

Behind the protective veil of colorblindness, groups are continuously reracialized in a way that reproduces the American racial order. Our task here is to examine some of the key political, economic, social, and cultural processes by which such racial ordering occurred in contemporary New York City prior to 1990, setting the stage for the Red Apple Boycott. Again, the racial order is a shared cognitive map that stands at the intersection of the discursive-ideological and social structural realms. That is to say, it is discursively constructed and reconstructed with social structural consequences that, in turn, fuel these constructions. The fact that Blacks are constructed as the most inferior, lowly group in the order means that they are subject to more numerous and comprehensive forms of exclusion than are Korean immigrants, who are triangulated between Blacks and Whites. Some of the processes of racial ordering involve White intentionality, some do not. What is important is their cumulative impact in reinforcing a certain structural relationship between Blacks and Koreans such that the former's misfortunes become the latter's opportunity and the stage for conflict is set.

Putting Blacks in Their Place

Since the turn of the century, in New York City as elsewhere, Blacks have been systematically kept apart from Whites through residential segregation. Residential segregation is fueled by and fuels the ongoing discursive construction (via the underclass myth and similar tropes) of Blacks as inferior, deviant, pathology-ridden beings. It literally seeks to put them in quarantine and cordon them off from Whites. It is tempting to take the spatial environment of cities for granted as the natural outcome of free market forces or individual preferences. Yet there is nothing natural about the racialization of urban space: it is the quintessential artifact of racial power (Goldberg 1993). As Kenneth Clark noted more than three decades ago, the "dark ghetto . . . [works] to confine those who have *no* power and to perpetuate their powerlessness" (1965, 11). Although the United States does not mandate racial segregation by law, as South Africa did during the apartheid era, it achieves by informal means a system of segregation so severe that many scholars have referred to it as American "apartheid." More than any other non-White group, Blacks have been the target of segregation. As Douglas Massey and Nancy Denton write: "No group in the history of the United States has ever experienced the sustained high level of residential segregation that has been imposed on blacks in large American cities for the past fifty years. . . . Not only is the depth of black segregation unprecedented and utterly unique compared with that of other groups, but it shows little sign of change with the passage of time or improvements in socioeconomic status" (1993, 2). The extremity and persistence of the residential segregation of American Blacks during the past century has truly marked them as a racial caste at the bottom of the racial order.

Residential segregation is a good example of how Whites, on occasion, do deliberately conspire to marginalize Blacks. In their book *American Apartheid: Segregation and the Making of the Underclass* (1993), Massey and Denton argue persuasively that residential segregation is the product of "a series of self-conscious actions and purposeful institutional arrangements" (2) on the part of Whites over the past century. The system of segregation in New York City and other major northeastern and midwestern cities was firmly established during the decades between the first "great migration" of southern Blacks to northern cities during World War I and the next major migration during World War II. During this period, banks systematically "redlined" or refused to grant home mortgage loans to Blacks. Real estate agents refused to show Black clients homes in White neighborhoods, instead steering them toward predominantly Black areas. White "neighborhood improvement" associations formed to ensure the racial purity of given areas, lobbying for favorable zoning regulations and building codes and policing the conduct of real estate agents. Restrictive covenants, contractual agreements among White property owners in a given area not to sell or lease to Blacks, were widespread until the U.S. Supreme Court ruled them unenforceable in 1948, by which time they had already done the work of constructing a thoroughgoing system of racial separation. Blacks who overcame these hurdles and dared to move into predominantly White areas were subjected to race riots, murder, beatings, verbal harassment, bombing, and arson. All of this suggests the intensity, scope, and deliberateness of White efforts to separate and stigmatize Blacks in American cities during the first half of the century.

Since World War II, federal government policies and deindustrialization prompted by global economic restructuring have worked together to further entrench the system of residential segregation in cities like New York. Federal tax, home mortgage, and highway construction policies have all permitted, indeed encouraged, middle-class White homeowners to move to the suburbs, simultaneously deepening the racial divide and reducing the cities' tax bases. At the same time, city governments have engaged in slum clearance, euphemistically known as "urban renewal," and have concentrated public housing in central cities (Squires 1998). As Adolph Reed Jr. (1988) points out, suburbanization and ghettoization are actually two sides of the same coin: suburban sprawl draws resources, jobs, and services away from urban centers, further impoverishing them. Deindustrialization, or the removal of heavy manufacturing jobs from the cities to the suburbs, the Sunbelt, or overseas, has also played a role in decimating the job and tax bases of central cities. The maintenance of residential segregation goes on, in part, behind the protective veil of colorblindness in the post-1965 era. The Federal Housing Authority, for example, defends its home mortgage practices on economic grounds, disclaiming racial motives. Yet Whites continue to use redlining, real estate steering, terror, and flight to maintain racial separation. Massey and Denton thus conclude that "systematic, institutionalized racial discrimination within urban housing markets" continues today, increasing the scope and depth of residential segregation (51).

New York City is one of the most highly segregated metropolitan areas in the nation (Massey 1998; Denton 1994; Massey and Denton 1993). Over the last few decades, due in part to White flight from areas adjacent to concentrations of Blacks, the level of White-Black segregation has remained quite high, unmatched by that between any other two groups (Mollenkopf 1993). With only slight variation by class, Blacks (including immigrants) remain largely confined to a handful of neighborhoods in upper Manhattan, the Bronx, central Brooklyn, and southeastern Queens (Mollenkopf 1993; Green and Wilson 1989). Several recent studies document the role that ongoing home mortgage discrimination has played in creating and reproducing this system of apartheid in New York City.[10] If the apartheid analogy seems extreme at first glance, consider the following events that occurred in New York City over the past fifteen years: the harassment of real estate agents who showed homes to prospective Black buyers in White areas in the early 1990s; the bombing of Black families' homes in the predominantly White area of Canarsie, Brooklyn, during the same period; the killing of a young Black man, Yusef Hawkins, by a group of White youths when Hawkins went to look for a used car in the White neighborhood of Bensonhurst, Brooklyn, in 1989; and the killing of Trinidadian immigrant Michael Griffith in 1986 by a group of White men who were incensed at seeing Griffith and his Black friends in their White neighborhood of Howard Beach, Queens.

There is evidence to suggest that these acts of terror were not the acts of isolated lunatics but that they in fact enjoyed considerable support within the White communities in question. According to one study, 51 percent of White (mostly Italian American) youths interviewed in Bensonhurst believed that neighborhoods should be racially homogenous, and 15 percent said they thought they had the right to physically prevent the entry of other groups onto their "turf" (Pinderhughes 1991, cited in Wellman 1993). The community of Bensonhurst indeed closed ranks after the killing of Yusef Hawkins, refusing to cooperate with the police investigation and hooting and throwing watermelons during Black protest marches through the area. This community reaction led scholar David Wellman to conclude that Hawkins's killers were merely "the informal enforcers of implicit community racial codes" (1993, 241).

Blacks are the only group in America that experiences this degree of residential segregation from Whites. The multiplier effects of residential segregation for Black people are many and profound: place of residence affects employment opportunities, the quality of public services, the availability of home and business mortgage loans and insurance policies, educational opportunities, and voting power. As the U.S. Supreme Court acknowledged over forty years ago, "separate is inherently unequal." Can Black people be said to enjoy equal protection under the law and equal rights if they are separated thus, to the point where they enter a White "township" at the risk of their lives? What is certain is that residential segregation marks Blacks as a separate and inferior caste, placing them at the bottom of the American racial order. It is not surprising, therefore, that the killings of Griffith and Hawkins came to be flashpoints around which the city's new Black Power movement (of which the Red Apple Boycott was part) mobilized.

Persistent Political Exclusion

The persistent exclusion of Blacks from meaningful political power in New York City is another aspect of racial ordering. Historically coopted by and subordinated within Democratic party organizations, Blacks in New York City remained on the outside looking in for most of the twentieth century. Mayor John Lindsay attempted partial minority incorporation during his two terms (1966–1973), but a powerful electoral/governing coalition comprising White corporate elites and middle-class, outer-borough White ethnics (especially Jews and Italians) took over following his departure. This coalition has ruled the city—with one important exception—from Mayor Edward Koch's first term (1978–1981) through the publication of this book during Mayor Rudolph Giuliani's second term (1998–2001), forestalling any significant degree of minority incorporation. Writing in the late 1980s, scholar John Mollenkopf indeed labeled New York City "the great anomaly" because it had not yet elected a minority mayor despite its significant minority population (Mollenkopf 1990). Mayor Edward Koch's legendary talent for demobilizing minority challengers during his three terms (1978–1989) helped to account for this anomaly. Beyond Gracie Mansion, Black underrepresentation has also been evident in other at-large offices and in the City Council.

Blacks have proven the crucial exception to the famous tradition of "ethnic" succession in New York City politics. Since the early decades of the twentieth century, when the Democratic machine, known as Tammany Hall, set up Black submachines to coopt and control Black political participation, Blacks have been persistent outsiders in city politics.[11] For much of the 1900s, the machine used its considerable powers over ballot access, voter registration procedures, judicial appointments, campaign fundraising, and drawing City Council district boundaries to keep Blacks at the margins of the city's political life. As a result, Blacks did not replicate the Irish, Italian, and Jewish trajectories from political powerlessness to political inclusion. Racial power has structured New York City politics more decisively than ethnic or religious intolerance ever did.

Mayor Edward Koch exercised nearly hegemonic influence over New

York City politics for three full terms. During this time, and especially toward the latter end of his stewardship, he was widely perceived as being anti-pathetic to Black interests. Although he began his career as a Greenwich Village reform Democrat, Koch eventually built an electoral coalition that excluded Blacks, used racial appeals to cement this coalition, and authored policies that disproportionately burdened Blacks. On the one hand, Koch's strategy for winning and retaining power involved pleasing the White corpo-rate elite with aggressive progrowth policies and appealing to the racial re-sentments of middle-class, outer-borough White ethnics. Koch billed himself as "a champion in City Hall" (Eichenthal 1990, 68) for Whites of middle- and upper-class status. On the other hand, Koch also took proactive measures to stymie Black opposition and perpetuate Black political exclusion. These mea-sures included nurturing a political climate hostile to Black aspirations; at-tempting to divide and conquer racial, ethnic, and class groupings; and using institutional power to demobilize and coopt potential challengers.[12]

In 1971, early in his career, Koch publicly opposed the construction of scatter-site public housing in Forest Hills, Queens, demonstrating his keen sense of how to play to the racial anxieties of White ethnics for his own political advantage. After he became mayor, Koch seemed to relish and even cultivate his reputation as anti-Black. During his twelve years in office, he launched a steady flow of rhetorical assaults on Black community leaders and activists, denigrating their motives, dismissing their grievances as spe-cial pleading and playing to stereotypical constructions of Blacks as overly demanding dependents seeking to be coddled by the state. He used color-blind talk not only to delegitimate Black protest of any kind but also to fan the flames of racial hostility for his political benefit. Rather than stepping care-fully with regard to the volatile issue of Black-Jewish relations, for example, Koch made public statements such as: "I find the Black community very anti-Semitic . . . My experience with Blacks is that they're basically anti-Semitic" (Auletta 1979). Koch's racial trash-talking and continuous suggestions that Black leaders exaggerated the extent of racism in the city thrilled nonliberal Whites fatigued with issues of minority empowerment even as they demor-alized Black leaders. Indeed, Koch's rhetoric promoted what Derrick Bell (1992) calls "racial bonding" among these Whites—a closing of ranks against minority demands—just as Reagan's rhetoric did on the national level. Koch in fact revered Reagan and invited him to Gracie Mansion as part of his ongoing flirtation with the Republican party.[13] Koch also tried to divide his potential opponents along racial, ethnic, and class lines. During his 1985 and 1989 mayoral campaigns, Koch aggressively courted the support of Latinos,

Asian Americans, Caribbean immigrants, and even middle-class Blacks as a counterweight to the growing political disaffection among low-income Blacks. These divide-and-conquer efforts were modestly successful.

Koch also resurrected Democratic party organizations as institutional instruments for amassing political power and maintaining Black exclusion. Regular reform cycles and the increasing influence of the mass media on political campaigns had progressively weakened the Democratic machine in New York City since its heyday in the 1920s and 1930s.[14] Although Koch began his career as a reform Democrat in the 1960s, he assiduously cultivated ties with party leaders during the 1970s and 1980s and helped to resuscitate their ailing organizations through generous patronage.[15] In return, party leaders not only supported his mayoral bids but also "promoted their own Black and Puerto Rican candidates, absorbed or coopted successful insurgents, and denied others access to the ballot" (Mollenkopf 1992, 127), thus thwarting potential minority challengers to Koch. Eventually, this alliance worked to Koch's detriment: machine scandals in the late 1980s contributed to his primary election loss to David Dinkins in 1989.

Finally, Koch did his utmost to preserve the Board of Estimate as a bulwark of mayoral power. From its creation by the City Charter of 1902 to its dismantling by U.S. Supreme Court decision in 1989, the Board of Estimate was the main counterweight to mayoral power in New York City, overshadowing the historically weak City Council. The Board of Estimate was composed of eight members: the five borough presidents (with one vote each), the mayor, the comptroller, and the City Council president (with two votes each). With critical decision-making powers over the budget, zoning, and planning, the Board of Estimate was a powerful player in the progrowth game. Although the Board was originally constituted as a check on mayoral power, Koch came to dominate it via the Democratic party organizations, which helped to vet candidates for the borough presidencies. In 1986, civil rights advocates challenged the Board's constitutionality, charging that equal representation on the Board for each borough violated the one person, one vote principle to the detriment of minority voters, who were overrepresented in certain boroughs and underrepresented in others. The Koch administration fought back, and the case went all the way to the U.S. Supreme Court. Koch stood to lose in more ways than one if the Court ruled against him: the Board was a bastion of his power and if it were dismantled, its powers would be transferred to the district-based City Council, which stood as a potential bastion of Black and minority power. Koch lost this war: in 1989, the Supreme Court ruled that the Board of Estimate was unconstitutional and ordered that it be dismantled. Voters promptly approved a new city charter transferring most of the Board's powers to the City Council.

Several factors—including residential segregation, past gerrymandering, and Koch's dominance over the Democratic machine—worked together to ensure that Blacks were not only kept out of Gracie Mansion but under-represented throughout city government during Koch's terms. At the start of Koch's third term in 1985, Blacks and Latinos, who together constituted about half of the city's population, held only 26 percent of City Council seats, 25 percent of the city's seats in the State Senate, and 30 percent of the city's State Assembly seats (Mollenkopf 1991, 335). By the end of the 1980s, Blacks and Latinos, who constituted 42 percent of the city's voting age population, still held only 29 percent of City Council seats (Mollenkopf 1997, 101). Black underrepresentation in boroughwide and citywide offices was even more striking. When David Dinkins became Manhattan borough president in 1985, he was the first non-White borough president in thirty years (since Percy Sutton held the Manhattan office during the 1950s). Dinkins was also the only Black member of the Board of Estimate. And when he was elected mayor in 1989, Dinkins became the first non-White citywide official in New York City history. (Even after the 1991 redistricting process improved Black representation in the district-based City Council, four out of five borough presidents, the council speaker, the mayor, and other citywide elected officials all remained White). The persistent political exclusion of Blacks in New York City through the late 1980s reflected the continuing operation of racial power in the "colorblind" contemporary era. This sheds some light on why Black efforts at empowerment eventually migrated outside of traditional political channels, resulting in the new Black Power movement of which the Red Apple Boycott was part.

Losing Out: Blacks in the Postindustrial Economy

Black economic marginalization is another artifact of racial power. Despite a sometimes booming local economy, most Blacks lost out economically relative to other groups in New York City during the 1970s and 1980s. Of course, the various dimensions of racial ordering work cumulatively and interactively. Thus residential segregation contributes to political exclusion; political exclusion renders effective resistance to economic marginalization impossible; economic marginalization intensifies residential segregation, and so on. The end result is that Blacks experience more comprehensive and more intense marginalization on a variety of fronts than any other single group, locating them firmly at the bottom of the racial order.

New York City's economy has been profoundly restructured since the 1960s (Mollenkopf 1992; Arian et al. 1991; Mollenkopf and Castells 1991; Netzer 1990; Sassen 1988). Technological innovations that permit the heightened mobility of capital have prompted economic restructuring in cities throughout the world, generating new international, national, and local divisions of labor. At the local level, restructuring consists of two intertwined processes: deindustrialization, or the removal of durable manufacturing and related goods-handling industries from central cities to the suburbs, the Sunbelt, or overseas; and the expansion of the service sector and its replacement of manufacturing as the main source of local employment (Arian et al. 1991). While most Rust Belt cities have suffered severe deindustrialization, New York City has been hit especially hard. Between 1965 and 1990, the number of Fortune 500 industrial firms with headquarters in Manhattan fell from 128 to 48, while manufacturing employment fell from 865,000 to 355,000 (Mollenkopf and Castells 1991, 7).

On the other hand, New York City's nodal position in the increasingly global economy has generated a service sector expansion greater than that in any other American city. The expansion in producer services such as finance, insurance, and real estate (FIRE) is directly tied to the decline in manufacturing, as Roger Waldinger notes: "Large corporations that have developed heavy foreign involvements find themselves more, not less, dependent on their external providers of business services. These services increasingly fall to a cluster of firms that are disproportionately based in the largest diversified urban centers . . . Paradoxically, the geographical spread of routinized manufacturing and information-processing activities increased the need for centralizing key control activities" (1996, 36). The service sector boom in New York City began during the 1960s, was interrupted by economic decline from 1969 to 1977, and took off again during the 1980s (Netzer 1990, 39). The preponderance of the five hundred thousand new jobs created in the city between 1977 and 1988 was in business services (Bellush 1990, 318).

The mutually reinforcing processes of restructuring and suburbanization have dramatically reconfigured the population of New York City since the 1950s. There has been a staggering exodus of Whites to the suburbs: approximately two million left the city between 1970 and 1980 alone (Bailey and Waldinger 1991, 55). At the same time, the proliferation of low-end service sector jobs has attracted unprecedented numbers of Caribbean, Asian, and Latin American immigrants to the city. White flight, Third World immigration, and internal migration by Blacks and Puerto Ricans have made New

York City a "majority minority" city for the first time in its history. Table 2.1 shows the city's population changes by race and nativity from 1980 to 1990.

If the restructuring of the city's economy and the diversification of its population are well-known facts, scholars disagree as to what consequences these trends have generated. Mismatch theorists such as William Julius Wilson (1987) argue that restructuring has produced a fateful mismatch between the minimal skills of Black urban residents and the high-skill demands of emerging service sector jobs, resulting in the emergence of the Black "underclass." Polarization theorists such as Saskia Sassen (1988) emphasize that restructuring has generated both high-end and low-end service jobs and argue that the latter have drawn poor, unskilled Third World immigrants willing to fill them.[16] In both perspectives, Blacks are shut out of the postindustrial economy by large-scale, impersonal economic forces rather than by race-related factors.

Roger Waldinger's 1996 book *Still the Promised City? African-Americans and New Immigrants in Postindustrial New York* gives the lie to these deraced accounts of how groups have fared in the city's postindustrial economy.

TABLE 2.1 POPULATION OF NEW YORK CITY BY RACE AND NATIVITY, 1980 AND 1990

	1980	1990
Native-born White	43.8%	35.3%
Foreign-born White	14.1	8.5
Native-born Black	16.5	19.6
Foreign-born Black	5.0	6.0
Native-born Hispanic	10.5	15.0
Foreign-born Hispanic	6.6	8.0
Native-born Asian	0.3	1.3
Foreign-born Asian	3.0	5.4

Source: Adapted from John Mollenkopf, *New York City in the 1980s: A Social, Economic, and Political Atlas* (New York: Simon & Schuster, 1993), 7.

Although Waldinger does not use concepts such as racial ordering or racial power, he places power, politics, and racism squarely at the center of his analysis.[17] Waldinger criticizes mismatch and polarization theorists for "depict[ing] faceless, impersonal structures inexorably performing their actions on an inert urban mass" and points out that in their work, these structures are "taken for granted, abstracted from any historical context, and divorced from the specific interests and forces that might have given them shape" (2). As an alternative, Waldinger suggests that we conceive of the postindustrial labor market as an "ethnic queue." Whites occupy the top position in this queue, native minorities occupy the bottom position, and immigrant groups get serially incorporated into the intermediate positions, where they establish and reproduce specific economic niches. The ethnic queue was established originally (and is maintained) by the tendency of employers to "rank entire groups of people in terms of their ethnic and racial characteristics" (3). Yet how it looks at any given time depends on a multitude of historically contingent forces, including the profile, magnitude, and timing of immigration flows and the efforts of racial / ethnic groups to establish, defend, and, where possible, improve their standing in this queue.

What follows is Waldinger's account of what has happened to Blacks in the postindustrial economy of New York City. When Blacks began migrating to the city during the first half of the century, Whites were firmly ensconced in private sector occupations up and down the labor queue. As a result, many Blacks entered the public sector, which was relatively open to them, especially after the passage of equal employment opportunity legislation in the early 1970s. By the time Whites started to leave the city in the 1970s and 1980s, Blacks were ensconced in the public sector and lacked the necessary networks to take over the private sector niches left by departing Whites. Blacks did fill some of the public sector jobs left open by Whites who departed during and after the fiscal crisis of 1975–1977, despite Mayor Edward Koch's dismantling of the city's public sector affirmative action plan.[18] By 1990, 28 percent of all employed Black New Yorkers worked in the public sector, where they constituted 36 percent of the city's total work force (111,227). The continued concentration of Blacks in the public sector left formerly White private sector niches open to incoming immigrant groups who possessed both the material resources and ethnic networks to succeed in them (think, for example, of Korean immigrants replacing Jewish and Italian merchants in Black neighborhoods). Although concentration in the public sector has sheltered some middle-class Blacks from overt discrimination and the vagaries of the business cycle, it has harmed the majority of other Blacks. The concentration of Black energies on networking within city government and the failure of Blacks to effectively penetrate any part of the private sector (including low-skilled jobs) have been two sides of the same coin. The big losers in the ethnic queue have been poor and undereducated Blacks, who end up lacking access to both public and private sector jobs.

By reminding us of the occupational roads not taken by Blacks, of the downside of the apparent boon of Black public sector employment, and of the linkage between Black economic absence and immigrant economic presence, Waldinger contributes significantly to our understanding of how group statuses (economic or otherwise) are relational. Wilson (1987) suggests that Black urban poverty must be caused by impersonal economic forces having nothing to do with racism, since the "significance of race" has been declining since the state adopted a formally race-neutral posture in the mid-1960s. Waldinger demonstrates that the scenario is in fact much more complex: the slotting of groups into (or out of) particular occupational niches in the ethnic queue is a product of the interaction of overt racism, group agency, restructuring, immigration flows, and other dynamics.

Other scholars and observers echo the point that old-fashioned racism—or discrimination based on the construction of Blacks (especially Black men) as undesirable (lazy, dishonest, unreliable) employees—still plays a key role in excluding Blacks from a variety of jobs, especially the most lucrative ones.[19] In his study of Black (under)employment in New York City during the 1980s, Thomas Bailey concludes unequivocally that "racism continues to play a much more important role in shaping Black employment opportunities than current popular explanations or policy priorities acknowledge" (1989, 81). Even the conservative business newspaper *Crain's New York Business*, not typically given to angst over racial injustice, proclaimed: "In 1989, one central, searing fact still influences the lives of so many of New York's black citizens: Race matters. As much as the American ethos suggests that anyone can make it, being black reduces the prospects for entrance and advancement in nearly every sector that defines the economic life of the city" (Beschloss and McNatt 1989). Between 1970 and 1980, the employment-to-population rate for Black men fell from 80.9 percent to 66.9 percent, dropping below that of any other group (Bailey and Waldinger 1991, 56). Between 1985 and 1991, Black men once again had the lowest labor force participation rate of any group (Rosenberg 1992, 19).[20] Studies suggest that even in the public sector, Blacks get the short end of the stick: they tend to be segregated in less prestigious city agencies and to draw lower salaries there than their White counterparts.[21]

If we look beyond the labor market, we can see that Mayor Edward Koch's fiscal, welfare, and economic development policies allocated most of the benefits of economic restructuring to the White corporate elite and most of the burdens to low-income Blacks and Latinos. Although city administrations constrained by progrowth bidding wars do not fully control the impact of restructuring on their economies, they can influence the distribution of benefits and burdens, either mitigating or aggravating the polarizing impact of change.[22] Koch used every instrument in his policy arsenal to fuel restructuring, hitched his political star to the economic winners, and shredded the safety net that might have saved the economic losers. When he first became mayor in 1978, Koch seized upon his post–fiscal crisis mandate for fiscal austerity and ran with it.[23] He balanced the city's operating expense budget by slashing social spending and holding down public wages, thereafter generating regular annual budget surpluses. To cut redistributive spending, he reduced the welfare rolls through stricter administration and dismantled the antipoverty apparatus that had been set up by Mayor John Lindsay. By 1981, the number of welfare recipients in New York City had declined to its lowest level in more than ten years (Savitch 1990, 260).[24] City spending, which had risen by 30 percent between fiscal years 1969 and 1976, declined by over one-third by the time Koch had been in office for several years.[25]

Even as he balanced the operating expense budget on the backs of the (mostly minority) poor, Koch used both capital and operating-expense budget funds to promote economic development and hasten New York's transformation into a corporate city (Mollenkopf 1992; Logan and Molotch 1987). Because power is highly centralized in New York City's political system—the city stands "at the centralized end of the continuum of executive influence over city government operations" (Mollenkopf 1992, 71)—corporate elites negotiating the city's dense and cumbersome development regulations actively sought out (and received) Koch's support for their agendas. Soon after taking office in 1978, Koch declared that "the main job of municipal government is to create a climate in which private business can expand in the city to provide jobs and profit" (Bellush 1990, 319). He proved as good as his word. Throughout his three terms, Koch provided hundreds of millions of dollars in tax benefits and incentives to developers. Insofar as tax benefits and incentives constitute what Michael Peter Smith (1988) calls "fiscal welfare" for developers, Koch took from the poor to give to the rich. From 1978 to 1983, capital budget spending to renew the city's infrastructure in service of development more than doubled, from $407 million to $866 million. During the same period, current operating expenditures in service of development increased by 72 percent (Bellush 1990, 321). Koch also took economic development policy-making out of the city bureaucracy and assigned it to a newly created deputy mayor for economic development who worked directly under him. He regularly adjusted zoning regulations to permit new corporate development projects; used the power of patronage to secure the Board of Estimate's support for new projects; and used public authorities to advance any projects opposed by the Board of Estimate or community groups. Together, the corporate elite and Mayor Koch orchestrated the development boom of the 1980s, during which new high-rises, hotels, and luxury condominiums sprang up to reshape Manhattan's skyline.

By the late 1980s, the cumulative effect of economic restructuring, ethnic queuing, and Koch's policies was to render most Blacks, especially the poor and undereducated, worse off in both absolute and relative terms. Between 1975 and 1990, both overall poverty rates and rates of income inequality rose substantially in New York City, as they did in the rest of the nation. From 1975 to 1987, the overall poverty rate in the city increased from 15 percent (20 percent above the national average) to 23 percent (almost double the national average). The rate of extreme poverty (income less than 75 percent of the poverty threshold) in New York City increased from 14 percent to 19 percent from 1979 to 1990 (Rosenberg 1992, 5). As Table 2.2 indicates, Blacks and Latinos were especially likely to be poor during the 1980s, with almost one in three Blacks and two in five Latinos falling under the poverty line.[26]

In addition, from 1977 to 1986, the ratio of total income received by the top

TABLE 2.2 POVERTY RATES BY RACE/ETHNICITY IN NEW YORK CITY, 1984–1987, 1990

	1984	1985	1986	1987	1990
Total	23.5%	23.9%	20.6%	23.2%	25.2%
White	9.0	9.7	8.9	8.4	11.6
Black	31.9	31.6	26.5	33.8	33.0
Hispanic	42.9	44.4	36.2	41.6	43.1

Source: Adapted from Terry Rosenberg, *Poverty in New York City, 1991: A Research Bulletin* (New York: Community Service Society, 1992), 7.

tenth of the city's population to that received by the bottom tenth jumped from 14.5 to 1 to 19.5 to 1 (Mollenkopf and Castells 1991, 11). The economic boom of the 1980s furthered income polarization because it occurred almost entirely within the advanced services sector. As John Mollenkopf observes, since "much of the boom . . . took the form of returns to financial assets rather than wages and salaries . . . [the benefits] were concentrated in upper middle class white areas, while losses or the least gains were concentrated in black and Latino areas" (1993, 43–44).

Thus the economic scenario for Blacks during Koch's three terms was bleak. Although some middle-class Blacks did well in the public sector, and a small number gained white-collar jobs in the private sector, most Blacks lost out economically during this time period. Increasing rates of overall and extreme poverty, deepening income inequalities, and persistently low labor force participation rates shaped the lives of most Black New Yorkers. Even the Commission on Black New Yorkers (appointed by Koch, who was suddenly anxious to court Black support just prior to the 1989 election) declared in its report that the Black community in the late 1980s was "a community in crisis" with regard to employment, education, and other socioeconomic measures.[27] What the report did not point out was how much the mayor's own priorities had contributed to this situation. But most Black leaders knew the score. Reverend Calvin Butts III of the Abyssinian Baptist Church in Harlem spoke for many when he declared: "During the twelve years [Mayor Koch] has been chief executive of the city, things have gone backwards for African-Americans" (New York Times, December 18, 1988). As we shall see, getting rid of Koch became the primary rallying cry of the Black Power movement that emerged in New York City during the 1980s.

Locating Haitian Immigrants

Immigrants who arrive in New York City get positioned not just in the labor queue but also in the overall racial order. Since the racialization of Haitian immigrants as Black bears directly on their participation in the Red Apple Boycott, I want to comment on it briefly here.[28] Whatever racial schemata may have pertained in their homelands, whatever their own subjective identities, immigrants tend to be lumped with one of the major native-born racial groups upon their arrival in the United States. Irish immigrants become White, Korean immigrants become Asian American, and Haitians become Black—in the eyes of the White American beholder, that is. According to Martha Giminez, this process, which she calls the "minoritization of immigrants" (1993, 43) or the racializing of nationality, reflects the dominance of the largely White core over the largely non-White periphery in the world system. Local racial ordering, in other words, reflects supranational racialization processes. Conflating Haitian immigrants with native-born Blacks keeps the racial order free of confusing and unwieldy ethnic, religious, national origin, linguistic, and cultural distinctions, even if it obscures vital differences between the two groups.

The story of Haitian immigration to the United States clearly reflects the dominance of the mostly White core over the mostly non-White periphery in the world system. According to Saskia Sassen (1988), the countries sending the most immigrants to the United States are those with whom the U.S. government has had or continues to have direct military, political, and financial ties. Haitian immigrant flows to the United States are indeed tightly linked to American involvement in Haiti (Glick Schiller et al. 1987). At least since the American invasion and occupation of Haiti (1915–1934), the U.S. government has involved itself heavily in Haitian affairs. It has been especially concerned about protecting American economic interests on the island and supporting indigenous dictatorships as regional counterweights to Fidel Castro's communist Cuba. As such, the U.S. government has had an indirect hand in fostering the political repression and economic devastation from which Haitian immigrants have fled since the 1960s.

The first major wave of Haitian immigrants that arrived in the United States in the 1960s consisted mostly of intellectuals and professionals who opposed the new regime of François "Papa Doc" Duvalier. The second wave, consisting mostly of unskilled workers and peasants, began in the early 1970s as a response to the intensifying political and economic hardship initiated by the rule of Jean-Claude "Baby Doc" Duvalier. Haitian immigration to the United States increased significantly each decade from 1960 to 1990: the number of legal immigrants between 1961 and 1970 was 37,500; the number between 1971 and 1980 was 58,700; and the number between 1981 and 1990 was 140,200 (Zéphir 1996, 5). Although estimates of undocumented Haitian immigration vary wildly, suffice it to say that the figures concerning legal immigrants do not tell the whole story. In the early 1990s, Haiti was the second largest source of Black immigration to the United States after Jamaica and the fifth largest source of immigrants to New York City following the Dominican Republic, Jamaica, China, and Guyana (New York City Department of Planning 1992). New York City has the largest concentration of Haitians in the United States, with Miami close behind. Estimates of the Haitian population in New York City vary considerably—from about 400,000 (Zéphir 1996) to 750,000 (New York City Human Rights Commission 1990)—in part because of the significant presence of undocumented immigrants.

Race has a different meaning in Haiti than it does in the United States. For Haitians, Blackness is a source of great pride.[29] To understand this, we need only glance back at Haitian history. When Jean-Jacques Dessalines led Haitian troops to victory over the French in the historic battle of La Crête-à-Pierrot in 1803, culminating a thirteen-year battle for independence, Haiti became the first independent Black nation in the Western Hemisphere. Having carried out the only successful slave revolt in modern history, Haitians became an inspiration to enslaved Blacks everywhere, including those in the southern United States. From its inception as a nation, then, Haiti stood as a global "symbol of Black power and Black freedom" (Zéphir 1996, 37). Blackness in this context connoted not biological inferiority but national greatness and pride. Although Haiti's population was diverse in terms of skin color at the time of the revolution, it is significant that the first postindependence constitution declared that "all Haitians whatever their shade shall be called black" (Nichols 1985, cited in Zéphir 1996, 38). Dessalines indeed created the Haitian flag by taking the white out of the French tricolor. After independence was won, he warned Whites to depart the island upon fear of death. Although contemporary Haitian society is stratified according to a complex and nuanced mixture of racial, class, cultural, and linguistic markers, the legacy of Blackness as a symbol of national pride persists.

However, when Haitians arriving in the United States get racialized as Black, they typically protest such classification, because Blackness here connotes inferiority and marginality. Lumped with native-born Blacks despite their protestations, Haitian immigrants must come to terms with what Susan Buchanan Stafford calls a "shift in the symbolic significance of color" (1987, 144). Indeed, racial ordering profoundly shapes the lives of Haitian immigrants, from their reception (or interdiction) to their social, economic, and political life upon settlement.[30] On the occasions when Whites do recognize Haitians as a distinct group, they usually depict them negatively and in a manner that resonates with constructions of native-born Blacks as diseased, dirty, and uncivilized. Alex Stepick (1997) argues that the American media denigrate Haitians more than any other group or nation: they routinely associate Haitians (whether in Haiti or the United States) with devastating poverty, illiteracy, illness, heathenism (voodoo), and a bastardized language (Creole). During the 1980s, the Center for Disease Control labeled Haitians an at-risk group for AIDS and the federal Food and Drug Administration banned the use of Haitian blood products. Subsequent scientific research suggests that the HIV virus was, in all likelihood, introduced into Haiti by Americans, Canadians, or Europeans (Stepick 1997, 35).

The differential treatment of Haitian and Cuban immigrants has been controversial since the early 1980s precisely because of its racial overtones. In 1968, the United States became party to the United Nations protocol relating to the status of refugees, which embraced the principle of *non-refoulement*—or the nonreturn of refugees whose lives or freedom might be threatened at home because of race, religion, nationality, political beliefs, etc. (Lawyers Committee for Human Rights 1990). Yet in 1981, President Reagan established the U.S.–Haitian interdiction program requiring the U.S. Coast Guard to stop and board unflagged vessels on the high seas and summarily return undocumented passengers to Haiti. At the same time, the United States was not only admitting immigrants from communist Cuba but granting them special treatment as political refugees. The Reagan administration argued that Haitians, unlike Cubans, were only economic refugees and therefore not protected by the principle of non-refoulement as laid out in the U.N. protocol. However, many critics, arguing that Haitians were fleeing both political persecution and economic hardship at home, accused the Reagan administration of racism. When the Tonton Macoutes, the former security police under "Baby Doc" Duvalier, took over after the dictator's fall in 1986 and instituted a fresh reign of terror, the argument about political persecution gained heightened credibility. Perceiving a racial double standard in the federal government's policy, Haitians living in the United States protested vigorously throughout the 1980s, demanding equitable and humane treatment for Haitian immigrants. Joseph Etienne, executive director of the Haitian Centers Council in New York City, put it this way: "People from Eastern Europe who seek asylum here are treated differently. But Haitians who come here in search of freedom are treated badly because we are Black. As far as Washington is concerned, Black people have no right to seek freedom" (*City Sun*, June 6–12, 1990). This is just one example of how the racialization of Haitian immigrants as Black has shaped the political activities of Haitian immigrants in the United States. As we shall see in Chapter 4, the Red Apple Boycott is another.

Cumulative Effects: The Scarcity of Black-Owned Businesses

Why have Korean immigrants succeeded in small business where Blacks have not? The answer lies in the cumulative and interactive effects of racial ordering processes, which position groups differently and relationally so that one group's misfortune becomes another's opportunity. The early literature on ethnic entrepreneurship denied such structural dynamics, arguing that all groups start on a level playing field and attributing group outcomes to differential internal resources. By this view, Asian immigrants have something that Blacks do not—namely, the right cultural stuff. They are modern day Horatio Algers.[31] Ivan Light (1972), for instance, argues that Asian (including Korean) immigrants' cultural solidarity enables them to set up rotating credit associations (*kyes*) with which they generate business start-up capital; Blacks, on the other hand, are too individualistic to do the same. However, subsequent research has challenged this perspective by revealing that Korean merchants do not use *kyes* as often as was thought (Light, Kwuon, and Zhong 1990); that Korean self-employment rates are higher in the United States than in Korea; that Caribbean Blacks engage in rotating credit associations in their native countries but do not appear to use them to generate business capital in the United States (Bonnett 1980); and that native-born Blacks once had a strong tradition of entrepreneurship that is now largely defunct (Feagin and Imani 1994; Butler 1991). Recent works on the topic present a more balanced picture that highlights the structural opportunities that immigrants enjoy as well as the material and cultural resources that they bring with them or develop once in the United States (Waldinger 1996; Aldrich and Waldinger 1990).

What is still missing in this literature is recognition of how all groups—both native-born and immigrant—get constructed as "races" and positioned in the racial order in a way that shapes each one's distinctive set of opportunities, constraints, and resources on an ongoing basis. Racial ordering in fact goes a long way toward explaining differential group outcomes where entrepreneurship is concerned. Korean immigrants find small business opportunities in poor Black neighborhoods precisely because Blacks are residentially segregated from other groups and because Blacks themselves cannot capitalize on those opportunities. In other words, Korean immigrant opportunities are direct products of the spatial and economic marginalization of Blacks in American society. Korean immigrants do not prevail over would-be Black entrepreneurs through head-to-head competition on a level playing field. They enter and take over the small business niche in Black neighborhoods because the niche is wide open.[32] But how has racial ordering led to low rates of Black entrepreneurship, on the one hand, and the propensity of Korean immigrants to undertake small business ownership, on the other? I will try to answer the first of these questions here and the second in the section below.

Blacks have one of the lowest self-employment rates of all U.S. ancestry groups, while Koreans have one of the highest. In 1990, in fact, Koreans had the single highest rate of self-employment out of ninety-nine U.S. ancestry groups. Table 2.3 indicates the magnitude of the disparity between the two groups' rates of self-employment as well as its increase over time.[33] In 1987 and 1990, Blacks constituted roughly 12 percent of the U.S. population but owned only 2.3 percent and 3 percent, respectively, of the nation's businesses. (Ahiarah 1993, 21; Feagin and Imani 1994, 564). Both the scarcity of Black-owned businesses and the disparity between Blacks' and Koreans' rates of self-employment are especially marked in New York City. For example, in 1989, New York City had 17,350 Black-owned businesses (only 1390 of which had paid employees), while Los Angeles had nearly two and one-half times the number of Black businesses per capita (Beschloss and McNatt 1989, 31). As of June 1990, the Black self-employment rate in New York City was only 3.4 percent, while that of the city's total labor force was 6.7 percent and that of Koreans was approximately 50 percent (*New York Times*, June 7, 1990). Fewer than 1 percent of the city's retail businesses were owned by Blacks in 1990, even though Blacks constituted roughly 25 percent of the city's population (New York City Human Rights Commission 1990).

The striking scarcity of Black-owned businesses is the cumulative result of a range of interactive racial ordering processes. During the early decades of the twentieth century, a significant pattern of Black entrepreneurship developed in many U.S. cities. However, the coercive drive toward residential segregation effectively undercut the tradition of Black business ownership by the time of World War II (Butler 1991). Rounded up and quarantined in urban

TABLE 2.3 SELF-EMPLOYMENT RATES AMONG BLACKS AND KOREANS IN THE UNITED STATES

U.S. Ancestry Group	1980	1990
Blacks	2.9%	3.7%
Koreans	16.1	24.3

Source: Adapted from In-Jin Yoon, *On My Own: Korean Businesses and Race Relations in America* (Chicago: University of Chicago Press, 1997), 18–19, 20–21.

ghettos with high rates of poverty, most would-be Black entrepreneurs could
not manage the financial risks of opening businesses in these areas—and they
had little chance of succeeding in White areas. Nor could they get start-up or
capitalization loans from banks. As a result, White immigrants entered and
took over the small business niche in these areas. By the 1930s, many of the
merchants in Harlem were Jewish or Italian immigrants. By the time White
ethnics started to abandon this niche in the 1960s (as their children moved up
the economic ladder and they themselves sought to move to the suburbs), the
few Blacks who might have had the requisite education, skills, and capital to
take their place had already established a niche in the public sector (Waldinger 1996). The remaining Black population lacked the resources (or access to
resources) to step in. When Korean immigrants began arriving in the United
States in significant numbers in the late 1960s, the small business niche in
poor Black urban neighborhoods was up for grabs.

The scarcity of Black-owned businesses remains crucially tied to persistent
Black economic marginalization. In the end, one's ability to start and sustain
a business comes down to whether or not one has the necessary capital.
Despite the fables about Korean *kyes* spinning straw into gold, people can
only pool what they have in the first place. Timothy Bates (1994) argues that
human capital endowments and financial capital are the key requisites for
business success among all groups, whether or not they have access to ethnic
networks. Most Blacks who are unemployed, underemployed, or employed
in low-wage jobs do not have the capital (or access to capital) to open businesses; nor do their friends and family. Discriminated against in the home
mortgage loan market, Blacks have low rates of home ownership relative to
other groups, which translates directly into greater difficulty in accumulating
wealth and securing business loans.[34] Even when Blacks do amass sufficient
start-up capital, "low owner equity investment from personal assets" (Chen
and Cole 1988, 121) leads to undercapitalization, which leaves businesses
highly vulnerable to economic downturns. That banks systematically dis-
criminate against Blacks in commercial lending clearly aggravates the problem. And when Blacks do get commercial bank loans to start businesses, the
burdensome terms of these loans often make business failure more likely. For
instance, banks often set higher interest rates for loans to Black entrepreneurs, or set up shorter maturity periods (Chen and Cole 1988).

Finally, discrimination against established Black-owned businesses by
banks and public agencies handicaps them in competition with their non-
Black counterparts. A study conducted in June 1988 reveals that private lenders in New York City approved 83 percent of loan applications from White

firms but only 68 percent of those from minority-owned firms (Hatchett 1990, 17–18; *New York Newsday*, June 15, 1990). Another study, conducted in 1990, shows that the Koch administration consistently discriminated against Black, Latino, Asian American, and women entrepreneurs in the granting of city contracts (*New York Amsterdam News*, March 7, 1992).[35] In sum, the scarcity of Black entrepreneurs in cities like New York is the cumulative and interactive result of racial ordering processes. Residential segregation constructs poor Black urban areas as captive markets, and economic marginalization and discrimination render most Blacks unable to capitalize on this opportunity.

LOCAL ORDERING: KOREAN IMMIGRANTS IN NEW YORK CITY

While Haitian immigrants get lumped with Blacks at the bottom of the American racial order, Korean immigrants get racialized as Asian Americans and triangulated between Blacks and Whites. Once again, imposed racialization has very little to do with how the immigrant group identifies itself upon arrival, since Haitian immigrants tend to identify simply as Haitians, and Korean immigrants as Koreans. As a result of such racial ordering processes, Korean immigrants find themselves in a disadvantaged position relative to Whites but in an advantaged position relative to Blacks. It is in this way that the very economic opportunities that are closed to Blacks become the ticket to upward mobility for Korean immigrants. To the degree that Korean immigrants also buy into the racial constructions that underwrite the racial order— that is, to the degree that they accept that Blacks deserve their lowly status because they are lazy, unintelligent, undisciplined, etc.—they become further implicated in American racial dynamics.

Who Comes and Why

Just as with Haitians, post-1965 Korean immigration to the United States is directly linked to American military, political, and economic involvement in the sending country.[36] Once again, the story begins with America's protracted efforts to influence economic development and shore up repressive anticommunist regimes in a non-White nation located on the periphery, resulting in significant migration from periphery to core. Consider the intensity and scope of American involvement in Korea over the last half-century. The United States liberated Korea from Japanese colonialism (1945), undertook the partition of Korea along with other major powers, governed South Korea through military rule (1945–1948), battled the Chinese and North Koreans during the Korean War (1950–1953), and exercised a dominant influence on the structuring of the postwar economy and polity. Since 1953, the United

States has maintained troops continuously in South Korea, viewing this nation as an important outpost of American hegemony during the Cold War years. Given the military, political, and financial influence that the United States has exercised over South Korea during the entire postwar period, Bruce Cumings (1981) indeed argues that the United States did not liberate Korea from Japan as much as it subjected Korea to a new kind of colonialism, American style. (This is a view that many Korean student radicals share.) Unsurprisingly, the United States is a preferred destination for Korean emigrants. As the new educated, skilled urban middle class generated by South Korea's export-oriented economic development has encountered employment shortfalls at home, many of its members have opted to come to the United States to fulfill what Kyeyoung Park (1997) aptly calls the "Korean American Dream."[37]

The United States has also exercised a profound cultural influence over South Korea during the postwar period. American films, videos, television programs, radio shows, and magazines continuously disseminate American culture throughout South Korean society. Kyeyoung Park identifies Koreans' fascination with and longing for the United States—what she calls "American fever" (*migukpyŏng*)—as a symptom of American "cultural colonialism" (1997, 29). Building on Bruce Cumings's account, Chungmoo Choi (1993) argues that continuing American influence has in fact kept Koreans in a kind of cultural limbo, trapped somewhere between the colonial stage and the postcolonial stage. She notes with approval that a student-led resistance movement in Korea has begun to challenge the official South Korean account of the United States as liberator, savior, and unqualified friend.

Significantly, American cultural influences imbue Koreans with a strong sense of racial positioning even before they emigrate. Themselves a racially homogeneous people—Park explains that Koreans use the same word, *injong*, for race and nation (1997, 144)—Koreans learn through American cultural productions that Whites are on the top and that Blacks are on the bottom in the American social order (Yi 1993). The equation of America with Whiteness is so strong in Korea that some Korean immigrants express surprise at the presence of so many non-Whites upon their arrival in the United States. In contrast to Haitian immigrants, Korean immigrants tend to accept the rules of the American racial order and come to themselves "assign Asians a status higher than that of African Americans and lower than that of white Americans" (Park 1997, 140). Some Korean immigrants, for example, use the word "nigger" (*gumdungyi*) among themselves as a way of putting distance between themselves and those at the bottom of the racial order (Yi 1993, 325).

If Korean economic development patterns have created a frustrated middle class eager to emigrate, and historical patterns of American influence have oriented them toward the United States, U.S. immigration policy has had the final say in who comes. America has a long, ignominious history of discriminatory legislation against Asian immigrants. The immigration acts of 1882, 1892, 1917, and 1924 are salient examples of state-sponsored civic ostracism. Even the immigration act of 1952, which removed the blanket ban on Asian immigration that had been established in 1924, instituted a system of racial quotas that depressed the volume of Asian immigration. It was not until after the civil rights movement that immigration law became truly colorblind with the passage of the Hart-Celler Act in 1965. An unanticipated result of this reform was that Asia, Latin America, and the Caribbean replaced Europe as the primary immigrant-sending regions to the United States. As Table 2.4 shows, Korean immigration increased steadily (with a few exceptions) from the late 1960s until 1987, when improved political and economic conditions in South Korea slowed the flow (Min 1996).

Most Korean immigrants have settled in Los Angeles or New York City. The New York metropolitan area contains the second largest concentration of Korean Americans in the United States, after Los Angeles. As of 1994, approximately 100,000 Korean Americans lived in New York City proper, with an estimated 150,000 to 200,000 living in the entire New York–New Jersey metropolitan area (Park 1997, 17; Min 1996, 37).

The occupational preference system laid out by the Hart-Celler Act of 1965 decisively shaped the profile of incoming Korean immigrants. Designed pursuant to economists' predictions that the U.S. economy would need more professional, technical, and managerial workers, these occupational preferences selected Korean immigrants from the urban, educated, and skilled middle and upper classes. Then, in 1976, in response to declining job opportunities and special interest lobbying, Congress downgraded occupational preferences so that fewer immigrants could enter via this mechanism (Ong and Liu 1994). By that time, however, there was a critical mass of Koreans living in America who could and did turn to family reunification provisions to perpetuate the flow of immigrants from similar class and educational backgrounds. Diminished reliance on occupational preferences has resulted in the increased diversification by class background of Korean immigrants to the United States since 1976 (Park 1997). Still, by the late 1980s, the majority of Korean immigrants coming to the United States were white-collar workers (Yoon 1997, 93). That most Korean immigrants have been relatively affluent and/or educated and skilled has had important consequences for

TABLE 2.4 KOREAN IMMIGRATION TO THE UNITED STATES, 1965–1990

Year	# of Korean Immigrants
1965	2,165
1966	2,492
1967	3,356
1968	3,811
1969	6,045
1970	9,314
1971	14,297
1972	18,876
1973	22,930
1974	28,028
1975	28,362
1976	30,830
1977	30,917
1978	29,288
1979	29,248
1980	32,320
1981	32,663
1982	30,814
1983	33,339
1984	33,042
1985	35,253
1986	35,776
1987	35,849
1988	34,703
1989	34,222
1990	32,301

Source: Adapted from Pyong Gap Min, *Caught In the Middle: Korean Communities in New York and Los Angeles* (Berkeley: University of California Press, 1996), 29.

their ability to take advantage of economic opportunities left open by Black marginalization.

Racial Triangulation

Upon their arrival in the United States, Korean immigrants are racialized as Asian Americans and triangulated relative to Blacks and Whites. As discussed above, the racial triangulation of Asian Americans takes place via two simultaneous discursive practices: relative valorization, by which White opinionmakers valorize Asian Americans as superior to Blacks on cultural grounds; and civic ostracism, by which White opinionmakers construct Asian Americans as permanently foreign and unassimilable on the same cultural grounds. Obviously, the ubiquitous model minority myth represents relative valorization. By celebrating Asian American "success," White opinionmakers implicitly assert that nothing is standing in the way of other non-White groups except their own bad habits or cultural deficiencies. Timothy Bates (1998) calls this "waving the immigrant report card in the face of indigenous minorities to demonstrate the sloth of underemployed and unemployed members of the latter groups". What is less obvious to most is that the model minority myth also does the work of civic ostracism. By lumping all Asian descent groups together and attributing certain distinctively "Asian" cultural values to them (including, importantly, political passivity or docility), the model minority myth sets Asian Americans apart as a distinct racial-cultural "other." Asian Americans are making it, the myth tells us, but they remain exotically different from Whites.[38] Beneath the veneer of praise, the model minority myth subtly ostracizes Asian Americans.

An article by journalist Michael Daly, entitled "Making It: The Saga of Min Chul Shin and His Family Fruit Store" (*New York*, December 20, 1982), provides a good example of how the mainstream media construct Korean immigrant store owners as "model minority" Asian Americans. The author presents Shin's life as a heroic epic. He writes of the "ordeal [that Shin] undergoes seven days a week" as a produce retailer; declares that the language of "hard work" is one in which Shin and his family are "fluent"; highlights the prejudice expressed by White wholesalers and customers against Shin; points out that Shin has barely any time to sleep or eat; and observes that illnesses and mental breakdowns are common among Korean merchants like him. The message here is that Korean immigrant merchants are hardworking, self-sacrificing, stoic figures whose struggle merits universal sympathy and admiration. The author's silences are conspicuous and significant. Despite the notoriety of Black-Korean conflict by the early 1980s, Daly does not mention that many Blacks believe Korean merchants treat them in a disrespectful, exploitative, and racist manner. What is implicit in this article is that Korean merchants do not deserve grief from anyone, that their valor places them beyond criticism. Both relative valorization and civic ostracism are at work in this article. On the one hand, Korean merchants are presented as succeeding on their own cultural steam, with no need for welfare or affirmative action; on the other hand, they are presented as so hard-driving and self-denying that they seem barely human. The construction of Asians / Asian Americans as self-immolating robots dates back to discussions of Chinese immigrant labor and Japanese kamikaze pilots during the 1800s and World War II, respectively.

Racial triangulation means that Korean immigrants are often marginalized as racial "others," but that they escape the severity and scope of the marginalization imposed on Blacks. Relative social acceptance by Whites is a good indicator of group position in the American racial order. Most Whites are more willing to date, marry, befriend, live among, and work with Koreans (and other Asian Americans) than they are Blacks. That Koreans are not forcibly segregated from Whites is a sign of their relative acceptance by Whites. Although many Korean immigrants new to New York City move into predominantly Asian / Korean areas such as Flushing and Elmhurst (both neighborhoods in the borough of Queens), they make this decision voluntarily for reasons of convenience and comfort. Indeed, Koreans who have lived in the city for a while and have saved up some money often move from these initial sites to White suburbs in Long Island or New Jersey (Min

TABLE 2.5 POVERTY RATES AMONG WHITES, BLACKS, AND
KOREANS IN THE UNITED STATES, 1980–1990

	1980	1990
Whites	7.0%	7.0%
Koreans	13.1	14.7
Blacks	26.5	26.3

Source: Adapted from In-Jin Yoon, *On My Own: Korean Businesses and Race Relations in America* (Chicago: University of Chicago Press, 1997), 97.

1996), where they do not confront the profound hostility awaiting Blacks who cross the urban-suburban line.[39] Only rarely do Koreans actually live in the Black neighborhoods where they own and operate stores. Asian Americans, on the whole, are quite segregated from Blacks in New York City; the two groups overlap only a bit, in southeastern Queens (Mollenkopf 1993). Heon Cheol Lee writes of New York City: "Most Korean merchants doing business in black neighborhoods in fact belong to three different communities: the local black community where they work, the suburban white community where they reside, and the metropolitan Korean community where they enjoy their social and communal life" (1993, 136). As a triangulated group, Koreans clearly enjoy greater freedom than do Blacks in choosing the spaces in which they reside, work, and travel.

Although aggregate figures can obscure as much as they reveal, it is worth noting that both poverty rates and median family incomes in 1980 and 1990 suggest Koreans' intermediate status between Blacks and Whites, as indicated in Tables 2.5 and 2.6. As a group, Asian Americans living in New York City in 1990 had higher median household incomes than either Blacks or Latinos. Elmhurst and Flushing, two communities with substantial Asian immigrant populations, had median household incomes that fell between those of affluent Whites and poor Blacks (Mollenkopf 1993, 19). While these figures do not constitute definitive proof of the racial triangulation of Korean immigrants, they are highly suggestive, especially when viewed together with other kinds of data.[40]

TABLE 2.6 MEDIAN ANNUAL FAMILY INCOMES AMONG WHITES, BLACKS, AND KOREANS IN THE UNITED STATES, 1980–1990 ($)

	1980	1990
Whites	21,014	37,152
Koreans	20,459	33,909
Blacks	12,627	22,429

Source: Adapted from In-Jin Yoon, *On My Own: Korean Businesses and Race Relations in America* (Chicago: University of Chicago Press, 1997), 97.

Small Business Ownership: Last Resort or Golden Opportunity?

Korean immigrant business success in New York City and other major urban centers is legendary. During the early 1990s, the Korean self-employment rate in New York City approximated 50 percent and was higher than that of any other group.[41] These kinds of figures, coupled with our national tendency to romanticize small business ownership as a bootstrapping activity, often obscure the fact that this occupational concentration is actually a mixed blessing for most Korean immigrants. Small business ownership is both a last resort and golden opportunity for them. As a recent immigrant group that is racially triangulated, Koreans often cannot participate equally with Whites in the open labor market, but they can take advantage of and benefit from Black residential segregation and economic marginalization. Racial ordering constrains Korean occupational choices, but not as much as it constrains Black choices.[42]

Since most Korean immigrants are educated, skilled, white-collar professionals, they view retail ownership as a form of status derogation and enter it reluctantly. As Min (1996) notes, the first cohort of Korean immigrants arriving in the late 1960s had every expectation of finding professional employment in the United States. Many had attended English-language and vocational schools in Korea in preparation for such jobs. Yet Korean immigrants have been excluded consistently from mainstream professional employment in the United States, in part because of their lack of fluency in English and in part because of racial discrimination. That second-generation Korean (and other Asian) Americans continue to face discrimination in the general labor market—often because they are constructed as culturally foreign, lacking in leadership skills, etc.—reminds us that racial as well as linguistic factors have contributed to this exclusion.[43] Korean immigrants who do find jobs in American companies often see racial discrimination as limiting their opportunities for promotion and move into entrepreneurship to escape this trap (Yi 1993, 106). Unlike earlier cohorts, Korean immigrants arriving in the 1980s have anticipated having to open small businesses and have come prepared (both psychologically and financially) to do so. Still, small business ownership remains a last resort for Korean immigrants. It is a shelter from and alternative to the broader labor market wherein they are disadvantaged, in part because of race, and it is a temporary status derogation endured for the sake of eventual upward mobility.[44]

The reluctance of Korean immigrants to own and operate stores in poor, urban Black neighborhoods is overdetermined by their adoption of prevalent social constructions of Blacks as lowly, dirty, and criminally inclined, and by their material concerns about crime. Stores like the Family Red Apple and Church Fruits in Flatbush are seen by Korean immigrants as especially undesirable both because they serve a primarily Black clientele and because they are located in a potentially high-crime (that is, low-income) area. In addition, the retail produce business involves exceptionally long work hours and strenuous manual labor. Produce stores in poor, urban Black neighborhoods indeed represent aggravated status derogation to white-collar Korean immigrants to the extent that they entail commerce, manual labor, *and* catering to the lowest racial caste. Unsurprisingly, research suggests that Korean greengrocers in Black neighborhood unanimously view their stores as temporary "stepping stone[s]" (Park 1997, 56) and aim to sell them as soon as possible so they can purchase higher-status stores (such as dry cleaning or gift shops, which are more capital intensive and less labor intensive) in high-status (namely, White) areas (Yi 1993; Kim 1981).

From another vantage point, however, small business ownership is clearly a golden opportunity for Korean immigrants, a reliable route to upward mobility that is effectively closed off to Blacks. As we have seen, this opportunity exists for Koreans (as it did for Jews and Italians) largely as a result of Black residential segregation and economic marginalization. Although Korean immigrants prefer to avoid Black areas as a rule, many are compelled to start their entrepreneurial careers therein, where financial barriers to entry are relatively low. In New York City as elsewhere, Korean small businesses are disproportionately located in Black areas (Min 1996, 65).[45] The Korean Produce Association of New York (KPANY) estimates that in 1990 most of the city's fifteen hundred Korean-owned greengroceries served Black neighborhoods (Lee 1993, 116). Once they have started up and consolidated businesses in Black areas, most Korean immigrants then experience upward mobility by selling their stores and purchasing more desirable ones in White areas and/or by facilitating their children's advance into professional jobs comparable or superior to those their parents had held in Korea.

How do Korean immigrants amass the capital to start up businesses? As mentioned above, the prior scholarly emphasis on the role of culture and kyes has given way to more balanced assessment of the varied sources of Korean immigrant capital, which include savings brought from Korea, savings earned in the United States (usually by working for a Korean store-owner), and money borrowed from friends and family (Aldrich and Waldinger 1990; Waldinger 1989a; Light and Bonacich 1988).[46] The occupational preferences elaborated in immigration policy have favored relatively affluent immigrants, and Koreans often come to the United States with a good deal of capital in anticipation of purchasing a small business.[47] The Korean government has accommodated this trend by raising steadily the amount of money that Korean emigrants may carry out of the country—from $1,000 to $3,000 for each emigrant and $10,000 per family in 1979, to $100,000 per family in 1981, to $200,000 per family by 1990 (Park 1997, 16). In addition, Koreans sometimes carry out more than is allowed by law (Yi 1993, 116). Some Korean immigrants refrain from seeking U.S. citizenship in order to retain significant property holdings in Korea.[48] Koreans who arrive in America with relatively little money usually amass start-up capital through some combination of saving wages earned in a Korean-owned store and borrowing money from friends and family. Min's 1992 survey of Korean merchants operating stores in Black areas in New York City shows that savings from U.S. earnings constituted an average of 47 percent of their business capital while money brought from Korea comprised an average of 22 percent (1996, 102). The owner of the Family Red Apple, Bong Jae Jang, borrowed money from his brother, other family members, and friends to purchase the store in 1988; Manho Park, the owner of Church Fruits, used a combination of savings and money borrowed from siblings and another Korean store owner to purchase his store (Lee 1993, 72–73).[49]

Education correlates positively with small business success for all groups, and Korean immigrants are better educated than most Americans (Bates 1994). The 1990 U.S. Census shows that 80 percent of Korean Americans twenty-five years and older (most of whom are foreign-born) finished high school and 34 percent completed four years of college; the comparable figures for all Americans are 75 percent and 20 percent (Min 1996). A survey of Korean merchants in New York City conducted by the Korean American Small Business Service Center (KASBSC) in the fall of 1986 shows that 70.3 percent of respondents received at least some college education in Korea and 5.6 percent also received graduate education there. More than two-thirds of the Koreans who ran stores on Church Avenue in the early 1990s had a college degree or more; one had been a high school principal in Korea (Lee 1993, 145). Although most Korean immigrants had held white-collar jobs in Korea, In-Jin Yoon (1997) points out that many knew friends or family members involved in entrepreneurship and suggests that this prior exposure enhanced their subsequent business success in the United States.

As in most things, success in small business breeds more success. During the early 1970s, Korean immigrants were struggling to establish a foothold in various retail industries in New York City and other major urban centers. By the early 1990s, Korean entrepreneurs dominated many of these same industries. What happened during the intervening years? Waldinger (1996) refers to this dynamic as niche formation and reproduction. Korean immigrants gradually built dense ethnic networks to circulate information and resources within the community and to facilitate the entry of a continuous stream of Korean immigrants into the retail trade. By dint of such networks, Korean immigrants have been able to take over entire urban retail sectors—such as greengroceries in New York City and liquor stores in Los Angeles. In 1990, an estimated 90 percent of the greengroceries in New York City were Korean-owned, including the Family Red Apple and Church Fruits (Rigg and Richtel 1990).

To maintain their retail produce niche, Korean immigrants in New York City have developed a range of wholesale and support services that improve their competitive advantage. Continuous immigration has helped to steadily expand Korean small business niches in New York City. From 1987 to 1991, the number of Korean-owned businesses in the New York metropolitan area increased from nine thousand to fifteen thousand. This growth was concentrated among retailers of produce, groceries, fish, imported Asian goods, dry cleaning, and nail services—all areas in which Koreans now enjoy a "virtual monopoly" (Min 1996, 53). Koreans have been so successful at dominating small business niches that intraethnic competition is now one of the most salient causes of Korean business failure.[50] Based on foreclosed Black opportunities in the first place, Korean small business niches make it even less likely that Blacks will be able to open stores in their own neighborhoods. Thomas Bailey and Roger Waldinger explain: "Since access to ethnic networks is based on particularistic criteria, and job information and assistance comprise scarce resources, the creation of these specializations involves a process of boundary creation and maintenance, restricting members of other groups from jobs or occupations within the niche" (1991, 48).

Exposing racial power means illuminating the American racial order and its tendency toward self-reproduction. It means denaturalizing our given surroundings and apprehending the structural and ideological dynamics related to race that so profoundly shape group outcomes in American society. This yields a very different picture of Black-Korean conflict than that proffered by the racial scapegoating argument. Proponents of the racial scapegoating argument argue that Korean immigrants get "caught in the middle" of Black-White tensions, and that Black collective action against Korean merchants is irrational, unproductive, and unfair. In other words, Korean immigrants' success bears no relation to Black marginalization, and the former are not implicated in any way in American racial dynamics. However, the notion of a racial order emphasizes that groups get racialized relative to one another on a continuous basis and that their fates are therefore crucially intertwined. Korean immigrants may be said to be implicated in the American racial order to the extent that their positioning within it determines their opportunities and constraints, and, more specifically, to the extent that they benefit from Black marginalization and buy into American racial constructions. This does not necessarily mean that Black collective action against Korean merchants is justified or fair. What it does mean is that we cannot summarily dismiss such action as irrational and wrong but must confront the important normative questions it raises about whether and to what degree intermediate groups share responsibility for the American racial order.

3

Black

Power

Resurgent

Does black nationalism exist only at certain historical junctures, or is it always there like the subterranean stresses which precede an earthquake? . . . Nationalism is an ever-present but usually latent (or unarticulated) tendency . . . The fact that black nationalism normally lies hidden just beneath the surface veneer of black America is over-looked by mass media which are geared to crises, scandals, and otherwise spectacular developments.

Robert Allen

If racial ordering implicates intermediate groups like Korean immigrants in its operation, then the presumption that Black collective action against Korean merchants is irrational clearly needs to be reexamined. Indeed, once we realize that the Red Apple Boycott was not an isolated incident but rather an aspect of an overall resurgence of Black Power activism in New York City during the 1980s, the conventional notion that the boycotters were venting their frustrations on Koreans *instead of* on Whites loses its cogency. The re-surgent Black Power movement in New York City was in fact a pointed response to continuing White dominance on the local scene, as personified by

Mayor Edward Koch. This is not to say that it was an inevitable occurrence, since, as social movement scholars have shown, oppression and injustice do not, in and of themselves, produce a collective response. But it is to say that these Black activists took action in the name of challenging White dominance or "racism" and that they drew upon a long historical tradition of Black nationalist resistance in doing so. Even as it confronted racial power, the resurgent Black Power movement in New York City was shaped by it both in terms of its imagination (it accepted the category "Black" and simply reversed its valence) and its aims and means (it explicitly challenged the racialization of urban space by adopting certain tactics and protest forms). In this chapter I introduce the reader to this movement; in the next chapter I situate the Red Apple Boycott within this movement, demonstrating that the boycott was not an isolated eruption of scapegoating but part of a larger manifestation of Black nationalist resistance to White dominance.

I begin this chapter by introducing the concept of a *frame repertoire*, which is intended to illuminate the historical continuities among movements in different epochs. I then briefly review the careers of two relevant collective action frames (Black Power and community control) before discussing the resurgent Black Power movement itself at some length. I then examine the social control tactics that Mayor Edward Koch employed against the movement and close with a brief account of the movement's culmination in the historic election of David Dinkins as the first Black mayor of New York City in 1989.

FRAME REPERTOIRES

Racial ordering has a long history in the United States, but so does racial resistance. One of the most striking aspects of the resurgent Black Power movement in New York City was its apparent connection to earlier periods of Black nationalist activity. This connection was especially clear with regard to how the activists "framed" or socially constructed their movement. Yet current social movement theory offers only limited help in conceptualizing this connection. For this reason, I introduce the concept of a frame repertoire here to help us appreciate the embeddedness of the resurgent Black Power movement within the historical tradition of Black nationalist resistance. Let me briefly comment on the notion of "framing," which is well established in the social movement literature, before I elaborate on my concept of a frame repertoire.

Starting in the 1980s, the field of social movement theory experienced something of a paradigm shift. Although the dominant paradigm, resource mobilization theory, has not been bumped from the stage altogether, it now has to share space with social constructionist approaches that emphasize culture, ideology, and meaning-production. The best known of the latter is probably that of David Snow, Robert Benford, and colleagues, who have taken Erving Goffman's notion of "framing" and applied it to the social construction of protest (Snow and Benford 1992; Snow and Benford 1988; Snow et al. 1986). According to Snow, Benford, and colleagues, activists engage in framing (or the creation of a collective action frame) for the purpose of mobilization. A collective action frame performs three functions: it punctuates or highlights a given event, issue, or condition as an intolerable problem; it attributes the problem to a given cause; and it articulates linkages among different aspects of the problem (Snow and Benford 1992, 137). By fashioning a frame out of people's preexisting cultural beliefs, activists generate a sense of collective identity and a mandate for collective action, thus facilitating mobilization. As Scott Hunt and coauthors (1994) point out, frames create a sense of groupness by helping people to situate themselves in relation to other actors and to clearly delineate the "identity fields" of protagonists, antagonists, and audience. A frame's efficacy at promoting mobilization depends on its "resonance"—or how well it explains the world, how well it explains people's actual experiences, and how well it speaks to people's existing beliefs (Snow and Benford 1992). Finally, activists seek different degrees of "frame alignment," depending on how much they seek to bring people's already existing beliefs into alignment with the movement's formal philosophy (Snow et al. 1986).[1]

Scholars typically depict framing within a given movement as an innovative, competitive, and disputatious process. Movement groups compete to see who can generate the most persuasive collective action frame and thereby win the most adherents over a particular issue or cause. William Gamson and David Meyer write: "[It is] comparatively rare that we can speak sensibly of *the* movement framing. It is more useful to think of framing as an internal process of contention within movements with different actors taking different positions" (1996, 283). Robert Benford discusses "frame disputes" wherein "social movement organizations devote considerable time to constructing particular versions of reality, developing and espousing alternative visions of that reality, attempting to affect various audiences' interpretations, and managing the impressions people form about their movement" (1993, 678). In Benford's account, then, organizations within the same movement squabble with one another publicly in a competitive bid for members. Participants, for their part, choose the organization whose particular angle on the issue they like the best.

But what are we to think when the same frames crop up from epoch to epoch, when they seem less products of ad hoc innovation than products of historical gestation? Many social movement theorists have addressed the organizational, structural, and tactical continuities that obtain among movements and across time. Charles Tilly has written about "repertoires of collective action," or sets of routine forms of protest that persist over time, for a generation (1995). Verta Taylor developed the concept of "abeyance structures" (1989; see also Rupp and Taylor 1987) to refer to the structural and organizational continuities among movements and to counter to what she calls the "immaculate conception" notion of social movement origins. However, there is little work on the cultural continuities among movements, which has prompted several theorists to call for research in this area (Johnston 1991; Gusfield 1981). Doug McAdam speculates about how enduring "cultural repertoires" might facilitate movement resurgence:

> Too often overlooked in structural accounts of movement emergence is the extent to which these established organizations/networks are themselves embedded in long-standing activist subcultures capable of sustaining the ideational traditions needed to revitalize activism following a period of movement dormancy. These enduring activist subcultures function as repositories of cultural materials into which succeeding generations of activists can dip to fashion ideologically similar, but chronologically separate, movements . . . The presence of these enduring cultural repertoires frees new generations of would-be activists from the necessity of constructing new movement frames from whole cloth. Instead, most new movements rest on the ideational and broader cultural base of ideologically similar past struggles. (1994, 43)

Along the same lines, Marc Steinberg (1995) discusses "repertoires of discourse" that generate ongoing, patterned dialogues between challengers and powerholders.

The concept of a frame repertoire builds on these ideas. A frame repertoire is, quite simply, a set of collective action frames that outlives specific movements, persists through time, and is continuously available to activists seeking to build a new movement. Each frame repertoire belongs to and is rooted in the cultural beliefs of a specific, fixed population. In other words, only persistently identified (and, quite often, persistently marginalized) groups that cohere continuously over time are the bearers of frame repertoires.[2] Black people living in the United States, for example, have a distinct frame repertoire consisting of various frames of integrationist or nationalist hues. Frames drawn from frame repertoires (repertoire frames) operate differently than, say, the kind of frames Benford (1993) discusses in his work on the nuclear disarmament movement. They do not mobilize previously unconnected people by presenting them with an innovative spin on an issue; to the contrary, they mobilize a given, preestablished population by resonating with the enduring, deeply held beliefs that already unite it. Activists seeking to get a new movement off the ground need not construct frames "from whole cloth"; they need only activate any of the available frames within a group's repertoire. Ready at a moment's notice, repertoire frames are like finely wrought swords waiting in their scabbards. They are powerful mobilizing weapons.

But there is still more to the story. In the nuclear disarmament movement, according to Benford, movement groups have to come up with innovative frames to distinguish themselves from their competitors. Within persistently identified and marginalized groups, on the other hand, the first imperative for activists is to appeal to the group's already existing collective subjectivity and oppositional consciousness—that is, to appeal to what the group has in common. In this context, a movement group that distinguishes itself too sharply from others narrows its appeal and undermines itself. Thus movement groups in these circumstances will use a repertoire frame not as a marker of distinction but as a mobilizing *umbrella* under which different movement groups can cooperate toward their common goal of mobilizing a specific population. The fact that most frames are exceedingly vague and abstract makes it possible for them to function this way. In the resurgent Black Power movement in New York City, for example, groups ranging from revolutionary nationalists to Pan-Africanists to militant integrationists gathered together under the umbrella frame of "Black Power." Of course, movement groups continue to pursue their respective agendas underneath the frame umbrella, since their second imperative is to have their own agendas and worldviews prevail over others'.[3] Over time, these centrifugal tendencies assert themselves with greater and greater force until the movement dissolves.

Repertoire frames crucially shape activists' decisions concerning the form and targets of protest. Scholars frequently note how much social structure and resource endowments impact the form that protest assumes (Piven and

Cloward 1979; Piven 1976). Sidney Tarrow, echoing French historian Marc Bloch, writes: "Particular structures give rise to characteristic forms of collective action" (1994, 35). Charles Tilly's notion of a repertoire of collective actions also emphasizes structural openings and resource capacities. Yet the form that protest takes and, relatedly, the choice of targets, are as much determined by the signifying work of frames as they are by social structural opportunities and resource endowments. No matter how favorable a structural setting may be to protest, no matter how many resources a group may possess, no matter how vulnerable a target may be to pressure, protest will not occur unless and until activists have, through framing, rendered that form of protest and that choice of targets meaningful and appropriate in the eyes of the participants. As Scott Hunt and coauthors write, "The constitution of targets of action is contingent on the establishment of their identity" (1994, 192). And identity construction, of course, occurs through framing. When protest forms and choices of targets persist from epoch to epoch (for example, Black retail boycotts against non-Black store owners), therefore, they reflect cultural continuities within a persistently identified and marginalized group as much as they do continuities in its structural position or resource capacities.

In sum, repertoire frames (as opposed to regular frames) are properties of persistently identified and marginalized groups. They persist through time, constituting an ongoing cultural resource to activists engaged in movement construction. When activated, they serve not to distinguish movement groups from one another but to provide them with an umbrella under which to coalesce, however precariously and briefly. They shape decisions about protest forms and targets, raising the likelihood that certain forms and targets will crop up over and over again in a particular group's tradition of resistance. The concept of a frame repertoire emphasizes the historical embeddedness of contemporary protests undertaken by persistently identified and marginalized groups. More specifically, it reminds us that Black resistance is as old as White dominance. Before moving on to the main topic of this chapter, I want to discuss briefly two repertoire frames that carried over from earlier epochs and shaped the resurgent Black Power movement in New York City.

BLACK POWER AND COMMUNITY CONTROL

Black Power and community control are two Black repertoire frames that have a distinctively nationalist hue. They call upon and resonate with long-standing and widely held Black nationalist beliefs that reinforce an enduring sense of collective identity among Black people. Rather than engaging in a full anatomy of "Black nationalism," I will proceed with a basic definition here.[4] Black nationalists believe that Black people within the United States constitute an oppressed nation or internal colony, and they exhort Black people to come together, take pride in their Blackness, liberate themselves, and take back power over their own lives.[5] This perspective is open-ended enough that everyone from pluralists to revolutionary nationalists to religious separatists can comfortably pledge adherence to it. Note that Black nationalism does not call for the repudiation of the imposed racial category of Blackness (as civil rights leaders espousing colorblind talk have), but instead embraces Blackness as grounds for unity and pride, thus transforming a badge of inferiority into a badge of honor. In this sense, racial power has shaped the ideational parameters of Black resistance. Or, from another perspective, Black nationalists are using the master's tools to try to bring down the master's house.

Black nationalism is not the dominant perspective among Black Americans; nor do all Black people embrace its tenets in toto. But most Blacks in America—not just the most downtrodden—appear to hold some Black nationalist beliefs to some degree. Robert Allen (1969) refers to the tendency toward Black nationalism as ever-present within the Black community, if usually latent. William Van Deburg asserts that Black nationalist beliefs have "percolated through all class-, age-, and gender-based divisions within the black community" (1992, 6). Recent public opinion surveys confirm that Black nationalist beliefs are widely held among middle-class Blacks, especially the college-educated (Tate 1993; People For the American Way 1992; Eisinger 1976). Since Black nationalist beliefs constitute an enduring oppositional consciousness to White dominance, it is telling that public opinion surveys consistently show a substantial gap between Black and White views on issues related to race. As Lee Sigelman and Susan Welch put it: "It is hardly an overstatement to say that blacks and whites inhabit two different perceptual worlds" (1991, 64–65).

Although Black nationalism is habitually presented as the antithesis of integrationism, this dichotomization can be misleading and should be qualified in most instances. In the real world, as opposed to the realm of pure ideology, groups and individuals often espouse a mixture of nationalist and integrationist sentiments, thus defying facile classification. Reality always overflows the boxes created by academic or political concepts. (This was certainly the case in the resurgent Black Power movement in New York City.) Still, the dichotomy is useful for heuristic purposes. I suggest that we think of Black nationalism and integrationism as two broad complexes of beliefs within the Black community, and that we recognize that repertoire frames can tap into and resonate with parts of both simultaneously. Rather than thinking of repertoire frames such as Black Power as appealing only to those who are avowed Black nationalists, then, we should think of such frames as appealing to different groups and individuals to varying degrees, depending on various contingencies.

The Black Power frame that emerged in the mid-1960s at the advent of the Black Power movement was, as the Kerner Commission aptly put it, "old wine in new bottles" (See *Report of the National Advisory Commission on Civil Disorders* 1968, 234).[6] That is to say, the slogan "Black Power" was new but the ideas behind it (that is, the underlying frame) were as old as the tradition of Black resistance in America. Black Power exhorted Blacks to come together as a nation or community, to take pride in their Blackness, and to struggle together for self-determination and liberation.[7] If White racism was the problem, Black Power was the solution. Introduced by Stokely Carmichael in a speech in June 1966, the slogan "Black Power" galvanized a turning away from the traditional civil rights agenda and a turning toward a Black nationalist agenda.[8] Though irrevocably tied to this historical moment, Black Power was, on another level, a resurrection of ideas that had been previously put forward by Marcus Garvey, Malcolm X, and others. Black Power was, in other words, a repertoire frame.[9]

Black Power was an effective repertoire frame in the mid-1960s because it appealed to an already established collective, resonated with longstanding and widely held beliefs within that collective, and provided a spacious umbrella under which differently oriented movement groups could cooperate or at least coexist. Despite their profound ideological differences, a wide variety of groups (CORE, SNCC, the Black Panther Party, etc.) gathered underneath the Black Power umbrella starting in the mid-1960s. What made this possible was that all of these groups held certain fundamental nationalist tenets in common; they were all rooted in the soil of Black nationalist beliefs. Whereas civil rights leaders advocated integration of Blacks and Whites into a single "beloved community," Black Power groups wanted Blacks to take pride in their Blackness and to resist duplicitous efforts to "assimilate" them or nullify their Blackness. They wanted Blacks to combat their mental, political, and economic colonization by Whites and to move toward self-determination and autonomy. Of course, each of these movement groups meant something different by Black "self-determination" and "autonomy" (ranging from repatriation to Africa to territorial separatism within the United States to world-wide socialism). The important point here is that the Black Power frame was vague enough to sustain different meanings, which enabled it to serve as an umbrella, marking off ideological space that all of these movement groups could occupy together. As we shall see below, this repertoire frame performed the same function in New York in the 1980s.

A second repertoire frame that played an important role in the resurgent Black Power movement in New York City was the community control frame.[10] Although it dates back to the 1800s, the community control frame gained visibility with the entrenchment of urban residential segregation during the 1900s. Where Black Power calls generally for Blacks to take back power over their own lives, community control calls more specifically for Blacks to take back control over institutions in their own (segregated) neighborhoods, such as schools, banks, political offices, and stores. We might think of community control as a place-specific application of the Black Power frame. Non-Black merchants, police officers, and teachers are seen in the community control frame as interlopers, agents of the White power structure who penetrate Black areas in order to keep Blacks in a dependent and subordinate position. Malcolm X elaborates on these ideas in his famous speech "The Ballot or the Bullet":

> We should control the economy of our community. Why should white people be running all the stores in our community? . . . Why should the economy of our community be in the hands of the white man? Why? If a black man can't move his store into a white community, you tell me why a white man should move his store into a black community . . . The white man has got all our stores in the community tied up; so that though we spend it [our money] in the community, at sundown the man who runs the store takes it over across town somewhere. He's got us in a vise. (Breitman 1965, 39)

Just as Black Power seeks to transform an imposed racial category into a source of unity and pride, so does community control seek to transform segregated Black areas into bases of solidarity and power. It seeks what Manuel Castells calls "the transformation of the space of exclusion into the space of freedom" (1983, 67). Like Black Power, community control is a response to racial power and is therefore shaped by it. The fact that Black participants in urban rebellions throughout this century have frequently targeted non-Black stores for looting or destruction is an index of how much the community control frame has shaped opinion within the Black community over time (Feagin and Hahn 1973; Skolnick 1969).

Like Black Power, community control is vague enough to sustain different meanings and thus provide an umbrella under which diverse movement groups can get together. This repertoire frame punctuates a problem, identifies who is to blame, and calls for action, but all in language upon which even Black capitalists and revolutionary nationalists can agree.[11] Throughout the twentieth century, community control has been associated with a repertoire of Black collective actions, including retail boycotts and picketing campaigns aimed at non-Black merchants operating stores in Black areas. New York City has been the most active crucible of Black nationalism in the United States at least since the days of Marcus Garvey's United Negro Improvement Association. During the 1930s, Black activists in New York City (and elsewhere) activated the community control frame in "Don't Buy Where You Can't Work" boycotts aimed at getting White store owners to hire Black clerks, as well as in "Double Duty Dollar" and "Buy Black" campaigns designed to encourage Black patronage of Black-owned stores. During the Black Power movement of the 1960s, Black activists in New York City activated the community control frame during numerous protest campaigns, including the one advocating school decentralization in Ocean Hill-Brownsville, Brooklyn. (In their period classic Black Power: The Politics of Liberation in America (1967), Stokely Carmichael and Charles Hamilton use the community control frame when exhorting Blacks to compel non-Black merchants to contribute to the community.) During the 1980s and 1990s, the community control frame has been activated in New York City in retail boycotts against Korean merchants. In all of these collective actions, ideologically diverse movement groups have cooperated under the generous rubric of community control. If we keep the history of this repertoire frame in mind, essentializing events like the Red Apple Boycott as simply "anti-Korean" or "anti-Asian" becomes highly problematic.

PHASE ONE: COMING TOGETHER

By activating repertoire frames such as Black Power and community control, the Black Power movement that arose in New York City in the 1980s reached back to and gained strength from the cultural legacy left by prior Black nationalist activities. The "carry-overs and carry-ons" (Gusfield 1981) between the Black Power movement of the 1960s and the resurgent Black Power movement of the 1980s were indeed numerous. The later movement drew upon the earlier movement's organizational structures, personnel networks, and tactical repertoires as well as its collective action frames. This is not to say that the Black Power movement of the 1980s sprang forth like Athena from Zeus's head, fully formed. In fact, it emerged in two relatively distinct phases. During the first phase, that of leadership mobilization, Black elected officials and activists from across the city came together and networked around several important political campaigns. During the second phase, that of mass mobilization, activists openly activated the Black Power and community control frames and took the movement into the streets, organizing in particular around incidents of racially motivated violence.

Those who came together during the first phase of mobilization included veterans of the civil rights movement, veterans of the Black Power movement of the 1960s, and ex-administrators of the antipoverty programs of the 1960s and 1970s.[12] What brought these diverse individuals together was a growing sense that something had to be done about the political and economic marginalization of Black people in New York City. Activist Jitu Weusi recalls that Mayor Edward Koch, who was seen as the personification of the racist power structure, served as a sort of "lightning rod" for this common effort.[13] Successive campaigns from the early to mid-1980s provided focal points around which Black leaders networked with one another, built cooperative relationships, and clarified their common agenda.

During this first phase of mobilization, Black elected officials led the way while Black activists (including many nationalists) played a supportive role—a situation that was reversed during the second phase of movement emergence. Why did Black nationalist activists, some of whom espoused revolutionary agendas, concern themselves with campaigns concerning local elected and appointed offices? According to Roger Wareham, who later helped to found the December 12th Movement, the revolutionary nationalist group that led the Red Apple Boycott, activists often see conventional politics less as an end in itself than as a step on the road toward more radical change:

ROGER WAREHAM: The electoral arena . . . that's the option that the United States put forth. People see that as an option in terms of, "You have to speak on my behalf." Now the question of whether the individual elected does that is different than the reason the people elected him, and, more often than not, the people get elected, that becomes something unto itself and removed from the reasons that people went out to vote: "We want you to represent us and speak in our interests." They get elected and they feel that they have to become universal and don't speak to the particular interests. But I think that the electoral motion is within the movement, because I think that for the people who are more politically conscious, the electoral motion is necessary because it exhausts the possibilities, that you can't win people over to the next stage until they have exhausted, at least in their mind, the possibilities of, "Have we tried this, have we exhausted it, have we done everything we can to make sure this works? It doesn't work" . . . It would be nice if you can get a candidate who will go in there and not simply take the job, but try to expose what's going on there and expose the contradictions. But more often than not, they get absorbed by the system.

Wareham's comments bring to mind what Robert Allen said of Black nationalism during the 1960s: "Anything workable goes—depending on specific conditions and the relation of forces—from legal struggle, to electoral politics, to direct action campaigns, to force. In short, what is required is a coordinated, multifaceted, multilevel struggle" (1969, 236). Again, we are reminded that conventional dichotomies such as "moderate vs. radical," "integrationist vs. nationalist," and "reformist vs. revolutionary" do not capture the complexity of real-life Black politics and should be used with caution.

The first important campaigns involved the Coalition for Community Empowerment (CCE), an organization formed by activists Al Vann and Roger Green in the early 1980s to promote Black nationalist candidates for elected office in Brooklyn. Vann (a veteran of the Black Power movement of the 1960s) and Green, together known as the "Brooklyn insurgents," ran for office as Black nationalists and wrested the State Assembly seats in the 56th and 57th Assembly districts (ADs) from regular Democratic incumbents. The aim of the Brooklyn insurgents was to establish a political power base in Brooklyn that was independent from Mayor Edward Koch and the Democratic machine as well as the moderate Black political establishment in Harlem.[14] Seeking Assembly seats appeared to be a sound initial strategy toward this goal, since ADs were small and relatively homogenous in racial terms (and therefore winnable) and the city's affairs were powerfully affected by the state legislature's decisions.[15] Prior to the dismantling of the Board of Estimate in 1989, the state legislature exercised an important check on mayoral power through its control of state-sponsored agencies such as the Metropolitan Transit Authority and the Urban Development Corporation and city agencies such as the Board of Education. Although the CCE's influence has never extended far beyond central Brooklyn, its early campaigns helped to bring ideologically diverse Black politicians and activists together and to generate momentum for subsequent contests across the city.

The struggle over the chancellorship of the Board of Education in 1983 also "brought together black political activists of a nationalist persuasion and black elected officials committed to black empowerment" (Green and Wilson 1989, 105). Upon the resignation of sitting Chancellor Joseph Macchiorala in

1983, CCE members and others demanded that Mayor Koch appoint Deputy Chancellor Thomas Minter (who was Black) as his replacement. Activist Jitu Weusi formed the Ad Hoc Committee to Elect Dr. Thomas Minter, whose explicit aim was to mobilize Blacks of all ideological persuasions to support Minter's candidacy. Although Koch ultimately bypassed Minter for a White candidate, the campaign intensified networking among Black activists and politicians and deepened their collective commitment to getting rid of the chief executive. Losing the battle increased their hunger for victory in the war. It was during the Minter campaign that Harlemite David Dinkins and Brooklyn-based nationalists first interacted on a sustained basis. For this reason, Weusi later called this campaign "the beginning of the struggle that ultimately led to Dinkins' victory in 1989" (Sleeper 1990, 280).

Many of those who had been involved in the Minter campaign came together again the next year to form the Coalition for a Just New York (CJNY), whose stated goal was to depose Koch in the election of 1985. The group was successful in constructing a broad coalition of Black leaders precisely because it built upon the networks generated by earlier campaigns. According to Weusi, CJNY achieved a new level of political unity among Blacks in New York City: "This [wa]s the first time in my memory that in New York City, the African-American community had a coalition that included all faiths and churches, elected politicians, appointed politicians, grass roots people, lawyers. You know, it was a very broad coalition, class lines and so forth. So, to me, that was like an accomplishment."[16] Two specific developments gave CJNY members cause for optimism as they approached the 1985 election. First, CCE and other groups had registered large numbers of new Black and Latino voters in New York City in preparation for Jesse Jackson's 1984 presidential campaign. Nearly 465,000 new Democrats were registered in the city between 1982 and 1985, over half of them in predominantly Black and Latino districts (Mollenkopf 1992, 115). Second, Jackson's campaign itself had helped to mobilize and encourage Black voters.[17]

Despite these promising developments, CJNY's candidate, Herman "Denny" Farrell, was badly defeated by Koch in the Democratic primary. Tensions between Blacks and Latinos, on the one hand, and between Brooklyn-based and Harlem-based Black leaders, on the other, contributed to the loss. Herman Badillo, a popular and well-known Puerto Rican politician, had declared his interest in running against Koch, but some CJNY members from the Harlem establishment had insisted on fielding a Black candidate. When they selected Farrell, the Manhattan Democratic party leader and assemblyman from the 71st AD, it seemed to many that his skin color was his main qualification. After all, Farrell lacked charisma, had no ties to Brooklyn-based Black nationalist leaders, and had none of Badillo's popularity. Black leaders who had supported Badillo's candidacy—including Assemblyman Al Vann, Reverend Calvin Butts III of Abyssinian Baptist Church, and attorney C. Vernon Mason—strongly opposed the endorsement of Farrell, fracturing the CJNY. Mayor Koch, in the meantime, targeted Black and Latino voters in particular, spending half of his $7 million war chest on field operations, mostly within minority areas (Mollenkopf 1991, 347). In the end, Koch trounced Farrell in both the Black and Latino communities, winning 41 percent of the Black vote, 58.2 percent of the mixed minority vote, and 62.4 percent of the Latino vote. Farrell's figures were 32.7 percent, 19.8 percent, and 17.8 percent, respectively (Mollenkopf 1993, 77, 82).[18] Although Black leaders were devastated by Farrell's defeat, the cloud did have a silver lining. That same year, David Dinkins won the Manhattan borough presidency on his third try, moving himself one step closer to Gracie Mansion.[19]

By the mid-1980s, Koch was widely perceived as the personification of the racist power structure, and Black leaders in New York City were determined to get rid of him by any means necessary. From 1987 to 1988, Wilbert Tatum, the editor in chief of the *New York Amsterdam News,* the city's leading Black weekly, wrote numerous front-page editorials that began: "This MAYOR MUST RESIGN OR BE REMOVED IF Blacks, Hispanics, and Asians are to have any hope of participating meaningfully in the life and economy of this city." The campaigns discussed above not only enhanced Black leaders' collective resources and deepened their resolve to get rid of Mayor Koch, but also convinced them of the need to go outside of the formal political system. If they took the movement into the streets, they could turn up the heat and pressure the system to change from the outside. On the topic of tactical flexibility, Jitu Weusi had this to say: "Twenty years ago I said electoral politics was a waste of time, but by ten years ago I was deeply involved in electoral politics. Now I feel the street has much value, and we must continue to protest in the street, but we must also play all over the board. In Zimbabwe, the folks came out of the bush and ran for office. We need to have that same kind of flexibility" (Jennings 1992, 32).

PHASE TWO: TAKING IT TO THE STREETS

After a group of White men chased Michael Griffith, a Trinidadian immigrant, to his death on a highway in Howard Beach, Queens, in December 1986, the resurgent Black Power movement entered its second phase.[20] By openly activating the Black Power frame at this point, movement leaders sought both to mobilize the Black masses by direct appeal to their nationalist beliefs and to construct an umbrella that would facilitate heightened cooperation among movement groups. Because the new movement sometimes gave the appearance of ambulance chasing and was characterized, at times, by manifest factionalism, many observers denied it the status of a bona fide social movement. Norman Fainstein and Susan Fainstein, for instance, argue that the movement was not a real movement because it was not "carried out under the auspices of established organizations," because its leaders did not assert "a specific set of objectives," and because they "failed to win much sympathy within the liberal white community" despite their best efforts to "imitate the style of Martin Luther King" (1991, 318–19). In other words, a movement that does not successfully emulate the civil rights movement is not a real movement but an assortment of chaotic activities. I take issue here both with the Fainsteins' description of this movement, which is inaccurate, and with their conclusions, which miss the point. The leaders of the new Black Power movement were not integrationists seeking White support for specific legislative goals but Black nationalists seeking to mobilize the Black masses in a pressure campaign against an oppressive system. That this movement did not look like the civil rights movement did not make it any less a movement.

Howard Beach: Resurrecting the Black Power Frame

The killing of Michael Griffith was the spark that set the new Black Power movement ablaze. Immediately afterward, activists openly resurrected the Black Power frame (which became the "master frame" for the new movement) and used it to exhort ordinary people into taking action.[21] The Howard Beach killing became a galvanizing event because Black activists punctuated it, via the Black Power frame, as a symbol of the overall degradation and powerlessness of Black people in New York City. Once again, this repertoire frame was used to encourage Black people to come together and fight racial oppression. One of the slogans of the new movement, "No Justice, No Peace!" which was seen and heard everywhere during the post–Howard Beach protests, signaled the militant and defiant tone that characterized the second phase of the movement's emergence. By resurrecting the Black Power frame through the spoken and written word, the leaders of the new movement quite deliberately and self-consciously attempted to reawaken the Black Power movement of the 1960s, which had died out by the early 1970s.[22]

Activist Elombe Brath, who later became a founding member of the December 12th Movement, recounts that he and his colleagues had resolved to do something drastic even before the Howard Beach killing:

> ELOMBE BRATH: A group of African nationalists and revolutionaries, or what have you, came together in about 1985 prior to the all of the Howard Beach stuff . . . to try to reconstitute the Black Power movement, because we felt there . . . was a tremendous setback both politically and socially, as well as economically [for Black people] . . . We started having some meetings, trying to put together a movement toward bringing about the Black Power movement . . . We felt that the quest for nationalism and Pan-Africanism was in sync with what the Black movements had started throughout the world and that had been crushed, or had been suppressed, and that was one of the reasons why we couldn't have any unity, we could not have a united front, so the best thing to put forward was demand for Black Power. This demand goes back into the last century . . . So we wanted to reconstitute that kind of movement because the movement went into a state of inertia and had not been really properly organized. It was almost dismantled between what the police were doing as far as rounding these people up in the '70s, forcing them into jail and forcing people out of the country, and the other ones being drugged. It was the kind of thing where you saw the movement almost disintegrate, although you saw how vital and vibrant it was in the '60s, so we wanted to go back to that. We wanted to get people starting to appreciate themselves, starting to have Black pride. That's why we wanted to start the Black Power movement.

As in the 1960s, the Black Power frame's vagueness, its ability to sustain many different meanings simultaneously, helped activists to construct a "united front," or what another movement leader called "a house big enough for everybody to hang their coat."[23] Movement groups with crucial ideological differences could gather under the umbrella of Black Power, united in their determination to mobilize the Black community against oppression. So, too, could ordinary Black people. Whether they were committed Black nationalists or relatively apolitical sorts, they could all find common ground in their outrage at the Howard Beach killing.

Because social space (churches, the media, residential areas) is highly racialized in New York City, movement leaders used primarily Black informational networks to get the word out.[24] Black talk radio, which one scholar calls an "autonomous information pipeline" (B. Wilson 1991, 24), has played a critical role in disseminating political news since its emergence in New York

City during the early 1980s. Radio has certain advantages over the print media: it is free to the user, it can get the word out immediately, and it can reach even those who are not literate.[25] One movement leader, Reverend Herbert Daughtry, frequently used the radio (in addition to his pulpit) to advertise his activities. He comments: "If I'm doing anything at all, the first place I want to go is WLIB [a Black-owned radio station]. That is far more important to me than the *New York Times* and other so-called White media."[26] Activists frequently appeared on Black radio programs to exhort listeners to attend specific protests and to maintain public visibility. Black newspapers and television programs also played a role in bringing the movement to the people. In these arenas, Black activists who were treated as criminal agitators in the mainstream press were accorded a basic respect.

Although we lack comprehensive data on Black public opinion in New York City during the general period of movement emergence, a telephone poll conducted by CBS and the *New York Times* from June 17 to 20, 1990, confirms that Blacks held oppositional beliefs toward the system.[27] We may surmise that these beliefs were not entirely a product of the movement and that they in fact enhanced their holders' receptiveness to the Black Power frame. Table 3.1 shows some of the results from this poll. The same poll also indicated that Blacks and Whites differed substantially about the prospects for Black advancement and the fairness of the city's judicial system. While 33 percent of Blacks doubted that Blacks living in New York City could overcome racial barriers to make real political and economic gains, only 15 percent of Whites felt this way. Moreover, 63 percent of Blacks felt that the courts were tougher on Black than White defendants, while only 28 percent of Whites agreed with this assessment. Another poll, conducted by the Medgar Evers Caribbean Research Center and the Gallup Organization in New York City in 1987, found that Caribbean immigrants and native-born Blacks concurred on the seriousness of anti-Black racism in New York City.[28] Without exaggerating the weight of these select findings, it does seem reasonable to conclude that the majority of Blacks living in New York City during the period of movement emergence viewed racism as a serious problem and that they were open, at least in principle, to what movement leaders were saying. Many Whites, on the other hand, accepted the tenets of colorblind talk and thought that the movement was much ado about nothing. Mayor Edward Koch spoke for them when he denounced the Howard Beach killing but insisted that it was an aberration and blamed Black leaders for making too much out of it.[29] Sometimes, of course, White commentators on the movement unwittingly supported Black activists' charges, as when one White reporter for the *Daily News* pointedly asked what Griffith and his Black companions had been doing in predominantly White Howard Beach in the first place.[30]

Soon after the Howard Beach killing, Black activists launched the first in a series of "Day of Outrage" protests designed to bring Black people out into the streets of New York City.[31] On January 21, 1987, a month or so after the killing, a group of officials and activists, including Assemblyman Roger Green, activist Sonny Carson, and lawyers Alton Maddox and C. Vernon Mason, led forty-five hundred people on a march from Brooklyn to Mayor Koch's home in lower Manhattan, where protesters chanted, "Mayor Koch, step aside, there ain't gonna be no genocide!" Black activists carried out a citywide, daylong boycott of non-Black-owned businesses to coincide with this march. Rhetoric about these activities ranged from mildly integrationist to emphatically nationalist, depending upon who was speaking, and to whom. Green, for instance, compared the daylong boycott to the Montgomery Bus Boycott of 1955 (which launched the civil rights movement), while Carson compared it to the more militant "Don't Buy Where You Can't Work" campaigns that took place in Harlem in the 1930s.[32] Despite their different emphases, both leaders sought to legitimate their activities by situating them within the historical tradition of Black resistance. In any case, the audience often adopted its own take on things, as when an audience at the Boys and

TABLE 3.1 BLACK AND WHITE OPINIONS ON RACIAL
FAIRNESS IN NEW YORK CITY, 1990
*Question: In general, do you think Blacks in New York City have
received their fair share, less, or more?*

	Total	White	Black
Fair	38%	45%	18%
Less	38	25	71
More	13	19	2
Don't Know / No Answer	11	11	9

Source: Data taken from the *New York Times*/WCBS telephone poll in New York City, June 17–20, 1990.

Girls High School in Brooklyn met Assemblyman Green's moderate comments with shouts of "Black Power!"

The politics of photo-ops can be quite revealing. The juxtaposition of two back-to-back press conferences about the Howard Beach killing suggests something of the complexity of relations between Black officials and activists (and the related tensions between moderate and radical agendas) during this stage of movement emergence.[33] During the first conference, Governor Mario Cuomo appointed Charles Hynes as special prosecutor for the Howard Beach case, a significant victory for movement leaders, who had demanded the appointment of such a prosecutor. As he made his announcement, Governor Cuomo was surrounded by Black elected officials, including Manhattan Borough President David Dinkins, Assemblyman Roger Green, State Senator David Paterson, and veteran politician Basil Paterson. Reverends Calvin Butts III and Herbert Daughtry were the only nonofficials present on stage. In one voice, these Black leaders praised Governor Cuomo and hailed his decision as a "people's victory." Shortly thereafter, this same group (minus Cuomo) held a second press conference at the State Office Building in Harlem before an overwhelmingly Black audience and Black media representatives. This time, they were joined on stage by Sonny Carson and other nationalist activists. Assemblyman Green's comments had acquired more of an edge by the time of the second press conference: "We recognize that the Governor has responded to pressure from the black community. And he can be sure that there will be greater pressure and higher expectations now" (*New York Times*, January 15, 1987). The first conference was pitched by Black elected officials (and Governor Cuomo) to a mixed audience while the second was pitched by a range of Black leaders to a Black audience.

As the new Black Power movement moved into the streets, activists gradually moved to center stage and elected officials moved off into the wings. This passing of the torch was marked by some tensions between the two groups. Activists and officials usually part ways at some point on what needs to be done and who needs to do it. Assemblyman Al Vann suggests that officials do more of the work while activists get most of the credit:

ASSEMBLYMAN AL VANN: The expectation that elected officials should necessarily be on the cutting edge of change as people perceive it, I think it's probably not accurate. I think our definition is, elected officials have to negotiate. A negotiator is a very important role . . . We are engaging in dialogue with power brokers from other groups, other races, et cetera, and so our value, our strength, has to be our ability to be informed, to use intelligent judgment, to be committed to our community, and to be able to negotiate, to know the issues, to use our leverage as elected officials. Elected officials have a very unique role that no one else has, and that is that we enact the laws. We create the public policy that affects everybody else in society. And so—never are we fully appreciated by our community, by the way—and so, we need to be augmented by other leadership, whether it is community activists . . . So, actually, there should not be a conflict or confrontation between elected officials and activists. It really should be an augmentation of support based on the revolutionary positions that others may make which would begin to have an effect in support of positions that we must take as elected officials.

Unsurprisingly, activist Omowale Clay, a founding member of the December 12th Movement, sees the division of labor differently. In his view, activists champion the people's causes while officials worry over their own political survival:

OMOWALE CLAY: I mean, politicians are a certain genre. My view is not to spend so much time dealing with them, because they're already owned by the Democratic party. That's who owns them. So, at some point in time they'll say something, at other points in time, they won't. You know what I mean. Sometimes some of them will be so treacherous as to be ostracized, but basically they walk upside down because they don't control their own politics.

Despite these differences of opinion, the relationship between Black activists and Black elected officials remained generally supportive throughout the 1980s, although some elected officials were critical of the activists' turn toward greater militance (symbolized by the open activation of the Black Power frame). It was only during the Red Apple Boycott in 1990, following the election of Mayor David Dinkins, that a serious breach opened up between the two groups.

Movement Groups Under the Black Power Umbrella

Who were the groups of activists who took the movement into the streets? They were as diverse in outlook and approach as movement groups had been in the Black Power movement of the 1960s. One activist, Reverend Al Sharpton, comments on this diversity: "Like the struggles in the '60s, I think they [movement activities] were multifaceted. You have those that operated at different levels from different ideologies. I think that all wanted to see more empowerment for Blacks and more fairness . . . [Today] some have different modus operandi, but I think the general goals are the same. I think that there's differences in approach and differences in reach. And I think that that was true in the '60s."[34] Yet it would be a mistake to interpret this diversity as prima facie proof of the movement's ineffectiveness or incoherence. L. P. Gerlach and V. H. Hine caution observers against this error:

> At first consideration, one might view organizational segmentation as a weakness, as a maladaptive characteristic for a movement . . . Outside observers may well see in such segmentation only something amusing—a sure sign of significant deficiencies in the movement and its members. In fact, observers, even professed students of the phenomenon, may focus so much on the fact of schism that they are misled into thinking that there is no movement, but only a collection of separate enthusiasms and divided efforts. In short, they miss the forest for the trees. Or, more accurately, for the diversity of the trees. (1970, 63)

In their work on the Black Power movement of the 1960s (and the Pentecostal movement), Gerlach and Hine explain that a "fragmented" leadership structure can be quite adaptive for a movement subject to persecution and repression. Their description of such a structure—it is "reticulated" (weblike, or characterized by crisscrossing lines of communication and allegiance that do not go through a central point), "segmentary" (composed of distinct cells or movement groups), "decentralized" or "polycephalous" (lacking a binding central authority), and composed of groups given to frequent fission, fusion, and recombination processes (1970, 33)—fits the resurgent Black Power movement in New York City quite well. The leadership structure of this movement was not bureaucratically organized but rather fluid, dynamic, and complex. In this section, I identify and describe some of the most important movement groups or centers of power, with special emphasis on the December 12th Movement, the organization that led the Red Apple Boycott. In the next section, I discuss what relations were like among these groups.

The December 12th Movement came into being during the planning of the post–Howard Beach protests in 1987. In the context of ongoing group fission and fusion processes, the December 12th Movement represented a new permutation or recombination of veteran Black activists. Founding member Elombe Brath recalls that the group of activists who would become the December 12th Movement first visited Michael Griffith's family together and then "decided to take it [the issue of the killing] up and then we started to meet. Eventually, we started to become involved in other things . . . and as a result of that, we started to put into motion a working relationship with a group of people, including lawyers and everything else."[35] Many of these

activists had worked together on an ad hoc basis earlier in the 1980s on issues
such as drug abuse and police brutality, but it was the Howard Beach killing
that led them to formalize their working relationship and establish a new
organization together.[36] Composed of nationalists, Pan-Africanists, and revolutionaries, the December 12th Movement became the most radical, hard-line
group in the resurgent Black Power movement.

Although the mainstream media frequently conflate the organization with
its infamous leader, activist Sonny Carson, the December 12th Movement is,
in fact, internally heterogeneous.[37] In fact, it is a coalition of three main cote-
ries of Black nationalist activities. The first coterie consists of Sonny Carson
and activists involved in the other organizations that he leads, including the
Committee to Honor Black Heroes and the Black Men's Movement Against
Crack. Carson, who led the Brooklyn chapter of CORE in the late 1960s when
it broke away from the national headquarters in order to pursue a more
militant line, is a traditional Black nationalist whose philosophy in some
ways mirrors that of Malcolm X during his early years. Carson, for instance,
views complete racial separation as the proper aim of the Black liberation
struggle and the only guarantee of Black self-determination. The second coterie of activists consists of Elombe Brath and activists involved in his Pan-
Africanist organization, the Patrice Lumumba Coalition.[38] Brath is a Pan-
Africanist committed to advancing the Black revolutionary struggle in both
Africa and the United States. The third coterie, finally, consists of former
members of the New York Eight, a militant group whose members were tried
and convicted on weapons possession charges (and acquitted of conspiracy
to commit bank robberies and jail breaks) during the early 1980s.[39] Former
New York Eight members such as Robert Wareham and Omowale Clay are
revolutionary nationalists whose philosophy echoes that of the Black Panther
Party of the 1960s and 1970s.

Structurally, the December 12th Movement is like a microcosm of the
resurgent Black Power movement. It is a coalition within a coalition. Its members (constituent organizations and individuals) share certain nationalist beliefs but retain their respective ideological identities and priorities. In this
way, the organization achieves what Elombe Brath calls the "synthesis of all
these various types of philosophical orientations all grounded in the rights of
self-determination."[40] Roger Wareham comments on this intraorganizational
diversity:

ROGER WAREHAM: [The December 12th Movement] is a movement and
the movement has—you know, it's not a party. The movement has a wide

variety of points of view and the fundamental commitment needed is to liberation for the Black nation and to defend the human rights of the people of African descent. And so, within that, you get a wide range, as you do in any sort of national liberation struggle.

As chair of the December 12th Movement, Sonny Carson is primus inter pares. However, collective decision making is the general rule. Carson notes that the coalitional structure nevertheless permits constituent groups considerable autonomy:

SONNY CARSON: I chair the collective. On the more weightier, the bigger decisions, I mean tasks, of course, there has to be a collective decision made so we have to have a collective role in making the decisions. But I also am the chairman of the Committee to Honor Black Heroes and I am the chairman of the Black Men's Movement Against Crack, and those are two organizations within the December 12th Movement, and so there are times where those organizations will be making their own moves and we don't have to have a collective decision.

What is surprising about this coalition is that the three main perspectives represented within it—Black nationalism, Pan-Africanism, and revolutionary nationalism—are highly distinct, albeit overlapping, ideologies. To grossly oversimplify, the first calls for the establishment of a separate Black nation, the second for the liberation of the African continent and diaspora from European domination, and the third for socialist revolution. How can advocates of these three perspectives work together in a single organization? The answer lies in the ideological common ground that all three share—fundamental beliefs in Black pride, unity, self-determination, etc.—and the fact that grand ideological differences about ultimate ends do not significantly affect the daily operations of a movement group.

Let's look more closely at these philosophical or ideological differences. Sonny Carson, who seems unperturbed by the potential contradictions between his ideology and those of his colleagues, proudly claims Malcolm X as his ideological progenitor:

SONNY CARSON: I'm not a socialist. I'm a Black nationalist and my philosophy is Malcolm X-ism. I believe that it's about freedom or death. I believe that it's about land. I believe that Black people have to be freed by any means necessary. I believe that all of the involvements that one is picturing today, where Blacks like Jesse Jackson and all of the rest of them are acquiescent to the customs of the system . . . are detriments to our progression. I believe that even the march on Washington, both of them, were an obstacle, a detriment, and a distraction. I believe that what the last march on Washington had done was to distract and to get a lot of the young people who could possibly be warriors later on identified by the FBI. I think that the whole object of voter registration is a cop-out and an accommodation to the kidnappers . . . The Black liberation that I am involved in is about, the bottom line, freeing our people by any means necessary.

Pan-Africanism, a philosophy that has a distinguished pedigree reaching back at least to W. E. B. Du Bois, places special emphasis on the unification of the African continent and the organic connectedness of the struggles of African people throughout the diaspora.[41] As Stokely Carmichael writes, "Pan-Africanism is grounded in the belief that Africa is one . . . [and] in the belief that all African peoples, wherever we may be, are one" (1971, 221). Pan-Africanists typically embrace revolutionary ideals, envisioning a united socialist Africa as the ultimate outcome of the Black liberation struggle. Elombe Brath talks about the Pan-Africanist organization that he founded:

ELOMBE BRATH: The Patrice Lumumba Coalition was founded on the 11th of November, 1975, the same year the People's Republic of Angola was founded. It was founded in order to organize the African community against an imposition by the media, the media establishment and the U.S. government to intervene into the affairs of Angola . . . So the Patrice Lumumba Coalition was founded by Pan-Africanists, people who have a long African nationalist history, because I have been involved in the struggle going back to 1956 . . . Subsequently, it also dealt with issues in South Africa, in Zimbabwe, and almost every county in Southern Africa you can actually think about, particularly Namibia, you know . . . As far as the domestic scene [in the United States], we analyzed the situation from both a class and racial position . . . how race is used in the United States to confuse [poor] White people who are also exploited, [as if] the reason why they are not getting more [is that] we people of color, the African population, is demanding more.

Revolutionary nationalists, finally, view Blacks living in America as an internal colony or nation subjected to both racial and class oppression. Black liberation, for them, means not only the eradication of racism but also the dismantling of capitalism. Like the Black Panther Party before them, revolutionary nationalists like Roger Wareham and Omowale Clay fight against "a two-headed monster: racism—the most brutal and heinous crime against Third World people's human rights; and ruthless class oppression under the yoke of the bourgeoisie" (from the December 12th Movement's newspaper,

Arm the Masses, October 1991). The following programmatic statement, representative of a revolutionary nationalist perspective, is printed on page two of every issue of *Arm the Masses,* just below the table of contents:

> What we believe:
> Revolutionary nationalism and socialism for the Black Nation, forty million Africans captured inside the racist, capitalist USA. The Black Nation is constituted by a distinct history and psychology shaped by racial and national oppression of its people and their resistance to national oppression; a historically-developed land-base concentrated in the southern USA; a common language shaped with its own cultural idiom; a common economic way of life, underdeveloped due to racism. Africans are mainly wage-slaves to capitalism who will never control the means of production, but all are subject to racist exploitation across class lines. The struggle of Africans inside the USA is a human rights struggle for self-determination, national liberation and the freedom to control African people's destiny free of Racism, Capitalism, and Imperialism.
>
> FREEDOM OR DEATH!

Omowale Clay says more about revolutionary nationalism:

> OMOWALE CLAY: Philosophically, I believe certainly in socialism. I believe that Black people are a nation in this country and have the right to self-determination, and that a nation is not a nation, in my view, that would be at all productive if it just mimicked the one that we are in now. And so, I would see socialism as an aim of that nation. It's not a prerequisite, but certainly that's where I would see it going to . . . We're a nation within this nation . . . very similar, in a sense, to a colonized nation. If we took Jamaica . . . or South Africa and, you know, we placed them inside the United States, I think that we would begin to see the same kinds of relationships.

Roger Wareham comments on the same:

> ROGER WAREHAM: Within the Black nation there is a class question which sometimes gets obscured because the racism in the United States is so great that no matter what class you're from, you are subject to attack, discrimination, and brutality regardless of your class origin or class that you belong to. In the final analysis, you cannot resolve anything without dealing with the class question . . . I think that there is a connection between the resolution of the class question and the resolution of the national question, even our national question. That one cannot be resolved without the other. The reality of a self-determining Black nation or independent Black nation, if

that's what that nation decides, is really tied to the question of the success of socialism inside the United States.

Because Wareham and colleagues claim to identify with other Third World people struggling against Western imperialism and racism, it is not surprising that *Arm the Masses* features regular commentaries on countries where communists are either in positions of power or contenders, such as China, North Korea, Cuba, and Peru. The July / August 1994 issue of the newspaper contains a full-page letter expressing condolences to the new North Korean president, Kim Jong Il, on the death of his father, Kim Il Sung. The letter requests permission to send a representative from the December 12th Movement to Kim Il Sung's memorial ceremony. (This letter is especially striking in light of Korean American accusations that the December 12th Movement is anti-Korean.) As part of their international efforts, revolutionary nationalists within the December 12th Movement founded Masses United for Human Rights, a group that works with the International Association Against Torture (a nongovernmental organization with consultative status at the United Nations) and the Organization of African Unity to mobilize international opposition to the oppression of Black people in the United States. The October 1991 issue of *Arm the Masses* observes: "The December 12th Movement continues to fulfill Malcolm's legacy to bring the human rights struggle of Africans in the United States into the international arena."

Why would activists committed to socialist revolution bother with protests like the post–Howard Beach marches or the Red Apple Boycott? In the 1960s, when critics assailed revolutionary nationalists in the Black Panther Party for engaging in such mundane activities as providing free breakfast programs, health clinics, and educational classes, group members retorted that a revolution is not built in a day. Consciousness-raising, they insisted, is a long-range, multifaceted process. Revolutionary nationalists in the December 12th Movement share this long-term perspective. Like the Black Panthers, Roger Wareham and colleagues see themselves as a vanguard party in the Marxist-Leninist-Maoist tradition, as this excerpt from the December 1991 *Arm the Masses* makes clear:

> The vanguard responsibility is to develop the correct political programs to combat the destruction of the masses by the bourgeoisie. The National Question must be approached scientifically and clearly make common sense to the masses. This struggle cannot be from a sectarian or doctrinaire position but must be developed cooly and calmly through mass political

education and an analysis of the concrete conditions of our people . . . The aim of bourgeois propaganda is to overkill the subconscious of those most disposed to the belief that the solution to their oppression is being Hollywood, a Ph.D., a two car garage, and making all-Pro. The net effect of this propaganda is that it becomes increasingly difficult for revolutionaries to organize the oppressed Black masses.

Thus the December 12th Movement see it as their mission to (re)educate and politicize the masses, to "decolonize" their minds, and to raise their consciousness until, finally, the time is ripe for revolution. This process involves debunking the "lie" of integration (and colorblindness) and awakening Black people to the immovable reality of White racism:

OMOWALE CLAY: I think that integration has hurt the question because it has reversed the question. It's like Black people had to do something to themselves to make them acceptable as an integration partner, that there was something wrong with us . . . You know, we had to talk differently, we had to act differently, we had to get rid of certain things to become part of the American melting pot . . . I always go back to; we were never asked whether we wanted to be associated with the United States. No, slaves were never given a plebiscite to determine their relationship . . . Even when we look at the Supreme Court decision in terms of *Brown v. the Board of Education* . . . separate but equal got translated to separate was the contradiction, and separate wasn't the contradiction, separate was certainly the contradiction in the theme of America, but the theme was never a reality . . . So, to chase that lie only led us down a terrible path. The reality was Black people didn't have a problem being separated from White people, Black people had a problem because of inequality . . . America never had any intention of integrating its ex-slaves. It's never integrated its masses of White, poor, working-class people into mainstream America. That's not the nature of capitalism.

Protest campaigns are important because they not only raise consciousness among Black people about racism but also awaken them to their own collective power. After all, since "the masses make revolution . . . [they] have to believe they can and must take control over their own lives. They must participate in their own liberation from beginning to end" (*Arm the Masses,* April 1992). This gives us crucial insight into why the December 12th Movement, as we shall see in the next chapter, refused to negotiate an end to the Red Apple Boycott, preferring instead to prolong the campaign. You don't have to be a socialist to appreciate the politicizing and mobilizing effects that protracted campaigns can generate within the Black community.

Another important center of influence within the resurgent Black Power movement was comprised of Reverend Al Sharpton and two of his close associates, attorneys C. Vernon Mason and Alton Maddox. Like Sonny Carson, Sharpton is a charismatic, well-known figure who tends to overshadow, in the mind of the public, both the organizations he develops and his various colleagues. He developed his oratorical skills at a young age and became a Pentecostal preacher during his preteen years. Up until 1992, when he toned down his appearance to run for the U.S. Senate, Sharpton's public uniform consisted of a flashy jogging suit and a large Martin Luther King Jr. medallion. As his sartorial choices suggest, Sharpton straddles the fence ideologically between the Black Power and the civil rights traditions. He preaches Black solidarity and empowerment but does not talk about separatism or revolution. He leads militant, defiant marches against racism, but calls upon the authority of Martin Luther King Jr. and eschews violence of any kind. Although he does not have a church of his own, Sharpton commands a large following through his organization, the United African Movement, and through his rousing weekly speeches at the Slave Theater in Brooklyn. He was probably the single most widely known leader of the new Black Power movement, and was seen by many as being the primary "go to" man after incidents like the Howard Beach killing.

Mason and Maddox, who work closely with Sharpton, often act as counsel for Black victims in highly publicized cases of racially motivated violence or police brutality.[42] Believing the legal system to be stacked against Blacks, they frequently use unorthodox tactics to secure favorable outcomes for their clients. During the resurgent Black Power movement, their maneuvering within the legal system complemented the direct-action tactics of Sharpton and other activists. When Mason and Maddox represented the surviving victims of the Howard Beach attack, for instance, they threatened to unleash mass demonstrations and / or withhold their clients' cooperation in the police investigation in order to pressure Governor Cuomo into appointing a special prosecutor. As we have seen, Cuomo did accede to this demand. The jury's final verdict in the case, handed down in December 1987, represented a clear victory for the activist-attorneys: three of the four defendants were convicted of manslaughter, while one was cleared of all charges.[43] The verdict also gave the resurgent Black Power movement a boost. As Charles Green and Basil Wilson observed: "Maddox and Mason have indicated that they are not just questioning the legitimacy of the justice system but are committed to building a political movement" (1989, 110).

Other veteran activists, such as Reverend Herbert Daughtry and Jitu

Weusi, also played important leadership roles in the resurgent Black Power movement. Once again, the personal reputations of these men clearly overshadow their shifting organizational affiliations and constitute the actual source of their political influence. Like Al Sharpton, Daughtry is a Pentecostal preacher who straddles the fence between the civil rights and Black nationalist traditions. Given these similarities, it is not surprising that Daughtry considers the younger Sharpton to be his heir apparent among the city's Black leadership cadre. In the mid-1980s, Daughtry founded the African People's Christian Organization, which espouses a Black liberation theology that "synthesiz[es] African nationalism, the teachings of Christ, and the necessity for fundamental political change" (Green and Wilson 1989, 73). He is presently the pastor of the House of the Lord Pentecostal Church in Brooklyn, where he leads a loyal congregation. Jitu Weusi, who played a prominent role in the Ocean Hill-Brownsville school decentralization conflict in 1968, is a self-described Black nationalist with strong ties to many other activists on the local scene. He founded The East, a cultural nationalist organization in Brooklyn, as well as an Afrocentric school, and he was actively involved in several of the electoral campaigns described earlier. Because both Daughtry and Weusi maintained good relations with most other Black activists in the city, they were able to serve as elder statesmen during the resurgent movement. Daughtry explains: "My role is to be able to communicate with all the forces in the community."[44]

Relations Among Movement Groups

Ever since the FBI's counterintelligence programs (COINTELPROs) decimated Black Power movement groups in the 1960s and early 1970s, Black activist circles in New York City have been marked by a certain degree of distrust and suspicion. Daughtry suggests that those in the resurgent Black Power movement struggled with this legacy: "People still had wounds from the '60s where they had been manipulated into fighting each other." Jitu Weusi comments on the same:

> JITU WEUSI: The '70s sort of brought in a cynicism. A distrust. Can I trust you? Do you trust her? Who's he? Do you know him? You know. There was the COINTELPRO revelation. Undercover operations and so on. So a sort of cynicism seeped into the movement, and had an impact. And then by the '80s, you know, you were trying to build these things again.

In this context, movement leaders worked only with those whom they trusted; ideological compatibility was a bonus but not a prerequisite. Since

these activists were subjected to ongoing persecution, harassment, and surveillance by the state, trusting someone else could literally be a matter of life
and death.[45] How did they know who was trustworthy and who was not?
Because many of the activist-led organizations in New York City's Black
community have been prone to the kind of fission and fusion discussed by
Gerlach and Hine (1970), reputations have attached to individual leaders
rather than to organizational entities per se. Individual activists who were
veterans of past struggles and who had been on the scene for a long time had
established good reputations (i.e., reputations for being trustworthy, being
team players, and having integrity), which served as social capital in their
dealings with other activists.

If you listen to these activists discussing how they chose with whom they
would work, you can appreciate the role that personal trust played in their
calculations. Daughtry explains: "From time to time, certain things erupt,
and you just call on certain people. You've been knowing people across the
years, it's normal, it's natural that you call on these people." Speaking for the
December 12th Movement, Omowale Clay states: "We try to work with everybody who we think has principles."[46] In other words, he and his colleagues used an integrity litmus test, not an ideological litmus test, during the
course of the movement. Jitu Weusi's assessments of other movement leaders
reflects a similar kind of evaluation. Of the December 12th Movement, Weusi
says: "I know the people. I think they've done good work. They've been
around for a long time."[47] And of Reverend Al Sharpton, he has this to say:

> JITU WEUSI: I think Reverend Sharpton, you know, I think he's done excel-
> lent work. I've known him since he was a kid . . . In fact, I met him the first
> time in 1968. A friend of mine who was a student at the high school that
> Reverend Sharpton attended invited me to their high school to speak. And
> after the speech, he said that, "Oh, I want you to meet this young guy, who's
> a reverend." He [Sharpton] was fourteen at the time. Nice young man, and
> that's when I met him. He's gone through a metamorphosis in his life. Done a
> lot of things, been around a lot of folks, but basically he's conducted himself
> in a very satisfactory manner . . . And since the mid '80s, when he more or
> less assumed the mantle, I think he's done a tremendous job.

To the extent that they trusted one another, then, activists were able to cooperate in planning and staging protest campaigns during the resurgent Black
Power movement. By the same logic, serious violations of trust created ir-
reparable damage and made further cooperation impossible. (It is in the
nature of trust, of course, that it takes years to build but only a day to destroy.)

When rumors surfaced in 1987 that Sharpton might have acted as an FBI informant, the December 12th Movement cut ties with him and refused to work with him thereafter.[48] This rift weakened the overall movement considerably.

Competition among individual activists to be "on the point" also created centrifugal strains within the movement. To be on the point was to be the primary "go to" man in times of crisis. Whoever was on the point was the chief troubleshooter for the community, the person who would take on the White power structure on behalf of the little guy. Black activists vied for this distinction not by emphasizing their respective ideological positions (which would only have narrowed their potential constituencies) but by trying to be in the right place at the right time. The first activist on the scene after a major race-related incident usually became the official spokesperson for the victim or victim's family and the point person for subsequent protests related to that event. Elombe Brath describes this dynamic with regard to the Howard Beach killing:

ELOMBE BRATH: Then of course there was the Michael Griffith killing, which Sonny Carson found out who the family was and went to them, and also was instrumental in taking Cedric Sanford [another victim of the attack] out of the police station when he saw that the police were too busy watching the ball game to even listen to what Cedric was telling them. And we had gone to the Griffith house the day after the thing happened. It happened on Saturday, we were there that Sunday, and we saw Sanford with his face all bandaged up. He had been beaten, and he told us exactly what happened.

Of course, who was on the point at any given time was ultimately a subjective determination, open to debate. Throughout the 1980s, the mainstream media tilted toward Sharpton. Sonny Carson, who coveted the distinction, responded by deriding Sharpton as a handpicked darling of the White establishment who would get mugged if he ever entered a housing project.[49] The important point here, in any case, is that the competition to be on the point strained relations among movement leaders.

Given these sources of tension, it is not surprising that cooperation among movement groups and individual leaders was ad hoc, limited, and transient—when it occurred at all. The following was a typical fact pattern for the resurgent Black Power movement: a dramatic incident of racially motivated violence or police brutality occurred; one or more movement leaders rushed to the scene; and some sort of leadership arrangement was worked out among these activists and enacted in subsequent protests relating to this

incident. Reverend Herbert Daughtry conveys just how ad hoc the process of
leadership formation actually was in many instances:

> REVEREND HERBERT DAUGHTRY: Sometimes . . . you form coalitions,
> which means that you're going to stay together for this particular issue.
> People outside of the community may not understand that . . . So you call on
> people to do things, and then sometimes it just ends up people come to the
> scene, you know . . . Sometimes there's a struggle for who's going to emerge
> as the leader. Sometimes people think that they have a corner on particular
> kinds of issues. Sometimes it's an international issue, and there are groups
> that feel that, "That's our issue" . . . so, sometimes you have internal strug-
> gles as to who is going to, you know, lead this, this struggle here. And so, we
> just sometimes come together. Sometimes if it's a particular issue, you say,
> well, "Oh, so and so and so, that's what they've been doing for years and
> years, so let me see what they're doing," you know. That had been some-
> times the way that I had tried to function. Most of the time, we sought again
> to keep, you know, keep some semblance of unity going.

Leadership formations for movement events thus varied substantially and
were contingent on numerous factors, including the nature of the specific
protests in question. One-day "Day of Outrage" demonstrations, for instance, required only loose cooperation among activists, while protracted
campaigns like the Red Apple Boycott required closer and more sustained
cooperation.

So was the resurgent Black Power movement characterized by internal
cooperation among movement groups or by conflict among the same? Was
the glass half full or half empty? The answer seems to depend upon where
one was standing in the overall picture. Movement statesmen like Daughtry
and Weusi, who worked assiduously to build bridges among movement
groups, claim that they were at least partially successful in creating a united
front. Daughtry explains why he resisted outside pressure to break ranks and
condemn Sonny Carson, despite their many disagreements:

> REVEREND HERBERT DAUGHTRY: [Carson's] got a role he's playing, you
> know. He's doing what he perceives to be a role . . . He's the commu-
> nity bulldog. He's been the ranking radical for as long as I can remember,
> and nobody's going to take that status from him. So he deliberately says
> things . . . Then guys like myself who know him, you know, who have been
> knowing him for years and years know that's a lot of, just a lot of mouth. And
> that if you get beyond that, you know, you find that he has a nice streak. I ain't
> going to say he's an angel or anything. But I'm saying that he ain't what

comes across . . . in verbiage. . . . So when people ask me do I know Sonny Carson, I say, yeah, I've been knowing him for over thirty years, and you know, never disavowed our relationship. Don't think I ever will. You know, because I know him. I know what he stands for. I know what he's trying to do. I don't agree, you know. We disagree and we have some knock-down, drag-out arguments from time to time. Almost come, have come to blows, but I understand that. So I'm not going to denounce him, you know, into the larger community . . . He trusts me. He calls me his minister. So that's where that is.

Where Daughtry appears to be speaking about disagreements within a family, Sharpton insists that the family was never more than a mirage. According to Sharpton, it was always every movement group for itself and unto itself:

REVEREND AL SHARPTON: Well, I think some alliances form based on agreement on an issue. For example, when Howard Beach happened, I became involved because the young man killed at Howard Beach, Michael Griffith's first cousin, worked for me . . . He called me in the middle of night and told me his cousin had been killed. I went to the house, and I was incensed at what happened. I called for the first two marches at Howard Beach. And other people got involved because they were outraged. So people from the NAACP to people that consider themselves revolutionary got involved. Now, that does not mean that we all agree ideologically. That does not mean that we all do things the same way. But all of us found ourselves at the same place protesting, because we agreed that issue was wrong. So once you get past that issue, it's not even that the coalitions break up. There never was a coalition . . . They all were together on that issue. So if somebody came in this room right now and knocked that wall down, you and I would be together trying to get out of here . . . When we get downstairs, we go separate ways. It's not that you and I split. We were never together . . . We just faced the same situation together. . . . So I think that is more truthful than what has been made of coalitions splitting up, because the fact is that a lot of them were never coalitions in the first place.

These two interpretations of what relations were like among groups during the resurgent Black Power movement are ultimately two sides of the same coin. The first emphasizes the cooperation achieved by diverse groups, the second emphasizes the diversity and autonomy of the groups who cooperated. Both confirm that the Black Power frame provided an umbrella under which different groups and individuals could motor around doing their own thing and, occasionally, work together.

However, centrifugal tendencies persisted and grew over time. Tensions among movement groups intensified, aggravated, in part, by Mayor Edward Koch's determined efforts to sow the seeds of division within the movement. Once Koch lost office in 1989, and the concrete goal that had bound movement groups together was accomplished, these centrifugal strains worsened and the movement began to dissolve. The Red Apple Boycott—organized by the December 12th Movement to the chagrin of the newly inaugurated Mayor David Dinkins—was generated by, and in turn fueled, the tensions between Black elected officials and relatively moderate activists, on the one hand, and hard-line nationalists, on the other. It was an outgrowth of the resurgent Black Power movement and, in some ways, the beginning of its end.

Defying Racialized Space: Transgressive Marches and Community Control Boycotts

As a persistently marginalized population, the Black community in New York City in the 1980s had a specific kind of resource profile when it came to collective action. Although it had only limited wealth and could not count on external support from the state or third parties such as the mainstream media, it nevertheless possessed considerable internal resources. Together, these internal resources—an established collective identity, shared beliefs, common social spaces and communication networks, activist networks, charismatic leadership, and, above all, people willing to put their time, labor, and physical safety on the line—amounted to a significant capacity for collective action.[50] Leaders of the resurgent Black Power movement maximized these resources by planning events that generated marked social disruption without demanding too much time or commitment from ordinary participants. Walking in a march, pausing to listen to a speaker at a rally, not shopping in a boycotted store—these were modest acts on an individual level, but they added up to something quite powerful at the collective level.

The resurgent Black Power movement was characterized by two principal forms of protest: marches and retail boycotts. Both forms of protest constituted what David Goldberg calls "resistance to racialized city space" (1993, 57). They represented alternative ways of challenging the most glaring artifact of racial power in New York City: the system of residential segregation. Where marches deliberately transgressed the boundaries of segregated space, retail boycotts aimed to transform segregated space into Black power bases, or arenas of community control. Again, Black resistance is in some ways shaped by the very force it seeks to challenge—namely, racial power. Or as Frances Fox Piven and Richard Cloward write: "Popular insurgency does not proceed by someone else's rules or hopes; it has its own logic and direction. It flows from historically specific circumstances: it is a reaction against those circumstances, and it is also limited by those circumstances" (1979, xi).

Most of the events in the movement fell into the first category. The Day of Outrage events, for example, were spatially transgressive marches. Sometimes marches were organized in response to a particularly egregious incident; sometimes they were planned well in advance to spotlight an issue of ongoing concern. Like many of the campaigns of the civil rights movement of the 1950s and 1960s (such as the Freedom Rides and the student sit-ins), these marches challenged the racialization of space by placing Black bodies in areas that were supposed to be lily White. Marchers usually convened in all-Black areas and then moved en masse into White-dominated areas (whether residential neighborhoods or business districts in Manhattan). Roger Wareham describes the first Day of Outrage, January 21, 1987, in which forty-five hundred marchers walked from Brooklyn across the Manhattan Bridge to Mayor Koch's home in lower Manhattan, disrupting traffic along the way:

ROGER WAREHAM: The Day of Outrage was to demonstrate the ability of an organized group to disrupt business as usual, and that people were going to have to understand that if the powers that be in New York City continued to enforce the kind of policies that were devastating to the Black community, that the Black community was going to make them pay for it in a sense that "you are not going to be able to do all the things that you want to do at your convenience." So the Day of Outrage was a very coordinated activity of maybe four or five thousand people. I think the *New York Times* described it as "with military type precision" in terms of what happened and the disruption with the trains, the bridges, all of that.

The White men who had chased Michael Griffith to his death had sent a clear message: "Black people enter Howard Beach at their own peril." Participants in the post–Howard Beach marches sent this message back: "We can and will go wherever we please in this city."[51] Unlike civil rights movement campaigns, of course, the marches in the resurgent Black Power movement were nationalist in rhetoric and defiant in tone. The resulting picture was one of a controlled threat, a torrent that might be unleashed—a picture reinforced by the ubiquitous slogan "No Justice, No Peace!"

The demonstrations set off by the murder of teenager Yusef Hawkins in Bensonhurst, Brooklyn, in the summer of 1989 were also spatially transgressive marches. On August 23, 1989, Yusef Hawkins and three friends went to predominantly Italian American Bensonhurst to look at a used car they had seen advertised in the paper. A group of forty White teenagers cornered

Hawkins and his friends, and one of them shot and killed Hawkins, who was unarmed. The resonance between the Bensonhurst and Howard Beach killings was unmistakable. Once again, a young Black man had been killed by a group of Whites for daring to enter a White residential area. Using the killing to punctuate both White racial violence against Blacks and the evils of residential segregation, movement leaders led marches right into the heart of Bensonhurst. White residents there lined the streets shouting: "Niggers, go home!" "You savages!" "Long live South Africa!" and "James Earl Ray!"[52] Some held watermelons aloft. One resident said to a journalist, "We don't like hundreds of blacks marching in the neighborhood, degrading the neighborhood"; another added, "We don't go into their neighborhoods to start trouble. They need to know Bensonhurst is ours" (*New York Newsday*, September 3, 1989). One White onlooker stabbed Reverend Al Sharpton in the shoulder, seriously injuring him. A week or so after the murder, movement leaders organized a "Day of Outrage and Mourning" in which approximately seventy-five hundred people marched from Grand Army Plaza across the Brooklyn Bridge to Manhattan during rush hour. Chanting "No Justice, No Peace!" the marchers carried two mock caskets, one for Yusef Hawkins and the other for Huey Newton, the founder of the Black Panther Party, who had just been killed in Oakland, California. The Bensonhurst killing reenergized the resurgent Black Power movement just weeks before the all-important Democratic mayoral primary in which David Dinkins was to challenge incumbent Mayor Edward Koch.

Where marches transgressed racialized boundaries, the second protest form characteristic of the movement, retail boycotts, sought to turn segregated spaces into areas of Black autonomy and control. Where marches typically evoked the general Black Power frame, retail boycotts evoked the more specific community control frame. Since community control is, like Black Power, a vague notion that can sustain different meanings simultaneously, retail boycotts in the movement varied somewhat in tone and agenda, depending upon which activists were at the helm. When Reverend Herbert Daughtry organized boycotts against local merchants (White, Korean, Arabic, etc.) accused of abusing Black customers, for instance, the events were brief, moderate in tone, and oriented toward specific, limited goals (a merchant apology, the construction of a scholarship fund for Black students, the hiring of Black employees, etc.). In contrast, boycotts organized by the December 12th Movement were protracted, defiant in tone, and uncompromising.[53] Both sets of boycotts were community control campaigns, but there was a world of difference between the two.

It is hard to say exactly how many people participated in the mass mobilization phase of the resurgent Black Power movement. Neither the estimates of activists nor those of city officials is necessarily reliable, since the former has a motive to exaggerate the numbers and the latter a motive to depress them. Even when activists and officials roughly concurred in their estimates, they only did so concerning specific events—for example, that several thousand Black people participated in the first Day of Outrage on January 21, 1987. Hence we are still left wondering about participation in the overall movement. Did each march draw an entirely new crowd or was there a substantial overlap among participants from march to march? The latter seems more likely, but it is difficult to prove. Popular participation in retail boycotts is even harder to measure. Consider the fact that nonactions (such as not shopping in a targeted store) count for participation, as do overt actions such as picketing. Moreover, Black support for the new resurgent Black Power movement did not necessarily directly correlate with Black participation in the movement. There is every reason to believe, in fact, that the number of Black New Yorkers who supported the movement was greater than the number of actual participants. Finally, there is the question of intensity of support for the movement, a matter that head counts (even if they were precise) tell us nothing about. It is reasonable to believe that some participants strongly supported the movement, while others did so only weakly, and that some endorsed particular movement events while repudiating others. Having pieced together the available data, I venture the educated guess that a sizeable minority of Blacks in New York City strongly supported the movement, while many more (probably a majority) partially supported it and partially opposed it, and a minority strongly opposed it. Again, this leaves the issue of head counts unresolved.

What about the participants' class backgrounds? The mainstream media frequently suggested that movement participants were restive members of the "underclass." Yet the reality was that participants in the resurgent Black Power movement—those who attended rallies and marches and joined boycott picket lines—came from a range of class backgrounds. Jitu Weusi comments on the mainstream media's tendency to depict movement participants as members of the lumpen proletariat:

JITU WEUSI: The mainstream press—they do things for their own objectives. And for the objectives of those who are financially supporting them. Not for the objectives of our community. And not for the objectives of providing truth. If you were to be around the movement for a sustained period of time, and you were to just casually interview and talk to the people, you would find that there's a tremendous cross section of people that are involved. There are retirees, people who have worked all their lives on a specific job, like postman or transit worker or whatever, and have retired. Now that they're in their late fifties or early sixties they have time, have income. And they can afford to go to Philadelphia for [the Mumia Abu-Jamal] trial. They can afford to go to Poughkeepsie for [protests about] Tawana Brawley. They can afford to go to Washington to picket Justice Thomas's home. You know what I'm saying? Now, they ain't going to go in the mainstream press and tell you that, "They got a bunch of retirees supporting them." See, they'd rather call them unemployed thugs and hoodlums, you know what I mean? Because that sounds better. That sounds more like what people want to hear, you know. But you find there are retirees. You would find there's a tremendously high level of professional people. You know. I'm a teacher. I have a degree. You find other people with teaching degrees. Nursing—the woman was head of CEMOTAP [Committee to Eliminate Media Offensive to African People], Betty Dobson, she's a registered nurse. Carol Taylor . . . she's a registered nurse, you know. See, there's a lot of professional people. Dr. McIntosh, he's a doctor. A lot of what I would call fringe middle class. Okay? Very rarely will you find unemployed, unskilled, you know. When the movement gets to that level, that's what you might call an uncontrollable level . . . But the sustained kind of thing that goes on from Howard Beach to Bensonhurst is by people who know what they're doing.

Roger Wareham concurs with Weusi about the limited but real class diversity among movement participants:

ROGER WAREHAM: [The participants are] working class. Certainly all have finished high school, some of them have finished college or done partial college . . . They do varied jobs. Secretarial jobs, there are clerical jobs, there are construction jobs, technical jobs. It's a typical working-class kind of range. And then there are people who are unemployed, given the nature of the economy . . . There is some [middle- or upper-middle-class support], not much. I think the appeal of the December 12th Movement and the type of issues that we deal with are geared more towards the working class, but the fact that we represent the issue of self-sufficiency and self-determination, I think, appeals across class lines.

According to Reverend Herbert Daughtry, relatively affluent Black people were typically reluctant to participate in demonstrations. The challenge, therefore, was to solicit their participation in other forms:

REVEREND HERBERT DAUGHTRY: I think that as it becomes heated, then those who have the most to lose . . . sometimes begin to back out. See, I understood that and didn't fight that. I think that there are some of our leaders who fight the middle class, or fight those who don't come out and take a stand. I thought it served our interest more effectively if, if people can't take a stand publicly that's all right, you know. You can be for us, you know. Do what you can. So there were people who were constantly in strategic places providing information. Well, I wouldn't want those people to come out, you know. And I discouraged any public posture from these people or any public activity from these people. So as issues sometimes become heated, and the forces that you struggle against become more and more powerful, then so often those, as I say, who have the most to lose, those with good jobs, those with programs, those with dah dah dah, whose prestige, whose wealth, whose mortgages depend on these associations, then they gonna thin out . . . And that's all right, if you understand that. And if you have a conversation with them where people would say, "Listen, I can't go with you on this one" . . . Fine. You don't have to, but, you know, give us some money, give us some information. If we go to jail, you know, we may need somebody to step out, you know, whatever. But don't just stay back . . . Do something. Don't you just, you know, sit and wait until we get finished shaking the apple tree and you run out with a bushel.

Many movement leaders were highly educated professionals (lawyers, graphic artists, adjunct professors, etc.) from middle-class backgrounds.[54] The majority of ordinary participants, on the other hand, were working poor or members of the lower middle class who had had some education and held steady if marginal jobs.[55] These were the segments of the Black community— not the hard-core unemployed and disaffected—who had a vision of something better and the wherewithal to fight for it.

SOCIAL CONTROL, KOCH STYLE

As a powerful three-term incumbent, Mayor Edward Koch enjoyed substantial latitude in dealing with the resurgent Black Power movement. The fact that Blacks did not play an important role in his electoral and governing coalitions increased this latitude. Koch used three principal social control tactics against the movement: he built up the repressive capacity of the New York City Police Department, engaged in ongoing rhetorical delegitimation of Black grievances, and orchestrated COINTELPRO-type undercover operations.

Koch and Police Commissioner Benjamin Ward were galvanized into action by the first Day of Outrage on January 21, 1987, which apparently caught them off guard. Roger Wareham explains:

ROGER WAREHAM: We [the December 12th Movement] had a rally at Koch's house in January of '87, right after Michael Griffith's killing, that was mainly organized by a lot of young people and we were part of it. We marched, the police were just totally caught by surprise. I think there were five, ten thousand people came out, and we marched and our security was carrying ax handles, and the police had a problem with that but couldn't do anything about it . . . and they said, "You can't march with that," and these people said, "We are going to." And one of the things that they [the police] could never really adjust to in terms of things that we were involved in with the December 12th group, was that when you have a lot of people in the streets, you can go where you want to go. And they would never know where we were going and we ended up down at Koch's house in the Village with about five to ten thousand people. And from that point, well, they had always had an attitude with some of us. Koch and Ward, who was the police commissioner, said they were not going to get caught by surprise again.

In May 1987, when Ward stated publicly that he sensed a "long, hot summer" coming, the comparison to the violent urban uprisings of the 1960s was lost on no one. Ward was clearly signaling the police force's siege mentality and its readiness to take action against the movement. From the summer of 1987 forward, Mayor Koch initiated a new riot training program for the NYPD. Police officers received special training on how to deal with riots and demonstrations, and they were regularly briefed about various movement groups, with a special emphasis on the ex–New York Eight members who were by this time part of the December 12th Movement.[56] In an unprecedented move, Koch and Ward arranged for all of the city's police commanders (those with the rank of captain or higher) to undergo crowd control training (*New York Times,* July 6, 1987). Frequently aggressive police behavior at movement events indicated that the newly trained officers saw themselves not merely as keepers of the peace but as active enforcers of social control and dissent management.

Koch also waged an ongoing rhetorical battle against the resurgent Black Power movement. Just as he had created a climate hostile to Black aspirations prior to the movement's emergence, so, too, did he seek to silence the movement through criticism and ridicule. Drawing heavily upon colorblind talk, Koch constructed the movement as an incoherent effort by racial rabble-rousers to extort scarce goods from the taxpaying public. Racism was no longer a problem, he intoned, and Black demagogues were seeking nothing less than preferential treatment for Black people. Thus Koch made the following comments in the aftermath of the Howard Beach killing: "They're [Black protesters] getting away with behavior that no one else can get away with without being denounced" (United Press International, January 21, 1987); "You know there are more whites assaulted in this town by blacks than the other way around"; and, "When a black is a victim, it's racist and when a white is a victim, it's robbery" (Japan Economic Newswire, December 24, 1987). Koch's transparent efforts to play to White resentment over affirmative action and other racial reforms went over especially well among middle-class White outer-borough ethnics, who were a vital part of his coalition. Through his "increasingly vitriolic and unrestrained attacks" (Mollenkopf 1992, 167) on movement leaders and activities, Koch consistently used the power and prestige of his office to condemn the movement.

The NYPD (under Koch's instructions) and possibly the FBI used COINTELPRO-type tactics to try to undermine the movement. Since trust was already a precious commodity among movement leaders, these tactics proved quite successful. In 1987, it was disclosed that since 1985 Commissioner Ward had maintained a "Black Desk," a special undercover operation in which agents monitored and taped Black radio programming and surveilled prominent activists. Ward and Koch insisted that the Black Desk was intended to target criminal activities as opposed to unpopular political activities. Roger Wareham talks about how the escalation in police surveillance and harassment appeared from the other side of the "desk":

ROGER WAREHAM: This was '87 or so, later that year, when the thing about the Black Desk came out—that the Black Desk was this undercover operation of the New York Police Department that was designed to deal with Black activists, and Ward and Mayor Koch got on T.V. and said, "We listened to WLIB, the Black radio station, and monitored it." They made the most extraordinary statement that I have ever heard. They said, "This really isn't about Black activists at all. It's really about the New York Eight." The folks that had been acquitted, right? "We have an ongoing criminal investigation of them"—which was, you don't, nobody announces that they have an ongoing criminal investigation . . . The Black Desk would reveal that they had special briefings out at Bennett Field and riot control and profiles of the people and stuff, which meant that there was an escalation of the state's response, of the state's reaction to more and more people getting active . . . We used to meet in schools; the schools we couldn't meet in any more, all the places that we were meeting in were no longer being open to us. People were getting pressure. We used to meet at Fort Greene Senior Citizens Center. The director said that, "I'm getting pressure from my board . . . if we let you meet there, our funding is going to be cut." So what it culminated in, . . . was that there was an attempt to isolate us and prevent people from meeting. At the same time, we were supposed to go up to Orange County for a retreat, like forty or fifty people, a few people went ahead. One of them was a New York Eight person, and the day before they went to make the trip, we sent a letter to the judge laying out all the stuff that had been revealed around the Black Desk and that it was clear that the police were trying to set up the New York Eight people for parole violation and could he intervene. The next day, these guys go up on their trip and they're stopped by the police going up to Orange County, and the police search their car three times and claim they found two weapons. So, bingo, now we're deferred to going seventy miles upstate to deal with people with a weapons charge. They ended up eventually being convicted of it.

Then, in January 1988, *New York Newsday* broke the story that Reverend Al Sharpton had occasionally worked as an undercover informant for the FBI.[57] Sharpton subsequently admitted that he had been an informant on cases related to his connections to the boxing world, but vehemently denied that he had ever informed on his colleagues within the movement. Once he admitted to having worked with the FBI, in any case, Sharpton became anathema to the December 12th Movement. Relations between the preacher and the organization had already been strained by events surrounding a Day of Outrage held on December 21, 1987:

ROGER WAREHAM: Sharpton was always very controversial, and many people had resisted for a long time his involvement and stuff because at that point, not that he was a police agent, but at best, he was an opportunist. He was a media freak and a hustler in terms of not really being committed to the liberation [of Black people]. It [the movement] was a vehicle for him in terms of his own self-aggrandizement. The only basis upon which he had been admitted to even participate in the Day of Outrage was the question of collective leadership, that once the decision was made that everybody was going to adhere to it, nobody was going to break ground. He did that on December 21st on the Day of Outrage because the plan was, there were only a few people who knew exactly everything that was going to happen, for security reasons. [Different] groups were given specific instructions in terms of where they were to go. Sharpton was with a group of people who wanted to be arrested, they wanted to have a symbolic arrest, civil disobedience. There were others, the majority sentiment was, "We don't need symbolic arrests, we've been arrested more than enough times," you know, but we made an allowance for that so that there was a group—Vernon Mason, Alton Maddox, some other people—who were going to be involved in the symbolic arrests. So they were supposed to go to the Clark Street subway station. Sharpton, in the middle of the demonstration, when they were going to Clark Street, decided that he didn't want to go there because he knew there was more media at Jay Street or Borough Hall. So he diverted his group to Borough Hall and when he got there—we told people to bring tokens because we didn't want people getting busted for jumping the turnstile—he jumped the turnstile. It was just crazy, so it ended up with sixty-five or seventy people getting arrested and that wasn't supposed to happen. It wouldn't have happened had he not gone to where he wasn't supposed to be. So that posed a very serious contradiction in terms of that he isn't going to adhere to stuff . . . So right after that, someone shouts, "He needs to be out of this," you know. The following week there was an incident in Bensonhurst . . . where two Black men who had been collecting bottles to turn them in had gotten beaten up by a group of Whites. They were chased and beaten up. Sharpton went on the radio and called for a demonstration in Bensonhurst. And the position of most of the people in December 12th was, "We do not want any part of this." We weren't going to get involved in it because causing a [spontaneous] demonstration in the middle of Bensonhurst is suicidal because there is no Black community to which you can retreat. The precinct is in the middle of a White area that is hostile to you, so that the only protection you have is if you say that the police are going to protect you because you can't do it yourself. At the last minute, we [the December 12th Movement] were forced to get involved because the people's assumption was that he was speaking for the entire group and . . . because we had demonstrated over the years that we don't take people into things if we cannot protect them. So at the last minute, literally, it was midnight the night before the demonstration, we said, "We've got to go there," which meant that at five or six o'clock that morning we had to go out and cover the whole area and just see what the whole setup was, and go there and rearrange the whole thing. I think in my own history, that was one of the more scary ones, being in Bensonhurst, because we were put in a situation where we were surrounded by hostile, racist [Whites] . . . and the police department was antagonistic to us . . . When I think of different situations that I've been in, arrested by the FBI, forty FBI agents with their weapons out. That was scary. Bensonhurst is right up there with it. Sharpton put us in that situation, you know. So at that point, it was clear. So there was another Day of Outrage scheduled for January of '88, but at that point it was clear that it was not going to happen. So that sort of split, and then just the day before the demonstration, *Newsday* came out with this revelation [about Sharpton acting as an FBI informant].

While they believed the *New York Newsday* story, December 12th Movement members also suspected that the FBI was up to its old "badjacketing" practices and trying to turn activists against one another.[58] In any case, the damage was done: the two main centers of power in the resurgent Black Power movement wanted nothing more to do with each other. Roger Wareham spoke for his entire organization when he said: "Sharpton is in a different category [than other activists] because I don't consider the police as part of the movement, and as far as I'm concerned, Sharpton is a police agent. He's an admitted police agent."[59] Although Jitu Weusi did not judge Sharpton as harshly, he acknowledges that the breach between Sharpton and the December 12th Movement was serious:

JITU WEUSI: It's unfortunate, the wedge that was driven between the groups. I understand why, though. In 1987, we did a Day of Outrage in the city. And every press account of that Day of Outrage—in the *New York Times,* the *Post,* the [Daily] *News*—everybody said how effective it was and how well done it was. The *New York Times* even went so far as to call it a "precision strike" . . . That scared a lot of people. That scared the powers that be. See, New York is a city that in order for it to be economically viable, it's got to run. Okay? It's got to run—the airports, trains, the taxis, the this, you know, it's gotta run. It runs twenty-four hours a day . . . And whenever a particular group can put New York in such a way that it can't function, that's scary . . . And that's what we did. And they [the powers that be] recognized that. And their situation on that was like, "Hey, we don't want this happening. And we're prepared to take whatever steps we have to take in order to make sure it don't happen." And so the mechanisms were put in motion to uproot that and divide it, you know, divide these [movement] groups. One of those mechanisms was the FBI story on Reverend Sharpton. I mean, I lived through the '60s. I lived through the Hoover FBI, and I know what they did. I'm not talking about hearsay. I got my 435-page FBI document from the government. I know the kind of things that went on. Why would a daily newspaper run a story like that? How would they get their information? See? If it wasn't designed to do something else . . . There was a powerful coalition [of movement leaders]. They wanted to break it up, that's what they do . . . It worked. They're still divided now.

Whether Sharpton did pass information about the movement to the FBI remains unknown today. What is clear is that the social control tactics deployed by Mayor Koch, Commissioner Ward, and the NYPD helped to sow the seeds of division within the resurgent Black Power movement. It was movement leaders, however, who would have the last laugh on Koch, in 1989.

MAKING HISTORY

Forged in opposition to Mayor Koch, the Black Power movement that arose in New York City in the 1980s contributed decisively to his defeat in the Democratic mayoral primary of 1989 by David Dinkins. Dinkins went on to defeat the Republican candidate, Rudolph Giuliani, and become the first Black mayor in New York City's history. The movement, in other words, helped to make history. Most mainstream observers failed to appreciate this connection. Denying that the movement was a real movement at all, they talked instead about the impact of "racial turmoil" on the election. In fact, the resurgent Black Power movement helped Dinkins both indirectly (by convincing Whites that Koch had become part of the race problem) and directly (by mobilizing Black voters in record numbers).

The Primary Election

Koch, who had appeared invincible after the 1985 election, seemed distinctly vulnerable by 1989. To begin with, the Wall Street crash in October 1987, known as "Black Monday," had abruptly halted the economic boom of the 1980s, weakening the mayor's progrowth allies and undermining his claims to have resuscitated New York City's economy. In addition, the demographic changes that had taken place in the city throughout the decade—specifically, the growth of Black, Latino, and liberal White populations relative to Catholic and conservative Jewish ones—did not favor the mayor (Mollenkopf 1993, 69–73). Koch's own strategies for minority demobilization began to backfire on him by 1989. Having reinvigorated the Democratic machine as a power base, Koch was seriously damaged when a series of machine scandals surfaced in 1986.[60] Richard Wade explains: "The number of forced resignations, quick exits, indictments, and prison sentences portrayed an ethical disarray in the very center of the administration" (1990, 285). The dismantling of the Board of Estimate in 1989 also weakened Koch, who had effectively consolidated his power over that important body. Finally, voters perturbed by increasing Black militance in the streets had gradually come to see the mayor's racial trash talking as part of the problem rather than the solution.[61]

At the same time, the scenario in 1989 augured well for David Dinkins. Jesse Jackson's 1988 presidential campaign laid an important foundation for Dinkins's mayoral bid by conducting voter registration drives in minority areas, consolidating a network of churches, elected officials, and unions geared toward grassroots mobilization, and raising the political hopes of Black voters (Mollenkopf 1993). Indeed, Jackson's showing was much stronger in 1988 than it had been four years earlier due in part to his ability to draw Black elected officials away from the ailing Democratic party organizations and to attract Latino voters during the later campaign. Jackson won the 1988 New York City Democratic presidential primary election with 45.3 percent of the total vote: he won 88.2 percent of Black ADs, 71.4 percent of mixed minority ADs, 63.5 percent of Latino ADs, 27.8 percent of White liberal ADs, 22.7 percent of White Catholic ADs, and 17.7 percent of outer-borough Jewish ADs (Mollenkopf 1993, 82). (Koch's candidate of choice, Senator Al Gore, finished a distant third behind Jackson and Michael Dukakis.) Most important, Jackson demonstrated in 1988 that a Black candidate could surpass the 40 percent mark so as to avoid a runoff election.[62] In many ways, Jackson's 1988 campaign served as a "testing ground" for Dinkins's mayoral bid in 1989 (Thompson 1990, 146).

Dinkins's primary election strategy was to reassemble Jesse Jackson's winning 1988 coalition of Blacks, Latinos, liberal Whites, and unions, thereby effectively bypassing Koch's key constituencies (corporate elites and outer-borough White ethnics). The fact that Blacks constituted only a third of Democratic primary voters in the city meant that Dinkins had to win the support of all of them, as well as that of a substantial number of White and Latino voters, in order to avoid a runoff. Table 3.2 shows the breakdown of New York City voters by race and ethnicity in 1989. It was especially crucial that Dinkins garner White support. Although Blacks and Latinos together constituted a near majority in 1989 and Blacks were more likely than any other group to vote in the Democratic primary, Whites still constituted the majority of voters in both the Democratic primary and general elections. Having been Manhattan borough president since 1985, Dinkins was accustomed to the tightwire act by which Black elected officials try to energize Black voters while at the same time reassuring White voters. His bilevel campaign strategy was part of this act:

> His strategy was to conduct a two-level campaign: one public, citywide, and directed at swing constituencies among Jews, white liberals, and Latinos, and a second relying on the networks extending around the major organizational players in the black community, especially black elected officials, black ministers, and black public sector trade unionists. The first campaign was highly visible to whites, the second much less so, but no less effective. His ability to conduct such a bifurcated dialogue was facilitated by racial segmentation in New York City's mass media . . . [and by] radio station WLIB,

owned by one of Dinkins' closest allies in the black community. He could speak to the black community through channels to which whites did not listen. (Arian et al. 1991, 199)

In addition, Dinkins's central campaign promise to safeguard New York City's "gorgeous mosaic" of racial, ethnic, and religious groups helped him to maintain his precarious tightwire act between Black and White expectations. As it happened, Blacks heard the campaign promise as a guarantee of racial justice while Whites heard it as a guarantee of colorblind peace. It was only after Dinkins took office in 1990 that the discrepancy between these two sets of expectations became clear and the tightwire act became impossible to maintain.

If Dinkins's campaign strategy was to persuade Whites that he would be a racial healer and Blacks that he would be their champion in Gracie Mansion, the resurgent Black Power movement helped him on both fronts. On the one

TABLE 3.2 VOTING STATUS BY RACE/ETHNICITY IN NEW YORK CITY, 1989

	Percentage of the Population	Percentage of Democratic Primary Voters	Percentage of General Election Voters
Asians	6.7	0.9	1.5
Blacks	25.2	34.2	26.8
Latinos	24.4	12.4	11.5
Whites	43.2	52.5	60.2
Liberal		14.1	17.5
Catholic		20.5	19.7
Outer-borough Jewish		13.4	13.5
Protestant/Other		4.5	9.5

Source: Adapted from John Mollenkopf, *New York City in the 1980s: A Social, Economic, and Political Atlas* (New York: Simon & Schuster, 1993), 97.

hand, the movement provided "a militant foil" (Haines 1988, 3) against which Dinkins appeared moderate, reasonable, and reassuring to Whites.[63] Historically, Whites have demonstrated a willingness to embrace moderate Black leaders as an alternative to more radical Black leaders. Black leaders who espouse colorblind talk and condemn their nationalist counterparts fare especially well in White opinion (the old Martin v. Malcolm phenomenon). Dinkins's "gorgeous mosaic" promise conjured up just the sort of images of racial harmony and brotherhood that many White voters find appealing. What the militance of the movement did, then, was "open the path for Dinkins, who suddenly bec[ame] much more attractive to the establishment" (*New York Times*, December 27, 1987). Thus Whites eager to put a stop to racial unrest in the city came to support the same candidate that the instigators of that unrest themselves endorsed.

On the other hand, the resurgent Black Power movement helped to generate great enthusiasm about Dinkins's candidacy within the Black community. This was not a preordained outcome. As a product of the Harlem political establishment, Dinkins in fact ran the risk of appearing too moderate, too staid, and too privileged to relate to the everyday concerns of most Blacks, especially those living in the "other" boroughs. The dismal performance of Herman "Denny" Farrell in the 1985 Democratic primary election proved that it took more than a Black face to get Black voters to turn out and vote. Because Dinkins had actively networked with Brooklyn-based Black nationalist activists throughout the 1980s, however, they turned out in force to campaign for him. Where Koch spent most of his campaign funds on media advertisements, Dinkins devoted many of his resources to building up a get-out-the-vote force involving several movement leaders. In June 1989, several months before the primary election, Jitu Weusi formed a group called African Americans United for David Dinkins, whose main aims were to foster a working relationship between Dinkins and Black nationalist activists, to register Black voters, and to get out the Black vote on election day:

JITU WEUSI: We [activists] had met with Bill Lynch [a Dinkins advisor] and he was worried about supporting Dinkins in the Black communities. And I told him that I would put together an activist group that would, you know, work on a grassroots-effective campaign . . . We put together a meeting of about 150 folks, and we strategized on how we could get grassroots turnout. And we did some things. We had some rallies, church rallies, community rallies in places like Queens, North Shore Queens, Bronx, Co-op City, northern Bronx, Brooklyn, different places. And we brought David into these places. And they were not places he had ever been to before. . . . Later on, several [members] became regular coordinators in his campaign. So we brought them [Dinkins's advisors] into these places, because, you know, they still had a more kind of party-oriented strategy. And our strategy was more of a mass-based, grassroots strategy . . . We brought him there with these rallies, brought out local leadership, hooked up David to local leadership. And as a result of that, that sort of prompted the kind of turnout, you know, we got in 1989.

Reverend Herbert Daughtry describes what he did to promote Dinkins prior to the primary election:

REVEREND HERBERT DAUGHTRY: When Dinkins decided to run, we had been close for a number of years. And I was one who urged him to run. Always liked him because he's really a decent guy. So I was there to help him to get elected. I think I played a pivotal role in getting him elected. I remember two things. I remember one time when he had hit the bottom. He'd gone out to Brooklyn and nobody was attracted, he wasn't drawing any crowds. Went out to Brooklyn, they was supposed to have this block gathering, masses of people were supposed to show up. When he went out there wasn't anybody out there. This was early in the day, Saturday. Then he was to come here to cap it off. So it became crucial that we had a crowd because now if the day ends with no crowd . . . So we knew we had to have a crowd. He was coming here with [Harry] Belafonte and Jesse Jackson, and what I did, what we did, I told him I wanted a sound truck and we got a big flat sound truck . . . and give out these flyers all over. But I went, we went around the community and I spent hours standing out there on the corner of Atlantic Avenue . . . telling people about the rally. They had to show up there, had to show up there, had to show up, right? Finally, when the rally came, it was packed, you know. People couldn't hardly get in this place. So that was critical.

The other critical point was Yusef Hawkins. How to deal with Yusef Hawkins. Right. And Yusef Hawkins's father was, he was kind of hard to deal with, and understandably so, in his pain, you know. He was very, very difficult. In fact, I remember being at the house with Sharpton and they were talking, and, you know, for me, I understand the pain, but it's, how do you not let your loved one die, you know? What do you do to perpetuate the memory? And how do you make something good come of that? Now, granted that can be misunderstood . . . That's where he and Jesse [Jackson] had this misunderstanding. At the funeral parlor . . . Jesse was trying to say, you know, "Well, Yusef Hawkins can be the catalyst for a political movement that will bring about tremendous change across the country. And so in that sense

he will live forever," you know. Just as Emmett Till became a kind of catalyst . . . [but] his father was not in a kind of mindset to hear any of that. So he
was very difficult to deal with. And Dinkins and Bill Lynch didn't know how to
deal with that, see. They didn't know whether to go out to the [Hawkins's]
house or not. They felt if they went out to the house and he [Dinkins] was
booed . . . If he didn't go out he was going to be criticized, you know. And
they called me and said, well, what do you think they should do, you know.
So they kind of dropped it on me. In fact, Bill Lynch said, "Well that's your
call" . . . And so here am I sitting right in this office here with this kind of
decision to make . . . I called Bill Lynch back and I told him, I say, "Let's go,
let's go . . . let Dinkins go out there, I think he should go." So he said, "All
right, he'll be about to pick you up. He'll drive right by Atlantic Avenue on his
way out to Brownsville and you and Dinkins can ride out there together." I
said, "Oh, Lord." And so he did, he come right by and, you know, right across
the street. So I jumped in the car and we went out there. And when we
reached there, the street was packed with young people, you know. Up and
down the street it was just packed. So when we were going into that street
and Dinkins was seen, and people started cheering, you know, I said, "Oh,
Lord," you know. And they were, "Yeah, yeah!" And we went inside and he
was well received by the family . . . the family, you know, was very, very
receptive, and so when we left and came on back to the church, I was
tremendously relieved.

As Daughtry suggests, movement leaders gave candidate Dinkins an instant
and invaluable credibility with the man and woman on the street.

When the Bensonhurst killing occurred in August 1989, it reenergized the
resurgent Black Power movement as described above. Many of the Black
activists who spoke at the post-Bensonhurst marches explicitly linked the
powerlessness of Black people in New York City to the incumbency of Ed
"Bull" Koch and urged Blacks to express their outrage at the voting booth.[64]
Alluding to Malcolm X's famous speech entitled "The Ballot or the Bullet,"
Daughtry spoke at a news conference during this period, addressing his
comments to Whites and Blacks alike: "The political structure must respond
equitably to protect its citizens. When that option is shut down, you leave
citizens no other option but the bullet . . . It's a state of emergency. We need to
do something about it . . . This is a political year. I believe it's time for New
Yorkers who believe in decency, who believe in fairness, who want to see a
better New York . . . to have a political change" (*New York Newsday*, August 25,
1989). Dinkins joined Sharpton and other movement leaders in blaming Koch
for the Bensonhurst murder, albeit with his characteristic caution: "I have

said that the tone is set on high, and I believe that" (*New York Newsday*, August 31, 1989). Koch did not help his own cause when he urged Blacks not to march in Bensonhurst because doing so would create tension and upset neighborhood residents. His comments provoked a flood of angry calls from Black listeners to WLIB talk radio shows. When Koch paid a condolence visit to Yusef Hawkins's family, he was booed so loudly by the Black mourners present that he had to retreat out of a side door after only ten minutes. Just days before the primary election, hundreds of Blacks marched outside of the mayor's home. During this march, one organizer exclaimed: "We feel Mayor Koch is the number one racist in the city. He epitomizes all forms of racism in this city" (*New York Times*, September 1, 1989).

Dinkins won the primary election, defeating Koch and two minor challengers to capture the Democratic nomination for mayor of New York City.[65] Table 3.3 shows the results by AD type. Dinkins did better among liberal Whites (44.6 percent) and outer-borough Jews (25.9 percent) than Jesse Jackson had in 1988 (27.8 percent and 17.7 percent, respectively). Among Latino voters, Dinkins did much better than Herman "Denny" Farrell had in 1985 (Dinkins won 60.4 percent of Latino ADs as compared with Farrell's 17.8

TABLE 3.3 DEMOCRATIC PRIMARY ELECTION RESULTS BY AD TYPE IN NEW YORK CITY, 1989

AD type	Dinkins	Koch
Black	84.8%	10.3%
Mixed Minority	65.1	26.8
Latino	60.4	31.8
White		
Liberal	44.6	46.0
Catholic	30.4	61.4
Outer-borough Jewish	25.9	67.2
Total	50.8	42.0

Source: Adapted from John Mollenkopf, *New York City in the 1980s: A Social, Economic, and Political Atlas* (New York: Simon & Schuster, 1993), 86.

percent) and only slightly less well than Jackson had in 1988 (63.5 percent). Finally, Dinkins did exceptionally well in turning out and securing the Black vote. He won 84.8 percent of the Black vote with 70.9 percent turnout, whereas Jackson had won 88.2 percent of the Black vote with 48.3 percent turnout in 1988, and Farrell had won 32.7 percent of the Black vote with 26.8 percent turnout in 1985 (Mollenkopf 1993, 82). While 41 percent of Black ADs had voted for Koch in the 1985 Democratic primary election, only 10.3 percent of them voted for him in 1989 (Mollenkopf 1993, 77). According to exit polls, a full two-thirds of Black voters felt that Koch favored Whites over Blacks (Arian et al. 1991, 82). The resurgent Black Power movement had clearly made an impact.

The General Election

In the late 1980s, New York City was overwhelmingly Democratic. In 1989, 69 percent of registered voters were Democrats, 14 percent Republicans, and 15 percent independents (Mollenkopf 1993, 61). Unsurprisingly, the Democratic primary winner was usually the presumptive winner of the general election. But the Democratic nominee had never before been Black. The question of the hour was the following: Would the traditional reluctance of some Whites to vote for a Black candidate keep David Dinkins out of Gracie Mansion? The Republican candidate, Rudolph Giuliani, was a former U.S. attorney for the Southern district of New York with a record of going after mafia dons, Wall Street insiders, and corrupt cops and Democratic politicians. Giuliani was not particularly well known or well liked, but as a White (Italian American) candidate with an anticrime reputation, he threatened to draw Reagan Democrats across party lines. In this context, Dinkins's supporters took nothing for granted and campaigned strenuously during the two months between the primary and general elections.

Giuliani's election strategy involved three tasks: pushing Dinkins off of the tightwire that he had been walking between Black and White voters, polarizing Black and White voters, and reconstituting Koch's electoral coalition as his own. Giuliani's political consultant, Roger Ailes, creator of the infamous Willie Horton television ad that sank Michael Dukakis's 1988 presidential bid, crafted a campaign that racialized nearly every issue while almost never mentioning race out loud. For instance, the campaign emphasized that Giuliani was a vigorous crime fighter who had prosecuted both the New York Eight and Koch's corrupt Democratic machine buddies (sending two messages at once: "Giuliani has it in for Black extremists," and, "As a Black person and a Democrat, David Dinkins would be soft on crime"). Tak-

ing a page out of Koch's book, the Giuliani campaign also played to stereotypes of Black criminality by claiming that Dinkins had committed with
impunity various misdoings such as neglecting to file federal income taxes
eighteen years earlier and engaging in tax evasion. Playing to White racial
anxieties behind the cover of colorblind talk was the Giuliani campaign's
rejoinder to Dinkins's "gorgeous mosaic" strategy.

Roger Ailes's ace in the hole was publicizing Dinkins's connections to
Black nationalist activists. When the Anti-Defamation League of the B'nai
B'rith broke the story that Jitu Weusi and Sonny Carson were on the Dinkins
campaign payroll (as part of the get-out-the-vote effort), Ailes saw his opportunity. Well aware that both activists had gained the reputation of being anti-
Semitic during the 1968 Ocean Hill-Brownsville school decentralization conflict, Ailes created a series of television ads reminding viewers of that earlier
conflict. One campaign ad referred to a notorious incident in which Weusi
had read a poem with strongly anti-Semitic overtones, written by one of his
students, on Julius Lester's WBAI radio show in 1968. The ad made no mention of the fact that Weusi had repeatedly disavowed and apologized for that
action in the twenty years since 1968. Another ad suggested that Carson was
blackmailing Dinkins with the threat of more post-Bensonhurst marches.
Clearly, this "teledemagoguery" (B. Wilson 1991, 43) suggesting that Dinkins
was beholden to Black "extremists" and "racists" was designed to promote
what Derrick Bell (1992) calls "racial bonding" among White voters (especially Jews). In this way, the very nationalist activists who helped Dinkins
win the primary became his Achilles' heel during the general election.

The Weusi/Carson controversy picked up steam as the general election
drew nearer. The practice of giving campaign workers "walking around"
money (discretionary funds for which they do not have to provide strict
accounting) was both legal and commonplace in New York City politics.
Nevertheless, the Dinkins campaign felt compelled to prove that Carson had
spent his walking around money ($9,500) for legitimate campaign purposes.
In an October 15 memo to the Dinkins campaign, Carson claimed that he had
used $7,100 cash to pay 140 full- and part-time workers for distributing flyers
prior to the primary election. Yet he could only provide receipts for the $2,700
that he had spent renting sound equipment trucks and other campaign vehicles. When asked about the charges of anti-Semitism at an October 19 news
conference, Carson stated: "I'm anti-White. Don't just limit me to a little
group of people" (New York Times, October 20, 1989). Carson's declaration, of
course, echoed James Baldwin's famous article "Negroes Are Anti-Semitic
Because They're Anti-White" (New York Times Magazine, April 19, 1967). Rev-

erend Herbert Daughtry explains that Carson was simply thumbing his nose at his critics, acting out the role of veteran bulldog: "He knew that he was going to alienate everybody. He knew he was going to be the baddest dude in town. He knew that everybody was going to talk about him. He knew that."[66]

If Sonny Carson had a scripted role to play in this situation, so did David Dinkins. Derrick Bell's fourth "rule of racial standing" seems relevant here: "When a black person or group makes a statement or takes an action that the white community or vocal components thereof deem 'outrageous,' the latter will actively recruit blacks willing to refute the statement or condemn the action. Blacks who respond to the call for condemnation will receive super-standing status. Those blacks who refuse to be recruited will be interpreted as endorsing the statements and action and may suffer political or economic reprisals" (1992, 118). Mindful of such dynamics, the Dinkins campaign moved swiftly to control the damage following Carson's press conference. First, Dinkins himself publicly denounced Carson's comments. Then he announced that both Carson and Weusi had resigned from the campaign of their own accord. (In reality, both had been asked to leave.) Dinkins then redoubled his campaigning in Jewish areas, pleading with voters to remember his long record of supporting Israel and other Jewish causes.[67] Where Jesse Jackson had alienated even liberal Jews with his support for the Palestinian Liberation Organization and his "Hymietown" comment in 1984, Dinkins had long cultivated the image of being pro-Jewish and a champion of religious and racial tolerance (for example, by denouncing Louis Farrakhan for his anti-Semitic statements in 1985 and strategically distancing himself from Jesse Jackson in 1988). Dinkins had in fact won the early support of most Jewish local officials in 1989, although he faced an uphill battle among outer-borough conservative Jews who had avidly supported Koch. To many Blacks, however, Dinkins's gestures to the Jewish community seemed obsequious and demeaning. Some asked whether Dinkins was selling out his own people in order to please Jewish voters. Dinkins, as always, was caught between a rock and a hard place.

Dinkins barely won the 1989 general election in an overwhelmingly Democratic town. He won 48.2 percent of the popular vote to Giuliani's 45.8 percent. It was the smallest margin of victory in a New York City mayoral election in more than eighty years (Arian et al. 1991, 199). Table 3.4 shows the results by AD type.[68] Overall, Dinkins won due to overwhelming support from Black voters and substantial support from Latino and liberal White voters. Strong support from labor—especially Dennis Rivera's Local 1199 of health and hospital workers, Stanley Hill's District 37 of municipal workers, Sandra Feldman's United Federation of Teachers, and Barry Feinstein's Teamsters local—also made an important difference in the outcome of the election.

In the end, the general election had a great deal to do with race. According to exit polls, almost every White voter who did not trust Dinkins to be fair to Whites voted for Giuliani. Indeed, 60 percent of Whites who thought he would be fair voted for Giuliani anyhow (Mollenkopf 1992, 185). Registered White Democrats defected at an astounding rate; nearly six out of ten Jewish voters cast their ballots for Giuliani. Although Arian et al. report that "the great majority of voters rejected the idea that race *per se* motivated their vote" (1991, 113), the authors nevertheless conclude that race impacted White voting in this election in three important ways: first, approximately 10 percent of voters acted out of "racism pure and simple"; second, approximately 39 percent of voters acted out of "race-based anxiety" or a concern that a candidate of another race might not treat their race fairly; and third, the rest acted out of concern about certain "race-correlated" agenda items such as crime and welfare (xi). Roger Ailes had read his audience well.

David Dinkins thus became the first Black mayor of New York City with

TABLE 3.4 GENERAL ELECTION RESULTS BY AD TYPE IN
NEW YORK CITY, 1989

AD Type	Dinkins	Giuliani
Black	89.0%	10.4%
Mixed Minority	76.7	22.4
Latino	73.6	25.4
White		
Liberal	48.5	50.0
Catholic	25.8	71.9
Outer-borough Jewish	29.3	68.6
Total	50.4	48.0

Source: Adapted from John Mollenkopf, *New York City in the 1980s: A Social, Economic, and Political Atlas* (New York: Simon & Schuster, 1993), 86.

the help of the resurgent Black Power movement. But the Weusi/Carson controversy proved a harbinger of things to come. The week Dinkins was inaugurated in January 1990, movement leaders held a celebration at Reverend Herbert Daughtry's House of the Lord Pentecostal Church in Brooklyn to commemorate Jitu Weusi's twenty-five years of service to the Black community. The transparent purpose of the event was to restore Weusi's honor after his forced departure from the Dinkins campaign. Assemblyman Roger Green spoke at the celebration: "When the attack occurred on Jitu, it was an attack on us . . . We want to see fundamental change built on these brothers who built years ago. We want to see that the people who made it possible are in power, that Jitu is not forgotten" (*New York Newsday*, January 17, 1990). But the newly opened chasm between the mayor and his militant former allies could not be closed so easily. With Koch gone, there was little common ground to hold the original movement coalition together.

The resurgent Black Power movement that arose in New York City during the 1980s was a direct response to racial power and was shaped by the latter in imagination and form. Drawing heavily upon the Black Power and community control frames, the movement was also deeply embedded in the historical tradition of Black nationalist resistance. These powerful repertoire frames carved out ideological space within which diverse movement groups could coexist and occasionally cooperate. However, centrifugal strains increased over the course of the movement, exacerbated by Mayor Edward Koch's assiduous social control efforts. In the end, the movement helped David Dinkins become the first Black mayor of New York City, but the price for this victory was Dinkins's relationship with Black nationalist activists. Just seventeen days after the new mayor was inaugurated, the Red Apple Boycott began, spotlighting the chasm between the mayor and the militants and rendering it, over time, too large to repair.

4

The

Red

Apple

Boycott

The question for Black folks to consider is this: Who is going to control the economic life of the Black community? This is the 1990s. People understand that this struggle we are presently engaged in is a continuation of our historical struggle for self-determination.

boycott flyer

Those who had voted for David Dinkins in the hope of greater racial harmony were quickly disappointed. Set off by the altercation between merchant Bong Ok Jang and customer Ghiselaine Felissaint, the Red Apple Boycott began on January 18, 1990, just seventeen days after Dinkins was inaugurated as the 106th mayor of New York City. Why did the December 12th Movement launch a boycott once Dinkins was in office? Revolutionary nationalist activists and moderate Black officials joined forces in the resurgent Black Power movement to oust Mayor Edward Koch, but they had never been more than temporary bedfellows. With the election over, the December 12th Movement went back to its regular grassroots work of educating and politicizing the Black community through campaigns like the Red Apple Boycott. The December 12th Movement did not direct the boycott at Mayor Dinkins—that is, they did not organize it in order to embarrass him or to put him on the hot seat. Nor, however, were they willing to cease their own political activities just because he was in office. After all, as revolutionary nationalists, they desired far more than a Black mayor in Gracie Mansion. As Lewis Killian writes, "Extremists serve to identify unresolved, and in that sense crucial, issues still facing the movement . . . Just as the extremist will not be taken in by illusions of progress, he refuses to accept a false peace" (1972, 47).

The Red Apple Boycott became one of the most protracted and publicized campaigns associated with the resurgent Black Power movement in New York City. Lasting nearly sixteen months, it was truly a movement within the larger movement. During the boycott, Black nationalists from the December 12th Movement worked with local Haitian and Caribbean activists to punctuate the alleged beating of Felissaint as a symptom of racial oppression and to mobilize Black people in Flatbush and throughout the city.[1] The resurrection of key repertoire frames—namely, Black Power and community control—proved crucial to their efforts. Although the December 12th Movement advocated a few proximate goals related to the incident (such as a merchant apology, the conviction of the Korean merchant(s) involved in the alleged beating, and the closing of the two Korean-owned stores), their long-term goal was to politicize, educate, and mobilize the Black community around the issue of Black disempowerment. The boycott was thus an oppositional campaign intended to arouse Black collective action against a racially oppressive system rather than a strategy to wrest goodies (such as small business start-up loans) from the state.

Proponents of the racial scapegoating argument would have us believe that the boycott leaders "used" Korean merchants in this instance to achieve extraneous political goals, that they misdirected the anger of the Black masses at this convenient, vulnerable target. However, as we shall see, the boycott leaders believed, à la the community control frame, that Korean merchants as a group were frontline representatives of the White power structure, and that individual Korean merchants who showed overt disrespect for Blacks rendered themselves legitimate targets of protest. In their worldview, Korean merchants were not pawns or proxy targets, but active participants, along with Blacks and Whites, in an ongoing racial war. Once again, rather than reducing the Red Apple Boycott to an episode of Black demagoguery and/or irrationality, it is important to keep our eye on the big picture. Racial power not only juxtaposed different groups within the racial order in New York City but also shaped the repertoire frames and protest forms of the Black Power movement that arose in response. If we situate the Red Apple Boycott within these dynamics, we can better understand the event itself and how and why it became a battleground upon which racial power and its challengers clashed.

I begin this chapter with a brief discussion of the Tropic Fruits Boycott of 1988, from which the December 12th Movement gleaned important lessons that it would apply in 1990. A snapshot glimpse of Flatbush, Brooklyn, follows. I then discuss the Red Apple Boycott in full, focusing on the consolidation of leadership, the framing of the protest, the mobilization of Haitian immigrants, and reactions within the Black community.

LESSONS LEARNED

We will see below that the December 12th Movement was determined to retain full control over decision making during the course of the Red Apple Boycott. To understand their resolve, we need to look back briefly at the Tropic Fruits Boycott of 1988, during which the December 12th Movement's agenda was thwarted by more moderate leaders in the Black community. What group members learned from the 1988 boycott was the need to maintain scrupulous control over a protest campaign in order to avoid being undercut by other leaders.[2] The Tropic Fruits Boycott began on August 27, 1988, following an altercation between a Korean store owner and two Black women shoppers at the Tropic Fruits store in Bedford-Stuyvesant, Brooklyn. The merchant accused the women of stealing; the women accused the merchant of racially motivated assault. Resurrecting the community control frame, the December 12th Movement punctuated the incident as evidence of Black powerlessness, attributed the situation to the White power structure and its Korean representatives, and exhorted Blacks to take back control over their community through collective action. As the picketing persisted, Korean American community leaders pleaded with Mayor Koch to get involved, but he declined. (We will see what happened to Mayor Dinkins when he tried this tack a few years later.)

The Tropic Fruits Boycott lasted for months, slowing the store's business to a mere trickle. But then Assemblyman Al Vann intervened. Vann, who represented the district in which the store was located, had nationalist / activist credentials dating back to the Ocean Hill-Brownsville school decentralization conflict of 1968 (another community control campaign). As cofounder of the Coalition for Community Empowerment (CCE), Vann had played an important role in launching the resurgent Black Power movement and getting Koch out of office. Yet he decided that the Tropic Fruits Boycott, while just, had gone on too long. He hammered out a settlement with the Korean store owner's advocates, who included representatives from the Korean American Small Business Service Center (KASBSC) and the Nostrand Avenue Korean Merchants' Association. The four-point settlement, dated December 21, 1988, stipulated that Korean merchants in the area would: 1) transfer their accounts to local Black-owned banks; 2) contribute to the Bedford-Stuyvesant Community Trust Fund for economic development; 3) hire and train Black youths from the area; and 4) take ethnic sensitivity courses. It also called on the store owner in question to publicly apologize to the two women shoppers. It is interesting to note that this agreement mirrored almost exactly the community rebate plan proposed by Stokely Carmichael and Charles Hamilton in the classic text *Black Power: The Politics of Liberation in America* (1967).[3] Vann believed in Black Power and community control as much as the December 12th Movement did, but he interpreted these notions differently than did the latter. The December 12th Movement refused to sign the settlement, but Vann's clout ensured its efficacy, and the picket line eventually dwindled. In the end, the December 12th Movement's radical vision of Black Power and community control was undercut by a more moderate vision of the same. The group would not be caught off guard in this way again.

Although the December 12th Movement resolved not to repeat the mistakes of the Tropic Fruits Boycott, the 1988 event foreshadowed the Red Apple Boycott in an important way. It indicated that Black elected officials, no matter how progressive, had different imperatives than radical Black activists. It also emphasized that the resurgent Black Power movement's coalition of officials and activists was intrinsically precarious and that the very officials whom Black nationalist activists had helped into office held the power to undermine or at least delegitimate the activists' efforts. Vann concedes that his intervention in the 1988 boycott damaged his relations with radical activists:

ASSEMBLYMAN AL VANN: It was sort of a serious conflict because I've always had good relationships and good credentials with the more revolutionary aspects of our community, 'cause I grew out of the movement, and I've always have good credentials and good rapport, even if we disagreed. This one [conflict] was rather cantankerous, and it did cause, on some level, a split between myself and some of the leaders of that particular boycott. But, be that as it may, I know what I was doing. I believe what I was doing was correct, and so I did it, and it worked, as far as I'm concerned. And, so that was the only negative fallout that I can think of.

The leading players in the Tropic Fruits drama—Al Vann and the December 12th Movement—would be replaced by Mayor David Dinkins and the December 12th Movement during the Red Apple Boycott. The mayor, who lacked Vann's nationalist credentials and long record of activism, would find himself facing an even more "cantankerous" situation than the assemblyman.

FLATBUSH: A TYPICAL GHETTO?

Black-Korean conflict always occurs in devastated, isolated all-Black ghettos . . . or does it? In some ways, Flatbush, Brooklyn, looks as we might expect: its Black majority is relatively poor and segregated from other groups, and many of its small businesses are owned by non-Black merchants who do not reside in the area. In other ways, however, Flatbush is a surprise. High levels of Black immigration (from Haiti and other Caribbean nations) into the area and incomplete White suburbanization have rendered the population of Flatbush somewhat heterogeneous in racial, ethnic, and class terms. The most compelling feature of Flatbush (for our purposes, at least) is its large Haitian population. Ghiselaine Felissaint, the woman shopper involved in the precipitating altercation, was Haitian, and, as we shall see, the December 12th Movement hoped to use the Red Apple Boycott as a vehicle for bringing Haitian immigrants into the resurgent Black Power movement.

Flatbush is centrally located in the borough of Brooklyn (see Figure 4.1). Lacking direct statistics on the area, we can use Community Board District 14 (which includes Flatbush) as a rough statistical proxy for Flatbush, keeping in mind, of course, that such a proxy does not give us a "felt" sense of Flatbush as a neighborhood.[4] Flatbush has experienced dramatic population changes in the last three decades. During the 1960s, most residents and shopowners in Flatbush were White. Then, during the 1970s, soaring levels of Caribbean immigration pushed the boundaries of Black areas in central Brooklyn outward into White areas, prompting Whites to move to White enclaves in southern Brooklyn or to the suburbs. As Table 4.1 indicates, from 1980 to 1990, the Flatbush area became less White and more Black at an even faster rate than the city as a whole.

These figures actually understate the extent of Flatbush's population changes for at least two reasons. First, Community Board District 14 also includes parts of the neighborhoods of Kensington and Midwood, which are Whiter than Flatbush itself. Second, these figures derive from the U.S. Census (1990), which typically undercounts both racial minorities as a whole and minority immigrants in particular (especially if the latter are undocumented). Note that Table 4.1 does not allow us to distinguish between native-born and

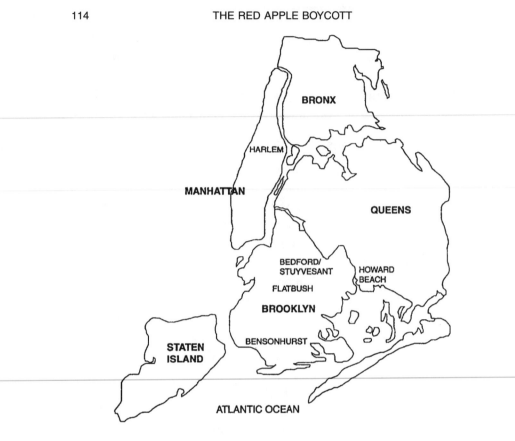

Figure 4.1. New York City

Source: Adapted from John Mollenkopf, *A Phoenix in the Ashes: The Rise and Fall of the Koch Coalition in New York City Politics* (Princeton: Princeton University Press, 1992), 45.

foreign-born Blacks. Taking these factors into account, we can surmise that Flatbush is significantly more Black and less White than these figures suggest (an educated guess that participant observation confirms).

Haitians are a dominant presence in Flatbush. In 1990, Haitians were the second-largest immigrant group (after Jamaicans) living in Brooklyn, whose population was 29 percent foreign-born. They were also the single largest immigrant group to have settled in Flatbush during the 1980s (New York City Department of City Planning 1992, 101, 199). By one estimate, 34 percent of the nearly eighteen thousand immigrants who settled in Flatbush between 1983 and 1987 were Haitians (*New York Times*, May 18, 1990). Because of the presence of undocumented immigrants, the precise size of the Haitian population in Flatbush is hard to gauge. Nevertheless, we do know that Flatbush is home to one of the largest concentrations of Haitians in New York City, which is, in turn, home to one of the largest concentrations of Haitians in the diaspora.

Impressionistic evidence suggests that Flatbush is segregated along both racial and class lines. Just a few blocks along Church Avenue away from the Family Red Apple store in either direction are two distinct worlds. If we head down Church Avenue away from Flatbush Avenue, we enter a mostly White, middle-class, residential area with freestanding homes, driveways, and lawns. If we walk toward Flatbush Avenue, we enter a markedly poorer, overwhelmingly Black area crowded with dilapidated walk-up apartment buildings and litter-strewn lots. These are sociologically important street-level distinctions that aggregate data usually obscure. Census tract household income figures also indicate that the area immediately surrounding the Family Red Apple and Church Fruits stores contains significant class disparities. As Table 4.2 shows, the four tracts immediately surrounding the two stores (506, 508, 510, and 512) contain residents of modest means who are markedly less affluent than residents of the other two tracts (522 and 524) located away from Flatbush Avenue.

Like other low-income, predominantly Black urban areas, Flatbush has

TABLE 4.1 POPULATION CHANGES IN COMMUNITY DISTRICT 14,
BROOKLYN, 1980–1990

Population Group	1980 (#)	1980 (%)	1990 (#)	1990 (%)
White Non-Hispanic	74,832	52.0	61,054	38.2
Black Non-Hispanic	44,285	30.8	64,662	40.5
Hispanic	17,234	12.0	22,372	14.0
Asian/Pacific Islanders	6,907	4.8	11,027	6.9
Korean	313	0.2	684	0.4
American Indian	127	0.1	307	0.2
Other Non-Hispanic	474	0.3	403	0.3
Total	143,859	100	159,825	100

Source: Adapted from Office of Community Board 14, *Neighborhood Information Kit* (Brooklyn, New York, n.d.), 12.

TABLE 4.2 ANNUAL HOUSEHOLD INCOME (IN THE 1,000s) IN SIX CENSUS
TRACTS, FLATBUSH, BROOKLYN, 1989

Tract #	# Households	Less than 20	20–39,999	40–75	More than 75
506	2146	43.01%	32.99%	17.76%	6.24%
508	4477	40.07	34.38	22.78	2.77
510	3164	36.00	37.20	24.30	2.5
512	2456	35.02	37.74	18.81	8.43
522	343	8.46	16.91	24.78	49.85
524	739	20.43	27.47	31.94	20.16

Source: Adapted from Office of Community Board 14, *Neighborhood Information Kit*
(Brooklyn, New York, n.d.), 11.

high rates of non-Black store ownership and, specifically, Korean storeowner-
ship. In April 1990, the Church Avenue Merchants and Business Association
(CAMBA) conducted a survey of stores located on Church Avenue in the five
blocks between Flatbush and Coney Island Avenues. This is the immediate
vicinity of the two boycotted stores. Of the sixty-seven storeowners surveyed, twenty-three were Korean, thirteen were Black, nine were Hispanic,
eight were Jewish, five were Indian, four were Chinese, three were Italian,
one was Greek, one was Polish, and the remaining few were unidentified
(Lee 1993, 69). Korean merchants who do business in Flatbush choose overwhelmingly to live elsewhere, fueling the Black nationalist notion that outsider merchants drain money out of the community.

A BOYCOTT GROWS IN BROOKLYN

The altercation between the Korean store manager, Bong Ok Jang, and the
Haitian woman customer, Ghiselaine Felissaint, sparked the Red Apple Boycott, much as the Howard Beach killing in 1986 had sparked the mass mobilization phase of the resurgent Black Power movement. Once again, activists
who were already mobilized and ready to move punctuated a specific incident of (alleged) violence against Blacks as an example of Black powerlessness and exhorted the Black community to engage in collective action. How
the Red Apple Boycott developed after the precipitating incident, however,

was entirely contingent on who ended up at the helm, who organized in opposition to the boycott, and the dialectical dynamics between opposing parties. After an initial sorting-out period, the December 12th Movement took control of the boycott, resolved not to repeat the mistakes of the past. The fact that they interpreted Black Power and community control in a hard-line nationalist fashion, and that they sought to nurture a Black oppositional stance toward the system rather than trying to get a bigger piece of the pie within it, had a decisive impact on the tone, course, and outcome of the event.

The day of the altercation started like any other day. Ghiselaine Felissaint, who worked as a home health care worker in Manhattan, routinely stopped at the Family Red Apple store (located just a block or so from the Church Avenue subway stop) on her way home from work. The store catered to Haitian customers, offering specialty items like plaintains. On Thursday, January 18, 1990, at about 5:30 in the afternoon, Felissaint stopped at the store to buy some fruit. The store was crowded with rush hour business. Minutes later, Felissaint and the store manager, Bong Ok Jang, were shouting at and grappling with each other. Felissaint ended up on the floor of the store.

What happened is a matter of vigorous dispute. As in Akira Kurosawa's classic *Rashomon*, the parties to the conflict constructed fundamentally different narratives about the same encounter.[5] Felissaint claimed that she had put her basket down to leave, having judged the line to be too long, when Jang accused her of shoplifting and demanded to inspect her bag. When she refused, Jang and two coworkers kicked and punched her, knocking her to the ground. Jang claimed that the incident began when Felissaint offered only two dollars for three dollars' worth of fruit. The cashier started to wait on the next person in line, at which point Felissaint became angry and threw a pepper at her. When Jang quietly asked her to leave, placing his hands gently on her shoulders, Felissaint simply laid down on the ground. By the first version, the merchant's arrogance, racism, and abusiveness caused the conflict; by the second, it was the customer's unreasonableness and unruliness that were to blame.

From that point forward, the available narratives converge. Haitian passersby, attracted by the commotion, slowly gathered on the sidewalk in front of the store. Then two transit police officers, followed by two NYPD officers, arrived on the scene. The arrival of an ambulance to carry Felissaint to the hospital a few minutes later sent a rumor racing through the mostly Haitian crowd that a Korean merchant had beaten a Haitian woman customer into a coma.[6] When the crowd in front of the store began calling for the merchant's arrest, one frightened Korean employee ran across the street to hide in Church Fruits, another Korean-owned produce store.[7] Eventually, Haitian community leaders Guy Victor and Philip Wilson Desir, who had been contacted by phone, arrived on the scene.[8] Using bullhorns, they managed to disperse the crowd—which had grown to about forty people by 7:00 p.m.—with assurances that they would pursue the matter further the next day.[9] The police charged the owner of the Family Red Apple store, Bong Jae Jang (Bong Ok's brother—that is, the wrong man), with third degree misdemeanor assault and issued him a desk appearance ticket.[10] After a day or so, the protest rekindled, due to an apparent miscommunication between Korean advocates and Haitian community leaders. This time the boycott targeted the Church Fruits store as well. By late Saturday afternoon, the crowd outside of the two stores had grown to approximately four hundred people. By Monday, January 22, the police had erected barricades around the stores.[11]

For a week or so after the precipitating incident, the leadership situation remained unclear. Different parties were feeling out the situation as the protest developed in a semispontaneous manner. Sabine Albert, a Haitian Flatbush resident who became a prominent leader of the boycott, describes the scene in front of Family Red Apple during these early days:

SABINE ALBERT: When I came from work on, this happened Thursday afternoon, and the store owners were still very arrogant. People were, you know, there were a couple of women with signs saying these people beat someone up. So I stopped and I asked them what was going on. And they told me this is what had occurred. And these people [the store employees] were like, they were throwing things at the people. I think their behavior did more to foster a state, you know, where people made the decision of, "Not only do you do this, but you have the nerve to come out and get, you know, superior" . . . [People] formed a crowd that Friday night. And eventually, what happened was, people just stayed. People just gathered around and it was like a really spontaneous thing. And then they closed their store around 7:30 or 8:00, and it was raining, and someone, you know, just out of the crowd said, "We'll be back tomorrow." And it was like a consensus. Everybody said, "Yes, we'll be back tomorrow." It rained all day that Saturday, the following day, and I was out there at 8:00 in the morning, and there were already people out there. And that's when we just pitched in, got some boards and whatever and just made some signs, and this is how it all began.

Guy Victor and Philip Wilson Desir, who were members of Haitian Enforcement Against Racism (HEAR) and other activist groups serving the Haitian immigrant population, were well known and respected among Flatbush residents. Building on their established reputations, they sought to channel the protesters' outrage into a constructive campaign that would pursue not only justice for Felissaint but also greater political and economic empowerment for Blacks living in Flatbush.[12] Via word of mouth (the Creole term is *teledjol*, meaning gossip network), Haitian newspapers, and, especially, the local Haitian-operated radio station, Radio Soleil, Haitian activists spread the word about the boycott and urged Haitians to join the picket line. Claude Celestin, a Radio Soleil employee and supporter of the boycott, recalls: "It was the radio. Suddenly, the next Sunday, we have a Haitian community program all day from 10:00 to 4:00 in the afternoon, and people went on the air to tell what happened . . . All the people were calling in saying there were other cases, there were victims like that."[13] Like an on-air town meeting, the radio call-in show provided a forum in which Haitians could exchange information, strengthen their sense of group identity, and encourage participation in the boycott.

Guy Victor and Philip Wilson Desir soon joined with other Black activists (including well-known Caribbean activists Ernie Foster and George Dames) to form the Flatbush Coalition for Economic Empowerment (FCEE), an organization devoted exclusively to running the boycott and picketing campaign.[14] Sabine Albert describes how the FCEE took on the daily tasks of operating the picket line:

> SABINE ALBERT: We started out as a group of people, you know, who were emotionally angry. But eventually we became organized, where it's clear that, "Hey, you know what, it's not necessary for all of us to take days off of work to be here. Some of us could be here in the morning, some of us could be here in the afternoon, some of us could be here on particular days. We don't all have to be here at all times." And then, you know, it even got down to numbers where we found out that if we had 15 to 20 people on the line, it was just as effective as having 150 to 200 people. So people were able to do more in terms of organizing.

The FCEE was a broad panethnic coalition comprised of groups such as the Alliance of Haitian Emigrants; the 131–141 Tenants' Association; the East 18th Street Block Association; Haitian Americans for Economic, Racial, and Social Justice; Friends of Ernie Foster; and Black Veterans for Social Justice. The organization's goals were to ensure that Felissaint received justice at the hands of the legal system, to compel local merchants to treat their customers

with respect, and to secure the city's help in promoting Black business development in Flatbush. Albert explains: "The Coalition for Economic Empowerment basically was more centered around bringing in business training and more speaking on the economic development of the people that lived
in the neighborhood."[15] When political entities such as the Brooklyn borough
president's office and the City Commission for Human Rights urged a negotiated settlement to the boycott conflict, the FCEE agreed to cooperate.

Then a radical turn of events rendered such negotiations impossible. The
December 12th Movement, which had come onto the scene soon after the
precipitating incident, assumed decisive control of the Red Apple Boycott. It
is difficult to say exactly how this happened because all of the activists declined to discuss such matters (an interesting fact in its own right), preferring
instead to project the image of a united front. Most Haitian activists simply
claim that the December 12th Movement offered to help out; December 12th
Movement people, on the other hand, say that their help was solicited.
What is clear is that the December 12th Movement did take over the operation within a few weeks of the precipitating incident. Activist Jitu Weusi,
who has strong ties to the organization, explains that the December 12th
Movement saw the boycott as (among other things) an important vehicle for
bringing Haitian and Caribbean immigrants into the resurgent Black Power
movement:

JITU WEUSI: [It had become] common knowledge, I guess you could say, to
the activist community that, you know, we were not being treated well in
these stores, and that with the least little bit of provocation, that we were
prepared to take action, okay? And there was another thing that was happening, too, and that was that there was an increasing number of immigrants—people of African descent moving into the central Brooklyn community. And there was an attempt to try to figure out how there could be more
communication between . . . African-Americans and different Caribbean
groups, okay? Well, this was the perfect outlet. See, we didn't realize how
much anger was in many of these folks [Caribbean immigrants] around
these stores . . . The stores became vehicles, okay? I remember the first
time when somebody had come and told us about the Church Avenue situation and all that. There was an argument. This woman, this Haitian woman
or something, and they were, they were ready to pounce on that. I mean,
they had troops, everything. You know, "Let's go out there, let's close the
store down," et cetera, et cetera. Okay. So that was sort of like, I guess you
could say, tailor-made for the activist community. And it didn't require long
for them to involve themselves in it, okay. Anyway, so that became like a

symbolic struggle between the activist community and the Church Avenue merchants.

The December 12th Movement formed a new organization, the Flatbush Frontline Collective (FFC), which gradually edged out the FCEE and took over the day-to-day tasks of maintaining the picket line, producing flyers, organizing rallies, etc.[16] Some FCEE members, including Sabine Albert, joined the new organization, while others departed from the scene. The more radical thrust of the Flatbush Frontline Collective was immediately apparent. Its members refused to negotiate a settlement and instead issued three unconditional demands: that Jang publicly apologize to Felissaint, that the system prosecute him and his coworkers to the full extent of the law, and that the Family Red Apple and Church Fruits stores close permanently. Where the FCEE sought concessions from the system (enhanced business opportunities for would-be Black entrepreneurs), the FFC sought to nurture an oppositional consciousness and sense of empowerment among Blacks.

The December 12th Movement's hard-line interpretation of community control alienated activists who favored a more moderate approach. Reverend Herbert Daughtry, who was on the scene early, considered getting involved. He had led numerous boycotts against White, Korean, and other merchants around the theme of community control. However, as Daughtry explains, he decided not to get involved in the Red Apple Boycott because he could not go along with the December 12th Movement's approach:

REVEREND HERBERT DAUGHTRY: I didn't agree with those persons who obviously had the leadership of that boycott . . . I think they wanted to put this person [Jang] out of business. That was their objective. I disagreed with that. That's never been my tactic, to put people out of business, but to bring people around to a better understanding and work together toward achieving mutually beneficial goals. And we have been able to do that. And so some of the people who are my friends, we started in a confrontational setting, you know. See, I think for me, you have to not only win the argument, your tactics must be designed not only to achieve an objective but also win the moral argument. So that it can stand the light of day. So that whatever, you know, I was engaged in I wanted to be able to argue it before the world . . . Once I saw that they were not about [that], that they had adopted a position of, you know, this store had to go, I sort of backed away from it.

Although it did exclude some moderate activists, the community control frame articulated by the December 12th Movement still provided a broad umbrella under which various groups could come together and cooperate. The Flatbush Frontline Collective was a loosely knit coalition in which constituent groups (organized mainly along ethnic/national origin lines) maintained considerable autonomy. Jitu Weusi explains that different groups did their own thing within the cooperative framework of the larger organization:

JITU WEUSI: There's three parts of leadership there . . . There was the Haitian leadership, that tried to deal with it from the perspective of their people, their community and so forth. There was a Caribbean leadership, that was trying to develop a political base in Brooklyn. Trying to, you know, use it as a mechanism to register their people to vote, you know, develop a sort of political perspective. And then there was the African American leadership, December 12th . . . which looked at it as a kind of a cause in terms of their political struggle.

Without centralized decision making or an explicit division of labor, these different groups managed the daily tasks involved in running the boycott, as Roger Wareham explains:

ROGER WAREHAM: It didn't really develop as a division of labor. Once the boycott started, it was just really making sure that the line was always staffed. I was about to say "manned." Manned, womanned . . . that there were always people. And mobilizations, when people got arrested, because there was a whole period of time [when] there was a very intense assault by the police either on the boycott line or [on picketers] when they left the boycott line because they knew where people lived. There were people getting arrested left and right. But there was no real division of labor. We had meetings in different places and people would speak to their constituencies . . . It was coordinated, but it wasn't a division of labor. It wasn't people working on antagonistic points.

Throughout the boycott, the December 12th Movement remained the primary leadership body. Roger Wareham comments: "I would say that for the extent of the boycott we were the ones who were there from the beginning to end. Some of the other ones at different points dropped out or were less active, so I would say that organizationally we were the ones who were most consistent."[17] Jitu Weusi concurs on this point:

JITU WEUSI: As I understand it, December 12th is more or less the—they did the foundation work . . . putting out the flyers, getting people out on the line, keeping the thing going. It's doubtful that the other two groups could have maintained it if it wasn't for December 12th, okay? But the other groups, you know, they sought to project their leadership. And of course their visibility was important in terms of keeping people out of the stores. So they were equally important. But the foundation work of the actual demonstrations was December 12th.

In fact, the December 12th Movement provided the other (predominantly immigrant) groups with everything from tactical suggestions to American history lessons, as Elombe Brath explains:

ELOMBE BRATH: [The December 12th Movement taught the Haitian and Caribbean groups] about mobilizing, how to organize rallies in the streets, marches. [We taught them how to] deal with the police, to let them know this is exactly what their rights were, and everything else that needed to be done that would help to maintain the longevity of the demonstration . . . They would not have known the whole history of the economic struggle that Black people had in this country, if it was not for us putting those pieces together for them.

Over time, the seams of the boycott leadership coalition started to show. As the city government, the mainstream media, and other parties intensified their criticism of the boycott and pressed for a negotiated settlement, the constituent groups in the FFC became increasingly wary of one another. Jitu Weusi explains:

JITU WEUSI: Relationships, as I understand it, were very touchy . . . Because you have the city, on the one hand, that was trying to undermine [the boycott]. So they were trying to play off people to get a settlement. And so, you know, relationships were very touchy. Rumor-filled. "Somebody's going to get so much and so much money. And they're going to sell us out," you know.

The mainstream media's insistent focus on Sonny Carson to the exclusion of Haitian and Caribbean leaders exacerbated tensions among the boycott leadership. As a notoriously outspoken Black nationalist, Carson made for much better copy than did a collection of indignant immigrants.[18]

The FFC thus transformed what had begun as a moderate, access-oriented, predominantly Haitian neighborhood protest into an uncompromising Black nationalist mobilization campaign. On February 7, Brooklyn Borough President Howard Golden and a multiracial group of thirty community, religious, business, and political leaders issued a statement calling for an end to the picketing and the commencement of negotiations with the FCEE concerning economic development in Flatbush. Although they had moved quickly, Golden and his associates had already missed their chance. By early February, the baton of leadership had passed into the hands of the December 12th Movement, who wanted nothing to do with negotiations. Although this uncompromising stand put Mayor Dinkins in an uncomfortable position, Roger Wareham explains that the boycott leaders were simply going about their own business, not trying to embarrass the mayor:

> ROGER WAREHAM: Our position was that it's not enough to have a Black mayor . . . Simply putting a Black man in place is not going to resolve our problems. The demand has got to be for him to be accountable to the community from whence he came . . . We weren't concerned about embarrassing him [with the boycott]. That wasn't the issue. The issue was that there had to be established in our community a view that if you don't respect the people there, you are going to pay the price of being put out of business.

Sonny Carson expresses impatience with the notion that boycott leaders had set out to make things difficult for Dinkins:

> SONNY CARSON: You know, the reason for the boycott was that a Black women was slapped. So, how, if that embarrassed the mayor, come on, I mean, how can you answer that? How can that embarrass anybody when the people out there were only coming to the aid or to the defense of a Black woman who represented an entire community, and that slapping insulted our entire community? So, I mean, the mayor being embarrassed, I mean, F the Mayor if that's the case. I mean, if you have to respond to that kind of allegation being presented deliberately to provoke division, then you deserve to be where you wind up being, because it should not have been embarrassing to anybody. The boycott didn't happen for no reason. We didn't just pick out one store and say, "We're boycotting you." I mean, there was some justification for it happening . . . So, the mayor being embarrassed is hogwash.

Regardless of the boycott leaders' intentions, the Red Apple Boycott did become a crisis for the young Dinkins administration—but only after the Korean American community and other vocal boycott opponents transformed the event into a test of whether or not the new mayor could stand up to Black militant activists.

COMMUNITY CONTROL AND CONSCIOUSNESS RAISING

As a central repertoire frame, community control calls up a long tradition of Black nationalist resistance to White dominance. As discussed above, the frame itself responds to and is shaped by racial power in that it embraces both the imposed category of Blackness and segregated space as potential bases for group solidarity and empowerment. By characterizing the Red Apple Boycott as a community control campaign, the December 12th Movement sought to tap into widespread nationalist beliefs in an effort to exhort the Black community to engage in collective action. The organization's members wanted to mobilize the Black community to punish the offending merchants, to defy and disrupt the power structure, to bring Black immigrants under the Black Power umbrella, and to raise Black people's consciousness about racial oppression in America. In their view, it all came down to helping Black people assume power over their own lives. Even for the revolutionary nationalists within the leadership, these were meaningful goals, small steps toward a revolution that would usher in a society free of both racial and class oppression. Roger Wareham suggests that members of the December 12th Movement maintained realistic expectations about what could be accomplished through the boycott:

ROGER WAREHAM: There are certain reforms that can be accomplished. The reforms that are tied not to the benevolent nature of the system, [but] to the amount of pressure and struggle that have been applied, so that our position always is that we accomplish most when people are in the streets and people are out demonstrating, protesting—whatever different forms that it takes to put pressure. Because it [protest] educates people to their own creativity, their intelligence, their power. And it's in that process that, you know, the system coughs up some things . . .

There's a twofold objective to protest. One is to heighten the awareness of your own people of their potential and their power, what they can do when they are organized, what they can do when they are disciplined. They can effect significant change. They have unlimited potential when they are organized and clear on objectives. Another goal is to demonstrate to the powers that be that, "We can mess up your stuff, we are fed up with it, we are not going to allow things to continue as they have been" . . . It's a real step forward in terms of getting people from the sense of the state's omnipotence or their own helplessness or inability to deal with things. You begin to break the . . . oppressed mentality. You begin to make a break of it and that can only come when you go outside the parameters that are set by the system, . . . You try to create a climate where you just have more room to function, you know, that sort of thing. You try to broaden the arena of rights that at least provide you with a better quality of life. I think we understand that this system fundamentally cannot address the basic human rights that people are entitled to, but if you struggle to push it as far as you can to make them live up to what they say they are about and to demonstrate that they cannot do that . . . It's not about reform as an end. Reform is a byproduct of a revolutionary struggle, and if you are clear about that, you don't get caught up into it as a goal.

Whatever their particular ideological dispensations, all boycott leaders agreed that raising consciousness was the single most important long-term goal of the Red Apple Boycott. The task was to move Black people from outrage over the alleged assault on Felissaint to a more comprehensive understanding of and opposition to racial oppression in American society. The leadership's decision to reject negotiations and put forward unconditional demands makes sense in light of this overarching goal. The longer the boycott went on, the more of a consciousness-raising function it could serve. Ten months after the boycott began, Sonny Carson declared: "I don't believe in negotiations. I don't believe in any kind of compromise. The only thing I see is these stores closing" (*New York Newsday*, October 10, 1990). Some observers saw the December 12th Movement's intransigence as evidence of mindless fanaticism; others suggested that the group was composed of criminal masterminds who had actually staged the initial altercation as a pretext for having a protest.[19] In fact, group members felt that their cause was just and adopted an uncompromising stand out of strategic considerations.

Constructing the "Other": Korean Merchants and the White Power Structure

Collective action frames stipulate a crucial opposition between "we" and "them," between friend and enemy, between right and wrong. A frame (re)defines a group as a collective subject and mobilizes it against an external target. The community control frame has called historically for Blacks to empower themselves by seeking to influence the practices and behavior of outsider (historically White) merchants within Black areas. According to this frame, outsider merchants constitute the long arm of White power reaching into the ghetto; they are frontline representatives of and beneficiaries of the White power structure that segregates Blacks and keeps them in a state of political and economic powerlessness. As such, outsider merchants must be compelled by Blacks to treat their customers with respect and fairness. It was precisely this logic that Black activists applied to Korean merchants during the Red Apple Boycott. As we will see, the boycotters were willing to (and did) patronize Korean-owned stores in Flatbush on an ongoing basis, despite their reservations about outsider merchants. When a particular Korean store owner exhibited what Black activists thought was open disrespect or abusiveness to Black customers, however, all bets were off. Through his or her own exercise of racist agency, that Korean merchant declared allegiance to the White power structure and denigrated Blacks, inviting community censure. The community control frame was thus used to construct offending merchants as antagonists to Black people, as outsiders who had repaid Black tolerance with racist abuse. In their view, the boycott leaders did not misdirect Black anger at an innocent bystander group; rather, they targeted for protest a few individuals who they thought had implicated themselves, by their own behavior, in a racial war—and all of this was part of a larger Black Power movement directed at the overarching reality of White dominance.[20]

From the start, boycott leaders punctuated the alleged beating of Felissaint as another example of the racist abuse and disrespect inflicted upon Black people by American society in general and by Korean merchants in particular. Arguing that Korean merchants as a group mistreated Blacks, and that the Family Red Apple and Church Fruits stores were notorious for such practices, boycott leaders insisted that it was time to draw the line with the most egregious offenders. As boycott leader George Dames put it: "The stores have become a symbol of what has happened across the city in terms of the lack of recognizing the humanity of black people. It was not an isolated incident, and people are realizing that it doesn't have to be tolerated" (*New York Times*, July 16, 1990). Activist Ernie Foster explicitly linked Korean mistreatment of Blacks to the community control frame, using language that evoked the "double-duty dollar" doctrine advanced by Black leaders in the early decades of the twentieth century:

> No one will spend six months on a boycott line for nonsense. We have a reason to be out there. The reason is that time and time again, the Koreans have been disrespectful to the community and to African people in the community as a whole . . . One thing about our community, the dollar goes around one time in Flatbush. You go to Bensonhurst, you go to Bay Ridge, any other community that is non-African, you will find out the dollar goes around three times. In this community . . . the dollar . . . goes into the hands of the Korean merchants and it goes out of the community.[21]

At a public hearing held by the Mayor's Committee investigating the boycott in Flatbush in June 1990, activist Yvonne Murray suggested that the two Korean merchants had brought the protest upon themselves through their own racist behavior:

> I have patronized those stores for small items, and I have had the disrespect paid to me, all right? So when this incident took place on Mrs. Felissaint, that was just the straw that broke the camel's back . . . Let me say this to you. It is not a Korean issue as it is being made to be here. The issue is respect, and when you disrespect a people, we are no longer going to sit around and allow folks to disrespect us. There are Koreans doing business all over this community, and they are doing business and they are not being boycotted. Those two stores are being boycotted because of their disrespect.

James Small, a professor at City College of New York and boycott supporter, echoes the point about Korean merchants repaying Black tolerance with abuse:

> JAMES SMALL: We don't have time to have nothing against Korean peoples. We're just saying, don't become a part of the exploitation, otherwise you're going to become our enemy and we're going to have to start fighting you, too. We don't want to do that. We shop with you. I mean, you ain't got sense enough to see that we're shopping with you and you're making millions off of us? And you ain't got sense enough to say, "Shit, I better build some relationship with these people, I'm making my life off of these people." Instead of treating us like we're animals. Something to be disdained. Just to get the money out of us. We may be poor but we're not stupid. I don't care who sells me my produce, just do it with the same respect that you'd want me to give you. I'm tired of colonialism. And you [Koreans] come from an oppressed society, you should be tired of colonialism. Don't imitate the colonialist that you just threw off your back.

Sonny Carson makes a similar point.

> SONNY CARSON: The boycotts weren't aimed at the Koreans themselves. The boycotts were aimed at the attitude of people coming into our community and taking advantage of what the system allowed them to have, to provide them a place to continue to rip us off, that the crackers had done before they got here. Their [Koreans'] attitudes were so arrogant, that they now, in some instances, thought that they could even resort to violence, and that wasn't going to be tolerated. In fact, we could have put an end to that in an hour. We could have blew up the stores, it don't make no difference. But they gave us an opportunity to organize our people, you understand? It

wasn't about the Koreans themselves, it was about their arrogance and them choosing to be like the people who they didn't realize were the enemies of our people . . . This time, it gave us an opportunity to organize and to organize and to organize and to carry it a little further.

Roger Wareham speculates that Korean merchants learn to be racist against Blacks before they even arrive in the United States:

ROGER WAREHAM: There wasn't any per se anti-Korean sentiment [in the boycott]. What developed was a sense after those incidents that the Korean merchants had bought into an attitude of Black people that was racist . . . And our view was that probably a lot of them came over with attitudes about Black folks that they had gotten from the United States Army in terms of just how you deal with niggers.

In sum, while boycott leaders claimed that the two Korean merchants' behavior was symptomatic of racism toward Blacks on the part of both Whites and Korean merchants in general, they took pains to emphasize that they were targeting the two merchants because their overt and egregious discriminatory behavior toward Black customers had empirically demonstrated where they stood in the American racial war.

Many boycott leaders expressed disappointment that Koreans, a people of color with a proud anticolonialist history, would choose to ally themselves with Whites rather than sympathizing with Blacks. James Small comments on this point in language that recalls the phenomenon of "Third World" consciousness from the 1960s:

JAMES SMALL: The thing that upsets us who have fought against it [racism] so heavily in America, it hurts us when we see brothers and sisters who come from colonial places where America has exploited them the way America has exploited Korea, exploited Japan, and then they come to America, where we have fought for them, and turn against us. It's a hurt for those of us who are conscious, even though people don't speak on that. If you look at our rhetoric of the '60s, you will not find a moment where we have not referred to our Asian brothers and sisters, and we have not raised their struggles and we have not talked about their exploitation and made it akin to our exploitation. And then when they begin to come over in large numbers after the '60s, we are thinking comrades are coming, and an enemy is coming. But that enemy is not conscious of its being an enemy. Nor is it conscious of us being a comrade and that becomes sad. Because we have not developed a way of communicating.

Activist Omowale Clay criticizes Asian American New Yorkers for rushing to the defense of the Korean merchants rather than evaluating the conflict impartially. Again, note the sense that Asian Americans have repaid Black openness with repudiation, that they have chosen to join the oppressor rather than their brethren of color in the ongoing racial war:

> OMOWALE CLAY: Basically, Asians across the city around the boycotts took a position that was racist. . . . We'll start with the only reason you're interested in what's happening in the Black community is because [the boycott] happened . . . A Black kid gets killed, you're not there, you don't give a fuck. Now what you give a fuck about is an issue, and your relationship to the issue is, you start from, you're right and we're wrong. So there's a lack of validity or legitimacy to your entree into this . . . It's not surprising then when some shit happens that you immediately take the side of the Asian . . . That was very unfortunate in terms of that, because it would have been very important during that period for some Asian Americans here to speak on the question that existed . . . We [Black people] always extended our hand first. Always. Our first entree is not the sword, it's the hand, even when it's to our detriment, it has been to extend the hand, you know. But that was very unfortunate at that time, almost monolithically, the Asian community took a position. People from Asia could have spoken, but, see, they felt themselves if they spoke, they would have been speaking directly against other Asians and anti-Asian sentiment that they thought the boycott was now feeding into. But you see, it's the demand of progressive people in politics in the midst of a storm, to come with what's politically correct because that is what endures. That's fundamentally what endures. The correctness of that. Not even what everybody sees at that moment, but of the correctness of it. I always felt that that was just a real reflection of the quality of the politics in the Asian community.

Sonny Carson expresses more indignation than regret or disappointment on this score. He articulates his opinion of Korean American choices with characteristic bluntness: "I don't care what kind of oppression the Koreans have had to suffer. All I know is that since they've been here, they have tried to subject us to their own brand of oppressions. I haven't run into any Koreans who are sympathetic to our position in this racist society" (*New York Newsday*, October 10, 1990).

Boycott leaders steadfastly denied that the Red Apple Boycott was racially motivated or driven by an anti-Korean animus. They saw the boycott as a struggle for racial justice, not as a racist campaign. Elombe Brath suggests that the December 12th Movement had presumptively positive feelings toward Koreans as another non-White people who had suffered various forms of colonialism. His grievance was not with Koreans per se, he explains, but rather with those Korean merchants who had, upon their arrival in the United States, allied themselves with Whites against Blacks:

ELOMBE BRATH: We sympathize with the Koreans. We sympathize with the struggle in South Korea now. We are, at least myself, and many other people in the December 12th Movement, also are very much in support of North Korea and Kim Il Sung. And also, when the progressive Korean group here in New York were protesting for unification, I participated in that, at the same time I was participating in the Church Street boycott. So it was never anything about being anti-Korean. It was the principle because we saw them as exploiters who had very little knowledge about the community and then insulted us by saying that Black people don't want to work.

Omowale Clay acknowledges that empowering Blacks may well mean wresting things from others who have benefited historically from Black disempowerment, but insists that this does not indicate the presence of any anti-Korean animus:

OMOWALE CLAY: The Koreans are not so much a threat to Black people, but the Koreans are a tool to be used against Black people in terms of their fight to be self-determined . . . People are in motion around the world because of the economics of it and their lack of control of their economics in that sense. So, in that sense, the Koreans found themselves in the Black community because the Black community has the least power to resist. To resist what? The control of their own community. Not so much keeping Koreans out per se, but the control of their own community. There's an international line in the world which says, "If you want to make some money, come to the Black community." Why? Because they open their arms, they'll buy it from you better than they'll buy it from themselves . . . [So] people come in and fill the void in that sense, and then that becomes a contradiction, because when you then begin to talk about doing for yourself, you immediately start to talk about not doing for some people who are now integrated into your situation.

Despite these disclaimers, some picketers did yell racial slurs at the Korean merchants, calling out: "yellow monkey," "fortune cookie," and "Why don't you go back where you belong?" We have seen that the construction of non-Black merchants in Black areas as outsiders predated the arrival of Korean merchants. Nevertheless, the effort of some boycotters to depict the

Korean merchants as foreigners clearly reiterated the practices of civic ostracism that shape the racial positioning of Asian Americans. According to Clay, it is important to distinguish activists from lay participants on this issue. Where unsophisticated lay participants sometimes expressed racist sentiments against Koreans, the activists sought to make them understand that their real enemy was the system, not Koreans themselves:

> OMOWALE CLAY: The issues around the boycott, I mean, they get distorted . . . They get distorted by some of the more backward elements in the community because that's the level of their consciousness. They don't see any further than that. They see—you know what the problem is, it's like a drunk who beats his wife. You know why? Because you're standing right in front of me . . . I don't see any further than that. Immediately you're here, I can do something about that . . . That's why there's a responsibility [on the part of activists] . . . [People who] have some politics [must help others] to understand that the Koreans in the Black community is a phenomenon that one can analyze and critique and historically look at and see what that is.

Reverend Herbert Daughtry explains that keeping protest rhetoric focused and accurate is challenging since popular emotions are invariably aroused:

> REVEREND HERBERT DAUGHTRY: The way the language was used [in the boycott], I think that they allowed it to get out of hand, right? . . . People out on the street hurting from a whole different series of abuses, you know. They don't have the refined language, you know, of trying to separate out one incident from another. So if it's a Korean store, people on the community level is upset with this particular store, they would not be careful to use language in which people could clearly understand that I mean this store. I would do that, you know. And it took me a long time and many struggles to try to refine my language so I could be very clear, and make me clear about what I'm talking about. But when people in the community, they're angry in the first place . . . They're not trying to hunt for nice language to express their grievances.

Thus boycott leaders sought to discipline participants' behavior, purge racist sentiments from the picket line, and keep the boycott focused on racial oppression in American society. In doing so, they were driven by both principled and strategic considerations. They believed that they were engaged in antiracist activism, and they did not want charges of their own "reverse" racism to undermine the legitimacy of their efforts.

The December 12th Movement's success at purging their activities of anti-

Korean sentiment and clarifying their political message improved over time. Consider flyers from the Tropic Fruits Boycott of 1988 and the Red Apple Boycott of 1990, respectively. The 1988 flyers make sweeping claims about Koreans in a scathing tone. Examples include: "The Koreans are agents of the U.S. government in their conspiracy to destabilize the economy of our community. They are rewarded by the government and financed by big business," and "All Korean merchants out of our community!" Even in 1988, however, boycott leaders distinguished between the role Korean merchants played and Koreans themselves. Thus one flyer read: "Be Clear! The Korean people are not our enemies, but these Korean merchants can never disrespect us and be used against us." Another stated: "The Korean boycott must be seen as an overall campaign to control our community and not a campaign against the Korean people." On the whole, flyers from the Red Apple Boycott differed from the earlier ones in that they moved farther away from anti-Korean sentiments, distinguished between the two merchants in question and other Koreans more clearly, and addressed more critical attention to the overall system of White dominance. It should be emphasized that many boycotters continued to shop in the other Korean-owned stores in the Flatbush area and that these stores picked up a good deal of the business lost by Family Red Apple and Church Fruits during the boycott. While anti-Korean animus was evident on the picket line, then, characterizing the boycott as *essentially* anti-Korean (as many observers did) seems to me a rhetorical sleight of hand that obscures what was really going on.

Constructing the Collective Self: The Black "Nation"

Persistent marginalization ensures that most Black people living in New York City share a certain inchoate sense of group identity. It is precisely this enduring collective subjectivity that permits repertoire frames like Black Power and community control to persist and operate as they do. The leaders of the Red Apple Boycott wanted to develop this collective identity or raise consciousness in two ways. First, they wanted to give Blackness a deeper meaning, to move Black people from a vague sense of having something in common to a strong sense of sharing community or nationhood with one another. The message: Black people would stand or fall together in the face of White racism. Second, they wanted to give Blackness a broader meaning, to bring Haitians, Caribbeans, and all peoples of the African diaspora under a common umbrella. The message: All Black people are united in a global struggle against White supremacy. The Black "nation" was thus de-territorialized: it referred not to a specific place but to the bond that held together all of the peoples in the African diaspora. Both the Black Power and community control frames proved useful in these consciousness-raising efforts.

To educate Black participants about where they stood, as Blacks, vis-à-vis a racially oppressive system, boycott leaders moved from focusing on the precipitating incident to focusing on the reaction of the political system to the boycott. Haitian activist Sabine Albert explains: "The first instance was to get them [Bong Ok Jang and his two employees] arrested, and then the more we stayed, the more things happened, and then it became our right to demonstrate."[22] This progression in focus from the incident to the system's reaction was chronicled vividly in boycott flyers:

- An FCEE flyer put out in January advertised a mass community meeting and urged Blacks to "boycott merchants who disrespect and don't support the community"
- A flyer invited people to a "black power street rally" on January 27 and urged them to "boycott all Korean stores"
- An FCEE newsletter put out in mid-February advertised "black power mass solidarity rallies" and mentioned the goal of establishing "businesses and institutions that are owned by Blacks within our Flatbush community that reflect our self-determination for our economic independence"
- An FFC flyer put out in February declared that "African people must control their own destiny," condemned "blatant disrespect and vicious attacks on Black people, women and children in particular, by Korean merchants," denounced "the business community that sucks our blood by draining the economic life of our people," and criticized the police and politicians
- An FFC flyer put out in early March invited area residents to "a people's victory celebration" marking the grand opening of the African People's Farmers Market, "controlled by AFRICAN people for AFRICAN people"; the flyer noted that invited speakers included Haitian activists Sabine Albert and Guy Victor[23]
- An FFC flyer put out in mid-March advertised a "rally for justice in support of the People's Struggle for Self-determination" and proclaimed "no sell out, no compromise, no negotiation"; the flyer made no mention of the Korean merchants or the two boycotted stores
- A flyer emblazoned with the slogan "No justice, no peace" invited people to a rally on April 9; the list of speakers included Sabine Albert, Omowale Clay, Ernie Foster, and Guy Victor
- A flyer put out in May advertised an emergency rally concerning the issuance of a court order compelling the picketers to remain at least fifty feet from the store entrances; slogans included "All power to the people" (the mantra of the

Black Panther Party), "Stand up and fight back!!!" and "No justice, no peace";
the flyer also stated: "the media has been attacking us with lies and
distortions of the facts concerning the issues relating to the boycott," and "the
racist power structure of New York City is attempting to deny the African
community their constitutional right to protest and demonstrate its legitimate
concern and outrage . . . [In] 1854 it was stated in the Dred Scott "decision"
that negroes had no rights that white folks were "bound by law" to respect . . .
[In] 1990, nearly 140 years later, Korean merchants of Red Apple and Church
Fruit markets and the city of New York are saying precisely the same thing
to us"[24]

- A flyer advertised a rally for May 19 and stated: "keep your eye on the prize,"
  and "in the spirit of Malcolm X and Jean-Jacques Dessalines . . . the boycott
  continues"; the flyer criticized the media, the city's "20th century negroes and
  flunkies," and "the Court's attempt to deny us our constitutional right to
  protest"; it made no mention of the Korean merchants or the two boycotted
  stores

- A flyer invited people to an August 2 community meeting to be attended by
  Sonny Carson and other December 12th Movement members; the flyer
  featured a picture of a clenched Black fist as well as the slogans "All power to
  the people," "African people unite: defend against all racist attacks," and "Join
  the Movement Brothers!"

As this chronological progression of flyers suggests, boycott leaders tried to
move participants from their initial outrage about Felissaint to a sense of immanent panethnic solidarity or nationhood in the face of White dominance.

If boycott leaders focused considerable attention on "the national question," they made no mention of socialism in either the Tropic Fruits or Red
Apple boycotts. As we have seen, several members of the December 12th
Movement are revolutionary nationalists who envision a revolution that will
usher in a society free of both racial and class oppression. Recall the blurb
printed on page two of every edition of the organization's newspaper, *Arm
the Masses*:

What we believe:
Revolutionary nationalism and socialism for the Black Nation, forty million
Africans captured inside the racist, capitalist USA. The Black Nation is constituted by a distinct history and psychology shaped by racial and national
oppression of its people and their resistance to national oppression; a
historically-developed land-base concentrated in the southern USA; a common language shaped with its own cultural idiom; a common economic way
of life, underdeveloped due to racism. Africans are mainly wage-slaves to

capitalism who will never control the means of production, but all are subject to racist exploitation across class lines. The struggle of Africans inside the USA is a human rights struggle for self-determination, national liberation and the freedom to control African people's destiny free of Racism, Capitalism, and Imperialism.

FREEDOM OR DEATH!

Given these ideals, the December 12th Movement's silence about the evils of capitalism was deafening in both the 1988 and 1990 boycotts. The flyer chronology above indicates what kind of rhetoric leaders used during the Red Apple Boycott. Consider, too, how the December 12th Movement described itself in a 1988 flyer entitled "Principles of Unity":

- The December 12th Movement is a Black human rights movement with progressive allies which believes Black people must be free by any means necessary and must use the tactics of civil disobedience, economic disruption, general strikes and mass resistance in the street to raise the political consciousness of the oppressed masses to struggle against racist oppression
- White racism exists and it's a common practice in all of New York—city, state, federal and private sectors—that affects commerce, education, social services, cultural, labor, and health institutions. As long as these conditions exist there will be no peace in New York City
- As an oppressed Black nation struggling for its human rights, we have the right to self-determination and national liberation and recognize and support this same right of all oppressed nations
- Political oppression is a concrete reality for millions of Blacks and other oppressed nations. Where there is political oppression, there must be political resistance. Political prisoners and POWs are descendants of the struggle against this oppression and must be supported politically and materially
- The right to defend ourselves by any means necessary. That an attack against one is an attack against all

Again, there is no mention of the organization's socialist agenda. Although the African People's Farmers Market that activists set up during both boycotts implicitly advanced the socialist ideal of communal ownership, it was pointedly advertised as a Black Power or Black nationalist institution—as "controlled by AFRICAN people for AFRICAN people."

The decision to focus exclusively on Black nationalist themes and to remain silent about the evils of capitalism was clearly a strategic one in both boycotts. While the Black Power and community control frames successfully brought together socialists and nonsocialists, Haitians and African Americans, etc., a socialist frame would have had a fragmenting effect among the leadership and lay participants. Simply put, socialist ideals are much less popular than Black nationalist ideals within the Black community. The integrity of the December 12th Movement itself has depended on glossing over ideological differences between Sonny Carson and his revolutionary colleagues. Roger Wareham explains that instilling a revolutionary consciousness in ordinary people is a long-term project:

> ROGER WAREHAM: There are some people who are very clear on the connection between race and capitalism. I think it's always the question of the nature of the attack and exposé, and is oftentimes a tactical question, because you have a long-range and a short-range program, and depending on the issue and what it is that you are trying to accomplish, who it is that you are addressing, you may tailor the question of what gets presented at that point in time. For people who consider themselves socialists or communists, the question always is, how do you begin to make the connection between the very different struggles of people . . . [and] the fundamental contradiction of capitalism and begin to get them to see that when you get to the bottom line of it, it's tied to the critical economic system that we live in?

Omowale Clay, too, sees protests such as the Red Apple Boycott as preliminary to or preparatory for the kind of full-blown global human rights movement that Malcolm X dreamed of:

> OMOWALE CLAY: They [actions like the Red Apple Boycott] are not deep protests, those are not deep protests. It's injustice. But our work is trying to raise up the question of the systematic nature of that. These are all reflections of denial of our human rights, you know. [We want] to establish that on a national level, that our rights as a people are being denied, and as Malcolm had said, this is not an arena to bring to resolve in civil court, because that is based on whether you are genuine citizens—then you can take these up to be actually redressed that way. . . . [The denial of our rights] is not a civil rights question, that's a human rights question. And to me, step two from that is our right to self-determination. If we can crystallize our movement as a human rights movement, then we've internationalized it, and internationalizing it is what raises the level of these particular incidents to a national level, raises the level of our particular communities to a national community and raises the level of our aspirations to those of the nations.

"Frame alignment"—taking people from where they are to where you want them to be, ideologically speaking—is a difficult, long-term project under any circumstances (Snow and Benford 1992). As Clay puts it, "Political consciousness is a cumulative question."[25]

The December 12th Movement also sought to bring Haitian immigrants into the Black Power fold by highlighting the immanent unity of all peoples in the African diaspora. Organization members actively nurtured relationships with Haitian activists and often featured Sabine Albert, Guy Victor, and others as speakers during rallies. In speeches and flyers, the December 12th Movement used "Black" and "African" interchangeably and glossed over national origin or ethnic divisions among Haitians, Caribbeans, and African Americans with slogans such as "African People Unite!" Members of the December 12th Movement self-consciously drew upon Haitian national mythology to inspire Haitian adherents, as when flyers exhorted Flatbush residents to participate in "the spirit of Malcolm X and Jean-Jacques Dessalines."[26] Then there was the time that Sonny Carson wrapped himself in a large red and blue Haitian flag during a May 10 demonstration on Church Avenue (Hornung 1990). For the December 12th Movement, gaining Haitian followers not only broadened their base of support but also helped to actualize their programmatic vision of an international Black struggle against White dominance.

Not all of the December 12th Movement's "nation building" efforts were exhortatory in the inspirational sense. As purveyors of Blackness, boycott leaders inevitably sought to act as arbiters of racial authenticity. Those involved in constructing (or reinforcing) a collective subjectivity usually end up labeling those who resist this project as deviant or wrongheaded. Boycott leaders indeed treated Blacks who crossed the picket line and shopped in the two Korean-owned stores as racial traitors, as pariahs who had cast themselves outside of the bounds of racial community through their actions. Negative sanctions included confronting those who crossed the picket line and calling them "Aunt Jemima," "Uncle Tom," "Negro," and other, nonracial epithets. Only those who had the "correct" position regarding the Black struggle were seen as genuine members of the Black nation.

HAITIANS: TRANSNATIONAL AND RACIAL TIES

Despite the dominance of the December 12th Movement within the boycott leadership, Haitian activists pursued their own distinct agenda during the course of the Red Apple Boycott. Sometimes this agenda overlapped with that of the December 12th Movement, sometimes it did not. As discussed in

Chapter 2, Haitian immigrants come to the United States with a highly na-
tionalistic sense of identity only to find themselves racialized as Black and
positioned at the bottom of the American racial order. In fact, the story is even
more complex. Haitians are culturally, linguistically, and religiously different
not only from African Americans but also from other Caribbean immigrants
in New York City. Thus they are "a minority within a minority, often viewed
simply as black by the white majority, but, at the same time, distinguished
within the black population from other black immigrants and from black
Americans" (Stafford 1987, 131). Flore Zéphir indeed suggests that Haitians,
as non-English-speaking Black foreigners, suffer from "triple invisibility"
(1996). In these difficult circumstances, Haitians have emphatically retained
and nurtured their identity as Haitians. At times, this has meant disidentify-
ing with other Blacks and pursuing their own group advantage.[27] At other
times, this has meant joining in racial solidarity with Blacks while retaining
their own Haitian identity. During the Red Apple Boycott, Haitians opted for
the latter course.

The key to understanding Haitian identity in America is to realize that it is
not ethnic but rather transnational. Nina Glick Schiller defines transnationalism as the construction of "social [and political] fields that link together their
[immigrants'] country of origin and their country of settlement" (1995, 111).
Haitians living in New York City have a transnational identity, which is to
say, they think of themselves as part of the Haitian nation rather than as a
bounded ethnic group within the United States. This has been true ever since
anti-Duvalier elites first fled Haiti in the 1950s and worked to depose the
dictatorial regime as exiles in New York City. To this day, Haitians in New
York focus a great deal of their political attention on what is going on in Haiti
and on U.S. policy toward Haiti and Haitian refugees/immigrants. Haitian
immigrant radio stations such as Radio Soleil in Flatbush, Radio Tropicale in
Hempstead, Long Island, and Radio Verité in South Orange, New Jersey, all
serve as "community bulletin boards" advertising news from Haiti, and as
"town halls for political debate among the Haitian diaspora" (New York Times,
August 20, 1993). Indeed, Haitians are often reluctant to naturalize insofar as
doing so signals a shift in orientation toward the United States (Zéphir 1996).
Both ongoing chain migration and the sending of remittances back to Haiti
continuously regenerate this transnational identification and consciousness
(Stafford 1987).[28] President Aristide acknowledged the vigor of Haitian transnationalism, of course, when he announced that Haitians abroad comprised
an additional administrative unit, Haiti's "Tenth Department."[29]

For many Haitians in Flatbush, the fact that Felissaint had been involved in the precipitating incident made the boycott a Haitian issue. They strongly empathized with Felissaint. As one boycotter put it: "It could have been my wife, one of my own relatives" (*New York Newsday*, January 24, 1990). Within the FCEE and later the FFC, Haitian activists repeatedly exhorted Haitian area residents to join the picket line in defense of one of their own. In effect, they used a (trans)nationalist frame to mobilize Haitians on the basis of their preestablished collective subjectivity. A few weeks after the Red Apple Boycott began, the federal Food and Drug Administration issued a ban on Haitian blood donations on the grounds that they were likely to be contaminated with the HIV virus. Together, the Red Apple Boycott and the FDA blood ban galvanized Haitians in New York City, intensifying their transnationalist consciousness and their willingness to engage in collective action. One Haitian boycott participant articulated the connection between Haitian transnationalism and support for the boycott:

> The first thing I'd like to say is that this boycott is not a racist boycott, it's not any issue involving race that—people in the community who are boycotting, they live there, it's not that they dislike Koreans, the fact of the matter is the people have felt that, look, this is enough, this is the straw that broke the camel's back. Now, Haitian people in America suffer a lot of injustices. Not only are we labeled as the people who brought AIDS, but we are also labeled as people who don't want to unite with other people, when that is not so. Being a Haitian student growing up in America, I suffered a lot of racism because I was Haitian . . . We have no justice, we have no respect, we get no equality. When you go to get a job or you go for a loan, simply because of the color of your skin you're discriminated against, all kinds of stereotypes are brought up in people's minds . . . The fact of the matter is, when you're Haitian, Dominicans will disrespect you, Americans will disrespect you, Koreans will disrespect you, all other groups will disrespect you.[30]

Claude Celestin, a Haitian boycott supporter and Flatbush resident, recalls: "[The blood ban] woke up a lot of people. Let me tell you, the kids—I have two kids born here. They didn't want to hear about Haiti. But since the FDA [ban], they are participating in the march. They listen to Haitian music now."[31]

During the boycott, the *City Sun*, the Black-oriented, Brooklyn-based weekly, ran a series of articles on Haitian political emergence in the city, entitled "Hidden Exiles No More: The Changing Face of the Haitian Diaspora in New York, Miami, and the Dominican Republic." One article in the series noted the application of transnational networks in local politics: "The networking that has developed among Haitian exiles in the United States not

only has helped alleviate conditions and usher in a new era for their com-
patriots at home, it now has become the infrastructure upon which Haitians
abroad are building strategies for empowerment. Demonstrations like the
one in New York City last April [about the FDA ban] are products of that
infrastructure. They are evidence of growing political agitation in a community that no longer is willing to be confined" (June 6–12, 1990). Ironically,
transnationalism had become a vehicle for Haitian involvement in local political affairs.

Even as they nurtured Haitian transnationalism, Haitian activists worked
with the December 12th Movement to promote racial consciousness and to
bring members of their community under the Black Power umbrella.[32] According to Reverend Philius Nicolas, a Haitian clergyman who opposed the
boycott, the December 12th Movement's community control frame resonated
strongly with Haitian immigrants:

REVEREND PHILIUS NICOLAS: I think one of the problems that we were
talking about, at least with several of the groups that were not for boycott,
but at least for remedy of relationship, was the Koreans are too self-centered. . . . Their businesses are family centered and they won't employ
anyone else in the community. The community felt that the Koreans do not
partake in the matter of generosity. If you come into a community, you are
making money in the community, at least part of the money, part of your
benefits, at least, should be somehow benefited also to the members of the
community. But the Koreans, they come and they only get, they don't put out.
That's the general feeling; they only get, they don't put out. They see everybody who comes into the shop as a shoplifter, because they are watching
everybody. The way they watch, the way they treat the buyers . . . That was
the general complaint we have in the whole community, not the boycotters,
the whole community.

Sabine Albert, who left Haiti when she was nine years old, was a paralegal
and part-time history and political science student at Brooklyn College when
the boycott began. She explains that the Red Apple Boycott politicized her
and prompted her to form an oppositional consciousness against the system:

SABINE ALBERT: I think that apart from a few people who we called in, you
know, like the December 12th Movement and . . . different people that we
would invite to speak at rallies, the bulk of the people were just people like
me, you know, who—I think as a result of this boycott, I'm more politically
active. Before, I used to go to school and go to work and that was it, but I

think the whole thing of going through this massive state of oppression on all levels to see how the media and the, you know, the establishment, they're able to work together, I think made not only myself, but a lot of people who were, you know, what you call "average Joes" in the neighborhood become more politically active.

(After the boycott, Albert continued to be active in various Haitian political groups and to maintain ties to December 12th Movement members.) Many Haitians involved in the boycott saw Black unity as the only rational response to global racial oppression:

CLAUDE CELESTIN: We all have the same fight. We are all fighting to survive, to get a job, and to make money and get some. If we don't benefit, we are thousands of Haitians and Jamaicans and Blacks living in the world, we don't get nothing . . . We are the same people, we are from Africa, we all came from the same background, so we have the same struggle, so it's good to get together. If one is fighting, it is a fight for everybody.

According to Haitian activist Guy Victor, Haitians recognize their debt to Black leaders such as Martin Luther King Jr., Malcolm X, and Medgar Evers, and they consider themselves to be "brothers and sisters in the struggle" with Blacks. Despite the best efforts of the "power structure" to divide Haitians and Blacks (as masters divided house slaves and field slaves), Victor insists that most Haitians "know what time it is" and reject this "mind game."[33]

Thus Haitians participated in the Red Apple Boycott both as Haitians and as Blacks, seeking to challenge the racialization of both groups at once. In this instance, transnational and racial considerations dictated the same course of action. The synergistic interaction of Haitian transnational and racial identities is evident in the following vignette. On April 20, 1990, as Dr. Emile Jean-Baptiste, president of the Haitian Biomedical Foundation, appeared before an FDA advisory council in Washington, D.C., to urge the FDA to repeal the ban on Haitian blood donations, Haitians in several U.S. cities held marches against the ban. In New York City, approximately ten thousand Haitians marched across the Brooklyn Bridge to the FDA's office in lower Manhattan, holding placards that read "Proud of our Haitian blood," and "Let's fight AIDS not nationality." Reverend Herbert Daughtry, one of the leaders of the resurgent Black Power movement, participated in that march. That same afternoon, on their way home to Brooklyn after the march, many Haitians went en masse to stand on the picket line in Flatbush, where placards of Malcolm X and the clenched fist of Black Power rose above the crowd.[34]

Not all Haitian leaders supported the Red Apple Boycott. Jean-Claude Belizaire, head of the Flatbush Haitian Center, and Reverend Philius Nicolas, pastor of the Evangelical Protestant Church in Brooklyn, both spoke out against the boycott early on because they judged the December 12th Movement's agenda to be too extreme and divisive. Belizaire, who favored a more conciliatory approach, exhorted Blacks to help themselves and, if necessary, to appeal to the state for help:

JEAN-CLAUDE BELIZAIRE: The Flatbush community does not belong to one group. It belongs to, it's a melting pot of different cultures and so on and so forth . . . [The boycotters] claimed that the Blacks don't own their business or they don't have the opportunities. Are they going to sit down and wait for everything to come to them? Or they have to go and get the opportunity. Because I remember once, a good friend of [then-governor Mario] Cuomo, in a speech said, "This is the land of opportunity." Okay? But, we cannot sit down and expect that the opportunity will come and fall in our laps. Okay? We have to go out there. We have to go out there and get it . . . This is something that should we sit down, meet with the bank officials, meet with the city officials, meet with the borough president's office, and meet with the [U.S.] Commerce Department, tell them we want to establish businesses, we want loans . . . If they do not listen, by going to them, or sending them letters, okay, we will protest. But we don't have to put this in front of the Koreans, we will protest in front of City Hall. We will protest in front of the borough president's office.

Reverend Philius Nicolas found himself in the awkward position of opposing the boycott when the majority of his all-Haitian congregation supported it. Like Belizaire, Nicolas was uncomfortable with the December 12th Movement's hard-line nationalist agenda. He explains that he supported the boycotters' right to protest but thought that they went too far in demanding the closing of the two stores.

REVEREND PHILIUS NICOLAS: I think the boycott should not have been started. There was an abuse at least by the Koreans' group, it was a fact, but at the same time they [Black activists] should build a way to deal with the boycott . . . Anything that happened we don't like, we have to have it make big noise, make boycott for every little thing that happens, [then we] will have boycott every day. I think some of the things that happened, which we consider as an abuse, at the same time they should build a way to compensate it, they should build a way to deal with it, to negotiate about it, to sit at the round table and talk about it and win the remedy. . . . Members of the church,

I'm sure some of them may have taken part in the boycott. They have a right to join in with the community if they feel like participating. If somebody comes and asks my advice, I would advise them, but they don't have to ask me advice on every little thing they want to do. All of the citizens in the community, they have the right to do whatever thing they feel, which is not a sin, which is their civil right . . . In some way I agree with the boycott, but I don't agree with destroying somebody for boycott. I agree with the boycott because sometimes if you do not make noise, they don't hear you. You have to make noise sometimes. But, at the same time, if you have to make noise, you don't need to have me close my church . . . You could still have boycott, but at the same time let the business go.

After Belizaire and Nicolas urged a negotiated end to the conflict during an early meeting in the Brooklyn borough president's office, they became targets of public vilification and received numerous death threats. Nicolas explains:

REVEREND PHILIUS NICOLAS: For me, as the minister of the church, when we learn about the problem, I started to take part, active part, at least sitting with the Korean community, with the police, with the officials in the community to see how we could bring an end to this problem . . . We [were] trying to negotiate. About seventy of us were in that meeting there, but, they [Black activists] pinpointed only to me and Belizaire, that we went to . . . negotiate on behalf of the lady, who was not represented, and we had [tried] to sell her out. They announced that they were going to blow my church away, kill me, and from that day I said, "Okay, enough is enough" . . . After Howard Golden's meeting, I stopped from everything, I only heard about it . . . On Sunday, over the radio, and it wasn't just something they say in the [Flatbush Haitian] community, they say that over the radio on . . . WLIB . . . we have people calling me and Belizaire all kinds of names. People . . . were calling, and friends calling friends, saying, "What happened to Pastor Nicolas? I heard he did something very bad" . . . Somebody called [Belizaire] and said that they have $15,000 to shoot me. He was going to shoot me and Belizaire.

Fearing for their lives, Belizaire and Nicolas withdrew from the conflict, leaving the December 12th Movement and their Haitian allies without public opposition within the Haitian community.

BLACK SUPPORT, BLACK OPPOSITION

Black responses to the Red Apple Boycott ranged from enthusiastic support to bitter condemnation. Participants stood at one end of the spectrum, organized opponents at the other, and the mostly silent, mostly passive majority fell somewhere in between. Although they did not endorse the boycott (and were often critical of it), the city's Black newspapers did depict it as a bona fide social movement for Black empowerment. This was in pointed contrast to the mainstream media's depiction of the boycott as a racial scapegoating cum criminal extortion campaign led by extremist hatemongers. Activists involved in the resurgent Black Power movement were fairly supportive of the boycott but stopped short of endorsing the December 12th Movement's uncompromising stand; most preferred not to comment on the boycott in public. Organized opponents, finally, denounced the boycott, whether in the name of colorblind talk, neighborhood use values, or a more conservative variant of Black nationalism. Clearly, Black opinion in New York City was anything but monolithic.

Boycott Participants

The Red Apple Boycott permitted a fantastic variety of forms and degrees of participation, ranging from attending marches and rallies, to standing on the picket line, to purchasing produce from the African People's Farmers Market, to not shopping in the two boycotted stores. People participated in different ways, to different degrees, for different amounts of time, and for different reasons. While rallies and marches regularly drew several hundred people, the picket line was often staffed by dozens or fewer, depending on the time of day and the day of the week. During work hours on weekdays, there were only a few people on the picket line; during evening hours and on weekends, the numbers increased substantially. The fact that business in the two stores trickled nearly to a halt during the course of the boycott indicates the efficacy of the picket line, even if it tells us nothing about the motives of customers who stayed away (did they support the boycott, or were they just reluctant to face harassment from picketers?). The picket line peaked in strength during the early months of 1990 and started to fade after the fall of 1990. An educated guess would put the number of all those who at any point participated in the Red Apple Boycott in the thousands, that of regular participants in the hundreds, and that of core participants in the dozens. Of course, numbers alone tell us much less than we want to know. Even if we had a precise head count of all those who participated in the boycott in some way or another, we still would not know their reasons for participating, the intensity of their commitment, or the extent of their agreement with the December 12th Movement's agenda. Obviously, not everyone who stopped to listen to a rally speaker or refrained from shopping in the two stores was an ardent Black nationalist.

Who were the boycott participants? People of both sexes and all ages participated. Most boycott participants were Flatbush residents, predominantly Haitians and Caribbeans. Haitians (boycott supporters and opponents alike) attest to the fact that the vast majority of Haitians living in the immediate area supported the boycott at some point, to some degree, and in some way. Sometimes Haitian households and kin networks participated together: Claude Celestin, for instance, got his wife and sister involved, and Sabine Albert persuaded her mother to participate. Judging from impressionistic evidence, most participants came from the working poor or lower middle class, as did the participants in the resurgent Black Power movement citywide. Occasionally, Black people came from other parts of the city to attend special rallies or boycott-related events. On the whole, though, the Red Apple Boycott was a neighborhood-based affair. According to Fitzgerald Lamont, a Haitian boycott participant, the mainstream media's suggestion that the boycott was the work of "outsiders" was preposterous and intentionally misleading.[35] Of course, as constructed and contested terms, "inside" and "outside" served more as rhetorical weapons than as objective markers of space and belonging.[36]

The Latitude of Acceptance

More Black people sympathized with the Red Apple Boycott than actively participated in it. As Doug McAdam et al. explain, "In the case of most movements, the size of the pool of recruits—the 'latitude of acceptance'—is still many times larger than the actual number of persons who take part in any given instance of activism" (1988, 705). How wide was the "latitude of acceptance" for the Red Apple Boycott within the Black community? We know that many Black people in New York City and elsewhere held vaguely nationalist sentiments at the time of the boycott, but this is hardly predictive of their opinions of this particular event. Pyong Gap Min's 1992 survey data suggest that many Blacks in New York City were critical of Korean merchants: 55.6 percent of Blacks agreed with the statement, "Korean merchants drain black economic resources by taking money out of the black community" while only 20 percent of Whites agreed; more than 40 percent of Blacks agreed with the statement, "Korean merchants in black neighborhoods become rich by exploiting Black people," while only 6 percent of Whites did (1996, 111).[37] Yet not all Blacks who were critical of Korean merchants supported the boycott. Some surely found the December 12th Movement's hardline strategy as objectionable as the merchants' alleged offenses.

Two public opinion polls concerning the Red Apple Boycott help us to define the latitude of acceptance a bit further. Table 4.3 shows the results of the first poll, conducted by *New York Newsday* / Gallup by telephone in New York City between June 1 and June 5, 1990.[38] The second poll, conducted by Pyong Gap Min in New York City between February and April 1992, shows similar results among Blacks, regardless of nativity. According to Min, 26.8 percent of native-born Blacks and 26.3 percent of immigrant Blacks supported the boycott (1996, 118).[39] Looking at these two polls, we can surmise that a sizable minority of Blacks supported the boycott, a sizable minority opposed it, and a nebulous intermediate group was undecided or had mixed feelings. Unsurprisingly, Black support for the boycott was much higher than that of any other group (more than four times higher than that of Whites, according to the *Newsday* / Gallup poll).

These public opinion polls may understate the boycott's latitude of acceptance among Blacks. To begin with, the phrasing of the questions in both polls was too crude and categorical to capture the complexities of Black opinion on this sort of topic. The significant number of "don't know" answers in the first poll may well indicate respondents' dissatisfaction with the available answer choices. If this poll had included answer options such as "saw both sides" or "sympathized with the boycott but thought it went too far," it might have provided us with much more revealing data. As it stands now, data from the first poll could support either of the following interpretations: 1) less than a third of Blacks supported the boycott; or 2) a majority of Blacks supported the

TABLE 4.3 SUPPORT FOR THE RED APPLE BOYCOTT BY RACE/
ETHNICITY, NEW YORK CITY, 1990

Question: Whom do you sympathize with in the boycott situation?

	Boycotters	Merchants	Don't Know	Haven't Heard Enough
Blacks	27%	37%	34%	2%
Whites	6	68	22	4
Asians	12	58	27	3
Hispanics	18	52	26	4
Total	13	58	26	3

boycott to some degree. Clearly, the first interpretation could be used to delegitimate the boycott; the second to legitimate it. My own interviews suggest that Black New Yorkers held complex, nuanced opinions about the boycott, sympathizing with certain aspects of it and dissenting from others— a picture that is not illuminated by either of these polls. A second problem with the polls is that they are snapshots in time: they do not provide longitudinal data. All available evidence suggests that Black support for the Red Apple Boycott peaked early and gradually diminished over time. Yet both polls were conducted well after the boycott's peak (the first poll was conducted in June of 1990 and the second in the spring of 1992), which suggests that both underestimate the latitude of acceptance for the boycott within the Black community.[40]

The Black Press

While some Black radio shows openly endorsed the boycott and urged listeners to participate, the city's major Black newspapers maintained a more detached stance. Still, the willingness of these papers to treat the Red Apple Boycott as a legitimate social movement, to treat the activists involved as credentialed leaders, and to communicate the latter's views via interviews and guest editorials distinguished them quite dramatically from the mainstream media.

The *New York Amsterdam News* typically sought to convey the boycotters' point of view without engaging in cheerleading. For example, the headline "Rallies Are Not Anti-Asian but for Justice, Organizers Say" (June 9, 1990) lent credibility to the activists' claims without openly endorsing them. The Harlem-based weekly also published guest editorials written by boycott leaders concerned with garnering Black public support. These often depicted the Red Apple Boycott as an integrationist rather than nationalist protest—a gesture aimed at the paper's relatively moderate, affluent readership. Thus Sonny Carson's guest editorial reminded readers that boycotts were a legacy of Martin Luther King Jr. and Rosa Parks (May 12, 1990). Attorney Alton Maddox's piece alluded to the Montgomery Bus Boycott of 1955 (September 29, 1990).

If the editors of the *Amsterdam News* maintained a relatively detached stance regarding the Red Apple Boycott itself, they were up in arms over the mainstream media's coverage of it. They especially objected to the mainstream media's appropriation of civil rights movement rhetoric and symbols for the purpose of condemning the boycott. When the mainstream media hailed Black high school teacher Fred McCray as a civil rights hero for leading his fifty pupils across the picket line in May of 1990, an editorial retorted that what happened was "not unlike the idea of Black school teachers in Montgomery, Alabama, leading their students to buses during the Montgomery Bus Boycott in order to break the boycott, rather than taking the children to march with their parents and neighbors in order to demand respect and equality" (May 19, 1990).

The *City Sun*, a progressive Brooklyn-based weekly with the motto "Speak truth to power," also castigated the mainstream media for their biased coverage of the boycott. One column, entitled "And So It Goes: Maintaining the Myths About Race," commented:

> The Flatbush boycott story is being used as a counterweight to Bensonhurst [the killing of Yusef Hawkins] (they've never shown as much emotion over Bensonhurst as over the boycott). The story takes some of the spotlight off Bensonhurst and, at the same time, lets the white media preachers say, "Look, there are Black racists, too, not just white ones. We've all got to work at brotherhood" . . . The New York City white media are a case study in the use of media power to define racial issues in a way that protects the status quo. Then they try to force the rest of us to live with their definitions. (May 23–29, 1990)

Another column, entitled "Blacks and Asians Have a Common History in America," continued the critique of the mainstream media's ideological shenanigans:

> The so-called mainstream media in New York City has been working overtime the last few months to pit Asians and Blacks against each other . . . The media mythmakers have played up or invented anti-Asian attitudes and violence on the part of Blacks, while at the same time casting Asians in the role of "model immigrants" able to find a place for themselves in the American Dream while Blacks continue to stumble blindly and hopelessly in the ghetto. The implicit—and increasingly explicit—message is that whatever problems Black Americans have, they sure aren't the result of white racism . . . The Korean boycott in Flatbush was a godsend to the media because it enabled them to praise Asians and condemn Blacks at the same time. The white media is doing this, not because they have any love for Asians—as a brief glance at history will show—but because they see it as an opportunity to use Asians as a tool to keep Blacks in their place. (June 6–12, 1990)

Like the *Amsterdam News*, the *City Sun* was more critical of the mainstream media's coverage of the boycott than it was enthusiastic about the boycott itself. The few editorials that directly addressed the boycott were, in fact, mildly disparaging. One, entitled "More Heat Than Light in East Flatbush," lamented the boycott's "ineffective, confused leadership" (May 16–22, 1990). Despite such criticism, though, the *City Sun,* like the *Amsterdam News,* treated the Red Apple Boycott as legitimate political activity, in pointed contrast to the mainstream media.

Other Movement Leaders

What did other leaders of the resurgent Black Power movement think of the Red Apple Boycott? Jitu Weusi, who maintained close relations with December 12th Movement people, endorsed it unequivocally. Reverend Herbert Daughtry, as we have seen, declined to get involved in the boycott once the December 12th Movement had taken control of the event. Yet he refrained from publicly criticizing the boycott and even appeared on CBS's *48 Hours* to explain the boycotters' perspective. Many of the other activists and politicians associated with the resurgent Black Power movement were somewhat critical of the boycott but refrained from saying much in public as the event was going on.[41] Maintaining a united front to the outside world was a sign of respect to their colleagues and a good way to avoid giving succor to the enemy.

Though supportive of the boycott in principle, Reverend Al Sharpton was critical of the December 12th Movement's hard-line agenda. However, he did not voice his criticism in public as the boycott was going on. Here he gently faults the boycott leaders for failing to distinguish adequately between the misdeeds of one or two particular Korean merchants and the essential badness of all Korean merchants:

REVEREND AL SHARPTON: Well, when the boycott started, it was some of the people that worked with my group that started it. Ollie McLean, Norman Reide, Ernie Foster, and we supported it from the beginning. I felt that people have the right to use their economic withdrawal to protest what they felt was a grievance or an injustice . . . I was getting ready to go on trial, because [State Attorney General] Bob Abrams . . . had tried to prosecute me, which we were successful in beating it in court. So we did not directly get involved, other than we sent a lot of people out and we supported Ernie and those that had started. Other groups became involved later on, but we always supported it. What I think occurred here, I think that it is always appropriate for people to protest an injustice. I think the fine line that had to be walked is, there's a difference between saying that I feel that a merchant did an injustice, as to saying that all Korean merchants or all Chinese merchants, all Black merchants are guilty. So I think a fine line sometimes became blurry. And that, I think, is unfortunate. But I think it was absolutely right that they fight an injustice, and I supported them.

Roger Green, whose successful run for the New York State Assembly under the auspices of the Coalition for Community Empowerment helped to galvanize the movement's leadership in the early 1980s, was one of the few movement leaders who expressed public criticism of the boycott as it was going on. Green explains that he wanted boycott leaders to repudiate anti-Asian sentiment more consistently and to promote a concrete and constructive agenda for Black empowerment:

ASSEMBLYMAN ROGER GREEN: The leadership of the boycott, in fact, were engaged in protest politics, but there was no program linked to it. So I had troubles with that . . . [There was] no specific agenda other than to protest the alleged beating of the Haitian woman, the elderly Haitian woman. Aside from that, there was no program. And I feel that protest has to be linked to a program in order to secure social transformation. Particularly if it's a legitimate grievance. And in this particular case the program of action should have been linked to the development of economic empowerment—a program for economic empowerment within the African American communities. So consequently, you know, essentially even in the statement that I prepared in response to this crisis, I talked about how this would have been addressed by us organizing and utilizing our energies for a program that talked about development of a Black entrepreneur class and the creation of programs that would serve as a catalyst in the development of African American commercial ventures and businesses like that.

Now, the other problem that I had was, and I said this, was I was gravely concerned about the expression of anti-Asian sloganeering. And I said that it would unleash a dangerous genie because historically in this country the same people that had exploited anti-Asian sloganeering, such as concepts of the "yellow peril," have also been actively involved in scapegoating African Americans, Native Americans, Latinos as well. And I expressed dismay and opposition to that. And that our leadership should confront them on that . . . I issued not only a public statement to the press, I issued a public statement to the leaders of the boycott. I was asked to speak at Erasmus High School, and I was in Albany, I couldn't speak, but I offered the statement myself. I wrote it out myself and sent it down. I spoke to Sonny Carson, who had wanted me to speak, and I told him that I was going to send this message down. And one of my staff persons went to the rally. He was not allowed to speak, but he did distribute copies of the statement. And the statement essentially expressed what I'm telling you. I said I defended the right of any people to protest, the constitutional right of any people to protest, number one. And that particularly for me I'm very sensitive to that, coming out of the African American experience, and that's a strategy that we have often used when we felt that we've been aggrieved. And then I went on again to say what I just told you. That we had to address the question of the frustration around economic powerlessness that our people were facing and I felt that was at the root of this demonstration. Number two, we needed a program, not just protest. To protest for protest's sake was not enough. We needed a proactive agenda and that it should be linked to the development of commercial businesses in our community. That we needed to avoid any expressions of anti-Asian sloganeering . . . The response from some of the folks was that they weren't engaging in any anti-Asian sloganeering, so there's obviously conflict over that within our community because some of the people that I'm very close with came back and said there were expressions of anti-Asian sloganeering. And these are people that are very progressive and radical in their politics and they told me this. And so that's why I put it in the statement that I articulated.

Thus movement leaders engaged in their own internal debate over the role that anti-Asian/anti-Korean sentiment played in the boycott. Assemblyman Al Vann, who promoted the negotiated settlement of the Tropic Fruits Boycott of 1988, defended the boycotters' right to protest as a matter of principle but worried quietly about its impact on coalition building with other racial and ethnic groups (a political strategy that Vann favors).

In sum, activists such as Weusi, Daughtry, and Sharpton supported the Red Apple Boycott (albeit with certain reservations), while elected officials tied to the movement thought it extreme, occasionally racist, and counterproductive. Mindful of the imperative to maintain a united front among movement leaders, neither group gave full voice to its reservations about or criticism of the boycott. Indeed, in response to the mainstream media's condemnations of the boycott, all movement leaders consistently emphasized that the boycotters had a constitutionally guaranteed right to protest.

Organized Black Opposition

Organized Black (or multiracial) opposition to the boycott was carried out by a handful of religious groups, civil rights organizations, neighborhood groups, and private individuals. Although these ideologically diverse groups opposed the boycott for different reasons, those who used colorblind talk to frame their position earned the most mainstream media attention. Challenging the boycott's Black Power thrust, these opponents spoke of Martin Luther King Jr.'s hope for a "beloved community" where Blacks and Whites would live side by side in harmony. Rejecting the notion of an immanent Black nation, they spoke of King's dream of a society in which his children would be judged not by the color of their skin but by the content of their character. To the extent that they articulated and reaffirmed the dominant discourse on race, these "colorblind" opponents of the Red Apple Boycott were celebrated by the mainstream media and held up as examples of "reasonable" Black people, as we will see in Chapter 6.

Self-described "racial harmony" marches exhorted Black New Yorkers to choose racial brotherhood and goodwill over racial antagonism. Often led by a multiracial team of Black, White, and Korean American clergy, these marches proudly donned the mantle of the civil rights tradition. On May 19, 1990, four months after the boycott began, the Brooklyn-based Coalition for Harmony, an ad hoc, multiracial group of clergy, held a service at St. Paul's Episcopal Church, led a march to the two boycotted stores, and held a "racial harmony" prayer meeting there on the sidewalk (United Press International, May 19, 1990). The next day, Norman Siegel, executive director of the New York Civil Liberties Union, and Michael Meyers, the leader of the New York City Civil Rights Coalition, led a multiracial group of one hundred people in a "unity march" past the two boycotted stores. Meyers, who is Black, led the marchers in singing the anthem of the civil rights movement, "We Shall Overcome." Speaking to the marchers, he declared: "We call upon New Yorkers who are black, brown, yellow, red and white to take a stand, to march and speak out against racism of any stripe and to affirm that we are all neighbors" (*New York Times*, May 21, 1990). Dozens of similar marches occurred during the course of the boycott. Again, the mainstream media consistently highlighted these events: Black people praying, singing, recalling Martin Luther King Jr., and denouncing the boycotters as racist made for reassuring copy.[42]

The most sustained and organized Black opposition came from the Congress of Racial Equality (CORE), led by Roy Innis, and Umma, a Flatbush-based Muslim patrol group dedicated to keeping the neighborhood free of crime. CORE, which first gained visibility by advocating nonviolent protest tactics such as the Freedom Rides during the civil rights movement, went nationalist in the mid-1960s as the Black Power movement was emerging. During the late 1960s, Sonny Carson, who was head of Brooklyn CORE, locked horns with Innis, the group's new national director. Carson ended up walking out of the 1968 CORE national convention. More than twenty years later, Carson and Innis clashed again during the Red Apple Boycott. By 1990, CORE, which still called itself a civil rights organization, had become a manifestly conservative group advocating Black self-help as the key to Black empowerment.[43] Headquartered in Manhattan, CORE needed "insider" allies in Flatbush to effectively oppose the Red Apple Boycott. Thus Innis teamed up with Ed Powell, the head of Umma, a group that also emphasized Black self-help, discipline, and personal responsibility as the antidotes to Black marginalization. Both CORE and Umma disparaged the boycott for emphasizing the system's victimization of Blacks and distracting Blacks from the urgent task of self-improvement. Although their criticism of the boycott came from a different place than did "colorblind" criticisms, the verdict was the same: the boycott had to be stopped.

Working together, CORE and Umma organized the "6:30 Shoppers," a group of Black Flatbush residents who demonstrated their opposition to the boycott by crossing the picket line and shopping in the two stores on a daily basis (at around 6:30 p.m.). Composed mostly of low-income Caribbean women who lived in the immediate vicinity of the two boycotted stores, the 6:30 Shoppers did not articulate programmatic ideological objections to the boycott. Instead, they framed their opposition in terms of the preservation of neighborhood use values. Simply put, they resented the picketers for disrupting the neighborhood, urinating on the street, littering, and making too much noise. Ed Powell spoke for them at the mayor's committee hearing held in Flatbush in June 1990: "The people of this community are distressed. Residents and merchants . . . have gone through hell. Bullhorns, loud music, often late into the evening, blocked sidewalks and streets, catcalls and coarse insults, chanting that reminds us that our streets and avenues are now their streets and avenues. Mr. Mayor, the people of North Flatbush are getting fed up." The 6:30 Shoppers did not appreciate being called "Aunt Jemimas" and other epithets for shopping in the two boycotted stores. One group member exclaimed, "Sonny Carson can't tell *me* how to be Black!"[44] In the spring of 1990, under the tutelage of CORE attorneys, the 6:30 Shoppers filed a federal class-action suit against Mayor David Dinkins and the New York City Police Department to compel the enforcement of a previously issued court order requiring the boycotters to remain at least fifty feet from the store entrances. In doing so, they joined a swelling chorus of critics determined to compel the new Black mayor to bring the boycott to an end.

Once again, as an explanation for Black-Korean conflict, the racial scapegoating argument misses the forest for the trees. It focuses narrowly on factors such as group proximity and Black frustration rather than contextualizing Black-Korean conflict within the broader racial dynamics that characterize contemporary American society. It is only by illuminating the forest, or exposing racial power, that we can grasp the full significance of the Red Apple Boycott. Racial power not only positions groups differently within American society but also shapes the resistance undertaken by subordinate groups. As a rejoinder to racial power, the resurgent Black Power movement in New York City was shaped by it in imagination and form. The same can be said about the Red Apple Boycott, wherein leaders activated the key repertoire frames of Black Power and community control to galvanize the Black community in Flatbush. Although their main concern was always with the White power structure, it would be misleading to say that boycott leaders used the two Korean merchants as proxies for that larger target. The December 12th Movement saw Korean merchants not as innocent bystanders but as active participants in the American racial war. Even so, they only initiated boycotts against merchants who were seen as especially abusive and disrespectful to their Black customers—merchants, in other words, who they felt had declared their racial allegiances through explicit actions. Once the Red Apple Boycott began, the December 12th Movement prolonged it as a political platform upon which to educate Blacks about racial oppression in America, as perpetrated by the neighborhood merchant or the city government. As we shall see in the next chapter, Korean Americans did not react to the boycott like passive victims or disengaged bystanders but rather mobilized vigorously against it in their effort to negotiate their own position within the American racial order.

5

The

Korean

American

Response

The Korean American community refuses to be victimized once again by being the target of frustrations for some New Yorkers. We will not stand idly by while storeowner after storeowner is railroaded into abandoning their businesses . . . Korean Americans are a first generation immigrant community, with little knowledge of and access to the often confusing American political system. In the past, we have thus often taken no action when confronted with ethnic conflicts . . . We can no longer afford to be so passive.
Sung Soo Kim, in a letter to Mayor David Dinkins

The Red Apple Boycott provoked an unprecedented countermobilization within the Korean American community in New York City. Korean American community leaders and merchant advocates had responded to previous Black-led boycotts against Korean-owned stores (including the Tropic Fruits Boycott of 1988) by trying to negotiate settlements behind the scenes. But the outbreak of the Red Apple Boycott was the proverbial last straw. It convinced Korean American community leaders that they had to take more decisive action to protect Korean merchants from future boycotts. Although a few merchant advocates explored the possibility of negotiating an end to the Red

Apple Boycott, Korean American leaders also moved ahead with community mobilization and collective action. If the December 12th Movement saw the Red Apple Boycott as an opportunity to mobilize and politicize Black people, Korean American leaders came to see it as an opportunity to say, with one voice, "We will not stand idly by." When Bong Jae Jang and Manho Park moved to sell their stores soon after the boycott began, Korean American community leaders dissuaded them, arguing that it was time for the Korean American community to take a stand and fight back. In this way, Jang and Park, like Felissaint, became reluctant heroes in a struggle not of their own making.

Most Korean American community leaders and merchant advocates saw the Red Apple Boycott as racial scapegoating, pure and simple. In their view, Korean merchants, who were just trying to make a living and were not involved in or responsible for American racial conflict, had been singled out because of their racial vulnerability. To mobilize opposition to the boycott within the Korean American community and the general public, Korean American leaders wove together two overlapping tropes or frames: that of resisting transnational-racial oppression (bigotry aimed at Koreans per se) and that of protecting the American creed (colorblindness, equal opportunity, etc.) and the "Korean American Dream."[1] I use the term "transnational-racial" to indicate that Koreans see themselves both as a transnational community and a distinct race. Recall that *injong* means both "race" and "nation" in the Korean language (Park 1997). For Haitians, transnational and racial identities are distinct: they see themselves as Haitian and also as Black (and are racialized as the latter in the United States). For Koreans, the two identities are conflated: they simply see themselves as Korean (although they are racialized as Asian Americans in the U.S. context). While the first frame exhorted Korean Americans to come together out of a transnational sensibility in defense of their interests, the second appealed more broadly to all those who believed that America was the land of equality and opportunity. Eventually, Korean American leaders came to see themselves as being caught between Black racist demagogues, on the one hand, and a Black mayor unwilling to criticize his own, on the other. Over time, therefore, the Korean American countermobilization shifted its focus from the boycott itself to the Dinkins administration's handling of the conflict, much as the boycotters shifted their focus from the precipitating incident to the response of the political establishment to the boycott. By galvanizing the Korean American community in New York City and persuading it of the urgent need for local political involvement, the countermobilization had a significant impact on the community's long-term political development. The message was clear: Korean Americans could no longer afford to think of themselves as racial bystanders; they had to get involved.

Getting involved, of course, meant protecting their collective position within the racial order and thereby the order itself. Using the hallowed notions of colorblindness, equal opportunity, and the American Dream—notions that celebrate and validate the American system—the Korean American countermobilization sought to return things to the status quo ante. Their efforts, in other words, tended to the restabilization of the racial order that the boycott sought to disrupt. Of course, Korean American leaders only had in mind protecting their group interest, not fortifying an oppressive system that keeps Blacks on the bottom of American society. The genius of racial power, as we have seen, is that it does not require intentionality on anyone's part to reproduce itself. As long as each group strives consistently to protect its own privileges, the racial order will be perpetuated. In the end, differential positioning creates differential stakes in the status quo: Blacks have an interest in challenging the racial order, while Korean Americans have a greater interest in protecting it.

In this chapter I examine the Korean American community's response to the Red Apple Boycott. I focus on the emergence and consolidation of leadership in the countermobilization effort, the leaders' articulation of two distinct if overlapping mobilizing frames, their shift in focus over time from the boycott itself to the Dinkins administration's handling of it, and, finally, expressions of dissent within the Korean American community.

FINDING THE "KOREAN COMMUNITY'S VOICE"

Composed mostly of post-1965 immigrants and their children, the Korean American community in New York City was still relatively young and, by most accounts, politically undeveloped when the boycott began. Business associations catering to small business owners abounded, but such associations were often fragmented by neighborhood and business type.[2] The result was a scenario of decentralized power wherein different community leaders wielded influence over different issues and geographical areas, but none wielded commanding influence throughout the community. The Korean American community's political underdevelopment was due in part to ongoing interference from the South Korean government. Through its influence over the Korean Consulate General, the Korean Association of New York (KANY), and newspapers such as the *Korea Times*, the Korean government maintained a powerful presence in New York City's Korean American community. The Korean Consulate General, for instance, handled immigration and naturalization issues, sponsored cultural events, and financed Korean American organizations, thus touching the life of every Korean immigrant in the city. According to John Kim, a 1.5-generation lawyer who helped organize the countermobilization effort, the Korean government's principal aim was to control Korean Americans' attitudes toward Korea and their potential influence over U.S. foreign policy toward Korea.[3]

> JOHN KIM: Well, they [the Korean government] are not taking any active role as far as American politics are concerned. They are more concerned about the Korean [American] community's political influence or orientation to Korean politics happening in Korea. For instance, under the Park regime, you know, they were trying to control the Korean community [in New York City] so the Korean Association and other private organizations, they didn't want any protest against them [the Korean government]. That actually has been continuing since then. So even under the present Kim regime, it's supposed to be civilian regime, but they are still using the Korean Association and other private groups . . . They select certain community leaders as members of this advisory board. Once you're recognized as a member of that group, they invite you to Korea to entertain . . . to special events and receptions, and things like that. Also, they are using the Korean media and the Korean Consulate General office. The Korean Consulate General is, for instance, handing out certain money to the Korean community . . . And then, they also control the Korean media, because Korean news organizations provide all the Korean news to these newspapers here. So these local newspapers tend to not report any comment or demonstration against the government . . . I think the main goal is, they don't want to see any active protest against the government. And then, the secondary goal would be . . . [using] these various community figures to influence the American politicians. I remember that the Korean Consulate office here was handing out certain donations each year to different community groups. Whenever there is an event organized by certain Korean groups, the Korean Consulate office donates some money.

Although the Korean government was, for the most part, unconcerned with U.S. domestic issues, its omnipresence in the Korean American community in New York City clearly stunted and distorted the growth of autonomous community leadership. In 1981, scholar Illsoo Kim wrote, "It is no exaggeration to say that the Korean Consulate General is the informal government of New York's Korean community" (1981, 228). His words still held some truth in 1990, nearly a decade later.[4]

In this context, Korean American efforts to respond to Black-led boycotts of Korean-owned stores had been ad hoc, fragmented, and reactive throughout the 1980s. Once a precipitating incident occurred, several merchant advocates would converge on the scene and sort out who was to take charge. Those who did not rise to the top would depart the scene altogether, conceding the conflict as the "turf" of another merchant advocate. (The parallel to the formation of boycott leadership is striking.) However, the imperative in the Red Apple Boycott was not to work out a deal for the Korean merchants in question but rather to rally the entire Korean American community in opposition to the boycott. This would require a kind of across-the-board cooperation that Korean American community leaders and associations had not yet achieved.

At first, Korean Americans responded to the Red Apple Boycott as they had its forerunners. Upon hearing of the precipitating incident, merchant advocates Michael Kang (president of the Korean Produce Association) and Sung Soo Kim (president of the Korean American Small Business Service Center) rushed to the scene.[5] Each offered to represent Bong Jae Jang and Manho Park in future negotiations related to the boycott. Like Black Power movement activists, then, Korean merchant advocates competed to be "on the point." For several days, both advocates acted as representatives for the two merchants when they met with police and attended neighborhood meetings called by concerned local officials. For instance, Kim accompanied Jang when he went to the police station to give a statement on the day after the altercation. According to Heon Cheol Lee (1993), however, Kang eventually emerged as the chief on-the-ground representative for Jang and Park.

Far from fading into the woodwork, Kim decided to represent the Korean merchants' cause to the Dinkins administration, the mainstream media, and the general public—that is, to the world "out there." During the first several months of the boycott, Kim wrote a series of impassioned letters to Mayor Dinkins, urging him to intervene personally in order to fulfill his campaign promise of protecting the city's "gorgeous mosaic" of racial, ethnic, and religious groups. Kim also granted numerous interviews to mainstream newspapers, in which he denounced the boycott as racial scapegoating and called upon the Dinkins administration to put a stop to it. In an interview with *New York Newsday*, for example, Kim stated: "Koreans are being scapegoated for a problem they neither created nor contributed to" (February 13, 1990). Kim's tireless efforts helped convince both the Korean American community and the general public that the boycott could not be tolerated.

As Korean American community leaders contemplated an all-out countermobilization effort, the absence of a suitable organizational infrastructure concerned them. Daniel Lee, who worked for the Korean Association of New York (KANY) during the boycott, explains how things looked:

> DANIEL LEE: I wouldn't call it a leadership struggle, you know, I'd call it a vacuum of leadership. Again, we don't have any Korean voice, you know, to address our own problems . . . There is no one organization that speaks for the interest of the Koreans here . . . including the Korean Association. You know, the Produce Association got involved because the stores being boycotted against were owned by the members of the Produce Association. I see why they think they want to get involved, and I see why they should get involved. I also see why some other organizations get involved, but, you know, again, the problem goes with the fact we don't have one central voice, we don't have one central organization that is capable of handling this umbrella kind of situation. As you know, we have many different functional, dysfunctional organizations in New York City.

Months after the boycott began, the KANY finally established itself at the helm of the growing countermobilization effort.[6] As the most important umbrella organization connecting Korean American organizations in the city, the KANY was well suited to the task. However, as Daniel Lee explains, the organization had to overcome considerable skepticism from within the Korean American community:

> DANIEL LEE: [Koreans] feel that this organization does not properly function and does not properly serve the needs and wants of the majority of the Koreans . . . Historically, we have seen a lot of internal squabbling among the top echelon of the leadership involved in that association, which has had a negative impact, turned a lot of people off, you know, fueled the apathy, and that type of thing. And also, there has been some talk of a mismanagement of, you know, of the office, mismanagement of funds and that the people who want to become president of the organization, they become president not to serve the needs of the Korean Americans, but to serve to become puppets, in fact, of the Korean government, and that type of thing. I don't know whether they're true or not, I'm not saying they're true, but there has been allegations.

The Red Apple Boycott became a hot issue in the KANY presidential campaign during the early months of 1990, with both candidates promising to improve Black-Korean relations if elected. Jong Duk Byun, who was elected president of the KANY in April 1990, began his term by organizing a cross-racial "goodwill mission" to Korea, forming the Ethnic Committee for Racial Harmony and Outreach in conjunction with the NAACP, and initiating other similar programs (Min 1996, 134–35). B. J. Sa, who was secretary general of the KANY when the boycott began, explains how the organization gradually asserted leadership over the countermobilization effort, creating order out of chaos:[7]

> B. J. SA: At that time, first stage, we have very—there's lots of problems because many people appeared as representatives. So it is no good. So we said, . . . "If you are approached by [anyone], you have to contact Korean Association first. And if any issues you have you faced, you have to report everything to the Korean Association" . . . [Then] we get together, we discuss completely, then we have to give answer even if it takes time . . . And also even I myself or somebody else attends a negotiation table with them, we can't say a yes or no right away. We have to come back and discuss again with the leaders, then you go back. Because the first words from you is not personal, it must be, you know, Korean community's voice . . . First time actually those things [incidents] that happened, many peoples appear. So even the city, they don't know who is [Korean] leaders . . . So now when I start working, we centralized all voice. "Okay, everybody get, come here. You're right, but we have to centralize and we have to discuss completely then go back to the negotiating table." So now the city says, "Okay, now we know who to contact first when we have such a problem." So now we are the Korean traffic control.

Sung Soo Kim and others continued their independent activities against the boycott, but the KANY set itself up as the official voice of the Korean American community. Composed mostly of immigrants and businessmen (and very few second-generation Korean Americans), the KANY adopted a hard-line stance against the Red Apple Boycott, President Byun's goodwill measures notwithstanding. With the December 12th Movement at the helm of the boycott and the KANY at the helm of the counteroffensive, the stage was set for conflict escalation.

RESISTING TRANSNATIONAL-RACIAL OPPRESSION

Korean American community leaders characterized the Red Apple Boycott as a racial scapegoating campaign that targeted Koreans as a distinct transnational-racial group and violated cherished American norms of color-blindness.[8] In other words, they used two overlapping frames to mobilize internal and external support for the countermobilization effort. First, they exhorted Korean Americans to act on their collective identity—their transnational identification as Koreans—in defense of their group interests. At the same time, they exhorted all Americans to defend the American creed and the "Korean American Dream" against the Black nationalist threat. During the first several months of the boycott, Korean American community leaders focused mostly on internal mobilization within the Korean American community. The task here was to reframe the boycott as a racist (rather than antiracist) campaign, generalize the sense of threat to all Korean Americans, and nurture a sense of collective identity and solidarity in the face of this threat. By situating the Red Apple Boycott in a historical trajectory of anti-Korean activity (comparing it, for instance, to the Japanese occupation of Korea from 1905 to 1945), Korean American leaders were able to channel the community's strong transnationalist sentiments into the countermobilization effort.

Korean American community leaders consistently punctuated the boycott as an example of how Koreans were oppressed as a transnational-racial group. Most Korean Americans were receptive to this message. B. J. Sa explains the majority viewpoint: "By using the Korean Brooklyn Flatbush case, they [the boycotters] like to call attention from the government to protect their interest for all Black communities or something like that. So we, some leaders of the Korean community sometimes say that we are used as a scapegoat."[9] Ben Limb, a Korean American lawyer who served on the Mayor's Committee investigating the boycott, says more about this viewpoint:

BEN LIMB: As to what was the root cause of this problem, there seems to be a general consensus among the members of the Korean community that it [the boycott] was racially motivated. They were sure about that . . . but as to how to resolve this matter, there was a variety of opinions. But the majority of them, regretfully, was based on rather a quick-fix type of approach rather than a well thought out, you know, approach to the problem . . . Their logic was rather simple and the word simple is the key to understanding the psychology of the general public in the Korean community. They thought that if these two store owners were, for example, Black Americans, they would not protest or boycott these two stores in the manner that they have done. They demonstrated and boycotted these two stores simply because they were Koreans. That was their [Koreans'] feeling, their analysis.

Since the boycotters had targeted Koreans qua Koreans, rather than responding to particular misdoings on the part of Jang and Park, all Koreans were at risk. Community leader Daniel Lee explains: "There was the feeling that the

Koreans across the board, not only those two particular store owners, but there was a sense of threat against all Koreans. A lot of people were pissed off and they felt threatened by it."[10] In an op-ed piece in the *New York Times*— entitled "As a Korean, I'm No Longer Neutral"—one Korean American wrote: "Since only Koreans are targeted, it concerns all Koreans living in the U.S. . . . The racism in Flatbush was not black vs. white; now it had to do with me . . . I was embarrassed to realize that until now I had seen racism as someone else's problem. It is now my problem, and it is everyone's problem" (May 19, 1990). The appearance of anti-Korean racial slurs on the picket line during the initial weeks of the boycott certainly lent credence to the racial scapegoating interpretation. Rector Paul Kim, who sympathized with the boycotters and dissented from the majority view within the Korean American community, expresses disappointment at the language used by some of the boycotters:

RECTOR PAUL KIM: You know, if their purpose was to get rid of Mr. Jang, the best thing would be to attack . . . [the] exploitation of [the community by] Mr. Jang's store or the beatings that people received and do a paper about how many people have been beaten or cursed or whatever, but obviously they came out with "Koreans are vampires," that kind of thing. So I think a lot of people felt frustrated by that, even though they might have understood that Mr. Jang could have beaten on this woman and that he should be punished for it. People felt that it was unfair [for] the boycotters to attack all the Koreans and present all of them as Mr. Jangs in every community. So, of course, later the boycotters came out saying, "We are attacking just Mr. Jang, not these [other] stores," but by that time, they lost it. Their message had gotten a crooked slant whether they intentionally wanted it or not.

While Paul Kim regretted the use of racial slurs and incendiary language in what he saw as an otherwise legitimate protest, many Korean Americans decided that the boycott was *essentially* anti-Korean and thus illegitimate.

How did Korean American community leaders convey their message about resisting transnational-racial oppression to Korean Americans across the city? Like Blacks and Haitians involved in the resurgent Black Power movement and the Red Apple Boycott, Korean Americans disseminated information primarily within their own distinct social spaces—the Korean language media, Korean churches, and Korean business and social networks. Although Korean Americans in New York City are geographically dispersed, they constitute a relatively small, cohesive community in which news travels quickly. The Korean language media—comprised of several television stations, three radio stations, and five major dailies—play a crucial role in maintaining community cohesion. As Pyong Gap Min (1996) notes, the great majority of Korean immigrants in New York City have limited English proficiency and are therefore dependent upon the Korean language media for most of their news. The Korean language media not only reinforce Korean transnationalism among Korean Americans (Kim 1981, 262) by continuously reporting news from Korea, but also promote a distinct Korean perspective on events in New York City.[11]

The most widely read Korean language daily, the *Korea Times*, was particularly active in disseminating the racial scapegoating message, generalizing the sense of threat, and exhorting Korean transnational-racial solidarity.[12] Published less than two weeks after the start of the boycott, one article in the *Korea Times* declared: "Koreans in New York should not be the sacrificial lamb" (January 29, 1990). Another article suggested that the boycott endangered all Koreans living in the United States.

> The boycotts of two shops, the "Red Apple" and "Church Fruits," have crossed a boundary, posing a great threat not only to thousands of Korean-owned shops but to all Korean immigrants in the U.S. If all the problems could be resolved by having the two shops shut down, it would be okay. However, this is not so. If they [Jang and Park] yield to the unjust demonstration and boycotts, these will surely spread to another Korean-owned shop. Perhaps they will spread throughout New York state. Then we would have no place to go. This is a common fear shared by all Koreans, which is why Korean organizations and individuals have been doing their best to help the two shops remain open. (May 19, 1990)

An editorial in another Korean language daily, *Sue Gue Times*, urged Koreans to defend themselves against transnational-racial oppression by shopping in the two boycotted stores:

> To counteract the increasingly violent picketers effectively, we Koreans should make a long line of visits to the two victimized stores and buy fruits and vegetables. The two Church Avenue Korean stores have now become pilgrims where we Koreans should visit to learn about the sufferings of racial prejudice. We should stretch sympathy to our compatriots by participating in the buy-merchandise campaign. All Korean ethnic organizations and individuals should share the sufferings and agony by participating in the buy-merchandise campaign. (May 25, 1990, cited in Min 1996)

Just as the December 12th Movement exhorted Blacks to express their collective solidarity by boycotting the two stores, so did Korean American community leaders and opinionmakers urge Koreans to express their collective solidarity by supporting them.

Korean American churches, vital centers of social and religious activity, also helped to get out the leadership's message. The power of the pulpit in the city's Korean American community is substantial. A remarkable 75 percent of Korean immigrant families in the United States were affiliated with a Korean American church in the early 1990s. In New York City alone, as of 1993, there were 230 such churches (Min 1996, 40–41). While many churches refrained from condemning the boycott—preferring instead to sponsor the kind of "racial harmony" marches described above—they did help to spread the word about the countermobilization effort. Attorney John Kim explains: "They [the churches] do not want to get involved politically, but when the Korean community needs to mobilize Korean people, we usually turn to Korean churches to inform them about the upcoming events and ask their pastor to announce the events at the Sunday church services."[13]

Community leaders' exhortations about resisting transnational-racial oppression were quite effective in mobilizing the internal resources of the Korean American community. As Mayer Zald and Bert Useem note about countermovements in general: "Since CMs [countermovements] are often linked to the elite and established order, they may have more resources (e.g., money and established organizations) available than movements, even while their repertoire of tactics is constrained by their class origins and commitment to order" (1987, 257). The KANY collected enough financial donations from Korean Americans (especially merchants and merchant associations) to keep Family Red Apple and Church Fruits open throughout the boycott—despite the fact that business in both stores slowed dramatically for many months.[14] Family Red Apple, which had made approximately $3,500 in sales per day prior to the boycott, made approximately $30 in sales per day during the boycott; Church Fruits, which had made about $4,500 in sales per day prior to the boycott, made about $50 in sales per day during the boycott (*Korea Times*, September 28, 1990). During the boycott, the two store owners, Bong Jae Jang and Manho Park, each received approximately $7,000 per month in donations channeled through the KANY. In addition, the Korean American landlords of the two stores building forgave Jang and Park their monthly commercial rents ($3,500 for the Family Red Apple and $3,100 for Church Fruits), and Korean merchants from across the city volunteered to work in shifts at the two stores (*Korea Times*, May 12, 1990; Min 1996). On October 20, 1990, the *Korea Times* reported that donations totaling $107,117.23 (including the foregone rent) had been collected for the two boycotted stores. By the end of the year, the total figure was $150,000 (Min 1996, 149). In keeping with the transnational sentiments fueling the mobilization, Koreans living in South Korea also held fundraisers to help out the two stores (Lee 1993). Due to this significant infusion of community resources, "the two stores took on the characteristics of public property" (Lee 1993, 183).

The road not taken often reveals something interesting. In this case, we should note that Korean American community leaders characterized the Red Apple Boycott as an anti-Korean rather than an anti-Asian campaign. They believed that the boycotters were targeting Koreans qua Koreans not qua Asian Americans, and that Koreans needed to respond as a transnational-racial community. The fact that most Korean American community leaders (and two-thirds of the community itself) were members of the first or 1.5 generations—and thus identified themselves as Koreans rather than as Asian Americans—helps to explain why they did not avail themselves of the established narrative of anti-Asian racism.[15] Regardless, other Asian American groups, pan-Asian organizations, the U.S. Civil Rights Commission, and the mainstream media consistently interpreted the Red Apple Boycott as an instance of anti-Asian scapegoating.[16] They situated the boycott within a historical trajectory anchored by such events as the U.S. government's exclusion of Chinese immigrants in 1882 and internment of Japanese Americans in World War II. Thus developed a strange disjunction between the terms in which most Korean Americans organizing against the boycott saw the conflict and those in which Asian American advocacy groups and others not directly involved saw it. All of these different narratives—the Black nationalist narrative of racial oppression, the Haitian and Korean narratives of transnational oppression, and the Asian American narrative of anti-Asian activity—met in this one event, investing it with multiple layers of contested meaning.

PROTECTING THE AMERICAN CREED AND THE "KOREAN AMERICAN DREAM"

The second framing strategy of Korean American community leaders was to exhort all Americans to defend the American creed and the "Korean American Dream" against the Black nationalist threat. By opposing the boycott, these leaders suggested, Americans could affirm their bedrock national ideals of equal opportunity, fairness, and colorblindness. They could guarantee the American Dream—the promise that hard work and persistence overcome all obstacles and result in success—for all, including Korean immigrants.[17] In sum, Americans could affirm their very national identity by opposing the boycott and supporting the Korean American countermobilization effort. By drawing heavily upon colorblind talk (including the model minority and underclass myths) to delegitimate the boycott, Korean American community leaders succeeded in winning widespread public sympathy for their cause.

This second mobilizing strategy was directed as much at Korean Americans as it was at Whites or other groups. There is evidence to suggest that Korean immigrants believe in the American creed and the American Dream even more ardently than do Whites. As mentioned in Chapter 2, Korean immigrants come to the United States having already absorbed American notions of racial hierarchy and a powerful belief in the American Dream. Some then interpret their subsequent experiences as an intermediate group in the American racial order as confirmation that those who try hard enough can overcome racial discrimination and get ahead.[18] One survey conducted by telephone in New York City in 1992 showed that 40 percent of Korean merchants strongly agreed with the statement, "In this country, anyone, regardless of race, sex, or national origin, can make it if he/she works hard." Only 14 percent of Whites strongly agreed with this statement (Min 1996, 122–23). The correlate to a belief in the American Dream, of course, is the belief that racial groups who do not fare well in American society are themselves to blame. Less inhibited by the norms of colorblindness than Whites, most Korean merchants readily admit to thinking that Blacks are less intelligent than, lazier than, less honest than, and more criminally oriented than Whites (Min 1996, 121). Several months after the Red Apple Boycott ended, the *Korea Times* published a ten-point code for Korean shopkeepers interested in avoiding future conflicts with Blacks (September 28, 1991, cited in Yi 1993). The code revels a great deal about how many Korean merchants view Black people:

1. do not use the term *gumdungyi* [nigger]
2. do not shout and do not point your finger to shoppers
3. do not behave like a rich person
4. participate actively in local affairs
5. do not chase shoplifters out of the store
6. restrain the use of a gun
7. study English and Spanish
8. do not answer with no

9.   always think that Black is beautiful
10. do not think that Blacks are naive

In the survey mentioned above, only 13 percent of Korean merchants agreed that "a large proportion of Black Americans are poor mainly because of racial discrimination," whereas 26 percent of Whites and 43 percent of Blacks agreed with this statement (Min 1996, 121).

If their views of Black people echo the underclass myth, Korean immigrants often accede to the mainstream media's depiction of themselves as a model minority. Clearly, they prefer to believe that Koreans get ahead because of their intrinsic virtues and not because they are relatively privileged in the American racial order. The *Korea Times* appears to emphasize Korean success stories over less cheerful tales as a way of promoting group identification and pride. Some Korean Americans, however, have come to recognize the model minority myth as a wolf in sheep's clothing. Sung Soo Kim, for example, believes that the mainstream media's reiteration of the model minority myth obscures the particular hardships facing Korean merchants—including crime, high commercial rents and taxes, unwieldy city regulations, and stiff business competition. As he put it in an interview with the *New York Times*, "We don't like people praising us" (December 27, 1990). Kyung Ho Koh, a 1.5-generation Korean American, observes that the model minority myth also divides communities of color and distracts Asian Americans from Asian-White discrepancies in status and wealth:

KYUNG HO KOH: Oh yes, that model minority [myth], when I was more naive, I used to take pride in that, but more and more, I was alerted to and learned . . . [that] what the media and politicians are trying to do by promoting that is actually a divisive strategy to pit groups against each other. And also, I think that the thing I don't like about that is that it makes other minority groups feel inferior, and I think that it intensifies hostilities towards the group that is the so-called model minority. And, I mean, it's one thing to receive some recognition for diligence and hard work, and making something out of your group in such a short period of time, but I think that model minority concept is really loaded with . . . "These are the people that made it. The African Americans, Latino Americans, what's wrong with you, you're not making it, and Asian Americans are. Is there something wrong with you, maybe?" . . . You know, what really bothers me about it is that the media is still controlled by Whites and what I think is distracting about it is that in a way, it tries to applaud us for achieving to a certain point, and they say, "You have achieved compared to these other groups." But what I find really distasteful about it is that it is not comparing us to what the Whites have achieved, and so it's very patronizing in that respect. It's like, "Yeah, you've gotten far," but of course the unsaid thing is you haven't and some people in that group will say, "You will never get as far as we've gotten."

Still, Koh concedes that many Korean Americans, including those of the second generation, find the model minority myth a hard habit to break:

KYUNG HO KOH: Even I buy into it sometimes, everybody buys into it sometimes. Let's face it, a lot of people buy into stereotypes, even when they know they shouldn't. And they try not to. I mean, my friends and I, sometimes we joke around because when we see something horrible or stupid that a Korean American did in the paper, especially if it's criminal, our initial bias is to say, "I can't believe a Korean American would do that." But, you know, let's face it, there are probably proportionately just as many crooks and thieves and this and that among Korean Americans as there are in any other group if you put them on the same kind of socioeconomic level. There's nothing morally superior about us, but by our own upbringing by Korean parents and maybe reinforced by this model minority [myth], sometimes even the best of people make misjudgments because of that.

While many 1.5- and second-generation Korean Americans express skepticism or ambivalence about the model minority myth, most first-generation Korean Americans put stock in it. Few complained when the mainstream media applied the underclass/model minority dichotomy in their analyses of the Red Apple Boycott.

In their effort to arouse internal and external opposition to the boycott, Korean American community leaders and opinionmakers argued that the boycotters were violating the American creed (colorblindness, fair play, free enterprise, equal opportunity, individual responsibility, etc.) and destroying the Korean American Dream by seeking to deprive another racial minority of the fruits of its labor. Note the evocation of the underclass/model minority couplet in this article from the *Korea Times:*

When we thought that our hard work was finally paying off after years of hardship, we face a great crisis. As a result of having been more diligent and frugal than any other ethnic group, we have established ourselves in a short period of time. Now that our children do well in school and we can afford to relax, an unexpected challenge hits us all. The boycotts and protests— though Blacks claim that they are aimed at specific shops and shop owners—are clearly aimed at all diligent and successful Koreans, whom they envy and dislike. Blacks are jealous of Koreans for leading a comfortable life and sending their children to good colleges while Blacks live in poverty. They suffer an inferiority complex. (August 28, 1990)

Chun Soo Byun, a leader of the countermobilization effort, reiterates the same underclass / model minority couplet in his comments:

CHUN SOO BYUN: The boycotter is aiming something. Aiming means they're trying to take advantage of the minorities such as Koreans. In other words, they do not want to work, do not want to earn anything. They want to just gain for nothing. So they want to enlarge the small kind of things, small tiny argument.

In a letter addressed to Mayor Dinkins, dated February 28, 1990, Sung Soo Kim suggested that the boycott threatened the quintessentially American ideal of free enterprise:

The Korean community understands the desires of Church Avenue residents for their economic self-determination, but it must not come at the expense of effectively killing off legitimate, tax-paying businesses. I am thus appealing to you once again for you to take charge of this tragic conflict. Koreans are not the ones denying Church Avenue residents an equal economic opportunity: we should not be the object of their discontent.

Finally, at the Mayor's Committee public forum in Flatbush in June 1990, Bong Jae Jang himself discussed the boycott's impact on his American Dream:

The reason why I came to America is that I had a dream that anybody who is willing to work hard can have their dream come true . . . I came here six years ago. During the last six years, I worked every day sixteen to eighteen hours a day, and only two years ago, I was able to buy this Red Apple store. In order to be able to buy this store, I had to experience indescribable pains and hardships that you cannot ever imagine . . . It was my sweat and tears and was a continuation of a long period of continuing hardship and suffering.[19]

It is easy to understand why these rhetorical appeals resonated with White audiences in particular. As ongoing national debates over affirmative action have revealed, many Whites disclaim responsibility for racial inequalities and believe that Blacks are seeking preferential treatment and a free ride on the backs of hardworking taxpayers. The Korean American countermobilization effort directly tapped into these beliefs. Monitoring mainstream media coverage of the boycott, Korean American leaders were gratified to find widespread public support for their cause. As we will see in the next chapter, the mainstream media overwhelmingly condemned the boycott as a racial scapegoating campaign that violated the American creed. As Pyong Gap Min puts it, "Korean community leaders in New York generally were satisfied with the mainstream media's treatment of Korean merchants as innocent victims and of Black boycott leaders as political opportunists" (1996, 107). The *Korea Times*, which frequently reprinted mainstream newspaper articles on the boycott for Korean American readers, expressed the hope that the mainstream media's fierce opposition to the boycott would shut the protest down.

Korean American clergy and second-generation Korean American groups also led numerous "racial harmony" marches against the boycott during the spring of 1990.[20] Celebrating the values of unity, harmony, and Christian brotherhood, these marches publicized and mobilized external support for the Korean American cause while avoiding the appearance of public demand making (which, as we will see, was a concern of many Korean Americans). The marchers consistently donned the mantle of the civil rights movement, thus legitimating their own position and delegitimating that of the boycotters à la colorblind talk. For example, participants in a May 1990 march organized by the Young Korean American Network and the Guardian Angels sang "We Shall Overcome" as they traveled through lower Manhattan.

By arousing internal and external public support via this second framing strategy, Korean American community leaders hoped to persuade Mayor David Dinkins to intervene in the boycott conflict. Indeed, they appealed to the mayor directly to protect the American creed and the Korean American Dream, citing his campaign promise to act as a racial healer and safeguard the city's "gorgeous mosaic" of racial, ethnic, and religious groups. Sung Soo Kim's first letter to Dinkins, dated January 24, 1990, pleaded with him to get involved:

It is with great urgency that I call upon you as the supreme leader of this great city to intercede in a grave ethnic conflict currently taking place in Brooklyn . . . This current turmoil reminds us of how sharp and defined are the edges of the interlocking pieces of New York's "gorgeous mosaic." Your mayorship recognized and celebrated the beauty of different pieces of ethnic mosaic; we thus look to you to translate your vision of harmony to reality by engaging in this tragic confrontation.

Similarly, Bo Young June, an official of the Korean Produce Association, wrote in a letter to Dinkins on March 1, 1990: "You are looked upon by many New Yorkers as a healer. It was under this premise that you were elected to lead our great city. What better opportunity to show your strength and ability?" (*New York Times*, May 7, 1990). As months passed and Dinkins refused to intervene personally, Korean American leaders gradually shifted their focus from the boycott itself to the city administration's discriminatory behavior toward the Korean American community. Especially after Dinkins instructed the NYPD not to enforce a court order seeking to move the picket line at least fifty feet from the store entrances (see Chapter 6), Korean American leaders became convinced that the mayor was selling them up the river to pander to Black extremists. At that point, they resolved to take the countermobilization effort to a new level.

THE PEACE RALLY FOR RACIAL HARMONY

In late spring of 1990, Korean American community leaders reassessed their options. Although their two framing strategies had mobilized considerable internal and external support for their cause, the boycott showed no sign of letting up. Direct appeals to Mayor Dinkins via lobbying (by the Korean Consul General, for example) and letter writing had not compelled his personal intervention in the conflict. Even the meeting that Korean American leaders had with President Bush in Washington, D.C., in June 1990 failed to yield results (Yi 1993). Shocked and outraged by the mayor's deliberate non-enforcement of the fifty-feet court order—the Dinkins administration appealed the order on the grounds that its enforcement might provoke violence and that the NYPD should not be involved in civil matters—the leaders of the countermobilization effort concluded that they were the victims of Black racism from above and below. They resolved to focus all of their energies on compelling Dinkins to enforce the court order. As Mayer Zald and Bert Useem point out, "Movement and countermovement each adjust their tactics as they gain responses from key constituencies, win or lose battles, appear to be achieving support, or gaining objectives" (1987, 259).

The Civil Rights Committee (CRC), a KANY body that had been created in February for the explicit purpose of resolving the boycott conflict, spearheaded the renewed countermobilization effort. Composed of a dozen or so businessmen, lawyers, professors, and other prominent community figures, the CRC self-consciously crafted itself as a body that could speak for the entire Korean American community. As Chun Soo Byun, the head of the CRC, explains, this meant excluding merchant advocates like Michael Kang and Sung Soo Kim, who might have been seen as representing their own interests rather than those of Korean Americans as a whole:[21]

> CHUN SOO BYUN: Both of them contributed a lot to the Korean community, but Mr. Kang was general secretary of Korean Grocer's Association, and Mr. Kim was the president of small business consulting firm, like that. And, again, they didn't represent the Korean community. They represent either their organization or they behave as individual mostly. And among them they didn't agree either, so that's why I managed everything under the name of the Korean community . . . When I organized the Civil Rights Committee, I excluded them because, you know, I want the fresh people join and give us fresh neutral ideas rather than old things. We were capable to analyze all the problems so just we made about fifteen prominent Korean leaders under the new organization. So I think we developed pretty much good ideas how to solve the problems.

Some CRC members came up with a plan to hold an unprecedented Korean American rally in front of City Hall to demand that Mayor Dinkins enforce the court order and intervene in the conflict. Although they strongly preferred behind-the-scenes tactics to overt demand making and worried about being seen as troublemakers, they felt that they had run out of options. As Jong Duk Byun, the president of the KANY, stated during the summer of 1990: "The Church Avenue riot has exhausted our patience. The only choice we have now is to demonstrate in order to accelerate the actions of the city government" (*Korea Times*, August 4, 1990).

The CRC's plan provoked a firestorm of controversy within the Korean American community. The debate played out vividly in the Korean language media throughout the summer. Although many Korean Americans felt that urgent measures were needed to stop the boycott, they were dubious about the rally idea. The main issue of contention was whether or not the rally would appear excessively confrontational, thereby generating negative repercussions for the Korean American community. Rally organizers wanted to emphasize the Korean American community's refusal to be victimized and its willingness to defend itself. As one opinion piece in the *Korea Times* said with reference to the rally: "We Koreans need to convey to the public that we love peace, but when unjustified oppression hits us, we will gather our strength to help each other" (May 11, 1990). Yet some Korean Americans worried that such stridency might backfire by alienating the White public and/or provoking some sort of Black retaliatory action. Second-generation Korean American groups, who tended to have some sympathy for the boycotters' cause, and Korean merchants, who were the most vulnerable to potential Black retaliation, were especially vocal in their criticisms. Chun Soo Byun recalls the controversy:

CHUN SOO BYUN: There was tons of arguments [about holding the rally] . . . And personally, I experienced it a lot. I didn't figure there would be that much criticism. Yet, I don't blame whoever opposed it who have different ideas because since we were not experienced at rally, they kind of feared backlash or backfire. Especially the store owners questioned me, "Mr. Byun, you don't have any experience doing business in Harlem area or dangerous area, how are you going to handle this case?" So I answered them, "Okay, if there is a backlash, say your house, your store is burnt by the Blacks or demonstrators, what is the percentage that is one out of million?" It could happen to any of the stores but whatever happens, it comes right to me. So I'm risking my life even though I don't have experience doing the business, risking my life living in this country over thirty years and do you think I'm just kidding or playing around? I am handling this matter with my honor with representing entire Korean community and I'm not doing it by myself. I have a full committee. So we are doing it for the best. So I want [them] to be quiet and support me.

Byun clearly saw himself as a champion of his people, defending Koreans against transnational-racial oppression. Here he compares himself with Kwan Soon Yu, one of the leaders of the legendary March First Movement undertaken by Korean subjects against Japanese colonial rulers in 1919:

CHUN SOO BYUN: From from the beginning, I insisted we are going to get ten thousand [at the rally]. So they [skeptics] questioned me, "How are you going to get ten thousand? I bet you can't get five hundred." So then I said, I convinced this way, "You have to make this as a movement. You yourself remember the March First Movement, 1919, in Korea? The leader was Yu Kwan Soon, you remember?" Okay. I questioned them, "Do you think Yu Kwan Soon estimated or expected that so many people are going to follow?" No. She didn't figure it out, she didn't have any figures. But she had the confidence, so she made the movement. So we as a Korean should make movement so that people could move.

According to CRC member Daniel Lee, there was dissension within the CRC itself on the subject of the rally, Byun's enthusiasm notwithstanding:

DANIEL LEE: The biggest concern of the people who opposed the rally is the fear itself. They fear that the rally will only further inflame the Blacks, because at that time, there was some talk, some rumors, that the Blacks will boycott all stores owned and operated by Koreans. So there was a lot of fear of that, but you know, you can't really let them blackmail us on that respect . . . The consensus was reached within the committee [to go forward], but there were also a lot of people within the committee who opposed it. There were also a lot of other organizations who thought this was a crazy idea . . . You know, I understand where the fear is coming from for the people who actually have stores in the Black neighborhoods and ghettos. The fear that their stores may be the next target for boycotts is a very, very serious concern. I did understand that. But for the good of the Korean American community as a whole, I felt, as well as other committee members for the rally, that we had to go ahead with the rally and then, you know, show our position . . . Some people felt that we should do more behind the scenes, maneuver, that type of thing, and some people are saying "Let the city handle it," you know, "Give more pressure to the city, New York City and the mayor and let them handle it." Some people were also against it because they don't like Chun Soo Byun.

Eventually CRC members reached a compromise solution: to proceed with the rally but to frame it as a "peace rally for racial harmony," scrupulously expunging signs of stridency or anger. By infusing the rally with the rhetoric and symbolism of colorblind talk, Korean American leaders hoped to win Korean American and White support without provoking Black retaliation. Chun Soo Byun comments: "The main reason why we say 'racial harmony' really is because we didn't want to [create] any new tensions, so that's why we named [the rally] very moderately. But the real aim was to stop the boycott, obviously."[22]

In this spirit, Korean American leaders planned for the rally to be reminiscent of civil rights movement protests from the 1950s and 1960s. Again, as in the "racial harmony" marches, Korean Americans appropriated the civil rights mantle to legitimate their own cause and emphasize how far the boycotters had strayed from the hallowed path of Martin Luther King Jr. Prior to the rally, organizers mindful of the need to filter out signs of bitterness and anger agonized over which slogans to permit. Three days before the rally, the president of the Korean Lawyers Association told the *Korea Times* that eleven out of the thirteen slogans selected by the CRC (including "Stop the racial attack," "We will overcome fear and hate," and "Stop the racial discrimination") might be offensive to Blacks and / or the general public (September 15, 1990). Another slogan—"Respect? You earn it, not demand it"—also failed to make the grade. The slogans that the CRC ended up authorizing were quite benign: "We are one," "Racial harmony," "Let's stop racism together," "Seoul brothers=soul brothers," "Malice toward none, charity for all," "Respect and unity" (Lee 1993, 97).

The rally organizers were willing to cancel the rally if Mayor Dinkins would agree to enforce the court order and intervene in the conflict. Yet events seemed to move them inexorably toward the public demonstration. When the Mayor's Committee released its long-awaited report on the Red Apple Boycott at the end of August, Korean American community leaders were deeply disappointed.[23] It is not that their expectations were high: many had complained months before that the two Korean American committee members, Reverend Michael Hahm and Ben Limb, were pro-Dinkins and out of touch with community sentiment. Still, they found the report's insistence that the Red Apple Boycott was not "race-based" disturbing. The *Korea Times* observed: "[The report] appears to have been influenced by politics in the way that it incorporates very diplomatic language and takes a middle stance. One wonders what good has come out of the study. If anything, Dinkins can no longer use the panel as an excuse to shield himself from the press . . . The coming September 18 peace convention [rally] is a good opportunity to trap the Dinkins administration, which has been making up excuses to run away from the problem" (September 1, 1990). Several days later, on September 5, rally organizers still willing to negotiate a deal met with representatives of the Dinkins administration. But the deal fell through. The rally would go forward as planned.

Even though the rally at City Hall was to be directed at Mayor Dinkins, Chun Soo Byun decided to invite him to speak at the event. The mayor's presence, he reasoned, would ensure considerable publicity for the rally:

CHUN SOO BYUN: I made new ideas to invite Mayor Dinkins to the rally and there was a new criticism among Korean community. "You invite him at the rally?" So I face all of the big problems then I answer this way. I said, "This rally, let's say you are making a movie. In order to make a movie we need a star. Without David Dinkins, we are making the movie without star . . . [To] get the people, to get the media, we need the mayor." Even *Korea Times* say, "Are you crazy? It is too crazy an idea." So I said, "Well, we'll see." Then I conveyed my idea to mayor's office. The mayor was surprised. He said, "What? The Koreans are talking to me and they are inviting me?" And Mayor Dinkins invited me [to a meeting]. And when he invited me, five Korean leaders went. We were scheduled half an hour talk, it last an hour and forty-five minutes. The final was I gave to Mayor Dinkins, "Mayor, you are in a very uneasy situation yourself politically, everything, so why don't you make this case as your own main breakthrough?" He said, "You're right." Then he agreed, he was so happy to be invited [and] at the same he was embarrassed.

Many of Byun's colleagues were dubious. On September 6, the CRC voted unanimously to place strict limits on Dinkins's role at the rally. They agreed to let him speak but excluded him from the formal list of guest speakers (*Korea Times*, September 14, 1990). An article in the *Korea Times* endorsed this decision: "Dinkins could use the rally as an opportunity to explain himself. Thus, we must not forget to set a limit to Dinkins's role at the rally. We must also criticize the incapacity of Dinkins and the New York City government, and press them for an immediate solution to the problem. The convention cannot be used by Dinkins for his political advantage, for he has shown himself to be indecisive and unreliable" (September 8, 1990).

As the rally approached, the *Korea Times* actively exhorted Korean Americans to participate. Its advertisements for the rally clearly demonstrate how Korean American leaders had shifted their focus from the boycott itself to the Dinkins administration's discriminatory handling of it. On September 5, 1990, the *Korea Times* ran a joint message with the New York Korean Radio Broadcast, Inc., entitled "An Announcement: A Plea to Korean Immigrants":

The boycotts by Black people in Brooklyn against Korean merchants have been going on for eight months. We have patiently waited for the city government to intervene in this act of racial discrimination, but it has done nothing and we now face the possibility of the boycott spreading and getting worse . . . We are stunned by the city government's and the police's claim that demonstrations are protected by law as a constitutional right. Freedom and rights are privileges enjoyed only when you do not harm other beings . . . We can no longer sit and be victimized. September 18 is the day we decided to have a massive peace rally to assert our rights. It will decide whether there is a place for us to live in this society . . . We plead with everyone to participate.

The next day, the paper ran a similar plea:

What are we to do when the law, the government, and the police do not help us? Korean leaders decided to use the peace rally to plead our case and accelerate their actions. Some Koreans opposed this, saying that it might backfire on us, which is exactly why we are planning it as a racial unity rally rather than a Korean-Black confrontation. Those who hesitated before should have no more hesitancy to participate, because it needs our support, our oneness to show others our power. Together we live and alone we die. Let us not think that one person makes no difference . . . Let each one of us come forward and assert our right. On September 18, let everyone close their shops and meet at City Hall. (September 6, 1990)

These appeals to the Korean American community were highly effective. The rally at City Hall on September 18, 1990, mobilized between six and eight thousand Korean Americans from all over the New York metropolitan area. It was the single largest gathering of Korean Americans in the city's history.[24] Although most Korean-owned stores remained open that day, many store employees were released from work so that they could participate. Korean American business associations, churches, and youth groups participated en masse, and some Korean American taxi drivers provided free rides to participants.

The rally speakers and participants reprised the two themes of resisting transnational-racial oppression and protecting the American creed and Korean American Dream. Some speakers compared the Red Apple Boycott to the Japanese colonization of Korea (1905–1945). Pyong Gap Min explains: " 'Just as we Koreans resisted the Japanese colonization' they [the speakers] argued, 'we should challenge unjustifiable black boycotts of Korean stores' " (1996, 152). Participants also joined hands to sing "Arirang," a traditional Korean folk song. At the same time, rally participants wore blue ribbons symbolic of racial harmony and carried American flags. Maxine Paige, a Black singer, delivered renditions of both "The Star Spangled Banner" and "We Shall Overcome," and Black clergy and representatives of CORE and the NAACP were featured speakers. Again, the banners and placards carried slogans such as "We are one," "Racial harmony," "Let's stop racism together," "Seoul brothers=soul brothers," "Malice toward none, charity for all," "Respect and unity" (Lee 1993, 97). Since the appellate court had upheld the fifty-feet court order a few days before the rally, vindicating the Korean American position, Mayor Dinkins's promise to finally enforce the court order did little to placate rally participants, many of whom booed heartily when he first ascended the stage. As we shall see in the next chapter, the Korean American Peace Rally for Racial Harmony played an important role in bringing the boycott to a close. It also marked a turning point in the history of the Korean American community in New York City, a kind of political awakening and "coming out" in local political affairs.[25]

DISSENTING VOICES

It would be easy to conclude that all Korean Americans were of one mind about the Red Apple Boycott. The consensus among prominent leaders, the amount of donations collected, the turnout at the rally, and the paucity of overt dissent all suggested that Korean Americans were powerfully united in their condemnation of the boycott. Even the debates about the rally plan were more strategic than substantive, and played out exclusively within Korean American social spaces, beyond the view of the general public. Yet such a conclusion about a monolithic Korean American response would be mistaken. Community leader Kyung Ho Koh comments:

> KYUNG HO KOH: I would say that there was a healthy diversity of opinion, and I think that's the way it should be. Obviously, a lot of people who own stores were of one opinion, and they are very supportive of the Korean store owners, very upset at the situation and boycotters, angry. And I would think that almost all Koreans had some sympathy for the store owners; I mean, only very few Koreans would say that they have no sympathy for the store owners, but there were some people who pointed out the negative faults of Korean American store owners, Korean Americans, maybe, in general, too. And maybe they wanted to focus more on our own responsibility for this situation happening, because to me, I would say that in this situation there are multiple responsibilities. So people are very supportive of the store owner, but focus mainly on what Blacks, Haitian Americans, did to make the situation worse. Maybe the minority of people who are critical of what was going on, maybe they focused more on what we Korean Americans don't do right, but I would say the majority of people were probably supportive of the store owners.

Although there is no extant data measuring the precise distribution of Korean American opinions about the boycott, there is evidence to suggest that a minority, composed mostly of highly educated, professionally employed members of the 1.5 and second generations, felt ambivalent about or expressed dissent from the majority opinion. While no Korean Americans sided with the boycotters against the merchants, a number of groups and individuals acknowledged legitimate grievances on both sides. They also expressed concern that the Korean American countermobilization effort (especially the rally) appeared excessively partisan and aggressive.

The generational divide within the city's Korean American community was concretely expressed in organizational terms at the time of the boycott. While the Korean Consulate General and most Korean American media and business organizations were dominated by first-generation immigrants, many political and social organizations—like Korean Americans for Social Concern, Coalition for Korean American Voters, and Young Korean American Network—were dominated by 1.5- and second-generation Koreans. The first set of organizations tended to be socially and politically conservative and oriented toward homeland politics; the second set tended to be more liberal and more oriented toward domestic affairs within the United States. As a result of having been born and/or raised and educated in the United States, many 1.5- and second-generation Korean Americans identified not only as Koreans but also as Asian Americans or people of color. They also had a basic familiarity with the history of Black disempowerment in the United States. For these reasons, they were more likely than their parents to identify with Black people as victims of racial discrimination and to sympathize with their grievances. During the Red Apple Boycott, some of them favored a more conciliatory posture by which Koreans would acknowledge their racism against Blacks, accept partial responsibility for helping to improve Black urban conditions, and seek to cooperate with Blacks in the struggle against White racism. Most of these suggestions were made within Korean American circles so as to preserve the appearance of a united front to the boycotters and the general public.

Kyung Ho Koh experienced considerable ambivalence about the boycott. Born in Seoul, Korea, Koh came to the United States in 1968, when he was five years old. Both of his parents were pursuing higher education in America. During his family's seven-year stay in Mississippi, Koh learned lessons about Black history that would later influence his perspective on the boycott:

KYUNG HO KOH: I lived in Mississippi, and you can't learn state history down there without learning about slavery and legalized segregation, the Klan, lynching, this and that. And I went to an all-Black school, a 98 percent Black school for two years in the South. I saw the poverty firsthand. But I think a lot of Korean Americans are ignorant of that. I mean they just know, "Yeah there was slavery, and look, the Civil War abolished it, and so what? There's Martin Luther King and the Civil Rights Act, so what?" And because of our own internalized racism, we uphold ourselves and either our ignorance or lack of respect for the history, I think that's sort of the root of the problems. That combined with our own self-centered goal of trying to get as much for ourselves and our families, and not really thinking about sharing it with people who are not in our own family, especially people who are not even in our own ethnic or racial group.

Koh explains that during the Red Apple Boycott, he was torn between sympathizing with the Korean merchants and faulting them for their racism toward Black people:

KYUNG HO KOH: The boycott, well, I'll tell you, I feel a couple of things. One is that as a person born in Korea and somewhat knowledgeable about Korean Americans and Korean lifestyle, and so on, different parts of the boycott hurt me and angered me and moved me. And I know that different people in my family have also had small businesses, my father in the past has had small businesses, and so on. And I know how much hard work you have to put into that, and stealing, no matter what the race of the person, I mean there is so much stealing going on, and it really puts a drain on you to be a surveillance person for theft. I know the frustration of well-educated people coming here and then having to be a merchant instead of what they were trained to be, say a journalist, or maybe they wanted to be a teacher in high school or college, well-positioned business people. I understand that frustration. Or a woman who might have led a more comfortable life maybe in Korea as a housewife, now having to put in twelve or sixteen hours a day working in the stores, and also being in charge of running the family, running the house. And I understand all that frustration and I have a lot of sympathy for that. And I can understand sometimes not being as patient or as courteous as we should be. But on the other hand, I think that there are negative things about Korean Americans in general, and about many of the people who are, unfortunately, the people who run the businesses, the small business operators. I think the majority of Koreans are racist. I think that the majority of Koreans really have a problem, especially accepting as equal Blacks and Latinos, and I've seen it in Korea and I've seen it here. I think my parents are some of the most liberal, and yet they are not completely bias-free either, but I have seen a lot of first-generation people who, if they were White, I would call them bigots or Ku Klux Klan sympathizers as far as their attitude toward Blacks . . . But also, unfortunately, I think, a lot of merchants who are in these neighborhoods are the scapegoats for the fact that the society isn't working in helping people in the underclass to receive education, receive job training, receive good family services. I think when you have broken a people historically like the African American race has been broken historically, I think that you not only have to say that they're equal, but you also have to make more of a positive effort to rehabilitate them, to make them feel genuinely equal and that they have opportunities, and that they can control their own destiny and succeed. And society as a whole, the government, all levels, just isn't doing a good job.

Concerned that the rally at City Hall would be confrontational and counterproductive, Koh decided not to attend. Yet he kept his reservations about the event to himself:

> KYUNG HO KOH: I don't think it would have been politically smart for any Korean American group to air publicly that minority view, because realism being that Korean Americans and all Koreans have sort of a touchiness about receiving public criticism. Maybe that's something we need to kind of grow up about, but I think that because Korean Americans and Koreans are so touchy about that, that if you're a group that is looking for support from the community, you're going to kind of commit suicide by being critical too loudly or too often. So I don't think it's politically smart.

In retrospect, Koh decided that his fears about the rally were unjustified and that the event had performed a service by promoting Korean American political expression and assertion:

> KYUNG HO KOH: Bottom line, I thought the rally was great. In a couple of ways I thought it was great, and I wasn't there, so maybe it's kind of weak of me to say, you know, I thought it was great. But I didn't want to go there, to be honest with you, because I was a little bit afraid of how it would be termed. If elements that are kind of intolerant of African American, Latin American customers were going to be the very vocal ones, I wouldn't have been comfortable there. Because there is a strong portion in the Korean American community who does see all our problems, the problems Korean American store owners face, and they want to throw most, if not all, the problems that they see at those two groups, Latin American and African American groups. And I don't feel that way, so I was a little bit afraid . . . From what I remember now, I thought it was tolerably balanced. It effectively stated more the grievances of the Korean Americans and what government could do about it . . . I was glad that it turned out that way, and seeing the media focusing on the fact that five or six thousand Korean Americans showed up, and it made the front page of the *New York Post* and so on. I think that was a good thing and I'm glad that some anger came out. Because too many times, mainstream media, elected officials, Whites, even Blacks, not only Koreans, but maybe Asians in general, they take us for granted in the sense of, "They don't complain, they don't say anything, they don't vote, they don't complain" . . .

And I think it's good every once in a while to flex a little muscle and show a little anger and show some criticism publicly. And I'm appalled, like as any lawyer, that this mayor did not enforce the fifty-feet court order . . . And I'm not even that conservative or traditionally Korean, but to me, that's a slap at Korean Americans.

Although his sympathies were divided during the boycott, Koh came out of the experience determined to promote Korean American political empowerment. After the boycott, he and other 1.5- and second-generation Korean Americans got together to form the Coalition of Korean American Voters, a nonpartisan group devoted to educating Korean Americans about the American political process and registering them to vote.

Members of Korean Americans for Social Concern (KASC) also sympathized with both sides in the boycott and favored a more conciliatory approach than that adopted by the rally organizers. At the time of the boycott, KASC was composed of about a dozen professionals. The head of KASC, a 1.5-generation attorney named Jenny Sook Nam Choo, explains, "It's basically postgraduate people who have done a lot of community work in college or during graduate school and want to continue that."[26] During the 1980s, KASC sponsored pro-Democratic voter registration drives within the Korean American community and participated in demonstrations against police brutality as a constituent member of the progressive pan-Asian organization Committee Against Anti-Asian Violence. Members of KASC responded to the Red Apple Boycott by seeking to educate the general public about the structural causes of the conflict and the legitimate grievances on both sides:

JENNY SOOK NAM CHOO: We've done mainly a lot of presentations to different groups, because whenever this thing [a boycott] comes up, they just really don't know who to turn to. I mean, even within the Korean community, there is really no spokesperson. Even people who can analyze what the situation is. So mainly I've done a lot of presentations all over the country. I mean, like one was at the National Asian-American Bar Association Conference in Houston. I went to speak a couple of times at Harvard Law School [on the boycott issue].

Although Choo is more self-consciously progressive than Koh, she, too, declined to voice her criticisms of Korean American community leaders to the general public.

Rector Paul Kim and Christie Huh (a married couple) were among the very few Korean Americans who voiced their dissent about the counter-

mobilization effort in public. If the Korean American church was an important vehicle for mobilizing the majority in opposition to the boycott, it was
also a vehicle for mobilizing dissent from the majority opinion. Kim is a
United Methodist minister who has worked in the Korean American community in New York City since the early 1980s. Huh served as the Asian American community liaison for the office of Comptroller Liz Holtzman during
the boycott and was involved in early mediation efforts sponsored by the
Brooklyn borough president's office and the city government. Although they
thought that the boycott was ultimately unfair to the Korean merchants, Huh
and Kim, both members of the 1.5 generation, opposed the Korean American
countermobilization effort (including the rally) on several grounds. First,
they argued that CRC/KANY officials (Chun Soo Byun in particular) were
doing the bidding of the Korean government and pursuing their own political self-interests rather than promoting democratic decision making within
the Korean American community or better relations between Blacks and
Koreans. According to Huh, the *Korea Times* was also "a mouthpiece of the
Korean government."[27] In addition, Huh and Kim thought that the countermobilization effort was unnecessarily divisive and one-sided. As an alternative, they formed the ad hoc Korean American Coalition for Community
Empowerment, which sought to avert future conflicts by building bridges
between Blacks and Korean Americans:

RECTOR PAUL KIM: We began meeting after the boycott started, after it
became a media issue, around April, May, after [the] Bensonhurst [trials]
occurred. Our major concern was with how the issue was being projected in
the media, as well as the lack of contact between the Koreans and the
Blacks around the issue. We started meeting in May, June of '90, and began
to talk about what are some things that we could do as Korean Americans . . . There were a couple, you know, young adult groups in the city,
Korean American organizations, youth organizations. Some of them began
to be worried about the issue, feeling that it was getting out of hand, and then
we also felt that we didn't like the Black-bashing that was happening because of the issue, and Koreans being drawn into that kind of formulation of
the problem. So, you know, we didn't organize even officially, it was an ad
hoc kind of a group. So we did begin meeting quite a bit in June, July, and of
course by that time, the Korean Association [KANY] was beginning to have
their own campaign. We began calling for a community-wide forum to deal
with the issue, as well as some kind of a citizen speak-out on this issue. But
the Korean Association was not interested in that.

As the rally approached, the Korean American Coalition for Community Empowerment went public with its criticism. Members even passed out leaflets discouraging Korean Americans from participating. Kim explains:

> RECTOR PAUL KIM: We felt that the Korean Association did not reflect the diversity of concerns within the business community, for one. As you know, when the opposition came out with the idea of holding this demonstration in May or June, Mr. Byun, the person who gets the credit for saying this, the way he says it, you know, the idea came to him because some White politicians mentioned to him that this issue would not go away, for him in one sense [it was an opportunity to] to make a political career for himself . . . It was not a community-based kind of reflection of how should we deal with this issue, and then the demonstration itself did not unite the Korean community. It did not come through a process of community realization or saying that, "This is the way we are going to deal with this issue and after this, the next step will be this." It was a onetime kind of thing, almost of a major reflection on just, "We've got to do something." But even the fact that we've got to do something was not something that was very—it didn't come out of consensus. You know, especially we were talking to a lot of the business people and they really didn't have the consensus. We had people who were saying, "We need to take this more slowly," you know, "We have to think of different ways. If it's a demonstration, maybe there are some different ways of telling the Blacks that we aren't against the Blacks, but we did not like the way we were being treated." The message had to be delivered in the right way. But the planning itself was very tightly controlled by the [Korean] Association. They did not allow even the Produce Association enough say in planning the whole thing. And when we look back, Mr. Byun got political mileage out of that, so he runs for City Council. You know, it was never an opportunity for us to meet with the Blacks. It kind of drove a wedge and, you know, even that store, Mr. Jang ends up selling it to another Korean, which was one of the first options that was mentioned in the beginning anyway.

Kim explains that he thought that the rally organizers were letting themselves be used by the White-dominated media to denigrate Blacks:

> RECTOR PAUL KIM: In the beginning, we felt that the demonstration was being orchestrated as an anti-Dinkins demonstration, and we felt that wasn't helpful. Being that Dinkins was early in his administration and . . . given December 12th going against Dinkins, we felt that to attack Dinkins in a very direct way would not be helpful to the cause. And so we wanted them to tone down the style of demonstration, the slogans, as well as what they were

really trying to get out of the demonstration itself. We felt that the demonstration was being egged on by some people who did not like Dinkins, who
wanted to use the issue to deflate the criticisms against the White community for the way they were treating them [Blacks], at least the way the Black
and White issue was coming out in the media then. Our group felt that we
[Koreans] were being used as a scapegoat in the whole issue and that the
demonstration itself was a way of, was being used by the White media to
scapegoat the Blacks, or at least use us as a way of putting down the Blacks
in one sense . . . Even as we were opposing the demonstration, we knew
that it would go on. So our next strategy was to tone down the slogans, so
that in the end they made it a peace march for peace and harmony, nothing
like "Down with Dinkins," as they were suggesting in the beginning.

Thus the striking picture of Korean American unity during the boycott covered over some ambivalence and dissent. Although dissenters were probably
a distinct minority, their generational status suggests that their views might
one day be those of the majority of Korean Americans.

When the Red Apple Boycott began, Korean Americans in New York City
did not sit idly by as passive victims. Instead, community leaders launched
an unprecedented countermobilization effort seeking to protect Koreans'
position in the racial order and to return things to the status quo ante. Over
time, they shifted their focus from the boycott itself to the Dinkins administration's handling of it. To mobilize both internal and external support,
Korean American community leaders used two overlapping framing strategies, one that focused on resisting transnational-racial oppression and one
that focused on protecting the American creed and the Korean American
Dream. By racializing Blacks as the shiftless underclass and Korean immigrants as a model minority, both tropes reinforced the relative positioning of
these groups within the American racial order. Both tropes were on display
at the Peace Rally for Racial Harmony, which marked an important turn
in both the political development of the Korean American community and
the course of the boycott. By tapping into cherished national ideals and the
dominant discourse on race—colorblind talk—Korean American leaders won
widespread support among the general public. As we shall see in the next
chapter, combined pressure from Korean Americans, the mainstream media,
and the rest of officialdom proved too much for the "neutral" Mayor Dinkins
to resist.

6

Manufacturing
Outrage

In this book I have sought to spotlight the role that racial power plays in shaping Black-Korean conflict. As we have seen, racial power both regenerates a distinct racial ordering that provides the parameters for group interaction and conflict, and shapes the imagination and form of Black resistance that arises in response to it. When targeted by Black protests, Korean American community leaders attempted to protect their collective interests through appeals to cherished national ideals and colorblind talk. In doing so, they reracialized themselves and Blacks in a way that buttressed the American racial order and their respective positions within it. In addition to generating and shaping Black-Korean conflict, racial power also governs interpretations of it. Here, racial power garbled and distorted the boycotters' message so as to delegitimate and ultimately silence it. Make no mistake about it: the Red Apple Boycott challenged the racial status quo. It gave the lie to colorblind talk and proffered a very different story about the persistence of racial oppression in American society. The challenge did not go unanswered. Mainstream journalists, pundits, and officials used colorblind talk to champion the Korean merchants, deflect charges of racism from the system, and condemn the boycotters as criminals, demagogues, and "reverse" racists. In this way, the boycott was silenced and the American racial order ritualistically reinforced.

An important aspect of this ritualistic reinforcement was forcing the new Black mayor to genuflect at the altar of colorblindness. Unlike its forerunners, the Red Apple Boycott became a crisis of historic magnitude precisely because mainstream opinionmakers turned it into a litmus test of Mayor David Dinkins's racial proclivities.[1] The stakes far transcended this particular neighborhood-based protest: Would the city's first Black mayor promote Black demagoguery and unrest or would he promote racial healing and harmony as he had promised? It was not only boycott leaders and Korean American leaders who used the event as a platform to make a larger point, but mainstream opinionmakers as well. Of course, as both the direct beneficiary of and supposed antidote to the resurgent Black Power movement, David Dinkins was between a rock and a hard place from the moment he was elected.[2] The ambiguity of his "gorgeous mosaic" campaign promise had helped him to walk the tightwire between Black and White expectations into Gracie Mansion. But the Red Apple Boycott brought his balancing act to an abrupt halt. Dinkins attempted to stay neutral in the conflict while vigorously pursuing behind-the-scenes negotiations. By manufacturing a sense of crisis around the boycott, however, mainstream opinionmakers generated the demand, à la Derrick Bell's fourth "rule of racial standing," that the mayor renounce his erstwhile allies in the name of colorblindness.[3] In the end, Dinkins submitted to the pressure and crossed the picket line personally to buy groceries in the two stores.

In this chapter I examine the mainstream media's role as purveyors of colorblind talk, the manufacturing of outrage over the boycott by editorialists and pundits, and the chorus of official voices that pressured Dinkins to intervene. I then briefly discuss the two governmental reports compiled on the boycott (by the Mayor's Committee and the City Council) and consider the implications of Dinkins's decision to cross the picket line and come out publicly against the boycott.

THE MAINSTREAM MEDIA AND COLORBLIND TALK

The mainstream media actively "manufacture consent" concerning the status quo—on racial and other matters (Herman and Chomsky 1988). The old-fashioned notion that the media objectively mirror reality is scarcely heard today. Even the notion of the media as aggressive watchdogs and champions of democracy has lost its luster (Martindale 1986). Many scholars now concur that the mainstream media exercise a conservative function in American society in that they interpret events so as to reinforce dominant beliefs and discourses and reproduce extant power arrangements (Cottle 1992; Schudson 1989). Edward Herman and Noam Chomsky, seminal articulators of this view, write:

> In contrast to the standard conception of the media as cantankerous, obstinate, and ubiquitous in their search for truth and their independence of authority, we . . . [see] the media as serving a "societal purpose," but not that of enabling the public to assert meaningful control over the political process by providing them with the information needed for the intelligent discharge of political responsibilities. On the contrary . . . the "societal purpose" of the media is to inculcate and defend the economic, social, and political agenda of privileged groups that dominate the domestic society and the state. (1988, 298)[4]

Those writing on the mainstream media's relationship to prevailing racial arrangements, in particular, reach the same conclusions (Martindale 1985; Hall et al. 1978).

Scholars who argue that the mainstream media reinforce the status quo fall into three major camps (Cottle 1992). Each camp or approach highlights a different set of imperatives shaping media behavior, but these imperatives are not mutually exclusive and probably occur in conjunction in the real world. The first approach, known as the political economy approach, emphasizes how the wealthy and powerful influence what gets reported and how they promote their own perspective(s) while marginalizing voices of dissent. Since the mainstream media are composed of large corporations dependent on advertisers for profits and government officials for information, their institutional self-interest lies in currying favor with these groups and perpetuating their power (Schudson 1989).[5] The second approach, the production studies approach, spotlights the impact that social relations, bureaucratic routines, and organizational practices within news organizations have on news coverage. Given journalists' hierarchical subordination to editors, their dependence on government sources, and their need to generate copy on short notice and on a daily basis, it is not surprising that they tend to assume rather than challenge dominant beliefs and arrangements (Hallin 1985; Fishman 1980).

The third approach, known as the culturalist approach, argues that the mainstream media operate within, are constrained by, and invariably reproduce the discursive-ideological frameworks that justify existing racial, political, and economic arrangements (van Dijk 1991; Hall et al. 1978). In other words, the media are conservative not only because they pander to the wealthy and because their internal practices discourage innovation but also because they remain entirely confined within dominant beliefs and discourses.[6] Mainstream media products are, in fact, windows onto contemporary (racial) meanings. As Simon Cottle writes: "The mass media are central purveyors of public 'texts,' the analysis and interpretation of which can provide insight into those historically specific forms of racialized meanings current at a particular point in time" (1992, 4). Of course, journalists and pundits engage in vigorous debates about race and other matters, but their debates always transpire within the parameters of dominant beliefs and discourses. For example, liberals and conservatives disagree about affirmative action, yet neither group questions the liberal-democratic premises that pervade American public discourse. Proponents of the culturalist approach focus on the "textual structures and strategies" (van Dijk 1991, 10) that journalists use to reinforce prevailing beliefs. Thus, with regard to race, these scholars scrutinize headlines, picture/story juxtapositions, stereotypical coverage of racial minorities, the absence of social and political critique, reliance on White authorities as "experts," and the marginalization of dissenting voices, among other things (van Dijk 1993). It should be emphasized that the culturalist approach does not necessarily attribute prejudiced attitudes or malignant intent to individual journalists. The problem lies in the operation of discourse, not the individual's psyche. Even journalists who fervently believe in their own impartiality work within the medium of prevailing ideas.

The culturalist approach is especially helpful in explaining why the mainstream media reacted to the Red Apple Boycott as they did. In a sense, the condemnatory response was predetermined, since the media do not evaluate events or issues de novo but rather view them through the lens of dominant beliefs. Using colorblind talk, the media denounced the boycotters and valorized their opponents, silencing the former's perspective and exploring the latter's with marked sympathy. As a result, the boycotters' political message about racial oppression and Black empowerment was garbled and distorted, and most of the general public remained in the dark as to what the event was about in the first place. Assemblyman Roger Green, who, as we have seen, was quite critical of the boycott, comments: "If the papers and the electronic media served as the main medium for informing the general public, and if they [the public] internalized all that the electronic media and what the major dailies projected, I would say that they're confused. Because I don't think there was any substantive discussion or dialogue about what that boycott was really about."[7] Of course, the media's role in shaping or reinforcing public opinion is especially powerful when it comes to racial issues, since most White Americans lack significant contact with non-Whites (especially Blacks) and therefore possess few alternative sources of information (van Dijk 1993). Observers who criticized the mainstream media for aggrandizing the Red Apple Boycott through extensive coverage seem to have missed the point. The media built up this particular boycott as a litmus test for the new Black mayor, and it was their manufacturing of outrage that compelled the mayor to take a stand against the boycott. In the end, the Red Apple Boycott was named, defined, delegitimated, and silenced by the discourse of racial power.

THE GOOD, THE BAD, AND THE COLORBLIND

The mainstream media developed an official line about the Red Apple Boycott soon after it began. This official line, manifest in both regular news coverage and editorials, held that the Black underclass was scapegoating the Korean model minority in a manner that violated the norms of colorblindness. Like the Korean American community's mobilizing tropes, this official line reracialized Blacks and Koreans in a way that reinforced the racial order. Representing the dominant majority's viewpoint on this "interethnic" conflict, the official line also reracialized Whites as neutral, disinterested observers who were only concerned with promoting fairness, justice, and the American way. In sum, the media depicted the Red Apple Boycott as a morality play featuring the good minority, the bad minority, and the colorblind enforcers. David Wellman has posed the question, "How, then, do white Americans deal with the racial situation—the troubles and aspirations of Black people—without putting themselves at a disadvantage and thinking of themselves as sons of bitches?" (1993, 207). In the case of the Red Apple Boycott, the media helped Whites to think of the boycotters as criminals and thereby let themselves (and prevailing social, economic, and political arrangements) off the hook. Again, racial power does not depend on a White conspiracy to function.

New York City is the undisputed media capital of the world. The sheer number and variety of media outlets in the city—each covering a distinct range of issues and targeting particular audiences—have earned it this title. The internationally respected daily the *New York Times*, which is geared toward affluent White professionals, shares newsstand space with tabloids geared toward lower-middle-class readers of all racial groups. Conventional citywide radio programs share the airwaves with local call-in shows concerning neighborhood activities in specific racial or ethnic communities. Mitchell Moss and Sara Ludwig note that the city's media have a "dual structure": "the so-called dominant media are geared to the broadest possible audience and consolidated so that a small number of firms control the major television channels, radio syndicates, and major daily newspapers . . . [while] a multiplicity of grassroots media outlets in New York City have emerged to counter the inadequate coverage and appeal of the mainstream, and often national, media" (1991, 264–65). In other words, one can find a little bit of everything in New York City's media market. My focus here is on both dominant/national and grassroots/local media outlets. Specifically, I examine the city's four major dailies at the time of the boycott—the *New York Times*, the *Daily News*, the *New York Post*, and *New York Newsday*—as well as selected television programs and magazines.

The Official Line in Regular News Coverage

Regular news coverage persistently depicted the Red Apple Boycott as the Black underclass's racial scapegoating campaign against the Korean model minority. The official line was more subtle here than in editorials and op-ed pieces, but nonetheless unmistakable. Haitian and Caribbean participants in the boycott were routinely overlooked, perhaps because they did not fit neatly into this good minority/bad minority trope. There were some variations in expressions of the official line in regular news coverage. For instance, the tabloid *Daily News* and *Post* were more enthusiastically biased than the more highbrow *Times*.[8] Also, liberal and conservative versions of the official line emerged, depicting the boycott as a social welfare problem and law and order problem, respectively. Still, the most striking aspect of the regular news coverage of the Red Apple Boycott was its univocality.

Of the four newspapers examined, the *New York Times* conveyed the official line most subtly. Because colorblind talk is hegemonic and ubiquitous, journalists can bring it up in the reader's mind through a few well-chosen cues. Van Dijk writes: "Because of the knowledge, beliefs, and mental models journalists and media users already have (and partly share) about the world, a large part of the information that plays a role in communication and mutual understanding remains implicit. The text is like an iceberg of information of which only the tip is actually expressed in words and sentences" (1991, 181). Hence the *Times* was able to characterize the Red Apple Boycott as a morality play between good and bad minorities without articulating this claim directly or in full. One news story, featuring the headline "Black Demonstrators March in 2 Brooklyn Communities," juxtaposed Mayor Dinkins's televised speech calling for racial harmony with Black protesters noisily chanting slogans in Bensonhurst and Flatbush (May 13, 1990). After briefly quoting one protester, the story introduced a Black man who sympathized with the Korean merchants and urged a negotiated end to the boycott. It then recounted vignettes about Bong Jae Jang's supporters, including one who gave him one hundred dollars, saying "Don't give up," and another who gave him an American flag and a sign saying "Bless the American dream." The accompanying photo showed marchers passing police clothed in riot gear.

Another *Times* story, featuring the headline "Racial Unity and Dissent in Brooklyn," covered one of the "racial harmony" marches led by boycott opponents (May 29, 1990). The subhead neatly summarized the story's perspective: "While Marchers Stress Love, Boycotts of Two Stores Continue." The story directly juxtaposed the "bitter boycott by a small group of blacks" and marchers pleading for "racial harmony." It also focused on one boycotter who "tapped incessantly with a spoon on a tin can and chanted, 'Boycott! Boycott!'" The story closed by quoting Fred McCray, the Black high school teacher who led fifty students across the picket line, as he vowed to "continue to speak out against racism." The media's glorification of McCray as a hero in the tradition of Martin Luther King Jr. brings to mind Derrick Bell's third rule of racial standing: "Few blacks avoid diminishment of racial standing, most of their statements about racial conditions being diluted and their recommendations of other blacks taken with a grain of salt. The usual exception to this rule is the black person who publicly disparages or criticizes other blacks who are speaking or acting in ways that upset whites. Instantly, such statements are granted 'enhanced standing' even when the speaker has no special expertise or experience in the subject" (1992, 114). As a Black man who publicly opposed the boycott in the name of colorblindness, McCray was indeed given "enhanced standing" by the mainstream media. Through all of these "textual structures and strategies"—juxtaposition, selective emphasis, choice of photos, choice of interviewees, etc.—regular news coverage in the *New York Times* implicitly disparaged the boycott as a violation of colorblind norms.

Tabloid newspapers relied heavily on headlining to convey the official line about the Red Apple Boycott. Headlines are arguably the most influential aspect of a news story. They quickly cue the reader to an operative discursive framework. In addition, headlines may be the only part of the story that is read, and they are often the part that is best remembered (van Dijk 1991, 150–51). Some tabloid headlines expressed overt bias. For instance, when Fred McCray, the celebrated transgressor of the picket line, dared boycott leaders to carry out their threat to expose his criminal background, the *New York Post* reported the story with headlines such as "Hero Teacher's Gutsy Reply to 'Jail Blackmail'" (May 1, 1990) and "Threats Thwart Boycott Busters" (May 16, 1990).[9] In August 1990, when Mayor Dinkins negotiated an end to a short-lived second boycott that had arisen in Brownsville, Brooklyn, the *Post* ran the headline "One Brooklyn Boycott Down—One to Go" (September 8, 1990). Other tabloid headlines were highly sensationalistic. Stories in the *Daily News* used headlines such as "Clash of Color: Family-Owned Grocery Is a Racial Battleground" (May 8, 1990). Television programs, too, used inflammatory titles.[10] CNN's *Crossfire* entitled its May 14, 1990, show "City on the Edge," and ABC's *Primetime Live* called its May 17, 1990, show "A City in Crisis." Van Dijk writes: "The presence of aggressive terms in the headlining of race relations . . . establishes an overall association between race relations and serious trouble and problems, if not violence" (1991, 56). Through the use of such incendiary language, tabloid and television news stories cued readers/viewers to associate the Red Apple Boycott with social disorders such as crime and rioting, thus reinforcing the notion that the boycott was the handiwork of the criminal underclass.

Some print and television news stories about the Red Apple Boycott made explicit use of the underclass and model minority tropes. One *New York Newsday* story, entitled "Singled Out for Their 'Success': Asians Battle Soaring Violence as 'Model' Immigrant Group," depicted the boycott as an example of such violence (June 29, 1990). On ABC's *Nightline*, reporter Jeff Greenfield attributed the boycott to "economic privation, the social pathologies within the inner city, measured by broken homes, births out of wedlock, lack of strong role models" (May 15, 1990). Greenfield, who did not proceed to explain what out-of-wedlock births had to do with a Black nationalist protest against two Korean-owned produce stores, seemed to think that the mere evocation of the underclass myth sufficed for analysis. Similarly, ABC's *20/20* built its story about the boycott around the characterization of Korean merchants as a "model minority" (September 14, 1990).

CBS's *48 Hours* offered an exceptionally fecund example of the mainstream media's take on the Red Apple Boycott. The episode about the boycott, entitled "Simmer in the City" (July 12, 1990), demonstrates how a news magazine show can go through the motions of being objective while aggressively promoting the official line.[11] The premise of the show is that reporters who spend an intensive two full days (forty-eight hours) on a story are able to cover every angle, discover all sides to the story, and really get to the bottom of things. Yet the boycott episode once again depicted the bad minority persecuting the good minority. It showed hardworking immigrants trying to achieve the American Dream and angry Blacks trying to prevent them from doing so. For instance, the program juxtaposed sympathetic clips of Bong Jae Jang (waking up at 5:00 a.m. in his tiny apartment, talking about his long work hours, looking bewildered and forlorn in his empty store) with unsympathetic clips of the picketers (shouting slogans, gesturing, leaning against the police barricades, looking angry and threatening). When a White reporter asked Jang why the boycott was happening, Jang shook his head, looked down, and responded, "I don't know, I don't know." Reporters indeed spent more time talking to Black opponents of the boycott (including those who crossed the picket line and Spike Lee, whose movie *Do the Right Thing* depicts Black grievances against Korean merchants as unfair and irrational) than they did talking to boycott leaders and participants. At the close of the program, with the song "New York, New York" playing in the background, a voice said, "It's about coming to America, and the American Dream. The dark side of the American Dream. And it's about the great American melting pot, and how this particular melting pot is boiling over." The last shot was that of a multiracial group of new citizens saying the Pledge of Allegiance during a swearing-in ceremony in Albany, New York. Through these various "textual structures and strategies," the program clearly characterized the boycott as a racist campaign that violated core American values.

We know that an official line has been established when it starts to govern ongoing media coverage so that journalists take newly emerging facts and try to fit them into this prevailing interpretation. Consider the news coverage of the beating of Cao Tuan on May 13, 1990, just blocks from the two boycotted stores. The day after the incident, a news story in the *New York Times*, featuring the headline "Blacks Attack 3 Vietnamese; One Hurt Badly," reported the following: "Shouting anti-Korean slurs, a mob of up to 15 black youths armed with a baseball bat, knives and bottles attacked three Vietnamese men on a Brooklyn street early yesterday and fractured the skull of one victim before fleeing into the night" (May 14, 1990). The article clearly implied that the attack was racially motivated and connected to the Red Apple Boycott. As it turns out, these characterizations were not accurate. Apparently, a young Black girl who was trying to impress her friends threw a beer bottle against the wall of an apartment building, inadvertently breaking Cao Tuan's window. When Tuan and two friends emerged from the building, a fight ensued and one Black youth hit Tuan on the head with a hammer. There is no evidence that anti-Korean slurs were spoken. The next day, the *Times* backtracked, reporting that a police investigation had determined that the incident "apparently had nothing to do" with tensions generated by the boycott (May 15, 1990). It seems likely that the reporter of the first news story rushed to judgment and tried to make the facts about the fight fit the official line about the boycotters being racist, threatening, and criminally inclined. By reiterating this official line throughout the boycott, the mainstream media helped to continuously reracialize Blacks and Koreans, reinforcing their respective positions in the racial order.

Indeed, the initial, inaccurate report on the Cao Tuan beating had an important impact on public opinion concerning the boycott. Newspapers, radio shows, and television programs reported the initial story nationwide and neglected to issue subsequent corrections or retractions once the truth was known. Most of the American public was thus (mis)informed that the boycott and its supporters had crossed the line into near-deadly violence. In fact, this misinformation prompted numerous Asian American advocates to speak out publicly against the boycott. Believing that the Black youths had targeted Tuan because they thought he was Korean, Asian American groups and individuals raised the specter of the brutal 1982 murder of Chinese American Vincent Chin in Detroit, and exhorted the public to denounce all forms of anti-Asian violence.[12] In an article in the *Village Voice* entitled "Doing the Right Thing: After Flatbush, Asians May No Longer Be the Silent Minority," Peter Kwong wrote of the Cao Tuan beating: "These incidents send chills down every Asian's spine: who will be the next victim of 'mistaken' identity?" (May 29, 1990). Virgo Lee, the director of Asian American affairs in the mayor's office, responded to the news story by calling a meeting of Asian American community leaders to discuss the issue (Min 1996, 154). The Committee Against Anti-Asian Violence, a progressive pan-Asian organization that had maintained a neutral stance during the boycott, referenced the Cao Tuan incident in a statement entitled "Towards Finding the Common

Ground," published in the August 1990 *Asian New Yorker.* More than thirty Asian American, Jewish, Puerto Rican, Black, and other organizations and individuals endorsed the statement, which read in part:

> Heated confrontations across color and class lines will continue as long as we have no positive program to address the racism and economic inequality that divides us . . . Should we defend our fellow Asians at all costs or seek to balance the needs of a multiracial society? . . . We recognize the legitimate concerns raised by the boycotters . . . [including] experiences of disrespect-ful and rough treatment . . . [and the] fundamental need for community control, political and economic empowerment in African American neighbor-hoods that have seen waves of immigrant-owned shops and a virtual ab-sence of Black-owned businesses. At the same time, in the face of escalating racist violence . . . we are also alarmed by the assault of a Vietnamese, Tuan Ana Cao, in Flatbush . . . Now is the time for us to jointly develop strategies to confront the underlying economic injustices that erode our unity and impede the political and economic empowerment of our communities.

Journalists, too, invoked the comparison with Vincent Chin (*New York News-day,* May 15, 1990). Even Mayor Dinkins publicly compared the incident to the racially motivated killings of Michael Griffith, Yusef Hawkins, and Vin-cent Chin. In this way, Asian American and other opinionmakers essen-tialized the boycott—which many Blacks thought of as a Black Power cam-paign and many Korean Americans thought of as an anti-Korean campaign—as an episode of anti-*Asian* violence. When the U.S. Commission on Civil Rights issued a national report a few years later entitled *Civil Rights Issues Facing Asian Americans in the 1990s,* the Red Apple Boycott was discussed under the section on "Anti-Asian Violence."

Editorialists, Columnists, and Pundits: Constructing a Crisis

The official line in regular news coverage paved the way for a vigorous campaign for mayoral intervention on the part of editorialists, columnists, and pundits. This campaign, waged with particular vehemence by the tab-loids, went beyond disparaging the boycott to criminalizing it. Condemning the boycotters as "criminals, deviants . . . [and] lunatics" (van Dijk 1991, 70), mainstream opinionmakers manufactured a sense of public outrage that eventually compelled the new mayor to cross the picket line himself.[13] By blasting the boycotters in the name of the downtrodden Korean merchants, these journalists avoided the appearance of overt racism and self-interest. Again, they almost never mentioned the role of Whites, as though Whites were neutral, disinterested observers who had no part in the conflict or stake in its outcome.

One strategy for manufacturing outrage involved vilifying the boycotters and sanctifying the Korean merchants, or reprising the good minority/bad minority theme with more force. One editorial in the *New York Post* declared: "On the one side are immigrants who are pursuing the American dream, using the time-tested recipe of saving money and hard work . . . On the other side are professional race-baiters like Sonny Carson, engaging in group defamation" (February 19, 1990). Michael Kinsley, the putative representative of the left on CNN's *Crossfire,* said simply: "You don't mediate between out and out racism on the one hand and a hardworking entrepreneur on the other. And that's what's going on" (May 14, 1990). Pundits frequently charged that the boycotters were too lazy to work for a living and were trying to extort money from Korean merchants.[14] For instance, former Mayor Edward Koch called the Red Apple Boycott "an organized hustle and extortion operation by Sonny Carson" (*Daily News,* May 16, 1990). Another editorial in the *Post* suggested that the "rabble rousers" had actually staged the precipitating incident as a pretext for extorting money from the merchants and thus avoiding responsible employment (August 29, 1990). In the same vein, an opinion column in the *Daily News* offered this advice: "Instead of picketing Korean stores and being angry, envious and resentful, blacks might be wise to take another approach. Take a look at how the Koreans have done it, and give it a try yourself. If you can organize a boycott or a protest, take it one step further. Organize your own grocery store. It might not make the network news, but it could send your kids to college" (May 23, 1990). Perhaps the most succinct rendition of the boycotters-as-parasites theme could be found in an editorial in the *Post,* entitled "Anti-Asian Bigotry" (May 24, 1990):

> We have condemned the anti-Korean boycott in Flatbush virtually since its onset for one overriding reason: It's clear the four-month-long and still-continuing campaign—judging from the rhetoric and fliers used by the boycotters themselves—has been motivated chiefly by racism. Racism is always wrong. And the effort by black racial agitators to deny hardworking immigrants the opportunity to make a living seems to us a direct challenge to the American dream . . . [The Koreans] labor long hours to make small businesses succeed; they pay taxes; their children excel in school, even when the parents don't speak English; they disdain welfare; and while they don't have an easy time getting bank loans, they often help each other with small start up loans. These immigrants, in other words, help subsidize the city . . . It seems to us that those whose constituencies are most dependent

on public expenditures—on the subsidies and social programs that are funded by tax dollars—should be particularly alert to the consequences of anti-Asian racism.

Thus mainstream editorialists, columnists, and pundits radically depoliticized the Red Apple Boycott, charging its leaders with everything from "reverse" racism to publicity-mongering to venality. Their suggestions that Blacks were only too ready to play the race card and to sponge off of others in order to avoid working resonated forcefully with prevailing neoconservative arguments against affirmative action, welfare, and civil rights law.

A second strategy for manufacturing outrage involved comparing the boycotters unfavorably with the venerable heroes of the civil rights movement, or emphasizing the good Blacks/bad Blacks dichotomy. Where civil rights movement leaders had been reasonable, fair, and righteous, the boycott leaders were irrational, hateful, and racist. In one *New York Newsday* column, entitled "When Boycotts Were for Just Causes," the author opined: "One of the saddest things about the boycott is that it cheapened the many legitimate protests of black people" (February 4, 1991). She then recounted her own memories of the Montgomery and Birmingham campaigns of the civil rights movement. Another article, in *New York: The City Journal*, entitled "Race: The Mess—A City on the Verge of a Nervous Breakdown," asked:

> Is there anything actually happening here, or has the city been hijacked by a traveling medicine show? The protests of the sixties, even the violent ones, had a moral and philosophical basis, but the tabloid-driven anger of recent years seems little more than show time. Is Al Sharpton ever *really* angry? Are the lawyers Alton Maddox Jr. and C. Vernon Mason really rebels or are they just drumming up business for their law practices? Is Sonny Carson really concerned about the rudeness of Korean shopkeepers or is he mostly interested in getting them to make contributions to "community" organizations of his invention? (Klein, May 28, 1990)

A later article in the same journal denounced Sonny Carson and his colleagues for hijacking the civil rights movement, abandoning integrationist goals, exploiting mass frustrations, and engaging in protest for protest's sake (Jacoby 1991). As we have seen, journalists enthusiastically touted boycott opponent Fred McCray as a hero in the civil rights tradition. Just like the good minority/bad minority trope, the good Blacks/bad Blacks trope allowed mainstream opinionmakers to blast the boycott while avoiding the appearance of racism.

The third and culminating strategy for manufacturing outrage involved comparing the boycotters with Ku Klux Klan members and/or Nazis. The message here was that Black racism was as deadly as any other brand. One editorial in the *New York Post,* entitled "New York Wakes Up to a Civil-Rights Emergency," stated the following (also quoted at the start of this chapter):

> While the conventions of journalism require reporters to convey both sides of a story, there can be no doubt where justice and decency lie in this dispute . . . Sometimes, one side is right and the other side is wrong—one party is the aggressor and the other party is the victim. When the Ku Klux Klan terrorized blacks in the Deep South, the KKK was guilty of criminal racism . . . At this point, the episode [the Red Apple Boycott] demands attention from the criminal-justice system. (May 9, 1990)

Another *Post* editorial, entitled "The Anti-Korean Campaign," declared: "Calling it a 'boycott' makes the effort sound like something out of the history of the civil rights movement . . . [when in] fact, it is far more similar to the Nazi agitation against Jewish shopkeepers in Germany during the 1930s" (April 23, 1990). An "editorial notebook" piece from the *New York Times,* entitled "Racial Boycotts, Then and Now: From Brown Shirts to Brooklyn," echoed this comparison (October 13, 1990). By comparing the boycotters to some of the most reviled racist wrongdoers in Western history, mainstream opinionmakers sought to convince the general public that core American values were very much at stake in this conflict.[15]

As public outrage mounted, the pundits directly pressured Mayor David Dinkins to keep his "gorgeous mosaic" campaign promise and intervene in the conflict. ABC's *Primetime Live* observed: "Dinkins's dream of colorblind opportunity is threatened by ugly racial disharmony" (May 17, 1990). An article in the *New York Times* characterized the boycott as "a test of the very image that helped elect him [Dinkins] as New York's first black mayor—that of a healer who could hold together the fractious city he calls a gorgeous mosaic." The same article discussed the view that "because of his reputation and his race, Mr. Dinkins should have particular power to resolve disputes like [this] one" (May 13, 1990). A columnist in the *New York Post* claimed that the boycott had "mushroomed into the biggest crisis—and the most important test—of Mayor Dinkins' young administration" (May 11, 1990). A columnist in *New York Newsday* mentioned the "gorgeous mosaic" promise more in the spirit of castigation than exhortation: "The inclusiveness of the politics of pleasing was thought to be Dinkins' great asset. After 12 years of Ed Koch, the city, it was said, needed a mayor with a smile button for a face. Dinkins would operate on the principle . . . that it is better to have troublemakers inside the tent spitting out . . . instead of outside the tent spitting in. What Dinkins is in the process of discovering is that a lot of his troublemakers are inside the tent spitting on him" (June 22, 1990). Finally, a column in the *New York Post,* entitled "The Law 'Won't Get Involved,'" compared the two Korean merchants to Jews who were victimized by Polish and Russian pogroms during the early twentieth century, pointing out that both groups were innocent victims of racial prejudice whom cowardly authorities refused to protect (May 17, 1990). If the mainstream media failed to instruct the general public as to what the Red Apple Boycott was really about, they did a fine job of manufacturing outrage about the event and putting Mayor Dinkins squarely on the hot seat.

THE CHORUS GROWS

Leading political and business figures throughout New York City joined the mainstream media in trying to dislodge Mayor Dinkins from his neutral stance toward the boycott.[16] Of course, the mayor was not the only official who adopted a position of neutrality. Black elected officials with ties to the resurgent Black Power movement (such as Congressman Major Owens and Assemblymen Al Vann and Roger Green) and White elected officials with large Black constituencies (such as Councilwoman Susan Alter, Assemblywoman Rhoda Jacobs, and State Senator Marty Markowitz, whose respective districts included Flatbush) refrained from taking sides publicly in the conflict.[17] Many other elected and appointed officials and business elites, however, denounced the boycott and joined the chorus of criticism directed at the mayor. Under mounting political pressure, Dinkins bought some time by appointing a committee to investigate the boycott (April), making a televised speech calling for racial harmony (May), and appealing the fifty-feet court order (May). But the tightwire act between Black and White expectations was getting increasingly difficult to maintain. The mayor's moment of reckoning was fast approaching.

The chairman of Community Board 14, Alvin Berk, was an early and ardent boycott opponent. Note the apocalyptic tone in his letter to Dinkins, dated February 16, 1990:

> These folks who would destroy community stability for the sake of empowerment are interpreting your administration's silent and measured reaction as a signal to redouble their efforts. In the absence of a critical statement from

the city's first African-American Mayor, their lies about what happened on Church Avenue are achieving currency by default. They are playing for time and they are getting it. And you, by your silence, are telling folks that the Dinkins administration may not be able to guarantee peaceful coexistence between different races. I am writing to tell you that time is running out. Police budget dollars are running out . . . New York City in 1990 cannot afford the social and economic cost of racially motivated strife . . . The working class and middle class people of NYC—the folks who elected you—will not tolerate an atmosphere of racism and lawlessness, whether in Canarsie, Bensonhurst, or Flatbush . . . You will be remembered as the mayor who presided over the beginning of the end.

Ironically, Berk's outspoken opposition to the boycott brought even more turmoil to Community Board 14. Some of the other members of Community Board 14, including George Dames and Ollie McLean, were involved in leading the boycott. Outraged that Berk had spoken for the board without first consulting other members, Dames, Ernie Foster, and others initiated an offshoot protest that involved disrupting regularly scheduled board meetings. This protest, which was led largely by Caribbean immigrants and those of Caribbean descent, called for more democratic decision making within the board and for the appointment of more Black members. It lasted for over a year.

Business elites in New York City also urged Dinkins to intervene in the boycott. As mayor, they argued, Dinkins had a serious obligation to preserve a favorable "business climate" in New York City.[18] Although the boycott was confined to one street corner in Brooklyn, international media attention threatened to extend its ramifications. What if the boycott were to discourage investors from locating or keeping their firms in New York City? Stephen Berger, executive director of the city's Port Authority, commented: "Those images [of the boycott] go out to the rest of the world on CNN. If you are an Asian businessman thinking of locating a factory in the United States, are you going to put it in Los Angeles or Miami . . . or New York, where they are picketing Asian businessmen? This is a double disaster. It's a bet against our future." Felix Rohatyn, a prominent financial leader credited with saving the city from disaster during the fiscal crisis of 1975–1977, also expressed concern: "If the virus of incivility keeps spreading, there will be no way to sustain even the current level of business activity and economic strength in the city" (Klein 1990, 36). These types of statements from prominent business figures helped to generalize the sense of threat associated with the boycott.

Those who had ignored the conflict suddenly worried about what impact it might have on their pocketbooks.

The judicial branch also weighed in on the boycott issue. Having failed to persuade Mayor Dinkins to intervene in the boycott, advocates for the two Korean merchants turned to another branch of government for help.[19] In April 1990, attorneys for Jang and Park filed a lawsuit charging the boycotters with obstructing their businesses.[20] In response, on May 3, State Supreme Court Judge Gerald S. Held issued a temporary restraining order requiring that the picket line be located at least fifty feet from the two store entrances.[21] In his ruling, the judge explained his reasoning and took a jibe at the mayor as well:

> The court must do a balancing act between the constitutional rights of the defendants to congregate, rally, and express their position, and the constitutional rights of the plaintiffs to pursue their opportunity to engage in commerce and make a living for themselves and their family . . . The court regrets the failure of the mayor of the City of New York to personally intervene and use the prestige of his office and his high standing in the community to convince the parties to bring a suitable end to this dispute.[22]

Dinkins responded in kind. He not only pointed out that the judge might have political motives for criticizing him ("I have personally intervened . . . I should think this distinguished jurist would understand these things . . . in particular since he was once a Republican district leader"), but also reminded reporters that the judge had once allowed a convicted swindler to evict senior citizens from a nursing home in Cobble Hill, Brooklyn (*Daily News*, May 11, 1990). After Stephen James, an attorney for the boycotters, unsuccessfully challenged the fifty-feet order in court, Dinkins instructed the NYPD not to enforce it. On June 4, 1990, attorneys for Jang and Park filed a lawsuit against the NYPD and the city seeking to compel them to enforce the court order. A few weeks later, CORE and the 6:30 Shoppers filed a federal class-action suit toward the same end. When Judge Held ruled on June 28, 1990, that the city and the NYPD had to enforce the order, Dinkins instructed Corporation Counsel Victor Kovner to file a notice of appeal that would trigger an automatic stay on the order pending the outcome of the appeal months later. Kovner advanced a twofold argument on appeal: that enforcement of the order might incite violence and aggravate the conflict, and that the police should not be involved in a civil (as opposed to criminal) matter.

The decision to appeal the fifty-feet court order cost Dinkins dearly in political terms.[23] Critics charged that he had chosen sides, that he had become a lawbreaker, that he had willfully defied the authority of the judiciary—all in the name of pandering to Black constituents. Pundits who had faulted him for indecision before now denounced him for blatant racial favoritism. One editorial in *New York Newsday* castigated the mayor for engaging in "the politics of pleasing" with regard to Sonny Carson (June 22, 1990). When Dinkins reminded his critics that he had condemned Louis Farrakhan for anti-Semitism in 1985 (that is, that he was sometimes willing to denounce Black extremists), his protestations fell on deaf ears (*New York Times*, May 13, 1990). At a public hearing held by the Mayor's Committee on the boycott in Flatbush in June 1990, Richard Izzo, an attorney for Jang, called for renewed pressure on Dinkins: "[The boycott] will only be stopped through political pressure, because through the legal process these merchants have won every battle. On the streets they are losing, and they are losing on the streets because that's not the judiciary's province. That's the province of the politicians."

As the controversy over the fifty-feet court order was unfolding, Dinkins decided on a major public relations move. On May 11, 1990, he would deliver an unprecedented televised speech on race relations. During the days leading up to the speech, Dinkins was coy with the press. He declared that "boycotts based on race ought not to be," yet refused to say whether or not this applied to the Red Apple Boycott (United Press International, May 1, 1990). He said he thought the Red Apple Boycott was a legitimate protest but that it should nevertheless end (*New York Times*, May 9, 1990). Caught on a tightwire between Black and White expectations, the mayor tried, in his televised speech, to ritualistically affirm colorblind talk without provoking Black nationalist activists (*New York Newsday*, May 12, 1990):

I am the mayor of all the people of New York. And my administration will never lead by dividing, by setting some of us against the rest of us, or by favoring one group over others. At the same time, and in the same spirit, we will never allow any group or any person to turn to violence or the threat of violence to intimidate others, no matter how legitimate their anger or frustration may be . . . Let us not permit the prejudice of a few—in Flatbush, in Bensonhurst, or anywhere else—to silence the good will of the rest of us. It's an old story, a cycle of immigration and discrimination that's as old as this city itself . . . New times bring new Americans who become new targets. And recently, too much venom has been injected into the lives of some of our newest Americans—Asian-Americans, especially Korean-Americans . . . I oppose all bigotry against anyone, anywhere. I abhor it; I denounce it; and I'll do anything—anything right and effective—to prevent it. I have clearly stated my views about the conflict between African-Americans and Korean-American store-owners on Church Avenue in Flatbush. I oppose any boycott based on race. I've instructed officials of my government to intervene and to facilitate settlement of this dispute . . . Whatever happened in that incident did not warrant this sort of ongoing intimidation. Boycotts can be an appropriate and effective response—but this one is not and the vast majority of the people in that community know it. I am personally prepared to mediate, to resolve this in a constructive, peaceful way.

These were the mayor's most negative comments on the boycott to date. Yet a few days later, Dinkins seemed to backtrack, declaring on a WCBS news radio show: "I believe the boycott has gone on too long, but it's important to remember that a picket is as American as apple pie" (*New York Post*, May 16, 1990). A columnist in the *Daily News* commented: "Mayor Dinkins is a day late and a dollar short in addressing the sorry state of race relations in New York . . . He simply isn't decisive enough" (May 17, 1990). On the whole, mainstream observers faintly praised the speech while at the same time urging the mayor to enforce the fifty-feet court order. Dinkins then unveiled a new public relations campaign designed to promote racial harmony through speeches, parades, and posters rendered in at least six languages. The slogan of the new campaign was: "New York Spirit: Respect and Unity."

While the televised speech did little to appease the mayor's critics, it did succeed in alienating some of his supporters. According to Reverend Al Sharpton, the speech was like "a James Brown record—talking loud and saying nothing" (*New York Newsday*, May 14, 1990). At the Slave Theater in Brooklyn, C. Vernon Mason addressed a crowd preparing to march in Bensonhurst and Flatbush: "I could not believe what this Negro said last night . . . [He is] a traitor . . . He is a lover of white people and the system. And last night he bashed black people. He ain't got no African left in him. He's got too many yarmulkes on his head."[24] As Mason spoke, the crowd chanted "Judas! Judas!" (*New York Times*, May 13, 1990). The rift between the mayor and the militants widened when Dinkins publicly scolded Sharpton for saying that the city would "burn" if the Bensonhurst trial did not end in murder convictions. Callers flooded the phone lines at WLIB, the city's largest Black radio station, to express their disappointment, frustration, and anger with the mayor. The reaction was so intense that Percy Sutton, the founder of WLIB's parent company, Inner City Broadcasting, and a longtime friend of Dinkins, proclaimed: "I will close down WLIB before I see it used by Blacks to attack Blacks" (*New York Times*, May 17, 1990).[25] This was but a prelude to the way that many Blacks would respond when Dinkins crossed the picket line several months later.

A TALE OF TWO REPORTS

Typically, executives appoint commissions in the midst of racial crises as a way of postponing meaningful government action indefinitely. By the time a commission finishes its investigation, the crisis has passed, and with it, the imperative for government intervention. As such, commission reports, which invariably contain a formulaic mix of recommendations about expanding social programs and enhancing law and order capability, do little more than provide ritualistic reassurance long after the crisis is over (Lipsky and Olson 1977; Feagin and Hahn 1973; Platt 1971). This is not quite how things worked out in the Red Apple Boycott. Because the boycott was a sustained conflict rather than a fleeting episode, the sense of crisis and calls for government action intensified over time. Indeed, a frenzy of expectations surrounded the release of the report of the Mayor's Committee investigating the boycott on August 30, 1990.[26]

Entitled "Report of the Mayor's Committee Investigating the Protest Against Two Korean-Owned Groceries on Church Avenue in Brooklyn," the report was issued in the seventh month of the boycott, as the fate of the city's appeal of the fifty-feet court order hung in the air and the Korean American community prepared for its Peace Rally for Racial Harmony. The report outraged mainstream observers (and the Korean American community) by directly challenging the media's official line about the boycott. Indeed, controversy over the report helped to force Mayor Dinkins's hand three weeks later, when he crossed the picket line to shop in the two boycotted stores. But the tale of the report did not end there. In mid-September, the City Council held its own public hearings on the Red Apple Boycott and thereafter issued another report whose primary purpose was not to reveal new facts but rather to criticize the Mayor's Committee report. As we shall see, the City Council report, which ritualistically affirmed colorblind talk in response to the controversial findings of the Mayor's Committee report, had the last word in the matter.

The very racial and ethnic diversity that made the Mayor's Committee appear representative and fair also made consensus difficult to achieve (the eight members were Black, Haitian, and Korean American). As Michael Lipsky and David Olson note, commission members "are apparently chosen for the diversity of interests they represent, while at the same time they are expected to agree on, and support, a meaningful report about a complex

problem with clear ideological overtones" (1973, 117). Laura Blackburne, the
Black cochair of the Mayor's Committee, comments on this dilemma:

> LAURA BLACKBURNE: It was important to the integrity of the process that
> we have diverse perspectives. But it was also very difficult for there to be a
> process, because working styles varied, points of view about what was
> important varied, and so the chairs had a serious and very difficult job of
> keeping the committee working and focusing and at the same time being
> respectful of the different work styles, the different perspectives, and man-
> aging the schedules of all of the people who had agreed to serve on the task
> force, who were very busy people . . . We reached agreement on the issues
> that were particularly difficult, and I think we did it in the fashion that negotia-
> tors and mediators do. We talked through it, worked through it, and tried to
> look at it from as many different people's perspectives as you could. I had to
> get out of my view and step into Ben Limb's [one of the Korean American
> representatives] view of the situation to really be able to be effective in
> getting the process to work.

Reverend Michael Hahm, the Korean American cochair of the Mayor's Committee, comments on the same:

> REVEREND MICHAEL HAHM: Well, when you have half Black and half
> Koreans, I try to be very objective, because I have lived here in this country a
> long time, and I have worked with the Blacks for a long time. Because in a
> way they are friends. We have worked together to fight against the racism in
> this country. But some of the Koreans who are rather new to the society, and
> so on, their sole interest was how they could protect the Koreans. My ap-
> proach was, we have got to work these things together, you know. And then
> later on, Haitian groups were added. A couple of Haitians [were] fine, but
> one Haitian was, we felt, strictly looking after the Haitians' interest. So you're
> bound to have a conflict.

In a sense, the Mayor's Committee simply recapitulated the clash of perspectives found in the boycott itself.

The three Korean American committee members found themselves in a
bind. Early on, it became apparent to them that the Black and Haitian majority on the committee wanted the report to be sympathetic to the boycotters
and to Mayor Dinkins. The Korean American representatives, who did not
want to be blamed for undermining the committee's work, felt trapped in
a process that they could neither influence significantly nor repudiate altogether. They successfully compelled revisions of an initial draft of the re-

port (which had called for Bong Ok Jang—now finally identified as the merchant who took part in the altercation—to apologize to Ghiselaine Felissaint), but they remained dissatisfied with the document. One Korean American committee member dropped out altogether, citing other commitments. Reverend Hahm nearly followed suit.[27] Ben Limb, the third Korean American representative, recalls the turmoil that preceded the release of the report:

> BEN LIMB: [Hahm] said that he was on vacation, and he went to Chicago. I spoke with his wife a couple of days preceding August 13th because so many important questions came up and I had to make a decision as to whether we should withdraw as a group or participate to the end. He was not available. I left a message over and over again with Mrs. Hahm, who said that her husband is staying in Chicago and he was not available and I had to make my own decision. When the whole thing was over, Michael told me that he was staying in New York, but for some reason, he would just not make himself available . . . I wanted to know whether we should participate to the end or withdraw, because we had to make a decision. There are some passages in the report which we could not accept. And if you compare the first draft with the second and third drafts and the final product, you may realize what changes have taken place during the last few weeks. At this time, I was the only one who was fighting for the, I mean, tried to represent what Korean Americans feel with respect to this particular, you know, incident. There were three representatives, three members . . . from Korean American community, and one virtually resigned because of his commitment to his business, and Reverend Michael Hahm and I were the only ones left. And at the final stage, Michael Hahm was not available and I had to deal with the situation. And I found out at one time that with or without the participation of Korean Americans in the committee, the report was going to go out. And also, if we withdraw from the committee, the blame will be placed upon us, that we have not tried hard with good faith to resolve the matter. So the negative, you know, consequences will be blamed upon Korean Americans.

In the end, Limb decided to remain on the committee and reluctantly stood in as acting cochair for the "vacationing" Hahm during the City Hall ceremony that marked the release of the report.

The most important finding of the Mayor's Committee's report was that the Red Apple Boycott was incident-based and not race-based—that is, that the boycott was a response to the precipitating incident rather than a racially motivated scapegoating campaign. The report's executive summary clearly states this finding:

The Committee found that there is no single, monolithic agenda proposed or followed by the protesters. Some focus only on justice for Mme. Felissaint, others on what they perceive as a history of disrespectful behavior by the specific Korean merchants involved, still others on wider issues of economic justice for Blacks in Flatbush and generally . . . The protest is multilayered. The Committee *does not see the protest as race-based.* Were race the primary agenda, other Korean merchants on Church Avenue would also be under protest. The Committee found, rather, that this protest and boycott are incident-based . . . Even so the Committee found disturbing evidence of distribution of some racist literature, and use of some racist epithets by some protesters. Seen largely at the beginning of the protest, the Committee does not attribute this literature or comments to any individual or group. (page 3, italics added)

By declaring that the boycott was not race-based, the report signaled that the protest was legitimate by colorblind standards and implicitly justified Mayor Dinkins's decision not to intervene in the conflict. It also protected the boycotters from prosecution under a New York state law prohibiting "race-based boycotts." Clearly, this was a critical finding in both political and legal terms.

Interestingly, the executive summary of the report, quoted above, misstated the committee's conclusions. The executive summary declared that the boycott was not race-based, but the main body of the report said something slightly different: "[The Committee] does not believe that the protest and grievances are based *primarily* on racial grounds. Because of its multilayered complexity, characterizing the protest as *solely* 'racial' or 'race-based' would not be accurate" (page 15; italics added). According to Ben Limb, committee members had negotiated carefully over these adverbs:[28]

BEN LIMB: Even the general characterization of this instance as to whether it was racial or nonracial, they were just yes or no situations. And I suggested that it's clearly racial in some part, at some time, during the entire instance, so at my suggestion, they [the other members] accepted the words "not solely racial," which means partly racial.

Despite the more nuanced language of the main body of the report, then, it was the stark finding of the executive summary that stayed with mainstream observers. Laura Blackburne comments:

LAURA BLACKBURNE: The only flaw in the report, in my view, was the hastily written summary that left out one very key small word that sent the press into a state of craziness in how they viewed the report . . . In the summary, it said something to the effect that the task force didn't believe the boycott was race-based . . . And in the body of the report it said "solely race-based," and the press went off on the notion that somehow we had ignored the elements of racism that we in fact identified when you read the body of the report. So, to that extent, I wasn't happy with what we produced because it's true that people are careless readers and lazy readers and they would like to get the essence of an issue, and that's what a summary is suppose to provide. And so that careless oversight on our part created the excuse for the hostile reception that our task force got.

The Korean American community was outraged by the language of the executive summary. Rector Paul Kim recalls that most Korean Americans heard only that the report had exonerated the boycotters. "You know, I don't know how many Koreans even got a copy of it [the report], probably none except for the [Korean language] media. So, the only thing that the [Korean language] media was emphasizing are those couple of points that this boycott was not racially motivated. That line, they really blew that up and said, 'Look, this report is,' you know, 'bogus.' "[29]

The Mayor's Committee report also declined to draw conclusions about the precipitating incident, criticized the Kings County (Brooklyn) district attorney and the mainstream media for their handling of the conflict, and defended Mayor Dinkins's neutral stance. Since Dinkins had originally charged the committee with a "fact-finding" mission, he raised expectations that the report would clarify finally what had happened between Jang and Felissaint, thus vindicating one side over the other. However, the report, citing several pending lawsuits related to the boycott, clearly disavowed this mission: "The Committee . . . did not interpret its task as deciding which *version* of fact or interpretation was 'right' or 'wrong' " (page 2). Instead, the report offered standard commission fare: the acknowledgment of grievances on both sides, a recommendation for negotiations, suggestions about programs to promote mutual respect and racial sensitivity as well as economic opportunity for Blacks.[30] The report also claimed that the Kings County district attorney had been delinquent in pushing the assault case against Bong Ok Jang through the system, and that this had aggravated and prolonged the boycott conflict. Mayor Dinkins, however, had acted appropriately by remaining neutral and trying to mediate between the parties (pages 25–26):

The press has fueled the fires with a full range of suggestions and demands, among them that the Mayor intervene personally in the conflict, become a negotiator, ply influence with "his community" (Black), and even shop in the boycotted stores . . . The Committee believes that the Mayor has acted properly to date in this matter and is aware of repeated and consistent efforts, through informal channels, to effect a solution . . . The Committee feels that primary attention in the press on Mayor Dinkins as the major mediator for the Church Avenue dispute has been misplaced. The Committee understands that community disputes end when the parties are prepared for them to end. Public officials, the press or others not directly involved may not be comfortable with this reality, but nevertheless the affected parties cannot be compelled to move on an outside timetable. It is the role of the Mayor to enable the healing process to commence, to set the stage for parties to begin their deliberations.

Overall, the report saved its harshest criticism for the mainstream media: "The Committee's analysis of the mainstream media coverage of the boycott generally reveals an overly simplistic and in some cases blatantly racist presentation of the issues to the public . . . Trends of depicting the protesters primarily as racist aggressors and the Koreans primarily as beleaguered victims were found" (page 31).

Critics blasted the Mayor's Committee's report as an exculpatory ritual on behalf of the boycotters and the mayor.[31] One *New York Newsday* columnist called the report "a specimen of the portentous nonsense you have to read not to believe" (August 31, 1990). An editorial in the *Daily News,* entitled "The Boycott Report: Worse than Useless," described it as "a tangle of cliches wrapped around a core of nonsense" (September 2, 1990). Where some resorted to ridicule, others went straight for the political jugular. An editorial in the *Daily News* excoriated the "gutless report that pandered to racists and came within a millimeter of elevating Dinkins to sainthood" (September 6, 1990), and a *New York Newsday* editorial called the report "a sorry attempt to exonerate Mayor David Dinkins' ineffective handling of the dispute" (September 11, 1990). Richard Izzo, an attorney for Jang, concurred: "This is the greatest whitewash since Tom Sawyer's fence. This is a partisan report in that it protects the mayor at all costs" (*New York Newsday,* August 31, 1990). Kings County District Attorney Charles Hynes, who was criticized in the report, expressed his confidence that the report was "universally rejected by everyone in the free world" (*New York Newsday,* November 8, 1990). Other commentators renewed their demand that Mayor Dinkins acknowledge the racial motivations of the boycotters and enforce the fifty-feet court order (*Daily News,* September 2 and September 5, 1990). Perceived as a leader who had broken the law, violated American ideals, and manipulated the committee to protect his Black extremist friends, Dinkins was in political trouble.

Poised on the brink of self-reinvention, the City Council of New York decided to join the controversy over the boycott and the Mayor's Committee report. In 1989, as we have seen, the U.S. Supreme Court ordered the dismantling of the New York City Board of Estimate on the grounds that equal representation for boroughs with different population sizes violated the one person–one vote principle nested in the Fourteenth Amendment. When voters then transferred the Board's immense powers over land use, franchises, contracts, planning, and the city budget to the City Council, they transformed the latter body from a rubber stamp into a powerful institutional check on mayoral power.[32] City Council Speaker Peter Vallone, who saw a chance for the City Council to flex its newly acquired political muscle, instructed Councilman Morton Povman (D-Queens) to set up a committee on the boycott.[33] Povman's committee held a round of public hearings on the boycott on September 12, 1990, and issued its own report a few months later, well after Dinkins had already crossed the picket line. An editorial in the *New York Post* applauded these moves: "The council's decision to hold public hearings on the ugly campaign waged against two Korean groceries in Brooklyn is a sign that the council may be ready to emerge as a full partner in city government" (September 14, 1990).

The primary aim of the City Council hearings and report was not to investigate the Red Apple Boycott anew but rather to castigate the boycotters and the Mayor's Committee report in what amounted to a ritualistic reinforcement of colorblind talk.[34] The transcript of the City Council hearings shows that speaker after speaker condemned the boycott as race-based, ridiculed the Mayor's Committee report, and demanded that Dinkins take a stand. State Assembly Speaker Mel Miller, for example, derided the Mayor's Committee report as a "term paper" that abdicated the government's moral responsibility to combat racism. Other speakers included Alvin Berk, chairman of Community Board 14; the Korean merchants and their attorneys; Roy Innis of CORE; Colin Moore, attorney for Felissaint; and Ollie McLean, Community Board 14 member and boycott leader.[35] Only a few speakers spoke in favor of the boycott, and none revealed any new information about the conflict. Laura Blackburne, who agreed to appear at the hearings to defend the Mayor's Committee report, recalls the hostile interrogation she faced:

LAURA BLACKBURNE: I would prefer not to [comment on the hearings] other than to say that for two and a half hours I sat in front of the collective ignorance of New York City and endured personal insults that were gratuitous and uncalled for, and with the exception of maybe two people who

participated in that panel, it was not an effort to add any enlightenment, and I
didn't perceive it that way. Many people had advised me not to lend my good
name to their charade, but I thought by not going, I would have given them
more credibility than they deserved . . . It was supposed to make a fool of me
and, indirectly, of the mayor. And most people, as I said, urged me not to
participate. And most people didn't expect me to participate. And once I participated, I think that they were limited even more by what they could say in
their report because most of their questions conveyed their utter ignorance
of the situation. And my responses so contradicted where they wanted to go
that even they couldn't twist it any further than they did.

The City Council's report, entitled "An Analysis of the Report of the Mayor's
Committee Investigating the Protest Against Two Korean-Owned Groceries
on Church Avenue in Brooklyn," proffered several major findings, including
the following (pages 6–8):

- Several members of the Mayor's Committee had the "appearance of potential
  bias," including cochair Laura Blackburne, who was told that Mayor Dinkins
  was thinking about appointing her head of the New York City Housing
  Authority prior to the release of the report; Karen Daughtry, whose husband,
  Reverend Herbert Daughtry, had expressed sympathy for the boycotters; and
  Philip Wilson Desir, who had been a boycott leader prior to his appointment to
  the committee
- The Mayor's Committee report did not contribute to fact-finding or the
  resolution of the conflict
- The mayor's decision not to enforce the fifty-feet court order "evidence[d] a
  bias in favor of appeasement of the protestors at the expense of the rights of
  the store owners and residents who wish to shop at the stores"
- The "conclusion that the protest is incident-based and not primarily racist is
  contradicted by the facts"

The City Council report was warmly received by the mainstream media (*New
York Post*, November 10, 1990). Indeed, its release months after Mayor Dinkins had crossed the picket line revived criticism of his handling of the conflict. In a column in the *Village Voice*, entitled "Can New York Endure the
Dinkins Mayorality?" Nat Hentoff wrote: "The character of some city administrations does not become clear for some time . . . What Dinkins has—and has
not done—with regard to this boycott is the clearest and most dismaying
illumination of his weakness and bumbling trickery. And more than anything else, his betrayal of elementary fairness and honesty during all those

months . . . makes me pessimistic about the immediate future of this city" (1990, 22).

CROSSING THE LINE

September 1990 began inauspiciously for Mayor David Dinkins. In rapid succession, the Mayor's Committee report provoked a firestorm, the City Council held its hearings on the boycott, the appellate court upheld the fifty-feet court order, and the Korean American community held its Peace Rally for Racial Harmony. A series of meetings with business leaders and public relations experts finally convinced the mayor that his administration would be irreparably damaged if he did not intervene (*Daily News*, September 22, 1992). Thus Dinkins crossed the picket line, shopped in the two stores, and initiated enforcement of the fifty-feet court order. Throughout his career, David Dinkins had complied with Derrick Bell's fourth rule of racial standing: he had denounced Louis Farrakhan as an anti-Semite in 1985, distanced himself from Jesse Jackson in 1988, and "let go" Jitu Weusi and Sonny Carson during the 1989 election campaign. At the same time, he had maintained decent relations with movement activists, thereby shoring up his support within the Black community. Pursuing these dual strategies, Dinkins had successfully walked the tightwire between Black and White expectations into Gracie Mansion. But the boycott conflict pushed him off of that tightwire.

On September 21, 1990, eight months after the Red Apple Boycott began, Dinkins crossed the picket line and bought fruit in both boycotted stores under the glare of press cameras. He insisted that he would have intervened earlier if he had known that negotiations would fail, and he criticized the boycotters' intransigence: "I think that we've gone to the ultimate limits of trying every way known to man to try to get people to be reasonable. There are some folks who don't want a resolution" (*New York Times*, September 22, 1990). The mayor's intervention marked the beginning of the end of the boycott. The picket line was weakened severely when the NYPD moved it back to fifty feet from the store entrances.[36] Shoppers flooded in from around the city as a way of endorsing and emulating the mayor's actions. The Family Red Apple store, which made approximately $3,500 in sales per day prior to the boycott and approximately $30 in sales per day during the boycott, made about $1,000 on September 25 and again on September 26. Church Fruits, which made about $4,500 per day before the boycott and $50 per day during the boycott made about $1,300 on September 25 and again on September 26 (*Korea Times*, September 28, 1990). Although a small number of activists kept the picket line alive for several more months, the boycott had clearly passed its peak.[37] December 12th Movement members remained defiant. When a jury acquitted Bong Ok Jang of third-degree assault on January 30, 1991, Sonny Carson called for a rally to protest the acquittal, declaring: "The boy-cott lives . . . The Black community has been let down again by the justice system that is supposed to represent everyone . . . We can no longer ask those people whose only interest is to criminalize us to defend us" (*New York Newsday*, February 8, 1991).

The image of a Black mayor crossing a Black picket line to shop in two Korean-owned groceries was ripe with symbolism. As it turned out, Mayor Dinkins's belated affirmation of colorblind norms did not repair his damaged reputation among Whites and Korean Americans, but only alienated Black supporters. From the boycotters' perspective, Dinkins had betrayed the struggle from which he himself had benefited. Upon seeing four hundred police officers arrive to enforce the fifty-feet court order, one boycotter said, "David Dinkins has come with the state to violate our constitutional rights" (*New York Times*, September 23, 1990). Colin Moore, attorney for Felissaint, added: "The city's supposed to be an impartial referee. Now the Mayor has not only declared the boycott to be illegitimate but has broken it himself. For the Mayor to condemn this method is for him to condemn the methods by which black people, including himself, gained power" (*New York Times*, September 22, 1990). Roger Wareham explains that he was disappointed but not surprised by the mayor's intervention:

ROGER WAREHAM: The best thing that he could have done was to just stay out of it. Of course, he put himself in it and then crossed the line, which then, you know, first he tried to duck away from it, then he took some heat for that. He should have just continued to take the heat for it. You know, for a long time they took a standoff position around whether they were going to enforce the court order or not, and then he caved in to the interests that put him in office. No, they didn't put him in office, that was always a contra-diction, he was put in office by the Black and Latino community, but the interests he served were the financial interests of New York City and he caved in to that.

Sonny Carson simply denounced Dinkins as a "traitor to his people" (*New York Newsday*, September 22, 1990). When he heard that the mayor's office was considering legal action against the boycott (pending ascertainment that it was indeed racially motivated) Carson responded: "Everything that hap-pens in America is racially motivated. Our people in this city are about to witness a contradiction that we cannot tolerate—that so-called black people are going to challenge the only means that we have used to survive in this country" (*New York Newsday,* September 27, 1990).

While boycott leaders and their supporters denounced the mayor as a racial traitor, other movement leaders, such as Reverend Herbert Daughtry and Reverend Al Sharpton, blamed the December 12th Movement for putting Dinkins in an untenable position and irreparably damaging his young administration. Daughtry expresses his frustration with Whites' expectations of Dinkins:

REVEREND HERBERT DAUGHTRY: Every time they force David Dinkins to make a statement against Farrakhan—and, oh, how many statements do you need to make? I mean, every time he says something, here come Dinkins. Say something, say something. There he come. How many times you need to say, "I disagree with the guy. That ain't my life, my actions, my politics. Everybody in the world know my action, my politics. I disagree." How many times you need to say that? So every time they force David Dinkins out to make a statement denouncing Farrakhan, the more enemies or the more [Black] people turn their backs on Dinkins.

At the same time, Daughtry criticizes the December 12th Movement for putting Dinkins in an impossible position:

REVEREND HERBERT DAUGHTRY: I came to see one of the reasons people always protest; it's easier to protest, you know. I mean you can always find something to protest about. And you can and it's easy. The harder thing is now to negotiate around what you've been fighting for, and that's when you leave yourself open for people accusing you of selling out, or whatever. When the revolutionary come in from the hill and say "I'm here to put my demands down" is when the revolutionary now run the risk of getting fired from his own people, from his own troops. It's easier to stay up in the hills and fire cannons, you know, shoot down on the enemy. What we did is that we were able to translate our energy into certain gains [electing Dinkins]. Now, what that meant is that people couldn't be out there demonstrating, you know, and I think that that's why some people were straining at the bit. They had nothing, they didn't have a program, they were not sophisticated enough or knowledgeable enough to know how now to take that political energy that they helped to generate and hack off a piece and do something, you know, for the people. And so they were kind of left to do nothing but criticize. So they started on Dinkins . . . That's a part again of some of my criticism of my fellow strugglers, is when do you negotiate for something?

You can't just live off protests, you know. People who put themselves on the line, people whose heads have been busted, people that you say, "Come on and go to jail with me," people who risk their lives, when do you say to them, "Here is a tangible return to what you have done?" . . . The people who were out there were not his [Dinkins's] friends. And they were as much about embarrassing him as anybody else. Because if they had a political sense as his friend, they could have clearly seen that this was becoming a hot link, this was going to be a political issue or had become a political issue, and did have the potential of helping to remove Dinkins from office. And that should have been a consideration that should have softened their position, brought them to a negotiating point, or something. But they didn't care about that.

Sharpton, too, criticizes the December 12th Movement for elevating Black nationalist dogma over Black people's concrete needs:

REVEREND AL SHARPTON: I think that, again, you have to deal with the differences in our community. I was very critical of Dinkins on some things. But in retrospect, David Dinkins never did anything different than what he said. He never told anybody he was an activist. So I think in many ways we put on him things that he never said he was going to do. David Dinkins was a clubhouse politician. So people would say, "Well, why didn't he do so and so at Crown Heights?" And "Why didn't he do so and so in other situations? Why did he cross the Korean boycott line?" Like he was Al Sharpton or, for that matter, Sonny Carson. He never was us. He never was an activist. He was a clubhouse politician. And I think that we should have expected from him based on his tradition, more than just be critical of him for not being like us . . . It is easy to sit back with the dogma, as many do, as an elitist, and say there are contradictions in the system and people shouldn't do this, that, and another. That's easy. It is harder to have to keep hospitals open because people are dying or make sure the school lunch is there for the kids. What he could do, though it was limited, was lifesaving for some of us in our community. And I think some of us are too elitist and dogmatic to understand it. You can't just write off the fact people need jobs and people need hospital care and people need education. To write that off on some utopian dream of revolution, to me, is not to have a real concern for people. Yes, you may want to change the entire system, but you should also have compassion for people while you are trying to change, to make sure they can survive. And that's what I see Dinkins's school of thought at, of making it better for people to have services of survival while we try to transform the system . . . My thing is that you cannot be so dogmatic that you're not functional, which is why you lose a lot of the mass of people, because, realistically, people are not going to do whatever can't handle their immediate problems.

The resurgent Black Power movement's coalition of radical activists, moderate activists, officials, and politicians was coming apart at the seams.

Dinkins never recovered fully from the Red Apple Boycott. Having alienated Whites, Korean Americans, and parts of his core constituency, the mayor was an easy target for Republican challenger Rudolph Giuliani in the 1993 mayoral election. In 1993, media strategist Roger Ailes once again helped Giuliani play the race card by transforming "the Korean boycott" (and subsequent movement events) into a major campaign issue. It is not hyperbolic to say that the Red Apple Boycott haunted Dinkins throughout his term as mayor and was one factor contributing to his loss in 1993. That year, Giuliani won a highly racially polarized election to become only the third Republican mayor of New York City since 1930. Color lines figured much more prominently than party lines in the election: Giuliani won 75 percent of the White vote and only 5 percent of the Black vote. White voters—especially middle-class Catholic and Jewish voters—turned out in greater numbers than in 1989 and gave less support to Dinkins than before (Mollenkopf 1997).[38] In addition, "black voters turned out in lower numbers; Latinos both turned out in lower numbers and defected from Dinkins, and white liberals defected" (Mollenkopf, 1997, 110). According to Omowale Clay, many Blacks who were disillusioned with the mayor simply failed to turn out to vote:

OMOWALE CLAY: So he crossed the picket line. That's unheard of. He crossed the picket line. Most of the Black people never forgave him for that. They didn't say it, you know, just subtly. How did it get measured? When Black people came out to vote, they did it. Were they into Giuliani? No, but they weren't into him [Dinkins]. They were not into him. And he could no longer inspire them to come out. In fact, he didn't inspire them initially. It was objective conditions, first Black mayor, there was nothing to say bad about him, but, shit, there was nothing to say good about him. But he rode on the coattails of being the first Black mayor. That wasn't enough the next time. He now had his own track record, and my view was that he didn't inspire Black people to come out and vote.

Thus David Dinkins made history again by becoming the first breakthrough Black mayor in American history to lose office after only one term.

One moral of this story is that racial power cleans up after itself. It inevitably generates protest by subordinated groups, but it also names, interprets, and ultimately silences that protest. As we have seen, mainstream opinionmakers transformed the Red Apple Boycott into a test of Mayor Dinkins's racial sympathies. They used colorblind talk to manufacture public outrage over the boycott, thereby forcing Dinkins to repudiate symbolically his erstwhile allies. The long-term implications of this scenario included the fragmentation of the resurgent Black Power movement coalition, the ascendance of a White Republican mayor, and the reinforcement of the racial order. The containment of the Red Apple Boycott raises an important question for students of American democracy. We often take open dissent on the part of dispossessed groups as an indication that they have some voice in American politics. Yet how meaningful is this "voice" if it is consistently garbled, distorted, and then silenced by mainstream opinionmakers and the dominant discourse? When is "voice" really voice?

CONCLUSION
Bitter
Fruit

Perhaps those of us who can admit we are imprisoned by the history of racial subordination in America can accept . . . our fate. Not that we legitimate the racism of the oppressor. On the contrary, we can only *de*legitimate it if we can accurately pinpoint it . . . Armed with this knowledge, and with the enlightened, humility-based commitment that it engenders, we can accept the dilemmas of committed confrontation with evils we cannot end.

Derrick Bell

Conventional accounts of Black-Korean conflict tell a story that is comfortable for us to hear. The story involves a group of aspiring newcomers caught in the crossfire of ancient feuding, a group of malcontents acting out of malice and rage, and a group of colorblind observers noting events from a distance. It depicts a Manichaean struggle between innocence and guilt in which the third-party observers are compelled by a sense of justice to intervene on behalf of the powerless. This story cheers us because it fixes the problem on a renegade minority, lets most of us off the hook, and reinforces our moral certainty in the face of racial conflict. What I have tried to show in this book is that this story also seriously misleads us.

Black-Korean conflict is the "bitter fruit" of the workings of racial power in contemporary America. It is the manifestation or outcome of processes of racialization, ordering, and resistance that permeate and constitute this society. The Red Apple Boycott was not a morality play between the forces of good and the forces of evil but a window onto dynamics of racial power and resistance that are usually hidden from us for one reason or another. I have sought here to expose these dynamics, to sketch the ways that racial power orders groups, conditions their resistance, and silences dissent through interpretive hegemony. This story is, of course, less cheerful than the conventional one. By implicating all groups within the racial order, it undercuts our moral certainty about who is right and wrong in conflicts such as the Red Apple Boycott. It also raises questions about how meaningful the political "voice" of subordinated groups is. Perhaps they can speak truth to power, but often they cannot make it listen.

At the University of California, Irvine, I teach an undergraduate course on "minority" politics. During the unit on Black-Korean conflict, I like to show the 1993 film *Sa-I-Gu* (April 29). Created by an outstanding team of independent filmmakers and scholars—Christine Choy, Elaine Kim, and Dai Sil Kim-Gibson—the film introduces us to Korean immigrant women devastated by the Los Angeles rebellion of 1992. It allows us to hear voices that are never heard, the voices of immigrant women of color, who describe their sorrow, loss, bewilderment, and anger in their own words. My students, the majority of whom are Asian American and many of whom are Korean American, feel for these women, and when the film projector goes off, there is a somber quiet in the room. At that point, I ask the class: What are other silenced voices that we should listen for? Should we watch a companion film about Black perspectives on Black-Korean conflict? If we had to create one, what would it look like? I try, in other words, to take the class from the point where they do not notice the absence of such a companion film to the point where they are constructing it themselves. I try to broaden their focus so that they see not only the suffering of one group but the suffering of both groups involved and the daunting moral dilemmas raised by their confrontation. Some students still cling to the racial scapegoating argument, unwilling to admit to any moral uncertainty. But others tell me that they are suddenly bewildered, that their cherished beliefs are shaken, and that they are not sure what to think about Black-Korean conflict anymore. Mission accomplished.

So what is to be done? It seems remiss for a study of a social "problem" to end without proffering practical suggestions for policymakers and / or activists. Having read about distressing issues, readers want to be told that things can be fixed. Yet I decline to make such suggestions because they would trivialize what I am trying to emphasize in this book: the somber reality of racial power in contemporary American society. I am not sure that understanding an issue leads automatically to knowing how to "fix" it. I am even less sure that policymakers seek solutions that are fair to all, or that academics who study events ex post facto have anything to teach activists. If the owl of Minerva flies at dusk, it also tends to fly close to the ground. My task here has been to shed some light on the dynamics of racial power that subordinate groups and condition and constrain their resistance. I respectfully leave the Monday morning quarterbacking to others.

This does not mean that there is nothing to be done—only that we need to come to terms with the magnitude of the problem before us and reject easy answers. As Derrick Bell (1992) suggests in the quote that opens this chapter, accepting the truth about racial power is not fatalistic or pessimistic but *realistic*. Realism of this kind is empowering. We need to know what we are up against. We need to acknowledge that racial distinctions and inequalities, embedded in our society for centuries, cannot be wished or educated away. We need to understand that they still constitute us most profoundly as a society and as individuals. Writing in 1903, W. E. B. Du Bois declared: "The problem of the twentieth century is the problem of the color line" (1989, 13). It seems likely that the problem of the twenty-first century will be that of the multiple color lines embedded in the American racial order. Thinking critically and speaking candidly about the contours of this order is only a first step, but it is a necessary one.

TIMELINE

Key Events Relating to the Red Apple Boycott

January 1, 1990	David Dinkins inaugurated as 106th mayor of New York City
January 18, 1990	Altercation between Bong Ok Jang and Ghiselaine Felissaint occurs; boycott begins; Bong Jae Jang arrested and charged with assault
April 20, 1990	Haitians demonstrate in front of Food and Drug Administration office in Manhattan to protest ban on Haitian blood products
April 21, 1990	Mayor Dinkins appoints committee to investigate the boycott
April 27, 1990	Bong Jae Jang and Manho Park file suit seeking to enjoin the boycott
May 3, 1990	New York State Supreme Court Judge Gerald Held issues a temporary restraining order against the boycott
May 10, 1990	The temporary restraining order becomes a permanent injunction barring the boycotters from picketing within fifty feet of the store entrances
May 11, 1990	Mayor Dinkins gives a televised speech on race relations
May 13, 1990	Cao Tuan beaten during altercation with Black youths in Flatbush
May 14, 1990	Teacher Fred McCray leads group of students across the picket line in Flatbush
June 4, 1990	Bong Jae Jang and Manho Park file suit to compel the NYPD and the city to enforce the fifty-feet court order
Early June 1990	Charges against Bong Jae Jang are dropped
June 26, 1990	New York State Supreme Court Judge Gerald Held orders the city to enforce the fifty-feet court order; the city appeals the decision
June 29, 1990	The Mayor's Committee investigating the boycott holds public hearings in Flatbush

July 7, 1990	Bong Ok Jang arrested and charged with assault
August 30, 1990	Mayor's Committee releases its report on the boycott
September 12, 1990	City Council committee holds public hearings on boycott
September 17, 1990	New York State Appellate Court denies city's appeal of fifty-feet court order
September 18, 1990	Korean American "Peace Rally for Racial Harmony" held at City Hall
September 21, 1990	Mayor Dinkins crosses the picket line and shops in the two stores
Late November 1990	City Council committee releases its report on the boycott
January 20, 1991	Jury acquits Bong Ok Jang of assault charges
May 30, 1991	Bong Jae Jang sells Family Red Apple store; picketing dies out

LIST OF INTERVIEWEES

Name	Position, Organization*	Date of Interview
Akyeampong, Kwasi	Congress of Racial Equality	June 27, 1991
Albert, Sabine	Flatbush Coalition for Economic Empowerment; Flatbush Frontline Collective; Haitian Enforcement Against Racism	August 25, 1992
Belizaire, Jean-Claude	Executive director, Flatbush Haitian Center	July 11, 1991
Benjamin, Playthell	Journalist; community activist	June 11, 1992
Blackburne, Laura	Cochair, Mayor's Committee	December 10, 1991
Brath, Elombe	Flatbush Frontline Collective; December 12th Movement; chair, Patrice Lumumba Coalition	August 28, 1992
Brathwaite, Ainsley	Member, 6:30 Shoppers	August 5, 1991
Byun, Chun Soo	Chair, Civil Rights Committee of the Korean Association of New York	September 2, 1992
Carson, Sonny	Flatbush Frontline Collective; chair, December 12th Movement	November 12, 1995
Celestin, Claude	Boycott participant; Radio Soleil employee	July 31, 1992
Cho, Milyoung	Committee Against Anti-Asian Violence	January 2, 1992

*The positions named indicate the interviewee's relationship to the boycott and / or capacity as expert and not necessarily his or her primary employment. This information is accurate for the time of the boycott (or, in a few cases, its aftermath) and not necessarily for the time of the interview. The interviews with Fitzgerald Lamont and Merle English were conducted by phone.

LIST OF INTERVIEWEES

Name	Position, Organization	Date of Interview
Choi, Christina	Deputy commissioner, Department of Employment, New York City	June 10, 1992
Chong, William	Chair, Asian Americans for Equality; Crisis Prevention Unit, State Division Of Human Rights	July 7, 1992
Choo, Jenny Sook Nam	Chair, Korean Americans for Social Concern	February 10, 1992
Clay, Omowale	Flatbush Frontline Collective; December 12th Movement	November 15, 1995
Cucinotta, Sharon	Church Avenue Merchants and Business Association	June 27, 1991
Daughtry, Herbert (Rev.)	House of the Lord Pentecostal Church	September 6, 1995
Desir, Philip Wilson	Flatbush Coalition for Economic Empowerment; Mayor's Committee	August 18, 1992
English, Merle	Staff writer, *New York Newsday*	August 6, 1992
Frank, Henry	Director, Haitian Centers Council	July 10, 1991
Green, Roger	Assemblyman, 57th District, Brooklyn; Coalition for Community Empowerment	March 13, 1992
Hahm, Michael (Rev.)	Cochair, Mayor's Committee	July 16, 1991
Han, Michael	Chair, Young Korean American Network	July 20, 1992
Haughton, Jim	Director, Harlem Fightback	January 22, 1992
Hornung, Rick	Staff writer, *Village Voice*	November 8, 1991
Huh, Christie	Korean American Coalition for Community Empowerment	April 15, 1992

Name	Position, Organization	Date of Interview
Ifill, Irwin	Director, Flatbush Workshop in Business Opportunities	February 19, 1992
Innis, Roy	Chair, Congress of Racial Equality	August 6, 1992
Izzo, Richard	Attorney for the Jangs	July 24, 1992
Kasinitz, Philip	Ph.D. candidate, New York University; researcher on Caribbean immigrants	December 2, 1991
Kharfan, Michael	Director, Community Assistance Unit	August 8, 1991
Kim, John	Civil Rights Committee of the Korean Association of New York	September 5, 1995
Kim, Paul (Rector)	Chair, Korean American Coalition for Community Empowerment	December 9, 1991
Kim, Sung Soo	President, Korean American Small Business Service Center	July 7, 1992
Kinzer, (Ms.)	Member, 6:30 Shoppers	July 31, 1991
Klempner, Joseph	Attorney for the Jangs	August 18, 1992
Koh, Kyung Ho	Chair, Coalition of Korean American Voters	June 29, 1992
Lamont, Fitzgerald	Boycott participant	April 13, 1992
Lee, Daniel	Civil Rights Committee of the Korean Association of New York	September 10, 1992
Lee, Virgo	Director, Mayor's Office on Asian American Affairs	October 29, 1991
Leid, Utrice	Managing editor, *City Sun*	April 4, 1992
Limb, Ben	Mayor's Committee	November 25, 1991
Liu, Mini	Cochair, Committee Against Anti-Asian Violence	January 10, 1992

LIST OF INTERVIEWEES

Name	Position, Organization	Date of Interview
Lyu-Volckhausen, Grace	Chair, African American / Korean American Alliance	April 16, 1992
Marin, Nancy	Member, 6:30 Shoppers	July 17, 1991
McQuillan, Michael	Office of Racial and Ethnic Affairs, Brooklyn borough president's office	July 1, 1991
Miller, Robert	Flatbush resident	July 21, 1992
Min, Pyong Gap	Civil Rights Committee of the Korean Association of New York; professor, Queens College, CUNY	August 17, 1992
Nicolas, Philius (Rev.)	Evangelical Crusade Church	October 17, 1991
O, Cao	Executive director, Asian American Federation	April 8, 1992
Pasanen, Glenn	African American / Korean American Alliance	September 18, 1992
Povman, Morton	Councilman, 24th District, Queens; acting chair, Committee on General Welfare, City Council of New York	August 20, 1992
Powell, Ed	Executive director, Umma; member, Community Board 14	July 22, 1992
Rosenberg, Mimi	Attorney, Legal Aid Society	April 10, 1992
Rubin, Gary	Director of national affairs, American Jewish Committee	October 17, 1991
Sa, B. J.	Secretary general, Korean Association of New York (KANY)	August 27, 1992
Sharpton, Al (Rev.)	Chair, National Youth Movement	September 13, 1995
Sherman, Robert	City Commission for Human Rights; staff, Mayor's Committee	July 19, 1991

Name	Position, Organization	Date of Interview
Simmons, Esmerelda	Director, Center for Law and Social Justice, Medgar Evers College, CUNY	November 20, 1991
Small, James	Professor, City College of New York; community activist	February 11, 1992
Smulyan, Betsy	Church Avenue Merchants and Business Association	July 15, 1991
(Unknown), Marie	Flatbush resident; member of Reverend Nicolas's congregation	January 29, 1992
Victor, Guy	Flatbush Coalition for Economic Empowerment; Flatbush Frontline Collective; Haitian Enforcement Against Racism	April 18, 1992
Vann, Al	Assemblyman, 56th District, Brooklyn; Coalition for Community Empowerment	July 20, 1995
Velez, Jose	Director, Flatbush Development Corporation	June 27, 1991
Walcott, Dennis	Director, New York Urban League	March 24, 1992
Wareham, Roger	Flatbush Frontline Collective; December 12th Movement	November 10, 1995
Weusi, Jitu	Chair, African Americans United for Political Power	August 30, 1995
Williams, Elaine	Director, Microloan Program, Economic Development Corporation	January 21, 1992
Williams, James	Flatbush Workshop in Business Opportunities	October 16, 1991

NOTES

Chapter 1: Exposing Racial Power

1. It bears repeating that the majority of those arrested for looting and other criminal activities during the Los Angeles rebellion of 1992 were in fact Latinos—mostly recent immigrants from Mexico and Central America. The media's preoccupation with Black-Korean conflict often obscured this fact.

2. I have chosen to use the terms "White dominance" (referring to a system of White advantage and privilege) and "racial power" (referring to the systematic tendency toward White dominance) rather than "racism" or "racial discrimination." In my view, the first two terms suggest systemic phenomena while the latter two suggest irrational prejudice on behavior or the part of individuals.

3. The Red Apple Boycott was also referred to as the Church Avenue Boycott and the Flatbush Boycott, alluding, respectively, to the street and the neighborhood where it occurred. The boycott actually lasted for well over a year, but most of the salient events took place in 1990.

4. A Brooklyn jury acquitted Bong Ok Jang of assault charges in January 1991.

5. In Chapter 4, I elaborate on the respective roles played by Black nationalist, Haitian, and Caribbean activists in the Red Apple Boycott. Note that these categories are overlapping rather than mutually exclusive. In this book, I focus primarily on Black nationalist activists of diverse national origins (African American, Haitian, Caribbean) and Haitian laypeople who participated in the boycott.

6. My argument is also applicable, with some modifications, to less organized events such as the Los Angeles rebellion of 1992. A substantial body of research indicates that most Blacks see urban rebellions as useful, legitimate, purposeful political activity (Eisinger 1976; Skolnick 1969).

7. Critical scholarship, whether conducted in mainstream departments, ethnic studies programs, or outside of the academy, self-consciously resists such cooptation, with varying degrees of success.

8. Middleman minority theorists originally sought to explain a distinct economic formation often found in feudal or colonial societies, in which racial or religious minorities concentrated in commercial niches, serving as middlemen between elites and masses (e.g., Jews in Europe, Asians in Africa, and the Chinese in Southeast Asia). For a general overview and summary of middleman minority theory, see Walter Zenner (1991). An important feature of this formation was the regular occurrence of conflict between the powerless masses and middleman minorities. During the 1980s, Edna Bonacich and colleagues explicitly applied the middleman minority theory to the study of Korean immigrant merchants in the postindustrial U.S. economy (Light and Bonacich 1988; Bonacich 1987; Bonacich and Jung 1982; Bonacich 1980). Pyong Gap Min's work continues this practice.

9. Lee talks about power, but he defines it quite narrowly (à la resource mobilization theory) as the material resources and mobilization capacity of a group *within given constraints*.

10. Heon Cheol Lee (1993) is one of the few scholars who distinguishes what he calls "conflict bases" from "conflict processes" with regard to Black-Korean conflict. He uses the resource mobilization approach to study the Red Apple Boycott as a social movement. I differ from Lee in three main respects. First, I take a social constructionist approach rather than a resource mobilization approach to collective action, and I do not think that the latter is adequate for understanding movements that have radical agendas and/or rely entirely on indigenous resources (Morris 1984; McAdam 1983). Second, I situate the Red Apple Boycott within a larger Black nationalist movement and the overall political landscape of New York City in the 1980s and early 1990s. Third, I elaborate a concept of racial power and conceptualize Black collective action as a response to the operation of racial power.

11. This echoes the collective behavior approach to collective action that held sway prior to the ascendance of resource mobilization theory in the 1970s.

12. The metaphor is Doug McAdam's (1983).

13. As mentioned in note 8 above, middleman minority theory addresses the formation and perpetuation of a certain kind of economic formation; host-middleman conflict is only one of its concerns. The racial scapegoating argument, on the other, hand, centrally addresses the venting of frustrations on any racially vulnerable group. For our purposes, these two perspectives are practically interchangeable, although they are analytically distinct.

14. Historically, the mainstream media and officialdom have depicted Black collective action as irrational and illegitimate (Feagin and Hahn 1973; Skolnick 1969). It was not only urban rebellions that were seen this way: the press depicted the civil rights movement as the work of troublemakers—especially during the movement's early stages and in the South. During the post–civil rights era, opinionmakers have routinely distinguished between integrationist protests (legitimate, constructive, and just) and nationalist outbursts (illegitimate, destructive, and unjust) in order to sanction the former and discourage the latter. It is worth noting that the great bulk of scholarly work on Black political activity since the 1970s has focused on electoral/conventional politics to the neglect of radical Black politics.

15. Edna Bonacich (1987, 1980, 1973) is unusual among middleman minority theorists for insisting that Black hostility is "reasonable" insofar as the interests of Blacks and Korean middlemen are objectively incompatible.

16. Although most Korean merchants think of themselves as Koreans/Korean Americans rather than as Asian Americans, Asian American advocacy groups adopt their issues as Asian American issues.

17. Of course, there are widespread genetic and phenotypical variations among human populations, but the construction of racial categories based on such variations and the investment of them with meaning is a social process. Once one is exposed to the social constructionist approach to race, one finds evidence of it everywhere—in the "one drop rule" concerning Blackness, in the shifting categories of the U.S. Census, in the manifest physical differences within all "racial" groups, etc.

18. Needless to say, there are other important axes of domination and power (such as class and gender) that overlap with and interact with race.

19. Here I am borrowing from Joe Feagin and Nikitah Imani (1994), where the authors dis-

cuss "cumulative, interlocking, and externally-amplified dimensions of discrimination" (562).

20. These ideas draw upon an earlier journal article of mine (Kim 1999).

21. Although I do not explicitly address the positioning of other groups (Latinos, American Indians, etc.) in this racial order, this is a decision of economy and not principle. The concepts I introduce here can be used to analyze the experiences of other groups as well. Since a truly robust account of the racial order would have to include more than the three groups discussed here, I invite the reader to think of this book as a preliminary investigation into this order.

22. Sonny Carson and other members of the December 12th Movement consistently refused to talk to academics researching the Red Apple Boycott (Lee 1993). For one thing, the group maintains a wary, defensive posture to thwart COINTELPRO-type tactics of repression. For another, group members have expressed skepticism about the ability of any Korean American to be impartial on the topic, and most researchers on this topic, including myself, have been Korean American. Without going into detail, suffice it to say that getting interviews with members of the December 12th Movement was a formidable challenge.

23. I employed a research assistant to search for articles about the boycott in selected Korean language newspapers and translate them into English.

Chapter 2: Racial Ordering

1. Filipinos were sometimes classified as "Malays," but they were also triangulated between Blacks and Whites. Chinese coming to Gold Rush California were the first Asian immigrants to be triangulated; the pattern was thereafter applied to subsequent streams of immigrants from other Asian nations.

2. I specify White "elites" because it was big businessmen rather than the White working class who benefited from the presence of Asian labor. Working-class Whites opposed the presence of Asian labor and played a crucial role in both the Chinese exclusion and Japanese exclusion movements.

3. My discussion of "colorblind talk" draws upon ideas articulated in Omi and Winant 1994; Bell 1992; and Gotanda 1991.

4. Klandermans (1992) identifies three interconnected levels of social construction in social movements: political culture, discourse, and collective action frame. My focus in this book is on the second and third levels, and the connection between them. As for political culture, colorblind talk is clearly rooted in the broader American political culture (i.e., in liberal-democratic or thought).

5. Although William Julius Wilson does not himself argue that racism has been eradicated in American society, his argument about "the declining significance of race" is frequently used by less precise observers to make just this point. It should be said that Wilson's work lends itself to this (mis?)appropriation. In *The Truly Disadvantaged* (1987), for instance, Wilson briefly mentions that racism might play a role in generating the urban underclass, but his entire substantive analysis concentrates on other (economic, social, and demographic) factors.

6. Here are a few examples of this trend. In *City of Richmond v. J. A. Croson Co.* (1989), the U.S. Supreme Court ruled that a "strict scrutiny" standard applied to remedial as well as

invidious racial classifications. In *Shaw v. Reno* (1993), Supreme Court Justice Sandra O'Connor, writing for the majority, stated, "Racial classifications of any sort pose the risk of lasting harm to our society." In the same opinion, Justice O'Connor compared the "balkaniz[ing]" impact of current redistricting efforts with that of past gerrymandering intended to disenfranchise Blacks. Advocates of California's Proposition 209, an anti–affirmative action ballot measure that passed in 1996, pitched the measure in the name of colorblindness and cited Martin Luther King Jr. as an authority for their cause.

7. The underclass myth is sometimes used to refer to Puerto Ricans as well as to Blacks. Again, my decision not to examine where other groups such as Latinos fit into the American racial order is one of economy and not principle. Many of the arguments that I make in this book can, I think, be applied, with appropriate modifications, to the experiences of Latinos and other groups.

8. See Adolph Reed Jr. (1992) for a cogent critique of the underclass myth.

9. It is precisely because they recognize the model minority myth as a rhetorical pillar of White dominance that scholars in Asian American Studies have denounced it for over a generation (Okihiro 1994; Hurh and Kim 1989; Suzuki 1989; Osajima 1988; Kim and Hurh 1983).

10. A recent ACORN (Association of Community Organizations for Reform Now) study of lending patterns by Manufacturers Hanover Trust (one of the largest banks in the city prior to its merger with Chemical Bank in the early 1990s) from 1985 to 1989 reads: "To the extent that MHT has made mortgage loans in New York City, a clear pattern of preference in lending to white applicants over blacks and non-whites is evident. Furthermore, the pattern of discrimination in lending appears to be a function of race only. In other words, low-income whites were better able to secure mortgage lending from MHT than were higher-income blacks and non-whites" (Valance, 1991a, 2). Another ACORN study of lending by all banks in the four largest boroughs of New York City (i.e., everywhere but Staten Island) during the same time period also found a "pervasive pattern of preference in lending to whites as against blacks and non-whites . . . [that was] a function of race and not of income" (Valance, 1991b, 2). A 1989 report by the federal Office of Thrift Supervision found that Black mortgage loan applications were rejected by savings and loans associations at twice the rates that White applications were rejected nationwide (Feagin 1994, 35). A 1991 Federal Reserve Board study demonstrated that Black and Latino applications for home mortgages were rejected at a higher percentage than those by Whites at all income levels during the fiscal years 1989 and 1990. According to this study, Black applicants faced a 29.4 percent rejection rate, whereas White applicants with the same income faced only a 15 percent rejection rate (*New York Amsterdam News*, February 1, 1992).

11. Despite the election of a Republican mayor once every several decades, the Democratic party is considered by most to be the main game in town. Although five parties have ballot lines (Democratic, Republican, Liberal, Conservative, and Right to Life), nearly 70 percent of registered voters register as Democrats, and only Democrats have a citywide structure of AD clubs and county party organizations (Mollenkopf 1992, 76). Each of the boroughs comprising New York City constitutes a county with its own Democratic party organization. The smallest units of party organization are the sixty New York State Assembly districts (ADs), which perform ward functions.

12. Having demonstrated that Black and Latino ADs (New York State Assembly districts) actually show higher registration rates than White ADs once youth and citizenship are taken into account, Mollenkopf argues that minority political power has lagged behind minority demographic presence because of both structural discrimination on the part of the political system and fragmentation among minority challengers (1991, 337–42). Mayor Koch worked hard to promote such fragmentation.

13. Koch's "flirtation with Republicanism blossomed into a courtship" when he received the party's endorsement for his 1981 mayoral race (Savitch 1990, 263).

14. In Manhattan, which was the only borough (or county) that lacked a viable political machine, Koch curried his own Black supporters and pointedly snubbed the Harlem-based Black political establishment in everything from political appointments to hospital closings.

15. Even prior to the 1977 mayoral primary runoff election with Mario Cuomo, Koch curried favor with Democratic regulars. During the 1982 gubernatorial race against Cuomo, Koch once again sought the support of the machine.

16. The increased availability of a third type of service sector job (relating to retail business) facilitated the economic adaptation of Korean immigrants in New York City and other major U.S. cities.

17. Let me briefly clarify the key differences between Roger Waldinger's approach and mine. First, Waldinger accepts racial categories as given while I adopt a social constructionist approach to race. Hence I pay attention to the ongoing reconstitution of racial categories and meanings as a crucial mechanism by which groups get differently positioned and treated. Second, Waldinger's notion of an ethnic queue applies specifically to the labor market, while my notion of a racial order applies more comprehensively to different aspects of life (residential, political, social, etc.).

18. Koch dismantled affirmative action hiring programs in city government and shifted equal employment monitoring from the City Commission for Human Rights to the Personnel Department, effectively making the latter self-monitoring. Even the Mayor's Talent Bank—a new computerized data base supposedly designed to foster affirmative action practices in municipal hiring—turned into a patronage mill, or, more precisely, "a computerized patronage-hiring system grafted onto an affirmative action program" (Mollenkopf 1992, 123). Rather than mitigating racial discrimination, the Mayor's Talent Bank helped ensure that only the right kind of minorities would be hired. Roger Waldinger points out: "By 1989, New York remained the only major city without a public sector affirmative action plan" (1996, 227).

19. Notwithstanding the claims of mismatch theorists, low Black male employment rates in New York City during the 1980s had less to do with the decline of manufacturing, in which Blacks were actually underrepresented, than with the loss of personal service jobs during the 1970s (Bailey and Waldinger 1991) and the persistence of racially discriminatory hiring and promotion practices in all sectors (Bailey 1989).

20. Labor force participation rates are more revealing than official unemployment rates because the latter overlook those who work part-time, are in job training, or are outside of the labor force altogether. Black men had very low labor force participation rates in New York City from 1985 to 1991. Black women had the highest rate of all women in the city during the 1980s; however, this edge was gone by 1991 (Rosenberg 1992, 19).

21. In the 1980s, Black municipal employees were largely segregated in low-paying city departments such as welfare, human services, health, and housing (Blank 1990). A 1989 report by the Community Service Society confirms that Whites held a disproportionate share of high-paying jobs in city government—both by occupying more jobs in high-paying departments such as police and fire and by occupying administrative / professional jobs in low-paying departments. In 1986, 80 percent of city employees earning less than $20,000 were Black or Latino, although these two groups together constituted 42 percent of the city's work force (*New York Times,* January 20, 1989).

22. See Paul Peterson (1981) for the argument that cities have to compete for industries via tax and regulatory incentives due to the increased mobility of capital associated with global restructuring; see John Logan and Harvey Molotch (1987) for a critique of this argument. Although progrowth ideology holds that economic growth benefits everyone and that cities have a "unitary" interest in local development, the fact is that growth produces clear winners and losers. Since economic restructuring is a global phenomenon, local executives have limited control over its effects: "The loci of pertinent decision-making are elsewhere—Congress, the White House, corporate board rooms, international currency markets, the Federal Reserve Board, etc." (Reed 1988, 152).

23. The story of the fiscal crisis of 1975–1977 is well known. The city's operating expense budget grew dramatically through the John Lindsay (1966–1973) and Abe Beame (1974–1977) years, regularly exceeding the city's revenues. Both mayors increased short-term borrowing to finance this budgetary gap. Lindsay initiated a moderate retrenchment program in city government, but Beame not only exaggerated expected revenues so as to balance the budget on paper, but also used the capital budget (financed from bond issues) to pay for current operating expenses. If these short-term measures and budgetary gimmicks made the city's financial status akin to a house of cards, the national recessions of 1969–1972 and 1973–1975 were the winds that came along and blew it down. Once the city's capacity to service its debt became dubious, the city's lenders closed down credit, prompting a full-blown fiscal crisis. The effects were immediate: the city lost one-sixth of its jobs and income during the economic slide that started in 1969, and the municipal payroll declined by 20 percent (sixty thousand jobs) between 1975 and 1977 alone (Mollenkopf 1992, 14). In an unprecedented move, the state government placed the city in political receivership, subjecting the city's affairs to direct oversight by state officials and corporate leaders. To fulfill the conditions of federal aid, the state also took over the administration of CUNY, paid most of the city's court and corrections systems costs, and increased its share of Medicaid coverage (Netzer 1990). Two organizations were formed to manage this oversight: the Municipal Assistance Corporation (MAC) and the Emergency Financial Control Board. Municipal union leaders were formally included in this process as well, although their power was arguably more symbolic than real. As a "profound consciousness-raising experience with regard to perceptions about the vulnerability of the local economy" (Netzer 1990, 53), the fiscal crisis had clear political ramifications. It left voters hungry for strong financial stewardship. Koch's 1977 campaign slogan addressed this yearning: "After eight years of charisma (Lindsay) and four years of the clubhouse (Beame), why not try competence?"

24. After 1983, Koch increased funding for nonprofit social service providers but continued to reduce spending on directly redistributive programs (Mollenkopf 1992, 7).

25. Figures are adjusted for inflation.

26. These racial/ethnic categories are mutually exclusive. Terry Rosenberg, who adopts the federal definition of poverty, uses data from the 1980 Census and the Current Population Surveys from 1985–1988 and 1991. The reader will of course note that Latinos have even higher poverty rates than Blacks according to Table 2.2. Puerto Ricans, perhaps the poorest of Latino groups, make up the majority of Latinos in New York City. A comparison of Black and Latino poverty rates in Miami (where most Latinos are relatively affluent Cuban Americans) would look quite different.

27. Despite this rhetoric, the report's recommendations on job training, employment, education, and economic development were uncontroversial. The report did not impress Black leaders, who saw it as a transparent public relations ploy on the part of Mayor Koch. Reverend Calvin Butts III of the Abyssinian Baptist Church in Harlem commented: "Mayor Koch is a very astute player in the game of racial politics . . . [Next] he'll probably find a Black pulpit to visit. Whenever he's in trouble, he runs to a Black church" (*New York Times*, December 18, 1988). The report produced no reforms or initiatives on the part of the city. A few years after the report's release, Elvin Montgomery, who had worked as an advisor to the Commission on Black New Yorkers, said,"The outcome of our study was a big fat zero. The city put it on a shelf and did nothing" (*New York Newsday*, June 15, 1990).

28. This discussion of the racialization of Haitian immigrants in the United States can be extended, with modifications, to the racialization of all Caribbean immigrants to the United States. Again, while there was Caribbean participation in the Red Apple Boycott, I focus in this book on Haitians, since they were the principal national origin/immigrant group constituting the mass base of the boycott.

29. This discussion draws heavily on Flore Zéphir 1996. See pp. 27–31 for a description of racial hierarchy in the French colony Saint-Domingue, which later became Haiti.

30. Haitians usually live in segregated Black areas in New York City. The largest Haitian concentrations are found in Brooklyn, Queens, and Manhattan, with working-class and low-income Haitians tending to settle in Brooklyn—Flatbush in particular (Zéphir 1996, 8).

31. Stephen Steinberg offers a persuasive critique of the Horatio Alger trope in his book *The Ethnic Myth: Race, Ethnicity, and Class in America* (1981).

32. Robert Boyd (1990) shows that Asian immigrant entrepreneurs do not push Blacks from entrepreneurial niches; Ivan Light and Angel Sanchez (1987) demonstrate that the presence of Asian immigrants lowers neither the rate of Black entrepreneurs in a given area nor the rate of returns for Black entrepreneurs.

33. In-Jin Yoon (and the original Census data that he draws on) distinguishes "African Americans" from various Black immigrant groups. To reduce terminological confusion, I refer to African Americans as Blacks in this table.

34. See note 10 above.

35. The first study was conducted by Interface, an independent research organization. The second study was conducted by National Economic Research Associates, Inc., and commissioned by the newly elected Mayor David Dinkins. Abraham May Jr., an official in the city's Office of Business Development under Mayor Edward Koch, pointed out that Koch's studied indifference toward Black-owned businesses shaped the city bureaucracy's approach to them during his three administrations: "It's benign arrogance. Be-

cause the mayor does not believe in set-asides, the commissioners tend not to care either" (Beschloss and McNatt 1989, 31).

36. There was only minimal Korean immigration to the United States prior to 1965 (Yoon 1997, 49–54).

37. Other factors prompting Korean emigration are the severe competition to gain entry into college and the high cost of college tuition in Korea (Yoon 1997, 76). Kyeyoung Park notes that immigrants consider it more acceptable to say that they are migrating for the sake of their children's education than to say they want to make more money (1997, 32).

38. For a more complete discussion of civic ostracism, see Kim (1999).

39. Korean residential patterns in New York City are fairly dispersed. Seventy percent of Koreans live in Queens, 9.5 percent in Brooklyn, 8.9 percent in Manhattan, 7.0 percent in the Bronx, and 4.2 percent in Staten Island (Min 1996, 38). Newly arrived immigrants tend to settle initially in Queens.

40. Median family income figures are frequently misleading. Historically, they have been used to suggest that Asian Americans as a whole are better off than Whites and to shore up the model minority myth. However, median family income figures distort the reality of Asian American economic well-being because they do not take into account such factors as household size, number of working household members, areal variations in the cost of living, and differences among Asian American subgroups. Some of these same distortions may be at work in the figures cited here.

41. Personal interview with S. Kim.

42. Compared with some European nations, the U.S. government poses few barriers to immigrant entrepreneurship via labor market policy (Aldrich and Waldinger 1990, 121–22).

43. Discrimination against Asian Americans in the workplace, ranging from wage discrimination to the "glass ceiling" phenomenon, has been well documented. See U.S. Civil Rights Commission (1992).

44. Small business ownership has not shielded Korean immigrants from all forms of White employment-related discrimination. Min (1996) gives examples of Jewish and Italian produce wholesalers in New York City using unfair pricing practices and uttering racial slurs against Korean merchants. By the mid-1980s, Korean dominance over the produce retail business had discouraged such practices.

45. Typically, Korean-owned stores are either located in ethnic "enclaves" (dense concentrations of businesses owned by members of a single racial/ethnic group, such as Koreatown in Los Angeles or Flushing, Queens) or dispersed in White, Latino, and especially Black neighborhoods.

46. In-Jin Yoon (1997, 44) distinguishes among Korean immigrants' ethnic resources (money, information, training, customs, labor, suppliers, and networks), class resources (private property such as education or wealth), and family resources (money and labor). Recent research has placed particular emphasis on class resources (Bates 1994a, 1994b).

47. This capital usually comes from savings, kyes, friends and family, or some combination of these.

48. An informal survey conducted by the Korean American Small Business Service Center in New York City in 1986 found that 35.2 percent of Korean merchant respondents were U.S. citizens and that 55.7 percent were U.S. residents. Reliable data on naturalization rates is notoriously difficult to come by.

49. None of the Korean merchants operating stores on Church Avenue at the time of the boycott had used bank loans to start up their businesses. They relied instead on family, friends, other Korean businessmen, and kyes (Lee 1993, 109). Min (1996) found that only 5.8 percent of his Korean merchant respondents in New York City used commercial loans as the main source of start-up capital.

50. The Korean Produce Association of New York, which played a leadership role within the Korean community during the Red Apple Boycott, was initially founded in order to plan store locations so as to reduce competition among Korean merchants.

Chapter 3: Black Power Resurgent

1. There are four types of frame alignment. From the least transformative to the most transformative, they are: frame bridging, frame amplification, frame expansion, and frame transformation (Snow et al. 1986, 467).

2. I developed the concept of frame repertoires with the historical tradition of Black nationalism in mind, but the concept can be applied to other groups who maintain a strong, coherent collective identity over time. These are often persistently marginalized groups.

3. See L. P. Gerlach and V. H. Hine (1970) for a discussion of the "split-level" nature of ideology in the Black Power movement of the 1960s (one level reflected common ground among movement groups, the other reflected differences among them).

4. For discussions of Black nationalism, see James Jennings (1992), William Van Deburg (1992), Alphonso Pinkney (1976), John Bracey et al. (1970), Robert Allen (1969), Floyd Barbour (1968), and Nathan Hare (1968).

5. As Benedict Anderson (1991) reminds us, all nations, established and envisioned, are "imagined communities." Moreover, nationalisms need not be intellectually rigorous or coherent in order to be politically potent.

6. See John McCartney (1992) for an overview of what he calls "black power ideologies."

7. Stokely Carmichael and Charles Hamilton's (1967) definition of Black Power as a group closing ranks before entering society is quite well known, yet many have criticized this definition as too reformist, moderate, and bourgeois (Allen 1969). Carmichael himself (later known as Kwame Touré) moved toward a more radical (revolutionary nationalist) definition of Black Power shortly after coauthoring the book with Hamilton.

8. The slogan "Black Power" became popular after Stokely Carmichael, the head of SNCC (Student Nonviolent Coordinating Committee), used it in a speech in Mississippi on June 16, 1966: "The only way we gonna stop them white men from whuppin' us is to take over. We been saying freedom for six years and we ain't got nothin'. What we gonna start saying now is Black Power!" (cited in Sellers 1973, 166–67). At the time, Carmichael was participating in the "March Against Fear" from Memphis to Jackson, undertaken to show support for James Meredith, a civil rights veteran who had integrated the University of Mississippi in 1962 and had been shot by a White sniper in early June 1966. The long-simmering tensions among the major civil rights leadership organizations were breaking out in the open by 1966 as SNCC and CORE (Congress of Racial Equality) openly espoused Black Power and repudiated the integrationist agenda.

9. The gap between Black and White opinions was quite evident on the issue of Black Power. Blacks tended to interpret Black Power favorably as a call for Black empower-

ment, while Whites interpreted it unfavorably as a call for Black supremacy. Black civil rights leaders were often as wary of the slogan as Whites (Aberbach and Walker 1970).

10. Although community control has come to mean something specific in the Black community, it is a general notion that is sometimes used to refer to administrative decentralization and grassroots decision making.

11. CORE, SNCC, the Black Panther Party, the National Urban League, and the NAACP (National Association for the Advancement of Colored People) all espoused community control in the late 1960s, although each group interpreted the repertoire frame in its own distinctive way.

12. Scholars disagree on whether the community-based antipoverty initiatives of the 1960s and 1970s fostered or impeded the development of Black political leadership in New York City. Charles Hamilton (1990) argues that these initiatives depoliticized Blacks by placing them on the powerless end of a "patron-client relationship" with the state. David Eichenthal, on the other hand, argues that "community-based antipoverty programs became training grounds for a new generation of Black and Latino leaders" (1990, 63).

13. Personal interview with Weusi.

14. Harlem, the historical seat of Black political power in the city, has been home to both moderate machine "pols" and nationalists like Marcus Garvey and Malcolm X throughout the twentieth century. With the growth of Brooklyn's Black population since the 1960s, some observers have noted a bifurcation between Black politics in Harlem (moderate, old-guard, institutionally oriented) and Black politics in Brooklyn (nationalist, brash, militant, outside of the system). While there is some truth to this distinction, it should not be overstated. Brooklyn has its share of Black regulars and Harlem has its share of radical activists.

15. Democrats have been the majority party in the New York State Assembly since the 1960s and members from New York City play an important leadership role within this legislative body. The state government initiates many policies that affect the city, and state aid constitutes a significant portion of the city's expense budget (Eichenthal 1990; Benjamin 1990).

16. Personal interview with Weusi.

17. Al Vann was the statewide coordinator and David Dinkins the Manhattan coordinator for Jesse Jackson's 1984 presidential campaign.

18. Unless otherwise noted, New York City election results are given by AD type (Black, mixed minority, Latino, liberal, Catholic, and outer-borough Jewish), following standard practice.

19. A moderate out of the Carver Democratic Club in Harlem, David Dinkins had held several patronage jobs, such as the head of the Board of Elections and city clerk. In 1973, Mayor Abe Beame appointed him deputy mayor, but Dinkins's failure to file income taxes the year before prevented him from taking the position. In 1977, Dinkins ran for Manhattan borough president and lost badly. In 1981, he ran again and fell short of victory by just 1 percent of the vote. In 1985, he won with 91 percent of the Black vote, 79 percent of the Latino vote, and 50 percent of the White vote (Arian et al. 1991, 39). Note that these figures reflect the popular vote, not votes by AD type.

20. Limited street protests occurred throughout Koch's reign. The Brooklyn-based Black United Front (BUF), founded by Reverend Herbert Daughtry, Jitu Weusi, Al Vann, and

Sam Pinn in the late 1970s to fight police brutality against Blacks, was at the helm of many of these protests. Three separate incidents—the police killings of fifteen-year-old Randolph Evans and businessman Arthur Miller and the attack on young Victor Rhodes by a Hasidic patrol in Crown Heights—prompted the formation of the BUF Constituent groups included Reverend Daughtry's House of the Lord, Black Veterans for Social Justice, Brooklyn CORE, and The East, a Brooklyn-based cultural nationalist organization founded and directed by Jitu Weusi. (In 1990, Black Veterans for Social Justice joined another ad hoc organization—The Flatbush Coalition for Economic Empowerment—that was briefly in charge of the Red Apple Boycott.) As Daughtry puts it, he wanted the BUF to be "a house big enough for everybody to hang their coat" (personal interview with Daughtry). The BUF was a classic "abeyance" organization that sustained Black nationalist activism during a politically inhospitable period (Taylor 1989; Rupp and Taylor 1987). During the winter of 1978, the BUF organized "Black Christmas," a boycott and picketing campaign intended to pressure downtown Brooklyn stores to establish a Randy Evans Memorial Scholarship for Black youth. In Daughtry's view, community control meant that institutions profiting from Black spending should give something back to the Black community. The BUF survived until the mid-1980s, when Daughtry left to form the African People's Christian Organization.

21. A master frame characterizes an entire movement, while specific collective action frames characterize individual campaigns within that movement (Snow and Benford 1992).

22. The FBI's counterintelligence programs (or COINTELPROs) used burglary, unauthorized surveillance and wiretapping, informants and agents provocateurs, bogus mail, disinformation campaigns, fabricated evidence, and even assassinations to decimate the Black Power movement of the 1960s (Churchill and Van der Wall 1988).

23. Personal interview with Daughtry.

24. According to *New York Newsday* (April 13, 1988), 47 percent of Blacks polled in New York City reported that the Black media were one of the sources they relied on for news, and 23.5 percent said that they were their most important source (cited in Moss and Ludwig 1991, 254).

25. According to one survey conducted from September 24 to December 16, 1988, WLIB had an (overwhelmingly Black) audience of about 30,400 people during every fifteen-minute period (*New York Times*, January 22, 1988). Black talk radio received a flurry of Black media and mainstream media attention in the late 1980s and early 1990s. See Karen Carillo, "The Politics of Black Talk Radio," *New York Amsterdam News*, February 29, 1992; Karen Carillo, "New York's Black Talk Radio: Voices of Cultural Resistance," *New York Amsterdam News*, February 22, 1992; William Schmidt, "Black Talk Radio: A Vital Force Is Emerging to Mobilize Opinion," *New York Times*, March 31, 1989; and E. R. Shipp, "WLIB: Radio 'Heartbeat' of Black Life," *New York Times*, January 22, 1988. Around the time of the boycott, attorney Colin Moore, who represented Ghiselaine Felissaint in cases relating to her altercation with Bong Ok Jang, did a twice-monthly radio show on WLIB called "Making It Legal." Reverend Al Sharpton appeared on WLIB to communicate with the Black community when the FBI informant story broke.

26. Personal interview with Daughtry.

27. The citywide poll surveyed 1047 people (including 484 Whites and 408 Blacks) by telephone. Blacks were first sampled at a higher rate, then weighted to reflect their actual

proportion of the city's population. The error rate is plus or minus three percentage points for results based on the entire sample.

28. Reported in *New York Newsday* (April 15, 1988), this poll surveyed 759 Black households by telephone in February 1988. The unprecedented level of Caribbean immigration to New York City during the 1980s helped to expand the movement's potential mass base. New York City has the single largest concentration of Caribbean immigrants in the United States (Massey and Denton 1993, 114). Excluding illegal immigrants, the city's Caribbean-born population increased by 127.5 percent during the 1980s (Mollenkopf 1993, 8), reaching almost one million in 1987 (Kasinitz 1992). Although many Caribbean immigrants were not eligible or registered to vote, they were clearly potential movement constituents, especially given their resource profile. While earlier waves of Caribbean immigrants were relatively well-off, highly skilled, and educated, those arriving in New York City during the 1980s tended to be poorer, less skilled, and uneducated. It is no accident that leaders of the resurgent Black Power movement in New York City often made allusions to heroes of Caribbean descent such as Marcus Garvey and Malcolm X.

29. Although individuals from all racial groups expressed outrage at the killing, Blacks were more likely than Whites to perceive a pattern of ongoing racially motivated violence against Blacks.

30. The reporter's query seemed to confirm Black activists' claims that New York City had an apartheid system akin to that in South Africa. For them, the analogy to South Africa was multivalent: first, it called on a Black diasporic perspective and internationalized the Black American struggle; second, it suggested (following Malcolm X) that America's treatment of Blacks constituted a human rights problem—something few White Americans wanted to hear.

31. While the overwhelming majority of participants in the post–Howard Beach marches were Black, some Latinos, Whites, and Asian Americans participated as well.

32. Carson's suggestion for a boycott slogan emphasized this historical referent: "Black folks don't buy and die where you can't live and work."

33. Some Black moderates were openly critical of the resurgent Black Power movement. Hazel Dukes, president of the New York City chapter of the NAACP, conveyed her opinion of the activists: "We [the NAACP] don't have time to be calling press conferences, whooping and hollering. The record is clear, we have freed a whole lot of people" (*New York Times*, January 10, 1988). On the other hand, Ben Chavis, who would later become the national executive director of the NAACP, participated in some movement protests.

34. Personal interview with Sharpton.

35. Personal interview with Brath.

36. Members of the December 12th Movement named the organization to commemorate an important march during this period.

37. Sonny Carson has been a public figure in New York City since the late 1960s, when he led Brooklyn CORE and participated in the Ocean Hill-Brownsville school decentralization conflict of 1968. In 1974, Carson was acquitted of attempted murder but convicted of second-degree kidnapping. Sentenced to prison in early 1975, he was released in September 1977. According to Carson, he had made a citizen's arrest of a man he had caught stealing precious African artifacts from him. Since that time, mainstream news coverage of Carson has typically referred to him as "a convicted kidnapper."

38. Patrice Lumumba was the late revolutionary leader of Zaire.

39. The New York Eight grew out of a 1970s group called Mobilization Committee Against Police Brutality. In October 1984, four hundred police officers raided the members' homes and claimed to have found dynamite and weapons intended for use in a planned jailbreak of two men then serving time for a 1981 fatal robbery of a Brinks armored car. New York Eight members were convicted of weapons possession and given probation, while they were acquitted of the more serious charges of conspiracy to rob banks and carry out a jailbreak. According to group members, they had acquired light weapons for self-defense purposes, and the dynamite and heavy weapons were planted by Howard Bonds, a group member turned informer (*Daily News,* July 12, 1987). The New York Eight were: Roger Wareham, Omowale Clay, Viola Plummer, Robert Taylor, Ruth Carter, Yvette Kelly, Collette Pean, and Coltrane Chimurenga. Viola Plummer is one of the most prominent female Black activists in New York City. She and other former New York Eight members run the Harriet Tubman-Fannie Lou Hamer Collective, a women's group and constituent organization of the December 12th Movement.

40. Personal interview with Brath.

41. See Tony Martin (1983) for a historical treatment of Pan-Africanism.

42. Guyana-born attorney Colin Moore, who served as counsel to Ghiselaine Felissaint in cases relating to her altercation with Bong Ok Jang, also handles these types of cases. He serves a largely Caribbean clientele in central Brooklyn.

43. The jury consisted of six Whites, three Asian Americans, two Latinos, and one Black.

44. This quote from Daughtry and those in the following section are drawn from a personal interview.

45. See below (section entitled "Social Control, Koch Style").

46. Personal interview with Clay.

47. Personal interview with Weusi.

48. See below (section entitled "Social Control, Koch Style").

49. Personal interview with Carson.

50. For discussion of internal resources used during the civil rights movement, see Doug McAdam (1983) and Aldon Morris (1984).

51. The second Day of Outrage occurred on December 21, 1987. Five hundred marchers disrupted rush hour traffic in Manhattan and paralyzed four Brooklyn subway lines by pulling the emergency stop cords, holding the doors open, and laying down on the subway platforms. Reverends Herbert Daughtry and Al Sharpton were arrested for standing on the subway tracks and charged with obstructing governmental administration. In another Day of Outrage in January 1988, two hundred people marched on the United Nations Plaza in midtown Manhattan to declare their solidarity with Palestinians and South African Blacks. Another Day of Outrage followed the Bensonhurst killing, which is described below.

52. James Earl Ray was the White man convicted of assassinating Martin Luther King Jr.

53. All of the December 12th Movement's four major boycotts were conducted against Korean-owned stores. Although the first two, which occurred in Harlem in 1980 and 1984, actually preceded the mass mobilization phase of the resurgent Black Power movement and the formation of the December 12th Movement, they were led by Sonny Carson and other future members of this organization. The two later boycotts, the Tropic

Fruits Boycott of 1988 in Bedford-Stuyvesant and the Red Apple Boycott of 1990 in Flatbush, drew upon and in turn contributed to the full momentum of the resurgent Black
Power movement.

54. Roger Wareham received a J.D. from Columbia University, taught for a time at the
Medgar Evers College Center for Law and Social Justice, CUNY, in Brooklyn, and is a
practicing criminal defense attorney. Coltrane Chimurenga, another December 12th
Movement member, attended Harvard University. Jitu Weusi, who has taught at Vassar
College and the John Jay College of Criminal Justice in New York City, is an adjunct professor of African American Studies at New York Technical College. Elombe Brath is a
graphic artist and researcher for a major television broadcasting company. Omowale
Clay has also worked as a graphic artist. Attorney C. Vernon Mason received his undergraduate degree from Morehouse College in Atlanta, his M.B.A. from Indiana University, and his J.D. from Columbia Law School.

55. Personal interview with Weusi.

56. If Koch thought of former New York Eight members as criminals, they explain their own
actions—including their trial for weapons possession and criminal conspiracy—with reference to an explicitly political agenda: "The strategic objective of the NY 8+'s political
trial was always subordinated to the strategic aim of the long march of revolutionary
war for socialism by the toiling Black Nation. Therefore winning or losing the trial was
not defined by the subjective outcome of sentencing the defendants, but rather what
were broader, higher goals and strategic objectives . . . The trial became a political forum
for the NY 8+ to conduct three to four months of political education around the rise of
fascism, its characters, form and the essence of its open attack against revolutionaries"
(*Arm the Masses,* October 1991).

57. Also during this period, Sharpton's reputation was tarnished when a grand jury found
that one of his clients, Tawana Brawley, had fabricated rape allegations against numerous White officials.

58. Badjacketing involves identifying an activist who has refused to inform on his colleagues
as an informer in order to create dissension and mistrust among activists (Churchill and
Van der Wall 1988).

59. Personal interview with Wareham.

60. In 1986, federal prosecutors swept through the Bronx and Queens Democratic organizations, charging numerous members of each with extensive corruption. Donald Manes,
the Queens party leader, committed suicide. As the prosecutions dragged on, the city's
mainstream media inundated the populace with news about the scandals. Eventually,
the Bronx Democratic organization, once the city's most powerful, became a political
"wasteland" (Wade 1990, 284). As a self-proclaimed champion of the city's machine,
Mayor Koch was clearly damaged politically by these scandals.

61. A campaign finance reform law passed that year handicapped incumbent Mayor Koch
by limiting primary campaign expenditures to $3.6 million and individual donations to
$3,000.

62. Since 1969, New York state law has required a runoff between the two top vote-getters in
a primary election for citywide office if no single candidate receives at least 40 percent of
the vote. This provision is intended to increase the probability of choosing a candidate
who can win the general election.

63. According to Herbert Haines (1988), radicals usually exert positive and negative "flank effects" on moderates simultaneously, thereby raising the important question of "net effect."

64. Eugene "Bull" Connor was the notoriously racist White police commissioner of Birmingham, Alabama, at the time of the civil rights movement. Connor's violent social control tactics against civil rights protesters in 1963 drew national condemnation and, ironically, promoted the civil rights movement's legislative agenda.

65. The other contenders were City Comptroller Harrison Goldin and Richard Ravitch, the former head of the Metropolitan Transit Authority.

66. Personal interview with Daughtry.

67. In 1989, Jews constituted about 30 percent of the Democratic primary electorate in New York City and 18 percent of the city's general electorate.

68. Votes for the Conservative, Liberal, and Right to Life ballot lines are not reported.

Chapter 4: The Red Apple Boycott

1. African Americans, Haitians, and Caribbeans could all be found in the boycott leadership and participant pool. In this book I focus primarily on native-born Blacks (whatever their descent) and Haitian immigrants. Although Caribbean immigrants played a role in the boycott, their participation is not explicitly highlighted here. This is a decision of economy, not principle.

2. It is typical for movement leaders to carry forward lessons from previous campaigns. The Southern Christian Leadership Conference and SNCC, for example, took lessons they had learned from the Albany Movement of 1961–1963 and applied them in the Birmingham protests of 1963, which made the latter a resounding success.

3. Carmichael and Hamilton write: "If a merchant wants customers from a black community, he must be made to understand that he has to contribute to that community. If he chooses not to do so, he will not be patronized . . . [Merchants should] also be made to understand that they face a boycott if they do not donate to the Black community" (1967, 172–173).

4. Community boards are the lowest level of government in New York City. The community board system, which took its present form in 1977, is a watered-down version of political and administrative decentralization experiments conducted in the 1960s. The city's fifty-nine community boards are "designed to facilitate more local planning and coordinated service delivery than are likely in a governmental structure composed of centralized and functionally specialized agencies" (Rogers 1990, 161). In theory, they serve as intermediaries between the public and city agencies on the issues of land use, zoning, service delivery, and community welfare. In practice, they handle complaints and requests about city services, recommend capital and expense budget priorities for the board districts, review zoning and land-use matters, and process applications for special events. Each board's fifty members are appointed rather than elected: City Council members from the area nominate half of the members, and the borough president makes all final appointment decisions. In 1988, only three of Community Board 14's fifty members were Black. By 1990, the number had risen to eleven, but this was still only 22 percent of the board's membership. Whites comprised only 38 percent of Community District 14's population in 1990, yet the chairman, the district manager, and thirty-nine of the board

members were White. Demographic flows had clearly outrun the pace of political succession.

5. *Rashomon* tells the tale of a rape / amorous encounter from the various perspectives of participants and observers. It is a discourse on the perspectival nature of reality.

6. The rumor was false. The hospital report showed that Felissaint was treated for a facial scratch, although she claimed that her injuries were more serious than the report indicated. Historically, exaggerated rumors have played an important role in galvanizing crowds and sparking collective action. This suggests a certain readiness among subordinated groups to credit accounts about the unjust or abusive behavior of the dominant group.

7. For background information on and detailed descriptions of the two boycotted stores, see Heon Cheol Lee (1993, 72–74).

8. My discussion here is partly based on personal interviews with Victor and Desir.

9. This estimate of crowd size is taken from a 70th Precinct police report dated February 6, 1990.

10. Despite Bong Ok Jang's objections, the police mistakenly charged his brother instead. The case of mistaken identity was not cleared up for several months (see Timeline).

11. Again, this estimate is taken from a 70th Precinct police report dated February 6, 1990.

12. Felissaint, who did not participate in the boycott at any time, expressed confusion and bewilderment over the conflict that grew out of her altercation with Jang. Her husband attended a few meetings held by boycotters but then dropped out.

13. Personal interview with Celestin. Celestin lived close to the two boycotted stores and had shopped at the Family Red Apple (the store had a different name before Bong Jae Jang purchased it in the late 1980s) for eleven years.

14. A sustained boycott and picketing campaign, unlike a march, requires the formation of a semipermanent leadership body.

15. Personal interview with Albert.

16. Creating a new organization helped to draw non–December 12th Movement activists into a working coalition and to convey the image of an entirely indigenous protest.

17. Personal interview with Wareham.

18. I rely on Jitu Weusi as a source of information here, since neither Haitians nor December 12th Movement members wanted to discuss tensions within the Flatbush Frontline Collective.

19. Michael Kharfan, head of the Community Assistance Unit, one of the city entities charged with trying to mediate the boycott, suggested the latter theory to me in a personal interview.

20. On the one hand, many Blacks feel that Korean merchants as a group tend to disrespect Black customers, and thus harbor ongoing and vague grievances against them. On the other hand, many Blacks feel acute and actionable grievances against particular merchants who have allegedly been abusive to Black customers on specific occasions. The second type of grievance taps into and is fueled by the former. Although Sonny Carson threatened to extend the boycott to other Korean stores in the city (as retaliation for the support they showed to Manho Park and Bong Jae Jang), he never followed through on the threat. It is worth noting that other Korean-owned produce stores located near Fam-

ily Red Apple and Church Fruits did well during the boycott and picked up much of the business lost by these two stores.

21. From the transcript of the public hearing held in Flatbush in June 1990 by the Mayor's Committee investigating the boycott. See Chapter 6 for a discussion of the Mayor's Committee and its final report on the boycott.

22. Personal interview with Albert.

23. To prove that they were more interested in doing for themselves than in asking the city for help, the December 12th Movement set up the African People's Farmers Market, a sidewalk produce stand, in late January 1990. The market, which originated during the Tropic Fruits Boycott of 1988, had been a regular weekend presence in Bedford-Stuyvesant since then. In 1990, it was set up in Flatbush every Saturday from 8:00 a.m. to 6:00 p.m. just blocks from the two stores. Overall, the market made a modest net profit during both boycotts (1988 and 1990). The funds helped defray the costs of maintaining a picket line (flyers, bullhorns, phone calls, etc.).

24. The flyer refers to *Dred Scott v. Sanford* (1857), in which the U.S. Supreme Court declared that no Negro, free or slave, could be a citizen. See Chapter 6 for a discussion of the fifty-feet court order.

25. Personal interview with Clay.

26. Dessalines, a slave who became one of Toussaint L'Ouverture's lieutenants (and later a general), is considered one of the founders of the Haitian nation. Malcolm X, of course, was of Caribbean descent.

27. Some Haitian immigrants, convinced of their superiority to American Blacks (whom they learn about via the American media in Haiti), respond to racial discrimination in the United States by breaking racial ranks and "evok[ing] symbols of French culture and Haitian history to distinguish themselves from black Americans and elicit favorable responses from whites" (Stafford 1987, 149). As one of Zéphir's informants said, "I may not go so far as displaying a Haitian flag in front of my window, but I want people to know that I am Haitian, not to expose onself to be in a state of inferiority" (1996, 45). Unsurprisingly, this practice of active dissociation offends many native-born Blacks.

28. According to Susan Buchanan Stafford, people from the same town in Haiti often live in residential pockets in New York City (1987, 140). According to a 1987 survey conducted in Haitian churches and community centers in New York City, 91 percent of those surveyed had sent remittances to relatives in Haiti during the past year (Dewind 1987, cited in Glick Schiller 1995).

29. Following the French model, Haiti's government consists of nine administrative departments. By creating the "Tenth Department," Aristide gave symbolic recognition to the role that Haitian emigrants have always played in Haitian affairs.

30. Carlos Montrevil, testifying in front of the Mayor's Committee at the public hearing held in Flatbush in June 1990.

31. Personal interview with Celestin.

32. On the interweaving of Haitian transnational and racial identities: Philip Wilson Desir, one of the early organizers of the Red Apple Boycott and a member of the Mayor's Committee investigating the boycott, later became the Haitian consul general in the United States.

33. Personal interview with Victor. Malcolm X popularized the house slave/field slave trope through his speeches.

34. Personal interview with Victor. The ban on Haitian blood products was rescinded in December 1990.

35. As of 1990, Lamont had lived in Flatbush for over ten years and many of his friends and relatives still lived there. Lamont chose to participate in the boycott personally rather than pursue mediation in his professional capacity, as a staff worker at the City Commission for Human Rights.

36. Many boycott opponents sought to delegitimate the protest by claiming that the December 12th Movement were "outsiders" because they were based in Bedford-Stuyvesant, Brooklyn. For boycott leaders, the relevant question was whether the group was inside or outside of the Black nation. The boundaries of this "imagined community" were more important than the geographical outlines of Flatbush or any other neighborhood.

37. Every Black person I interviewed, without exception, recounted that he or she or a friend or family member had been mistreated by a Korean merchant on at least one occasion. This finding is confirmed by countless newspaper stories, roundtables, talk shows, etc. As for nationwide Black attitudes on community control, 56 percent of respondents in the 1984 National Black Election Survey supported the idea of "shopping in Black-owned stores whenever possible" (Tate 1993, 155).

38. The total N for this poll was 1018, and the error rate for the total sample was plus or minus 3 percent.

39. Pyong Gap Min's poll did not include Asians or Hispanics.

40. Murray Edelman's comments on opinion polls are on point here: "Because opinion is constructed and volatile, all indicators of it are problematic. Poll reports are therefore another device for the reduction of ambiguity to clarity. Polled individuals are abstracted both from their everyday lives and from political discussion and action shared with others. Their opinions are therefore also abstract—not necessarily related to any course they would pursue when involved in political activities different from answering an interviewer" (1964, 207–08).

41. It is very likely that movement leaders were willing to criticize the boycott to an outsider like me because I was interviewing them well after the boycott had ended.

42. Private individuals also expressed their opposition to the boycott from a "colorblind" perspective. As mentioned above, Erasmus Hall High School teacher Fred McCray became a mainstream media hero when in the name of integrationism he led fifty of his students across the picket line to shop in the Family Red Apple store in May 1990. The mainstream media also widely reported the story about an anonymous Black Flatbush resident who sent Bong Jae Jang a one-hundred-dollar bill and a letter stating, "I cannot apologize for the treatment my brothers and sisters are giving to my Korean brothers. Instead, I can only suffer, I can only feel pain as my Korean brothers and sisters feel . . . I only ask that you truly feel forgiveness in your heart."

43. CORE's philosophy as of 1990 was a confusing amalgam of conservative Black nationalism and integrationism, reflecting the organization's winding historical trajectory. On the one hand, Roy Innis promoted Black self-help above all other solutions to Black disempowerment. On the other hand, in an interview with the *Korea Times*, he criticized the

boycotters from an integrationist perspective: "It reminds me of the civil rights movement of the 50s and 60s, at which point in time Whites refused to obey court orders to respect the civil rights of Blacks. But now Blacks are the ones refusing to obey the court
order to respect the civil rights of the minority. That is shocking" (September 7, 1990).
44. Personal interview with Kinzer.

Chapter 5: The Korean American Response

1. This phrase is the title of a recent book by Kyeyoung Park (1997).
2. Kyeyoung Park (1997) identifies three types of organizations in the Korean American
   community in New York City: occupational, local, and religious. These categories are not
   mutually exclusive. For example, the Flatbush Korean Merchants' Association was both
   an occupational and local or areal organization.
3. First-generation refers to the foreign-born who emigrated to the United States; second-
   generation refers to those born in the United States of first-generation parents; 1.5-
   generation, in Korean American parlance, refers to those who were born in Korea but
   raised and educated partially or primarily in the United States.
4. The election of a greengrocer as president of the KANY in 1978 was seen as a step in re-
   orienting the organization from homeland affairs to domestic affairs in the United States.
   Previous presidents had been community leaders with strong ties to the Korean government (Min 1996).
5. Founded in 1974, the Korean Produce Association of New York provided Korean produce retailers with various business services and information and protected their collective interests vis-à-vis (mostly White) wholesalers at Hunts Point Market and city
   agencies (Min 1996). The Korean American Small Business Service Center, founded in
   1986, lobbied the city to relax regulations pertaining to small businesses and counseled
   Korean merchants who had violated existing regulations. Since there was some overlap
   in their membership, the two organizations were somewhat competitive.
6. See Pyong Gap Min (1996, 134) for a discussion of the KANY's response to previous
   Black boycotts against Korean stores.
7. Former KANY officials often became heads of Korean American small business associations. B. J. Sa, for instance, went from being secretary general of the KANY to being president of the Korean Produce Association of New York, and Daniel Lee went from being
   an official at the KANY to being head of the Korean Association of Flushing.
8. While some Korean Americans felt that racism on the part of Korean merchants contributed to Black-Korean conflict, they were reluctant to break community ranks and state
   their opinions to the general public. (See section below entitled "Dissenting Voices.")
   When the newly elected president of the KANY, Jong Duk Byun, publicly declared that
   Korean merchants should get more involved in Black community activities, many
   Korean Americans deemed this sort of internal criticism inappropriate.
9. Personal interview with Sa.
10. Personal interview with Lee.
11. Although transnational identification could be found among both Haitian and Korean
    immigrants, each group's relationship to its homeland government was distinct. Until
    the election of President Aristide, Haitians considered themselves involuntary economic

and political refugees / exiles strongly opposed to the homeland government. In contrast, Koreans have been voluntary economic migrants supportive of the Korean government. This has made an important difference in each immigrant group's posture toward domestic American politics and American foreign policy toward its homeland.

12. Like the other Korean-language daily newspapers, the *Korea Times* was published in Seoul, airmailed daily to John F. Kennedy Airport, and reproduced in the New York City office, where editors supplemented the original copy with local news items and advertisements (Kim 1981, 264). Due to practical limitations, the *Korea Times* is the only Korean-language media source discussed here. According to Pyong Gap Min (1996), the other Korean-language dailies in New York City concurred, to varying degrees, with the *Korea Times*'s depiction of the Red Apple Boycott.

13. Personal interview with J. Kim.

14. The Korean Produce Association of New York and the Flatbush Korean Merchants' Association initiated the collection of donations for the two merchants; the KANY eventually took over the operation (Min 1996).

15. It is well documented that Asian American panethnicity or consciousness is less common among immigrants than among subsequent generations (Wei 1993; Espiritu 1992).

16. Historically, Asian American panethnicity or consciousness has peaked following episodes of violence which appear to threaten the racial group as a whole (Espiritu 1992). What appeared as one such episode related to the boycott—the beating of Cao Tuan in May 1990 (see Chapter 6)—prompted Asian American advocacy groups to express concern about the boycott. Overall, Asian Americans seem to have had mixed responses to the Red Apple Boycott. Recall that the public opinion poll discussed in Chapter 4 indicated that more Asian Americans than Whites expressed sympathy with the boycotters. While conservative Chinese American groups supported the Korean merchants (for instance, the president of the Chinese Consolidated Benevolent Association took a busload of Chinatown residents to cross the picket line in May 1990), progressive ones such as the Chinese Workers and Staff Association expressed sympathy with both sides and remained neutral (Kwong 1990).

17. The fact that those writing about Korean immigrants frequently allude to the American Dream—think of Kyeyoung Park's *The Korean American Dream* and Nancy Abelmann and John Lie's *Blue Dreams*—suggests that they are seen by Whites and Koreans alike as a shining example of how the American Dream is supposed to work (or, alternatively, of how it can go awry). It is worth noting that neither Korean American opinionmakers nor the mainstream media talked about the Haitian and Caribbean immigrants on the picket line with reference to the American Dream. Rather than seeing the boycott as a clash between the American Dreams of several immigrant groups, they chose to characterize it as the Black underclass scapegoating innocent Korean immigrants.

18. Compared with Korean immigrants, 1.5- and second-generation Korean Americans tend to perceive more racial discrimination, to be more skeptical about the possibility of overcoming it, and to recognize commonalities among groups of color. See the section below entitled "Dissenting Voices."

19. Jang spoke at the hearing with the help of a translator.

20. Korean American and Korean clergy and community leaders proffered many other "racial harmony" gestures. See Pyong Gap Min (1996) for an overview of how Korean

Americans sought to improve their relations with Blacks with a little help from friends in Korea. Reverend Henry Hong led a group of forty Black ministers on a nine-day church tour of Korea in October 1990; the trip was funded by donations from Korean merchants in New York City and churches in Korea. That same month, the chancellor of Kyung Hee University in Korea pledged one hundred scholarships worth a total of $1.5 million to Black students from New York City who wished to study in Korea. In a letter to Mayor David Dinkins, the chancellor wrote: "The reason I am doing this . . . is that I firmly believe all mankind must transcend nationality, racism, religion, ideology and political system" (*New York Newsday,* October 27, 1990). However well-intentioned, these gestures of goodwill did more to enhance public support for the Korean American cause than they did to build bridges to the boycotters. Hearing of the offer of scholarships from Kyung Hee University, Sonny Carson retorted: "We aren't interested in handouts from Koreans or anyone else . . . We can do it on our own. The Koreans take money out of our community every night. Why should I be overjoyed that someone in Korea wants to give money to someone? First of all, the Koreans must respect our community" (*New York Newsday,* October 27, 1990). Elombe Brath comments on the Black ministers' trip to Korea: "They [Koreans and Korean Americans] don't know the first thing about the history of this country, about how Black people worked to build this country and then after being totally exploited, never got reparations, never got forty acres and a mule as promised, and yet instead of trying to understand that, they joined in with the rest of the racists in contempt of the Black community. To prove the point, when they wanted to remedy it [the boycott], what did the Korean leaders do? They wanted to take Black people from this country to Korea, to learn Korean culture, when the question was not about learning Korean culture, because the Koreans have a beautiful culture like many other people do . . . It was for the Koreans to learn the culture of this country, not for Black students to be taken out by these various reverends and some Black traitorous people, because of some money they got, and went along with that, and didn't even reason it out . . . What good would that do? All it would do is bring them back as to be able to intervene on behalf of the Korean community, which still did not address the economic exploitation [underlying the boycott]" (personal interview with Brath).

21. Chun Soo Byun was elected president of the Korean American Association of Flushing in 1989. For a description of this organization, see Kyeyoung Park (1997).

22. Personal interview with Byun.

23. See Chapter 6 for a discussion of the Mayor's Committee report on the boycott.

24. Almost all of the rally participants were Korean American. According to Chun Soo Byun, Chinese Americans were too divided over the boycott to participate in a meaningful way (see note 16 above). One scheduled Chinese American speaker sent a proxy in his place and Byun, irritated at the substitution, refused to let him speak. The only non-Korean Asian American speaker at the rally was Charles Wong, who spoke as a member of the U.S. Commission for Civil Rights rather than as a representative of the Chinese American community (personal interview with Byun).

25. Some scholars suggest that Blacks and Koreans are equally oppressed in American society since the former lack economic power and the latter lack political power (Chang 1994). This conclusion seems a bit facile to me. To begin with, whether or not Blacks have meaningful political power continues to be hotly debated by scholars (Browning, Marshall,

and Tabb 1997; Reed 1992; Reed 1998). Also, Korean Americans' lack of political power is a demonstrable result of small numbers and immigrant status (low rates of naturalization, registration, and voting) and may therefore be amenable to change over time in a way that Black economic marginalization is not. Comparing the political power of a predominantly foreign-born group that constitutes less than 1 percent of the U.S. population (Koreans) with that of a predominantly native-born group that constitutes 12 percent of the U.S. population (Blacks) seems to me to be comparing apples and oranges. It makes more sense to recognize that both groups are politically marginalized, albeit in different ways and for different reasons. Clearly, in any given instance, the political power of a particular group is difficult to gauge. For example, was the Korean American Peace Rally for Racial Harmony a sign of Korean American political strength because it mobilized the community and influenced public opinion? Or was the fact that it occurred at all a sign of Korean American political weakness with regard to the city administration?

26. Personal interview with Choo.

27. Personal interview with Huh.

Chapter 6: Manufacturing Outrage

1. Despite the entreaties of Korean American leaders and other concerned parties, Mayor Edward Koch refused to get involved in the Tropic Fruits Boycott of 1988. He neither promoted a resolution to the conflict nor took a public stand against it (*New York Times*, July 30, 1990). Yet Koch received little if any public criticism for his nonengagement. As a White mayor, he was not subjected to Derrick Bell's fourth rule of racial standing (see note 3 below). Indeed, since he was famously antipathetic toward Black activists, he had nothing to prove to anyone on this score.

2. For discussion of the distinctive dilemmas facing Black mayors, see Rufus Browning, Dale Marshall, and David Tabb (1997), Adolph Reed Jr. (1988), Rod Bush (1984), and Mack Jones (1978).

3. Once again, this rule holds the following: "When a Black person or group makes a statement or takes an action that the white community or vocal components thereof deem 'outrageous,' the latter will actively recruit blacks willing to refute the statement or condemn the action. Blacks who respond to the call for condemnation will receive superstanding status. Those blacks who refuse to be recruited will be interpreted as endorsing the statements and action and may suffer political or economic reprisals" (Bell 1992, 118).

4. Herman and Chomsky (1988) are talking about the media's coverage of international affairs here, but their insights apply to media coverage of internal affairs as well.

5. The mass media and the state are linked by mutual need and influence. Elected officials, who are highly dependent on favorable media coverage, seek to influence the mass media directly (through press conferences, news releases, and media consultants) and indirectly (through the regulation of licenses, taxes, labor policies, and access to foreign markets). In turn, the mass media, which are dependent on officials for information and regulatory dispensations, seek to influence officials through laudatory or critical coverage (Cottle 1992).

6. The mainstream media typically espouse "liberal" as opposed to "conservative" positions, but both of these perspectives are actually conservative insofar as they are con-

tained within the parameters of colorblind talk and do not fundamentally challenge the status quo. I am mindful here of Todd Gitlin's observation that discussions of dominant ideologies often act "as if cultural hegemony were a substance with a life of its own, a sort of immutable fog that has settled over the whole public life of capitalist societies to confound the truth of the proletarian telos" (1979, 252). To avoid this error, I attempt to describe the precise discursive and political mechanisms by which the mass media's coverage of the boycott reinforced the racial order.

7. Personal interview with Green.

8. *New York Newsday* went out of business in the early 1990s. Many New Yorkers who read more than one daily newspaper read both a tabloid and a more highbrow paper like the *Times* (Moss and Ludwig 1991, 247).

9. The latter story contained a picture of a Black woman buying produce at one of the boycotted stores, accompanied by the caption "Brave buyer," and another picture of a Black boycotter talking to a policeman, accompanied by the caption "Finger pointing." Fred McCray, whose fame peaked when ABC Nightly News made him "person of the week" for crossing the picket line, said on the *Joan Rivers Show* (May 17, 1990) that he had been a heroin addict and had served a two-year prison term for drug possession.

10. For discussion of the techniques by which television coverage conveys normative judgments, see Robert Entman (1990, 337–38).

11. In a critical review of this program, one journalist wrote in the *City Sun:* "Mr. Jang assumes the on-screen role of the individual against the mob, a very American sort of hero" (July 12, 1990). Sabine Albert was dismayed that a *48 Hours* reporter had followed her around for two days, only to use one brief clip of her talking in the final program (personal interview with Albert).

12. Chin was murdered by two unemployed White auto workers yelling anti-Japanese epithets. When the two men were released on probation with light fines, Detroit's Asian American communities reacted in disbelief. Eventually, the case galvanized Asian Americans across the country, leading to unprecedented pan-Asian mobilization, organization, and political activity (Espiritu 1992). To this day, Vincent Chin is a symbol of both anti-Asian violence and Asian American panethnicity.

13. The reference here is to Edward Herman and Noam Chomsky's *Manufacturing Consent* (1988). Murray Edelman argues that the government sometimes inflates a threat to justify an expansion in its authority: "The belief in a crisis relaxes resistance to governmental interferences with civil liberties and bolsters support for executive actions, including discouragement or suppression of criticism and governmental failure to respond to it" (1977, 48). In the Red Apple Boycott, it was the mass media that generated a sense of crisis in order to compel and justify social control efforts on the part of the Dinkins administration. Jerome Skolnick draws an interesting parallel between this type of elite hyperbole and the hysteria that collective actors are often accused of: "While the beliefs underlying a riot may frequently be inaccurate or exaggerated, they are not necessarily more so than, for example, commonly held beliefs about racial minorities by dominant groups, the perception of foreign threats to national security . . . A measure of irrationality . . . is an element of many routine social processes and institutions *and* forms of collective behavior . . . [The] difference may be that established institutions are usually in a more advantageous position from which to define 'rationality' " (1969, 255).

14. During the Red Apple Boycott, lawyers for the two Korean merchants alleged that a Black political operative named William Banks had attempted to extort money from them in exchange for stopping the boycott. Sonny Carson denied any connection to Banks, who could not prove that he was representing the boycotters when he made the offer. This situation prompted the Federal Bureau of Investigation to revive its investigation of charges that Carson had attempted to extort money from the Korean merchant involved in the Tropic Fruits Boycott of 1988. No criminal charges were ever filed against Carson for attempted extortion with regard to either boycott (*New York Newsday*, September 13, 1990).

15. These analogies also mobilized Jewish opposition to the boycott. Gary Rubin, the director of national affairs for the American Jewish Committee at the time, opposed the boycott on the grounds that Sonny Carson was anti-Semitic (personal interview with Rubin).

16. Although Mayor Dinkins adopted a public stance of neutrality, his administration worked hard to end the conflict behind the scenes. The City Commission for Human Rights sponsored several neighborhood meetings in the aftermath of the precipitating incident. Per the mayor's instructions, the Community Assistance Unit also investigated the conflict and sought to mediate between the parties. In addition, Deputy Mayor Bill Lynch, sometimes described as Dinkins's liaison to the Black nationalist community, worked hard to bring the December 12th Movement to the negotiating table. Various other governmental bodies—including the Brooklyn borough president's office, Councilwoman Susan Alter's office, Assemblywoman Rhoda Jacobs's office, the New York State Division on Human Rights, the New York State Martin Luther King Institute on Nonviolence, and the Community Relations Service of the U.S. Department of Justice—also attempted to mediate between the parties during the early stages of the boycott.

17. The two boycotted stores were located in the 40th City Council district, represented by Councilwoman Susan Alter; the 42nd Assembly district, represented by Assemblywoman Rhoda Jacobs; the 20th State Senatorial district, represented by State Senator Marty Markowitz; and the 11th U.S. Congressional district, represented by Congressman Major Owens.

18. One does not have to be either a Marxist or a public choice theorist to recognize that economic elites, who are permanently mobilized and organized as few other groups are, wield immense political power at the municipal level (Castells 1983; Peterson 1981; Jones 1978). Recently, students of urban politics have sought to combine a traditional emphasis on the systemic power of business elites with more openness to the significance of political activity from below. John Mollenkopf, for instance, suggests "a vocabulary for analyzing politics and state action that reconciles the political system's independent impact on social outcomes with its observed systemic bias in favor of capital" (1992, 37).

19. Dissatisfied with the city government's response, Korean American leaders also lobbied state and federal officials on the boycott issue. As mentioned in Chapter 5, Korean American leaders held an unprecedented (albeit somewhat unproductive) meeting with President George Bush in June 1990. These lobbying efforts prompted the FBI to reopen an old investigation of Sonny Carson (see note 14 above) and persuaded the Civil Rights Division of the U.S. Justice Department to launch an investigation into whether the boycott violated the civil rights of the two Korean merchants (see note 23 below).

20. There were several other criminal and civil suits pending as well. In addition to the crim-

inal case against Bong Ok Jang, there was a criminal case pending against a Black woman protester whom Manho Park's wife claimed had assaulted her in early February. Mrs. Park also filed a civil suit against the woman, claiming that the quarrel had prompted her to take pills to calm down, which in turn forced her to have an abortion in order to avoid having a baby with birth defects. Felissaint filed a civil suit against her alleged assailant in May, seeking compensation for emotional and physical harm. Although the police had arrested Bong Jae Jang, the Family Red Apple store's owner, shortly after the altercation in January, it was not until the end of May that the Kings County District Attorney's office interviewed Felissaint for the first time and discovered that they had charged the wrong man. In early June, charges against Bong Jae Jang were dropped. In early July, Felissaint identified Bong Jae Jang's brother and the store's manager, Bong Ok Jang, as her assailant in a police lineup; he was promptly arrested and charged with third-degree misdemeanor assault. Colin Moore, Felissaint's attorney, and the Kings County District Attorney's office exchanged accusations about who was responsible for the delay in discovering the mix-up. The story of the mix-up probably increased public sympathy for the Korean merchants, who seemed to be victims of both Black racism and official incompetence.

21. In New York, the State Supreme Court is the trial court, and the Appellate Court is the highest court. If enforced, the fifty-feet court order would have moved the picketers from the storefront sidewalks to the middle of Church Avenue, a busy thoroughfare. When the NYPD finally began enforcing the order in late September, they moved the picket line to a nearby street corner, where its efficacy was greatly diminished.

22. As David Goldberg writes: "In its claim to universality and objectivity, the law effaces the being of legal agents . . . It effaces agency itself . . . [thus] commanding anonymously" (1993, 204). The next day, Judge Held stayed his order to allow for mediation efforts. On May 7, with no settlement in sight, he reinstated the order. A few days later, Bong Jae Jang's attorney agreed to court-sponsored mediation, but the boycotters' attorney declined to participate.

23. In mid-May 1990, the Civil Rights Division of the U.S. Department of Justice announced that it would not get involved in the boycott because the protesters were simply exercising free speech and not using force or the threat of force. This finding, which might have been seen as validating Mayor Dinkins's position, did not receive significant media coverage.

24. Mason was tapping into the feeling shared by many Blacks that Dinkins had succumbed to Jewish pressure in his denunciation of Louis Farrakhan in 1985, his implicit repudiation of Jesse Jackson in 1988, and his "letting go" of Jitu Weusi and Sonny Carson in 1989.

25. Despite this criticism from some Blacks, a *New York Times* / WCBS telephone poll conducted from June 17 to June 20, 1990, suggested that the mayor still retained substantial support among Blacks citywide. When asked, "Do you approve or disapprove of the way David Dinkins is handling relations between Whites and Blacks in New York City?" 83 percent of Blacks said they approved, 11 percent said they disapproved, and 6 percent said they didn't know or gave no answer. For Whites, the numbers were 66 percent, 23 percent, and 11 percent, respectively. However, the same poll suggested that Black respondents may have expressed support for Dinkins at least in part because they believed that he was unfairly persecuted by the system. When confronted with the statement

"Some people say the government deliberately singles out and investigates black elected officials in order to discredit them in a way it doesn't do with white officials," 77 percent of Blacks responded that this statement was "true" or "might possibly be true," while only 16 percent said that it was "almost certainly not true," and 7 percent said they didn't know or gave no answer. For Whites, the numbers were 34 percent, 57 percent, and 9 percent, respectively. The citywide poll randomly sampled 1047 adults (including 484 Whites and 408 Blacks) by telephone. Blacks were first sampled at a higher rate, then weighted to reflect their proportion of the city's population. The margin of error was plus or minus 3 percent for the entire sample.

26. On August 4, 1990, an altercation between a Korean merchant and three Black women occurred in the R & N Fruit and Vegetable Market in Brownsville, Brooklyn. Anticipating trouble, the merchant closed the store and promptly sold it to another Korean immigrant. When the new owner reopened the store a few weeks later, he was greeted by a picket line. One of the organizers of this boycott, Norman Reide, who often worked with Reverend Sharpton, was also involved in the Red Apple Boycott. What might have been another public relations disaster for Mayor Dinkins turned into a small victory when his personal mediation efforts quickly produced a negotiated settlement between the merchant and the boycotters. At least two factors made the R & N Fruit boycott easier to resolve than the Red Apple Boycott: first, the change in store ownership (of which the boycotters had not been aware); and second, the fact that the December 12th Movement had not yet become involved. The mass media praised the mayor for his role in ending the R & N Fruit boycott even as they renewed their call for him to do the same in Flatbush.

27. Piecing together the evidence, it appears that Hahm dropped out of sight (as described just below by Ben Limb) not because he personally thought that the report was pro-Black but because he faced considerable pressure from the Korean American community to ensure that the report was sympathetic to the Korean merchants.

28. Cochair Reverend Michael Hahm explains that his understanding of Blacks' and Koreans' common experience of racial oppression prevented him from seeing the boycott as essentially or even primarily "race-based":

> I knew that this was a racial issue, but knowing Blacks so many hundred years in this country, they were discriminated against, I cannot bring myself to say to Blacks that, "You Blacks are racist to Asians." I know there is very much racism involved there, but that is one of those things that if someone comes to me and say that, "You are racist," I assume that maybe we are all racist in one way or another. I am the one that is always fighting against the racist, to survive as Asian American in a White society. And if someone comes to me and say that, "You are racist," I am really going to resent that. Because that's the one that I am fighting against . . . I'm a United Methodist minister, and I myself have been discriminated because I'm an Asian, even in the churches and so on. My coworkers are the Blacks. They were the people that I could join hands together to fight this racism against White people. So in a way they became my colleagues and my friends. I understand them, they understand me. I have that background experience. I know more about the Blacks, the struggle, civil rights, and the many years of enslavement, and all that history, I

think, maybe more than anybody. In a way that we as the Koreans are coming from the same kind of background. We fought the Japanese and so on, and a lot of Koreans think that as they come to this country they think they are White, but they will soon discover that we are not White. White people don't care whether we are Koreans, or Chinese, or Japanese, or Blacks. We have to do double—"How many Ph.Ds do you carry?" . . . and that is the reality in this society. I try to tell my own kids, it's kind of tough things to say, but the sooner we learn to be prepared to deal with this issue, the better. I don't mean to suggest that to be sarcastic about all this thing, but realistic is maybe the word. (personal interview with Hahm)

29. Personal interview with P. Kim.
30. The Mayor's Committee report emphasized Haitian participation in the boycott, but it did not discuss the December 12th Movement's leadership role. Members of this organization refused to speak at the public hearing held by the committee in Flatbush in June 1990 or otherwise cooperate with the committee's preparation of the report.
31. An unusual *New York Newsday* editorial wondered about the uproar: "The negative editorial outcry that followed the release of the panel's findings seemed to ignore the history of such panels, at least in New York City. A panel appointed by the mayor to study a problem confronted by the mayor is expected to come back with a report acceptable to the mayor. Remember the panel named by former Mayor Edward I. Koch to study the problems faced by blacks in the city? . . . [There is an] informal mandate that has come to be expected of mayoral panels: no unpleasant facts, solutions the mayor can live with, no blame on the mayor, and a report the mayor can point to as evidence that the problem is not his fault" (September 4, 1990).
32. Joseph Viteritti commented on the transfer of power: "The key determinant of mayoral power in New York City will be the way the council chooses to respond to its newly defined constitutional role" (1990, 424).
33. Personal interview with Povman.
34. As Michael Lipsky and David Olson (1973) point out, official committees tend to beget other committees that contradict their predecessors out of political motivations.
35. Like the Mayor's Committee report, the City Council report did not mention the December 12th Movement, whose members refused to participate in either set of public hearings.
36. On September 22, the day after the mayor crossed the picket line, police officers found eighteen Molotov cocktails (gas-filled soda bottles topped with cloth wicks) on the roofs of the Family Red Apple store and adjoining businesses. Although the perpetrators were never found, and the explosives were never linked to any of the boycotters, the discovery helped to make heightened social control efforts by the NYPD appear necessary and legitimate.
37. Manho Park eventually changed the name of his store but kept it open for business. In May 1991, Bong Jae Jang sold his store to another Korean American, who promptly renamed the establishment.
38. A referendum on the future of Staten Island drew large numbers of White Catholic and Jewish voters to the polls in 1993 (Mollenkopf 1997, 110).

BIBLIOGRAPHY

Abelmann, Nancy, and John Lie. 1995. *Blue Dreams: Korean Americans and the Los Angeles Riots*. Cambridge: Harvard University Press.

Aberbach, Joel D., and Jack L. Walker. 1970. "The Meanings of Black Power: A Comparison of White and Black Interpretations of a Political Slogan." *American Political Science Review* 64 (2): 367–88.

Ahiarah, Sol. 1993. "Black Americans' Business Ownership Factors: A Theoretical Perspective." *Review of Black Political Economy* 22 (2): 15–39.

Ahn, Chong Sik. 1991. "An Alternative Approach to the Racial Conflict Between Korean-American Small Business Owners and the Black-American Community in the New York Metropolitan Area." In *The Korean-American Community: Present and Future*, edited by Tae-Hwan Kwak and Seong Hyong Lee. Masan, Korea: Kyungnam University Press.

Aldrich, Howard E. 1973. "Employment Opportunities for Blacks in the Black Ghetto: The Role of White-Owned Businesses." *American Journal of Sociology* 78 (6): 1403–25.

——, and Albert J. Reiss, Jr. 1976. "Continuities in the Study of Ecological Succession: Changes in the Race Composition of Neighborhoods and Their Businesses." *American Journal of Sociology* 81 (4): 846–66.

——, and Roger Waldinger. 1990. "Ethnicity and Entrepreneurship." *Annual Review of Sociology* 16: 111–35.

Allen, Robert L. 1969. *Black Awakening in Capitalist America: An Analytic History*. New York: Doubleday & Co.

Altshuler, Alan A. 1970. *Community Control: The Black Demand for Participation in Large American Cities*. Indianapolis: Western.

Anderson, Benedict. 1991. *Imagined Communities: Reflections on the Origin and Spread of Nationalism*, rev. and ext. ed. London: Verso.

Arian, Asher, et al., eds. 1991. *Changing New York City Politics*. New York: Routledge.

Armstrong, Regina. 1989. "New York and the Forces of Immigration." In *Future Shocks to New York*. New York: The Citizens Budget Commission.

Auletta, Ken. 1979. "The Mayor." *New Yorker*. September 10 and September 17.

——. 1982. *The Underclass*. New York: Random House.

Bailey, Ronald W., ed. 1971. *Black Business Enterprise: Historical and Contemporary Perspectives*. New York: Basic.

Bailey, Thomas R. 1987. *Immigrant and Native Workers: Contrasts and Competition*. Boulder: Westview.

——. 1989. "Black Employment Opportunities." In *Setting Municipal Priorities*, edited by Charles Brecher and Raymond D. Horton. New York: New York University Press.

——, and Roger Waldinger. 1991. "The Changing Ethnic/Racial Division of Labor." In *Dual City: Restructuring New York*, edited by John Mollenkopf and Manuel Castells. New York: Russell Sage Foundation.

Baldwin, James. 1955. *Notes of a Native Son*. Boston: Beacon.

——. 1967. "Negroes Are Anti-Semitic Because They're Anti-White." *New York Times Magazine.* April 19.

Banton, Michael. 1983. *Racial and Ethnic Competition.* Cambridge: Cambridge University Press.

Barbour, Floyd B., ed. 1968. *The Black Power Revolt: A Collection of Essays.* Boston: Porter Sargent.

Basch, Linda, et al. 1994. *Nations Unbound: Transnational Projects and the Deterritorialized Nation-State.* New York: Gordon and Breach.

Bates, Timothy, and Darrell L. Williams. 1993. "Racial Politics: Does It Pay?" *Social Science Quarterly* 74 (3): 507–22.

Bates, Timothy. 1994a. "Social Resources Generated by Group Support Networks May Not Be Beneficial to Immigrant Owned Small Businesses." *Social Forces* 72 (3): 671–89.

——. 1994b. "An Analysis of Korean-Immigrant-Owned Small-Business Start-Ups with Comparisons to African-American and Nonminority-Owned Firms." *Urban Affairs Quarterly* 30 (2): 227–48.

——. 1998. "The Bootstrap Paradigm: Using Self-Employment as a Strategy for Maintaining Poverty Among Minorities." Paper presented at the Conference on Social Science Knowledge on Race, Racism, and Race Relations, McLean, Virginia, April 26–28.

Bell, David A. 1985. "The Triumph of Asian-Americans: America's Greatest Success Story." *New Republic.* July 15 and July 22.

Bell, Derrick. 1987. *And We Are Not Saved: The Elusive Quest for Racial Justice.* New York: Basic.

——. 1992. *Faces at the Bottom of the Well: The Permanence of Racism.* New York: Basic.

Bellush, Jewel. 1990. "Clusters of Power: Interest Groups." In *Urban Politics, New York Style,* edited by Jewel Bellush and Dick Netzer. Armonk, N.Y.: M. E. Sharpe.

——, and Dick Netzer. 1990. "New York Confronts Urban Theory." In *Urban Politics, New York Style,* edited by Jewel Bellush and Dick Netzer. Armonk, N.Y.: M. E. Sharpe.

Benford, Robert. 1993. "Frame Disputes Within the Nuclear Disarmament Movement." *Social Forces* 71 (3): 677–701.

Benjamin, Gerald. 1972. *Race Relations and the New York City Commission on Human Rights.* Ithaca: Cornell University Press.

——. 1990. "The State/City Relationship." In *Urban Politics, New York Style,* edited by Jewel Bellush and Dick Netzer. Armonk, N.Y.: M. E. Sharpe.

Bergsman, Joel. 1971. "Alternative to the Non-Gilded Ghetto: Notes on Different Goals and Strategies." *Public Policy* 19 (2): 309–22.

Berk, Richard A., and Howard E. Aldrich. 1972. "Patterns of Vandalism During Civil Disorders as an Indicator of Selection of Targets." *American Sociological Review* 37 (5): 533–47.

Berube, Maurice, and Marilyn Gittell, eds. 1969. *Confrontation at Ocean Hill-Brownsville: The New York School Strike of 1968.* New York: Praeger.

Beschloss, Stephen, and Robert McNatt. 1989. "A Broken Trust: Many Black Professionals Are Turning Their Backs on Corporate New York and Changing the Rules of Gain." *Crain's New York Business.* October 30.

Blalock, Hubert M., Jr. 1967. *Toward a Theory of Minority Group Relations.* New York: John Wiley & Sons.

Blank, Blanche. 1990. "Bureaucracy: Power in Details." In *Urban Politics, New York Style,* edited by Jewel Bellush and Dick Netzer. Armonk, N.Y.: M. E. Sharpe.

Blauner, Robert. 1969. "Internal Colonialism and Ghetto Revolt." *Social Problems* 16 (4): 393–408.

Bluestone, Barry, and Bennett Harrison. 1982. *The Deindustrialization of America: Plant Closings, Community Abandonment, and the Dismantling of Basic Industry.* New York: Basic.

Bogen, Elizabeth. 1987. *Immigration in New York.* New York: Praeger.

Bonacich, Edna. 1973. "A Theory of Middleman Minorities." *American Sociological Review* 5 (37): 583–94.

——. 1980. "Middleman Minorities and Advanced Capitalism." *Ethnic Groups* 2: 211–19.

——, Ivan Light, and Charles Choy Wong. 1980. "Korean Immigrants: Small Business in Los Angeles." In *Sourcebook on the New Immigration: Implications for the United States and the International Community,* edited by Roy Simon Bryce-Laporte. New Brunswick, N.J.: Transaction.

——, and Tae Hwan Jung. 1982. "A Portrait of Korean Small Business in Los Angeles: 1977." In *Koreans in Los Angeles,* edited by Eui-Young Yu et al. Los Angeles: Koryo Research Institute and Center for Korean-American and Korean Studies, California State University.

——. 1987. " 'Making It' in America: A Social Evaluation of the Ethics of Immigrant Entrepreneurship." *Sociological Perspectives* 30 (4): 446–66.

Bonnett, Aubrey W. 1980. "An Examination of Rotating Credit Associations Among Black West Indian Immigrants in Brooklyn." In *Sourcebook on the New Immigration: Implications for the United States and the International Community,* edited by Roy Simon Bryce-Laporte. New Brunswick, N.J.: Transaction.

——. 1990. "West Indians in the United States of America: Some Theoretical and Practical Considerations." In *Emerging Perspectives on the Black Diaspora,* edited by Aubrey W. Bonnett and G. Llewellyn Watson. Lanham, Md.: University Press of America.

Boyd, Robert L. 1990. "Black and Asian Self-Employment in Large Metropolitan Areas: A Comparative Analysis." *Social Problems* 37 (2): 258–72.

——. 1991. "Black Entrepreneurship in 52 Metropolitan Areas." *Sociology & Social Research* 75 (3): 158–63.

Bracey, John, Jr., et al., eds. 1970. *Black Nationalism in America.* Indianapolis: Bobbs-Merrill.

Branch, Taylor. 1988. *Parting the Waters: America in the King Years, 1954–63.* New York: Simon & Schuster.

Breitman, George, ed. 1965. *Malcolm X Speaks.* New York: Grove Weidenfeld.

Brimmer, Andrew F., and Henry S. Terrell. 1971. "The Economic Potential of Black Capitalism." *Public Policy* 19 (2): 289–308.

Browning, Rufus P., Dale R. Marshall, and David H. Tabb, eds. 1984. *Protest Is Not Enough: The Struggle of Blacks and Hispanics for Equality in Urban Politics.* Berkeley: University of California Press.

——, eds. 1990. *Racial Politics in American Cities.* New York: Longman.

——, eds. 1997. *Racial Politics in American Cities,* 2d ed. New York: Longman.

Bryce-Laporte, Roy S. 1972. "Black Immigrants: The Experience of Invisibility and Inequality." *Journal of Black Studies* 1: 29–56.

Burgess, J. A. 1985. "News From Nowhere: The Press, the Riots and the Myth of the Inner City." In *Geography, the Media and Popular Culture,* edited by J. A. Burgess and R. A. Gold. London: Croom Helm.

Bush, Rod, ed. 1984. *The New Black Vote.* San Francisco: Synthesis.

Butler, John Sibley. 1991. *Entrepreneurship and Self-Help Among Black Americans: A Reconsideration of Race and Economics.* Albany: SUNY Press.

Carmichael, Stokely, and Charles Hamilton. 1967. *Black Power: The Politics of Liberation in America.* New York: Vintage.

Carmichael, Stokely. 1971. *Stokely Speaks: Black Power Back to Pan-Africanism.* New York: Random House.

Carson, Sonny. 1972. *The Education of Sonny Carson.* New York: W. W. Norton & Co.

Castells, Manuel. 1983. *The City and the Grassroots: A Cross-Cultural Theory of Urban Social Movements.* London: Edward Arnold.

Chan, Sucheng. 1991. *Asian Americans: An Interpretive History.* Boston: Twayne.

Chang, Edward T. 1991. "New Urban Crisis: Intra-Third World Conflict." In *Asian Americans: Comparative and Global Perspectives,* edited by Shirley Hune et al. Pullman: Washington State University Press.

——. 1994. "Jewish and Korean Merchants in African American Neighborhoods: A Comparative Perspective." In *Los Angeles—Struggles Toward Multiethnic Community: Asian, American, African American and Latino Perspectives,* edited by Edward T. Chang and Russell C. Leong. Seattle: University of Washington Press.

Chang, Jeff. 1994. "Race, Class, Conflict and Empowerment: On Ice Cube's 'Black Korea'." In *Los Angeles—Struggles Toward Multiethnic Community: Asian, American, African American and Latino Perspectives,* edited by Edward T. Chang and Russell C. Leong. Seattle: University of Washington Press.

Chen, Gavin M., and John A. Cole. 1988. "The Myths, Facts, and Theories of Ethnic, Small-Scale Enterprise Financing." *Review of Black Political Economy* 16 (4): 111–23.

Cheng, Lucie, and Yen Le Espiritu. 1989. "Korean Businesses in Black and Hispanic Neighborhoods: A Study of Intergroup Relations." *Sociological Perspectives* 32 (4): 521–34.

Cherry, Robert. 1990. "Middleman Minority Theories: Their Implications for Black-Jewish Relations." *Journal of Ethnic Studies* 17 (4): 117–38.

Cho, Sumi K. 1993. "Korean Americans vs. African Americans: Conflict and Construction." In *Reading Rodney King/Reading Urban Uprising,* edited by Robert Gooding-Williams. New York: Routledge.

Choi, Chungmoo. 1993. "The Discourse of Decolonization and Popular Memory: South Korea." *Positions* 1 (1): 77–102.

Churchill, Ward, and Jim Van der Wall. 1988. *Agents of Repression: The FBI's Secret Wars.* Boston: South End.

Clark, Kenneth. 1965. *Dark Ghetto: Dilemmas of Social Power.* New York: Harper & Row.

——. 1972. "The Negro Elected Official in the Changing American Scene." In *Black Political Life in the United States,* edited by Lenneal J. Henderson Jr. San Francisco: Chandler.

Cloward, Richard A., and Frances Fox Piven. 1972. *The Politics of Turmoil: Essays on Poverty, Race and the Urban Crisis.* New York: Pantheon.

Cohen, Jean L. 1985. "Strategy or Identity: New Theoretical Paradigms and Contemporary Social Movements." *Social Research* 52 (4): 663–716.

Coles, Flournoy A., Jr. 1973. "Financial Institutions and Black Entrepreneurship." *Journal of Black Studies* 13 (3): 329–49.

Cone, James. 1991. *Malcolm & Martin & America.* Maryknoll, N.Y.: Orbis.

Connolly, Harold X. 1977. *A Ghetto Grows in Brooklyn.* New York: New York University Press.

Cottle, Simon. 1992. " 'Race,' Racialization and the Media: A Review and Update of Research." *Sage Race Relations Abstracts* 17 (2): 3–57.

Crenshaw, Kimberlé. 1995. "Race, Reform, and Retrenchment: Transformation and Legitimation in Antidiscrimination Law." In *Critical Race Theory,* edited by Kimberlé Crenshaw et al. New York: New Press.

Cross, Malcolm, and Michael Keith, eds. 1993. *Racism, the City and the State.* London: Routledge.

Crowder, Ralph L. 1991. " 'Don't Buy Where You Can't Work': An Investigation of the Political Forces and Social Conflict Within the Harlem Boycott of 1934." *Afro-Americans in New York Life and History* 15 (2): 7–44.

Cumings, Bruce. 1981. *The Origins of the Korean War.* Princeton: Princeton University Press.

Daly, Michael. 1982. "Making It: The Saga of Min Chul Shin and His Family Fruit Store." *New York.* December 20.

Daniels, Roger. 1962. *The Politics of Prejudice: The Anti-Japanese Movement in California and the Struggle for Japanese Exclusion.* Berkeley: University of California Press.

——. 1972. *Concentration Camps USA: Japanese Americans and World War II.* New York: Holt, Rinehart & Winston.

——. 1976. "Majority Images—Minority Realities: A Perspective on Anti-Orientalism in the United States." *Prospects* 2: 209–62.

Danzig, David. 1966. "In Defense of 'Black Power.' " *Commentary* 42 (3): 41–47.

Delgado, Richard. 1994. "Critical Race Theory." *Sage Race Relations Abstracts* 19 (2): 3–28.

Denton, Nancy. 1994. "Are African Americans Still Hypersegregated?" In *Residential Apartheid: The American Legacy,* edited by Robert Bullard, J. Eugene Grigsby III, and Charles Lee. Los Angeles: UCLA Center for Afro-American Studies.

DeWind, Josh, and David Kinley. 1986. *Aiding Migration: The Impact of International Development Assistance on Haiti.* New York: Immigration Research Program, Center for the Social Sciences, Columbia University.

DeWind, Josh. 1987. "The Remittances of Haitian Immigrants in New York City." New York. Unpublished report for Citibank.

Dinnerstein, Leonard. 1987. *Uneasy at Home: Antisemitism and the American Jewish Experience.* New York: Columbia University Press.

Doctors, Samuel I., ed. 1974. *Whatever Happened to Minority Economic Development?* Hinsdale, Ill.: Dryden.

Drennan, Matthew. 1991. "The Decline and Rise of the New York Economy." In *Dual City: Restructuring New York,* edited by John Mollenkopf and Manuel Castells. New York: Russell Sage Foundation.

D'Souza, Dinesh. 1995. *The End of Racism: Principles for a Multiracial Society.* New York: Free Press.

Du Bois, W. E. B. 1989. *The Souls of Black Folk.* New York: Penguin. First published in 1903.

Dymally, Mervyn. 1972. "The Black Man's Role in American Politics." In *Black Political Life in the United States,* edited by Lenneal J. Henderson Jr. San Francisco: Chandler.

Dynes, Russell, and E. L. Quarantelli. 1968. "What Looting in Civil Disturbances Really Means." *Trans-Action* 5 (6): 9–14.

Echols, Alice. 1980. *Daring to Be Bad: Radical Feminism in America*. Minneapolis: University of Minnesota Press.

Edelman, Murray. 1964. *The Symbolic Uses of Politics*. Urbana: University of Illinois Press.

———. 1977. *Political Language: Words that Succeed, Policies that Fail*. Orlando: Academic.

Edsall, Thomas Byrne, and Mary D. Edsall. 1991. *Chain Reaction: The Impact of Race, Rights, and Taxes on American Politics*. New York: W. W. Norton & Co.

Eichenthal, David K. 1990. "Changing Styles and Strategies of the Mayor." In *Urban Politics, New York Style*, edited by Jewel Bellush and Dick Netzer. Armonk, N.Y.: M. E. Sharpe.

Eisinger, Peter K. 1976. *Patterns of Interracial Politics: Conflict and Cooperation in the City*. New York: Academic.

———. 1977. "Understanding Urban Politics: A Comparative Perspective on Urban Political Conflict." *Polity* 10 (2): 218–40.

Entman, Robert M. 1990. "Modern Racism and the Images of Blacks in Local Television News." *Critical Studies in Mass Communication* 7: 332–45.

Espiritu, Yen Le. 1992. *Asian American Panethnicity: Bridging Institutions and Identities*. Philadelphia: Temple University Press.

Essien-Udom, Essien Udosen. 1962. *Black Nationalism: A Search for an Identity in America*. Chicago: University of Chicago Press.

Fainstein, Norman I., and Susan S. Fainstein. 1974. *Urban Political Movements: The Search for Power by Minority Groups in American Cities*. Englewood Cliffs, N.J.: Prentice-Hall.

———. 1980. "The Future of Community Control." In *Urban Politics: Past, Present, & Future*, edited by Harlan Hahn and Charles Levine. New York: Longman.

———. 1985. "Economic Restructuring and the Rise of Urban Social Movements." *Urban Affairs Quarterly* 21 (2): 187–206.

———. 1991. "The Changing Character of Community Politics in New York City: 1968–1988." In *Dual City: Restructuring New York*, edited by John Mollenkopf and Manuel Castells. New York: Russell Sage Foundation.

Falcon, Angelo. 1988. "Black and Latino Politics in New York City: Race and Ethnicity in a Changing Urban Context." In *New Community* 14 (3): 370–84.

Fantasia, Rick, and Eric Hirsch. 1995. "Culture in Rebellion: The Appropriation and Transformation of the Veil in the Algerian Revolution." In *Social Movements and Culture*, edited by Hank Johnston and Bert Klandermans. Minneapolis: University of Minnesota Press.

Feagin, Joe, and Harlan Hahn. 1973. *Ghetto Revolts: The Politics of Violence in American Cities*. New York: Macmillan.

Feagin, Joe. 1991. "The Continuing Significance of Race: Antiblack Discrimination in Public Places." *American Sociological Review* 56: 101–16.

———. 1994. "A House Is Not a Home." In *Residential Apartheid: The American Legacy*, edited by Robert Bullard, J. Eugene Grigsby III, and Charles Lee. Los Angeles: UCLA Center for Afro-American Studies.

———, and Nikitah Imani. 1994. "Racial Barriers to African American Entrepreneurship: An Explanatory Study." *Social Problems* 41 (4): 562–84.

Ferree, Myra Marx, and Frederick D. Miller. 1985. "Mobilization and Meaning: Toward an Integration of Social Psychological and Resource Perspectives on Social Movements." *Sociological Inquiry* 55 (1): 38–51.

Ferree, Myra Marx. 1992. "The Political Context of Rationality: Rational Choice Theory and

Resource Mobilization." In *Frontiers in Social Movement Theory*, edited by Aldon D. Morris and Carol McClurg Mueller. New Haven: Yale University Press.

Fields, Barbara J. 1982. "Ideology and Race in American History." In *Region, Race, and Reconstruction*, edited by J. Morgan Kousser and James M. McPherson. New York: Oxford University Press.

———. 1990. "Slavery, Race and Ideology in the United States of America." *New Left Review* 181: 95–118.

Fine, Gary Alan. 1995. "Public Narration and Group Culture: Discerning Discourse in Social Movements." In *Social Movements and Culture*, edited by Hank Johnston and Bert Klandermans. Minneapolis: University of Minnesota Press.

Fireman, Bruce, and William H. Gamson. 1979. "Utilitarian Logic in the Resource Mobilization Perspective." In *The Dynamics of Social Movements: Resource Mobilization, Social Control, and Tactics*, edited by Mayer N. Zald and John McCarthy. Cambridge, Mass.: Winthrop.

Fisher, Robert. 1992. "Organizing in the Modern Metropolis: Considering New Social Movement Theory." *Journal of Urban History* 18 (2): 222–37.

Fishman, M. 1980. *Manufacturing the News*. Austin: University of Texas Press.

Fogelson, Robert M. 1970. "Violence and Grievances: Reflections on the 1960s Riots." *Journal of Social Issues* 26 (1): 141–63.

Foner, Nancy, ed. 1987. *New Immigrants in New York City*. New York: Columbia University Press.

Foner, Philip S. 1970. *The Black Panthers Speak*. Philadelphia: J. B. Lippincott.

———. 1975. "Black-Jewish Relations in the Opening Years of the Twentieth Century." *Phylon* 36 (4): 359–67.

———, and Daniel Rosenberg, eds. 1993. *Racism, Dissent, and Asian Americans from 1850 to the Present: A Documentary History*. Westport, Conn.: Greenwood.

Foucault, Michel. 1986. "Disciplinary Power and Subjection." In *Power*, edited by Steven Lukes. New York: New York University Press.

Franklin, Charles Lionel. 1936. *The Negro Labor Unionist of New York*. New York: Columbia University Press.

Fratoe, Frank A. 1986. "A Sociological Analysis of Minority Business." *Review of Black Political Economy* 15 (2): 5–30.

Frazier, E. Franklin. 1937. "Negro Harlem: An Ecological Study." *American Journal of Sociology* 63 (1): 72–88.

Freeman, Jo. 1973. "The Origins of the Women's Liberation Movement." *American Journal of Sociology* 78 (4): 792–811.

Friedman, Monroe. 1991. "Consumer Boycotts: A Conceptual Framework and Research Agenda." *Journal of Social Issues* 47 (1): 149–68.

Fusfield, Daniel, and Timothy Bates. 1984. *The Political Economy of the Urban Ghetto*. Carbondale, Ill.: Southern Illinois University Press.

Gamson, William A. 1968. "Stable Unrepresentation in American Society." *American Behavioural Scientist* 12: 15–21.

———, Bruce Fireman and Steve Rytina. 1982. *Encounters With Unjust Authority*. Homewood, Ill.: Dorsey.

———. 1988. "Political Discourse and Collective Action." In *From Structure to Action: Compar-*

ing Movement Participation Across Cultures, edited by Bert Klandermans, Hanspeter Kriesi, and Sidney Tarrow. International Social Movement Research, vol. 1. Greenwich, Conn.: JAI.

———. 1989. *The Strategy of Social Protest,* 2d ed. Homewood, Ill.: Dorsey.

———. 1992. "The Social Psychology of Collective Action." In *Frontiers in Social Movement Theory,* edited by Aldon D. Morris and Carol McClurg Mueller. New Haven: Yale University Press.

———, and David Meyer. 1996. "Framing Political Opportunity." In *Comparative Perspectives on Social Movements,* edited by Doug McAdam et al. New York: Cambridge University Press.

Garcia, John A. 1986. "Caribbean Migration to the Mainland: A Review of Adaptive Experiences." *Annals of the American Academy of Political and Social Science* 487: 114–25.

Garner, Roberta. 1997. "Fifty Years of Social Movement Theory: An Interpretation." In *Social Movement Theory and Research: An Annotated Bibliographical Guide,* edited by Roberta Garner and John Tenuto. Lanham, Md.: Scarecrow.

Gaventa, John. 1980. *Power and Powerlessness: Quiescence and Rebellion in an Appalachian Valley.* Urbana: University of Illinois Press.

Geltman, Max. 1970. *The Confrontation: Black Power, Anti-Semitism, and the Myth of Integration.* Englewood Cliffs, N.J.: Prentice-Hall.

Gerlach, L. P., and V. H. Hine. 1970. *People, Power, Change: Movements of Social Transformation.* Indianapolis: Bobbs-Merrill.

Geschwender, James A. 1968. "Civil Rights Protest and Riots: A Disappearing Distinction." *Social Science Quarterly* 49 (3): 474–84.

Giminez, Martha. 1988. "Minorities and the World-System: Theoretical and Political Implications of the Internationalization of Minorities." In *Racism, Sexism, and the World-System,* edited by Joan Smith et al. Westport, Conn.: Greenwood.

Gitlin, Todd. 1979. "Prime Time Ideology: The Hegemonic Process in Television Entertainment." *Social Problems* 26 (3): 251–66.

Glazer, Nathan, and Daniel P. Moynihan. 1963. *Beyond the Melting Pot: The Negroes, Puerto Ricans, Jews, Italians, and Irish of New York City.* Cambridge: MIT Press.

Glick Schiller, Nina. 1977. "Ethnic Groups Are Made, Not Born." In *Identity and Ethnicity,* edited by George L. Hicks and Philip E. Leis. North Scituate, Mass.: Duxbury.

———, et al. 1987. "Exile, Ethnic, Refugee: The Changing Organizational Identities of Haitian Immigrants." *Migration World* 15 (1): 7–11.

———. 1995. "The Implications of Haitian Transnationalism for U.S.-Haiti Relations: Contradictions of the Deterritorialized Nation-State." *Journal of Haitian Studies* 1 (1): 111–23.

Goldberg, David Theo, ed. 1990. *Anatomy of Racism.* Minneapolis: University of Minnesota Press.

———. 1993. " 'Polluting the Body Politic': Racist Discourse and Urban Location." In *Racism, the City, and the State,* edited by Malcolm Cross and Michael Keith. London: Routledge.

Gooding-Williams, Robert, ed. 1993. *Reading Rodney King/Reading Urban Uprising.* New York: Routledge.

Gordis, Robert. 1967. "Negroes are Anti-Semitic Because They Want a Scapegoat." *New York Times Magazine.* April 23.

Gordon, Paul, and David Rosenberg. 1989. *Daily Racism: The Press and Black People in Britain.* London: Runnymede Trust.

Gotanda, Neil. 1991. "A Critique of 'Our Constitution is Color-Blind.' " *Stanford Law Review* 44 (1): 1–68.

Gould, Stephen Jay. 1996. *The Mismeasure of Man,* rev. and exp. ed. New York: W. W. Norton & Co.

Green, Charles, and Basil Wilson. 1987. "The Afro-American, Caribbean Dialectic: White Incumbents, Black Constituents and the 1984 Election in New York City." *Afro-Americans in New York Life and History* 11 (1): 49–65.

——. 1989. *The Struggle for Black Empowerment in New York City: Beyond the Politics of Pigmentation.* New York: Praeger.

Green, Shelley, and Paul Pryde. 1990. *Black Entrepreneurship in America.* New Brunswick, N.J.: Transaction.

Greenberg, Cheryl Lynn. 1991. *"Or Does It Explode?" Black Harlem in the Great Depression.* New York: Oxford University Press.

Greenberg, Edward S., et al., eds. 1971. *Black Politics: The Inevitability of Conflict.* New York: Holt, Rinehart and Winston.

Greenstone, J. David, and Paul E. Peterson. 1973. *Race and Authority in Urban Politics: Community Participation and the War on Poverty.* Chicago: University of Chicago Press.

Gurr, Ted Robert. 1970. *Why Men Rebel.* Princeton: Princeton University Press.

Gusfield, Joseph. 1981. "Social Movements and Social Change." In *Research in Social Movements, Conflict and Change* 4: 317–39.

Hacker, Andrew. 1992. *Two Nations: Separate, Hostile, Unequal.* New York: Charles Scribner's Sons.

Haines, Herbert. 1988. *Black Radicals and the Civil Rights Mainstream, 1954–1970.* Knoxville: University of Tennessee Press.

Hall, Stuart, et al. 1978. *Policing the Crisis: Mugging, the State, and Law and Order.* London: Macmillan.

Hall, Stuart. 1988. "New Ethnicities." In *Black Film, British Cinema,* edited by Kobena Mercer. ICA Documents, vol. 7. London: Institute of Contemporary Arts.

Hallin, D. C. 1985. "The American News Media: A Critical Theory Perspective." In *Critical Theory and Public Life,* edited by J. Forrester. Cambridge: MIT Press.

Hamill, Pete. 1990. "The New Race Hustle." *Esquire.* September.

Hamilton, Charles V. 1990. "Needed, More Foxes: The Black Experience." In *Urban Politics, New York Style,* edited by Jewel Bellush and Dick Netzer. Armonk, N.Y.: M. E. Sharpe.

Hare, Nathan. 1968. "How White Power Whitewashes Black Power." In *The Black Power Revolt,* edited by Floyd Barbour. Boston: Porter Sargent.

Harris, Abram. 1936. *The Negro as Capitalist: A Study of Banking and Business Among American Negroes.* Philadelphia: American Academy of Political and Social Science.

Hatchett, David. 1990. "Minding The Store." *City Limits.* December.

Heller, Celia S., and Alphonso Pinkney. 1965. "The Attitudes of Negroes Toward Jews." *Social Forces* 43 (3): 364–69.

Hellwig, David J. 1977. "Afro-American Reactions to the Japanese and the Anti-Japanese Movement, 1906–1924." *Phylon* 38 (1): 93–104.

Henderson, Lenneal J., Jr., ed. 1972. *Black Political Life in the United States*. San Francisco: Chandler.

Hentoff, Nat, et al. 1969. *Black Anti-Semitism and Jewish Racism*. New York: Richard W. Baron.

Hentoff, Nat. 1990. "Can New York Endure the Dinkins Mayoralty?" *Village Voice*, Dec. 11.

Herman, Edward S., and Noam Chomsky. 1988. *Manufacturing Consent: The Political Economy of the Mass Media*. New York: Pantheon.

Hill, Herbert. 1965. "Racial Inequality in Employment: The Patterns of Discrimination." *Annals of the American Academy of Political and Social Science* 357: 30–46.

Hill, Richard Child. 1984. "Fiscal Crisis, Austerity Politics, and Alternative Urban Policies." In *Marxism and the Metropolis*, edited by William K. Tabb and Larry Sawers. New York: Oxford University Press.

Hirsch, Eric L. 1986. "The Creation of Political Solidarity in Social Movement Organizations." *Sociological Quarterly* 27 (3): 373–87.

———. 1990. "Sacrifice for the Cause: The Impact of Group Processes on Recruitment and Commitment in Protest Movements." *American Sociological Review* 55: 243–54.

Holden, Matthew, Jr. 1972. "The Crisis of the Republic: Reflections on Race and Politics." In *Black Political Life in the United States*, edited by Lenneal J. Henderson Jr. San Francisco: Chandler.

Holloway, Harry. 1968. "Negro Political Strategy: Coalition or Independent Power Politics." *Social Science Quarterly* 49 (3): 534–47.

hooks, bell. 1992. *Black Looks: Race and Representation*. Boston: South End.

Hornung, Rick. 1990. "Fear and Loathing in City Hall." *Village Voice*. May 29.

Hsia, Jayjia, and Marsha Hirano-Nakanishi. 1989. "The Demographics of Diversity: Asian Americans and Higher Education." *Change*, November / December: 20–27.

Hunt, Scott, Robert Benford, and David Snow. 1994. "Identity Fields: Framing Processes and the Social Construction of Movement Identities." In *New Social Movements: From Ideology to Identity*, edited by Enrique Laraña, Hank Johnston, and Joseph Gusfield. Philadelphia: Temple University Press.

Hurh, Won Moo, and Kwang Chung Kim. 1989. "The 'Success' Image of Asian Americans: Its Validity, and Its Practical and Theoretical Implications." *Ethnic and Racial Studies* 12 (4): 512–38.

Ikemoto, Lisa. 1993. "Traces of the Master Narrative in the Story of African American / Korean American Conflict: How We Constructed 'Los Angeles.' " *Southern California Law Review* 66: 1581–98.

Jacoby, Tamar. 1991. "Sonny Carson and the Politics of Protest." *New York: The City Journal*. Summer.

Jaynes, Gerald, and Robin Williams Jr., eds. 1989. *A Common Destiny: Blacks and American Society*. Washington, D.C.: National Academy.

Jencks, Christopher, and Paul E. Peterson, eds. 1991. *The Urban Underclass*. Washington, D.C.: Brookings Institution.

Jenkins, J. Craig, and Charles Perrow. 1977. "Insurgency of the Powerless: Farm Workers' Movements, 1946–1972." *American Sociological Review* 42: 249–68.

Jennings, James. 1992. *The Politics of Black Empowerment: The Transformation of Black Activism in Urban America*. Detroit: Wayne State University Press.

——. 1992. "New Urban Racial and Ethnic Conflicts in United States Politics." *Sage Race Relations Abstracts* 17 (3): 3–36.

Jensen, Richard J., and Cara J. Abeyta. 1987. "The Minority in the Middle: Asian American Dissent in the 1960s and 1970s." *The Western Journal of Speech Communication* 51: 402–16.

Jo, Moon H. 1992. "Korean Merchants in the Black Community: Prejudice Among the Victims of Prejudice." *Ethnic and Racial Studies* 15 (3): 395–411.

Jo, Yung-Hwan, ed. 1980. *Political Participation of Asian Americans: Problems and Strategies.* Chicago: Pacific / Asian American Health Center.

Johnson, James, Jr., and Melvin Oliver. 1989. "Interethnic Minority Conflict in Urban America: The Effects of Economic and Social Dislocations." *Urban Geography* 10: 449–66.

Johnston, Hank. 1991. *Tales of Nationalism: Catalonia, 1939–1979.* New Brunswick, N.J.: Rutgers University Press.

——, Enrique Laraña, and Joseph Gusfield. 1994. "Identities, Grievances, and New Social Movements." In *New Social Movements: From Ideology to Identity,* edited by Enrique Laraña, Hank Johnston, and Joseph Gusfield. Philadelphia: Temple University Press.

——, and Bert Klandermans. 1995. "The Cultural Analysis of Social Movements." In *Social Movements and Culture,* edited by Hank Johnston and Bert Klandermans. Minneapolis: University of Minnesota Press.

Jones, Delmos J. 1979. "Not in My Community: The Neighborhood Movement and Institutionalized Racism." *Social Policy* 10 (2): 44–47.

Jones, Mack H. 1972. "A Frame of Reference for Black Politics." In *Black Political Life in the United States,* edited by Lenneal J. Henderson Jr. San Francisco: Chandler.

——. 1978. "Black Political Empowerment in Atlanta: Myth and Reality." *Annals of the American Academy of Political and Social Science* 439: 90–117.

Kain, John F., and Joseph J. Persky. 1969. "Alternative to the Gilded Ghetto." *Public Interest* 14: 74–87.

Karp, W., and H. R. Shapiro. 1969. "Exploding the Myth of Black Anti-Semitism." In *Black Anti-Semitism and Jewish Racism,* edited by Nat Hentoff. New York: Baron.

Kasarda, John. 1986. "The Regional and Urban Redistribution of People and Jobs in the U.S." Paper prepared for the National Research Council Committee on National Urban Policy, National Academy of Science.

Kasinitz, Philip. 1992. *Caribbean New York: Black Immigrants and the Politics of Race.* Ithaca: Cornell University Press.

Katz, Shlomo, ed. 1967. *Negro and Jew: An Encounter in America.* New York: Macmillan.

Katznelson, Ira. 1981. *City Trenches: Urban Politics and the Patterning of Class in the United States.* New York: Pantheon.

Kaufman, Jonathan. 1988. *Broken Alliance: The Turbulent Times Between Blacks and Jews in America.* New York: Charles Scribner's Sons.

Keely, Charles B. 1980. "Immigration Policy and the New Immigrants, 1965–76." In *Sourcebook on the New Immigration: Implications for the United States and the International Community,* edited by Roy Simon Bryce-Laporte. New Brunswick, N.J.: Transaction.

Killian, Lewis, and Charles Grigg. 1964. *Racial Crisis in America: Leadership in Conflict.* Englewood Cliffs, N.J.: Prentice-Hall, Inc.

Killian, Lewis. 1972. "The Significance of Extremism in the Black Revolution." *Social Problems* 20: 41–48.

Kim, Claire Jean. 1999. "The Racial Triangulation of Asian Americans." *Politics and Society* 27 (1): 105–38.

Kim, Elaine. 1993. "Home Is Where the Han Is: A Korean-American Perspective on the Los Angeles Upheavals." In *Reading Rodney King/Reading Urban Uprising,* edited by Robert Gooding-Williams. New York: Routledge.

Kim, Illsoo. 1981. *New Urban Immigrants: The Korean Community in New York.* Princeton: Princeton University Press.

Kim, Kwang Chung, and Won Moo Hurh. 1983. "Korean-Americans and the 'Success' Image: A Critique." *Amerasia Journal* 10 (2): 3–23.

Kim, Shin. 1991. "Conceptualization of Inter-Minority Group Conflict: Conflict Between Korean Entrepreneurs and Black Local Residents." In *The Korean-American Community: Present and Future,* edited by Tae-Hwan Kwak and Seong Hyong Lee. Masan, Korea: Kyung Nam University Press.

Klandermans, Bert. 1984. "Mobilization and Participation: Social-Psychological Expansions of Resource Mobilization Theory." *American Sociological Review* 49: 583–600.

——. 1986. "New Social Movements and Resource Mobilization: The European and the American Approach." *Journal of Mass Emergencies and Disasters* 4: 13–37.

——, Hanspeter Kriesi, and Sidney Tarrow, eds. 1988. *From Structure to Action: Comparing Social Movement Research Across Cultures.* Greenwich, Conn.: JAI.

——. 1989. "Grievance Interpretation and Success Expectations: The Social Construction of Protest." *Social Behaviour* 4: 113–25.

——. 1992. "The Social Construction of Protest and Multiorganizational Fields." In *Frontiers in Social Movement Theory,* edited by Aldon D. Morris and Carol McClurg Mueller. New Haven: Yale University Press.

Klein, Joe. 1990. "Race: The Mess. A City on the Verge of a Nervous Breakdown." *New York.* May 28.

Koch, Nadine, and H. Eric Schockman. 1994. "Riot, Rebellion, or Civil Unrest? Korean American and African American Business Communities in Los Angeles." In *Community In Crisis,* edited by George O. Totten III and H. Eric Schockman. Los Angeles: USC Center for Multiethnic and Transnational Studies.

Kuo, Wen H. 1979. "On the Study of Asian-Americans: Its Current State and Agenda." *Sociological Quarterly* 20: 279–90.

Kushnick, Louis. 1991. "Race, Class and Power: The New York Decentralization Controversy." In *Black Communities and Urban Development in America, 1720–1990,* edited by Kenneth L. Kusmer. New York: Garland.

Kwang, Chung Kim, and Won Moo Hurh. 1983. "Korean Americans and the 'Success' Image: A Critique." *Amerasia Journal* 10 (2): 3–22.

Kwong, Peter. 1987. *The New Chinatown.* New York: Hill and Wang.

——. 1990. "Doing the Right Thing: After Flatbush, Asians May No Longer Be the Silent Minority." *Village Voice.* May 29.

Laguerre, Michel S. 1984. *American Odyssey: Haitians in New York City.* Ithaca: Cornell University Press.

Lang, Kurt, and Gladys Lang. 1961. *Collective Dynamics.* New York: Crowell.

Laue, James H. 1965. "The Changing Character of Negro Protest." *Annals of the American Academy of Political and Social Science* 357: 119–26.

Lawyers Committee for Human Rights. 1990. *Refugee Refoulement: The Forced Return of Haitians Under the U.S.-Haitian Interdiction Agreement.* New York: Lawyers Committee for Human Rights.

Lee, Heon Cheol. 1993. "Black-Korean Conflict in New York City: A Sociological Analysis." Ph.D. diss., Columbia University.

Lee, G. Jiyun. 1991. "Racism Comes in All Colors: The Anti-Korean Boycott in Flatbush." *Reconstruction* 1 (3): 72–76.

Lee, Sharon M. 1989. "Asian Immigration and American Race Relations: From Exclusion to Acceptance?" *Ethnic and Racial Studies* 12 (3): 368–90.

Lewinson, Edwin R. 1974. *Black Politics in New York City.* New York: Twayne.

Lewis, Oscar. 1966. *La Vida: A Puerto Rican Family in the Culture of Poverty—San Juan and New York.* New York: Random House.

Light, Ivan. 1972. *Ethnic Enterprise in America.* Berkeley: University of California Press.

——, and Angel A. Sanchez. 1987. "Immigrant Entrepreneurs in 272 SMSAs." *Sociological Perspectives* 30 (4): 373–99.

——, and Edna Bonacich. 1988. *Immigrant Entrepreneurs: Koreans in Los Angeles, 1965–82.* Berkeley: University of California Press.

——, Im Jung Kwuon, and Deng Zhong. 1990. "Korean Rotating Credit Associations in Los Angeles." *Amerasia* 16 (1): 35–54.

——, Hadas Har-Chvi, and Kenneth Kan. 1994. "Black/Korean Conflict in Los Angeles." In *Managing Social Conflicts,* edited by Seamus Dunn. Newbury Park, Calif.: Sage.

Lipsky, Michael. 1968. "Protest as a Political Resource." *American Political Science Review* 62: 1144–58.

——, and David J. Olson. 1973. "Riot Commission Politics." In *Ghetto Revolts,* 2d ed., edited by Peter H. Rossi. New Brunswick, N.J.: Transaction.

——. 1977. *Commission Politics: The Processing of Racial Crisis in America.* New Brunswick, N.J.: Transaction.

Lo, Clarence Y. H. 1992. "Communities of Challengers in Social Movement Theory." In *Frontiers in Social Movement Theory,* edited by Aldon D. Morris and Carol McClurg Mueller. New Haven: Yale University Press.

Logan, John R., and Harvey L. Molotch. 1987. *Urban Fortunes: The Political Economy of Place.* Berkeley: University of California Press.

Lukes, Steven. 1974. *Power: A Radical View.* London: Macmillan.

Lyman, Stanford M. 1971. "Strangers in the City: The Chinese in the Urban Frontier." In *Roots: An Asian American Reader,* edited by Amy Tachiki et al. Los Angeles: UCLA Asian American Studies Center.

Macchiarola, Frank J., and Joseph G. Diaz. 1993. "Minority Political Empowerment in New York City: Beyond the Voting Rights Act." *Political Science Quarterly* 108 (1): 37–57.

Martin, Tony. 1983. *The Pan-African Connection: From Slavery to Garvey and Beyond.* Cambridge: Schenkman.

Martindale, Carolyn. 1986. *The White Press and Black America.* New York: Greenwood.

Marx, Gary T. 1967. *Protest and Prejudice: A Study of Belief in the Black Community.* New York: Harper & Row.

——. 1971. *Racial Conflict: Tension and Change in American Society.* Boston: Little, Brown and Co.

Massey, Douglas S., and Nancy A. Denton. 1993. *American Apartheid: Segregation and the Making of the Underclass.* Cambridge: Harvard University Press.

Massey, Douglas S. 1998. "Why Racial Segregation Matters." Paper presented at the Conference on Social Science Knowledge on Race, Racism, and Race Relations, McLean, Virginia, April 26–28.

McAdam, Doug. 1983. *Political Process and the Development of Black Insurgency, 1930–1970.* Chicago: University of Chicago Press.

———. 1988. "Micromobilization Contexts and Recruitment to Activism." *International Social Movement Research* 1: 125–54.

———, John D. McCarthy, and Mayer N. Zald. 1988. "Social Movements." In *Handbook of Sociology,* edited by Neil J. Smelser. Newbury Park, Calif.: Sage.

———. 1994. "Culture and Social Movements." In *New Social Movements: From Ideology to Identity,* edited by Enrique Laraña, Hank Johnston, and Joseph Gusfield. Philadelphia: Temple University Press.

———. 1996. "The Framing Function of Movement Tactics." In *Comparative Perspectives on Social Movements,* edited by Doug McAdam et al. New York: Cambridge University Press.

———, et al. 1996. "Introduction: Opportunities, Mobilizing Structures, and Framing Processes." In *Comparative Perspectives on Social Movements,* edited by Doug McAdam et al. New York: Cambridge University Press.

McCarthy, John D., and Mayer N. Zald. 1977. "Resource Mobilization and Social Movements: A Partial Theory." *American Journal of Sociology* 82: 1212–41.

McCartney, John T. 1992. *Black Power Ideologies: An Essay on African-American Political Thought.* Philadelphia: Temple University Press.

McGurn, William. 1991. "The Silent Minority: Asian-Americans' Affinity with Republican Party Principles." *National Review.* June.

McPherson, James A. 1991. "Out of Many, a Few." *Reconstruction* 1 (3): 83–87.

Meier, August. 1963. "The Civil Rights Movement." *Current* 42: 35–41.

———, and Elliott Rudwick. 1968. "Negro Protest and Urban Unrest." *Social Science Quarterly* 49 (3): 438–43.

———. 1973. *CORE: A Study in the Civil Rights Movement, 1942–1968.* New York: Oxford University Press.

———, et al., eds. 1991. *Black Protest in the Sixties: Articles from the New York Times.* New York: Markus Wiener.

Melucci, Alberto. 1980. "The New Social Movements: A Theoretical Approach." *Social Science Information* 19: 199–226.

———. 1981. "Ten Hypotheses for the Analysis of New Movements." In *Contemporary Italian Sociology,* edited by D. Pinto. Cambridge: Cambridge University Press.

———. 1985. "The Symbolic Challenge of Contemporary Movements." *Social Research* 52: 781–816.

———. 1989. *Nomads of the Present: Social Movements and Individual Needs in Contemporary Society.* Philadelphia: Temple University Press.

Miles, Jack. 1992. "Blacks vs. Browns." *Atlantic Monthly* 270 (4): 41–68.

Miles, Robert. 1989. *Racism.* London: Routledge.

Min, Pyong Gap. 1986–1987. "Filipino and Korean Immigrants in Small Business: A Comparative Analysis." *Amerasia Journal* 13 (1): 53–71.

———. 1988. *Ethnic Business Enterprise: Korean Small Business in Atlanta.* New York: Center for Migration Studies.

———. 1991. "Korean Immigrants' Small Business Activities and Korean-Black Interracial Conflicts." In *The Korean-American Community: Present and Future,* edited by Tae-Hwan Kwak and Seong Hyong Lee. Seoul: Kyungnam University Press.

———. 1996. *Caught in the Middle: Korean Communities in New York and Los Angeles.* Berkeley: University of California Press.

Mollenkopf, John. 1990. "New York: The Great Anomaly." In *Racial Politics in American Cities,* edited by Rufus P. Browning, Dale Rogers Marshall, and David H. Tabb. New York: Longman.

———. 1991. "Political Inequality." In *Dual City: Restructuring New York,* edited by John Mollenkopf and Manuel Castells. New York: Russell Sage Foundation.

———, and Manuel Castells. 1991. Introduction to *Dual City: Restructuring New York,* edited by John Mollenkopf and Manuel Castells. New York: Russell Sage Foundation.

———. 1992. *A Phoenix in the Ashes: The Rise and Fall of the Koch Coalition in New York City Politics.* Princeton: Princeton University Press.

———. 1993. *New York City in the 1980s: A Social, Economic, and Political Atlas.* New York: Simon & Schuster.

———. 1997. "New York: The Great Anomaly." In *Racial Politics in American Cities,* 2d ed., edited by Rufus P. Browning, Dale Rogers Marshall, and David H. Tabb. New York: Longman.

Molotch, Harvey. 1979. "Media and Movements." In *The Dynamics of Social Movements: Resource Mobilization, Social Control, and Tactics,* edited by Mayer N. Zald and John McCarthy. Cambridge, Mass.: Winthrop.

Moore, Linda Wright. 1990. "Can the Press Do the Right Thing? How Your News Looks to Us." *Columbia Journalism Review* July / August: 21–24.

Morris, Aldon D. 1984. *The Origins of the Civil Rights Movement: Black Communities Organizing for Change.* New York: Free Press.

———, and Carol McClurg Mueller, eds. 1992. *Frontiers in Social Movement Theory.* New Haven: Yale University Press.

Morris, Milton D. 1975. *The Politics of Black America.* New York: Harper & Row.

Morsell, John A. 1965. "The National Association for the Advancement of Colored People and Its Strategy." *Annals of the American Academy of Political and Social Science* 357: 97–101.

Moss, Mitchell, and Sarah Ludwig. 1991. "The Structure of the Media." In *Dual City: Restructuring New York,* edited by John Mollenkopf and Manuel Castells. New York: Russell Sage Foundation.

Mottl, Tahi L. 1980. "The Analysis of Countermovements." *Social Problems* 27 (5): 620–35.

Moynihan, Daniel P. 1965. *The Negro Family: The Case for National Action.* Washington, D.C.: U.S. Department of Labor.

Mueller, Carol McClurg. 1992. "Building Social Movement Theory." In *Frontiers in Social Movement Theory,* edited by Aldon D. Morris and Carol McClurg Mueller. New Haven: Yale University Press.

Muraskin, William. 1972. "The Harlem Boycott of 1934: Black Nationalism and the Rise of Labor-Union Consciousness." *Labor History* 13 (3): 361–73.

Murray, Charles. 1984. *Losing Ground: American Social Policy, 1950–1980.* New York: Basic.

Myrdal, Gunnar. 1962. *An American Dilemma: The Negro Problem and Modern Democracy*, 20th anniv. ed. New York: Harper & Row.

Nagel, Joane. 1986. "The Political Construction of Ethnicity." In *Competitive Ethnic Relations*, edited by Susan Olzak and Joane Nagel. San Diego: Academic.

Naison, Mark D. 1974. "Communism and Black Nationalism in the Depression: The Case of Harlem." *Journal of Ethnic Studies* 2 (2): 24–38.

Nakanishi, Don T. 1985–1986. "Asian American Politics: An Agenda For Research." *Amerasia* 12 (2): 1–27.

——. 1989. "A Quota on Excellence? The Asian American Admissions Debate." *Change* November/December: 39–47.

"Negro-Jewish Relations in America: A Symposium." 1966. *Midstream* 12 (9).

Netzer, Dick. 1990. "The Economy and the Governing of the City." In *Urban Politics, New York Style*, edited by Jewel Bellush and Dick Netzer. Armonk, N.Y.: M. E. Sharpe.

New York City Department of City Planning. 1992. *The Newest New Yorkers: An Analysis of Immigration into New York City During the 1980s*. New York: New York City Department of City Planning.

New York City Human Rights Commission. 1990. *Report of the Mayor's Committee Investigating the Protest Against Two Korean-Owned Groceries on Church Avenue in Brooklyn*. New York: New York City Human Rights Commission.

Newman, Dorothy K., et al. 1978. *Protest, Politics, and Prosperity: Black Americans and White Institutions, 1940–1975*. New York: Pantheon.

Oberschall, Anthony. 1973. *Social Conflict and Social Movements*. Englewood Cliffs, N.J.: Prentice-Hall.

——. 1979. "Protracted Conflict." In *The Dynamics of Social Movements: Resource Mobilization, Social Control, and Tactics*, edited by Mayer N. Zald and John McCarthy. Cambridge, Mass.: Winthrop.

Offe, Claus. 1985. "New Social Movements: Challenging the Boundaries of Institutional Politics." *Social Research* 52 (4): 817–68.

Office of Community Board 14. n.d. *Neighborhood Information Kit*. New York.

——. n.d. *Statement of Community District Needs, Fiscal Year 1993*. New York.

O'Hare, William P., and Judy C. Felt. 1991. *Asian Americans: America's Fastest Growing Minority Group*. Washington, D.C.: Population Reference Bureau.

Okihiro, Gary Y. 1994. *Margins and Mainstreams: Asians in American History and Culture*. Seattle: University of Washington Press.

Olzak, Susan. 1983. "Contemporary Ethnic Mobilization." *Annual Review of Sociology* 9: 355–74.

Omi, Michael, and Howard Winant. 1994. *Racial Formation in the United States: From the 1960s to the 1980s*, 2d ed. New York: Routledge & Kegan Paul.

Ong, Paul, Kyeyoung Park, and Yasmin Tong. 1994. "The Korean-Black Conflict and the State." In *New Asian Immigration in Los Angeles and Global Restructuring*, edited by Paul Ong, Edna Bonacich, and Lucie Cheng. Philadelphia: Temple University Press.

Osajima, Keith. 1988. "Asian Americans as the Model Minority: An Analysis of the Popular Press Image in the 1960s and 1980s." In *Promises and Prospects for Asian American Studies*, edited by Gary Y. Okihiro et al. Pullman: Washington State University Press.

Ottley, Roi. 1943. *'New World A-Coming': Inside Black America*. New York: Literary Classics.

——, and William J. Weatherby, eds. 1967. *The Negro in New York: An Informal Social History.* New York: Oceana.

Park, Kyeyoung. 1995. "The Reinvention of Affirmative Action: Korean Immigrants' Changing Conceptions of African Americans and Latin Americans." *Urban Anthropology* 24 (1–2): 59–92.

——. 1996. "Use and Abuse of Race and Culture: Black-Korean Tension in America." *American Anthropologist* 98 (3): 492–99.

——. 1997. *The Korean American Dream: Immigrants and Small Business in New York City.* Ithaca: Cornell University Press.

Parrillo, Vincent N. 1982. "Asian Americans in American Politics." In *America's Ethnic Politics,* edited by Joseph S. Roucek and Bernard Eisenberg. Westport, Conn.: Greenwood Press.

Peller, Gary. 1995. "Race-Consciousness." In *Critical Race Theory,* edited by Kimberlé Crenshaw et al. New York: New Press.

People for the American Way. 1992. *Democracy's Next Generation: A Study of American Youth on Race.* 1992. Washington, D.C.: People for the American Way.

Perry, Stewart E. 1972. "Black Institutions, Black Separatism, and Ghetto Economic Development." *Human Organization* 31 (3): 271–78.

Peterson, Paul. 1981. *City Limits.* Chicago: University of Chicago Press.

Pinkney, Alphonso. 1976. *Red, Black and Green: Black Nationalism in the United States.* Cambridge: Cambridge University Press.

——. 1978–1979. "Recent Unrest Between Blacks and Jews: The Claims of Anti-Semitism and Reverse Discrimination." *Black Sociologist* 8 (1–4): 38–57.

Piven, Frances Fox, and Richard A. Cloward. 1971. *Regulating the Poor: The Functions of Public Welfare.* New York: Vintage.

Piven, Frances Fox. 1976. "The Social Structuring of Political Protest." *Politics and Society* 6 (3): 297–326.

——, and Richard A. Cloward. 1979. *Poor People's Movements: Why They Succeed, How They Fail,* rev. ed. New York: Vintage.

——, and Roger Friedland. 1984. "Public Choice and Private Power." In *Public Service Provision and Urban Development,* edited by A. Kirby et al. New York: St. Martin's.

——, and Richard A. Cloward. 1992. "Normalizing Collective Protest." In *Frontiers in Social Movement Theory,* edited by Aldon D. Morris and Carol McClurg Mueller. New Haven: Yale University Press.

——, and Richard A. Cloward. 1995a. "Collective Protest: A Critique of Resource-Mobilization Theory." In *Social Movements: Critiques, Concepts, Case-Studies,* edited by Stanford M. Lyman. New York: New York University Press.

——, and Richard A. Cloward. 1995b. "Movements and Dissensus Politics." In *Cultural Politics and Social Movements,* edited by Marcy Darnovsky et al. Philadelphia: Temple University Press.

Platt, Anthony, ed. 1971. *The Politics of Riot Commissions, 1917–1970.* New York: Macmillan.

Portes, Alejandro, and Ruben G. Rumbaut. 1990. *Immigrant America: A Portrait.* Berkeley: University of California Press.

——, and Min Zhou. 1992. "Gaining the Upper Hand: Economic Mobility Among Immigrant and Domestic Minorities." *Ethnic and Racial Studies* 15 (4): 491–522.

Posadas, Barbara M. 1982. "The Hierarchy of Color and Psychological Adjustment in an Industrial Environment: Filipinos, the Pullman Company, and the Brotherhood of Sleeping Car Porters." *Labor History* 23 (3): 349–73.

"Race and Hispanic Origin for the United States: 1990 and 1980." 1991. *Census and You* 26 (9): 3.

Rawls, John. 1971. *A Theory of Justice.* Cambridge: Belknap Press of Harvard University Press.

Reed, Adolph, Jr. 1988. "The Black Urban Regime: Structural Origins and Constraints." In *Comparative Urban and Community Research* 1: 138–88.

———. 1992. "The Underclass As Myth and Symbol: The Poverty of Discourse About Poverty." *Radical America* 24: 21–40.

Reiss, Albert J., Jr., and Howard Aldrich. 1971. "Absentee Ownership and Management in the Black Ghetto: Social and Economic Consequences." *Social Problems* 18 (3): 319–38.

Report of the National Advisory Commission on Civil Disorders. 1968. New York: Bantam.

Ricketts, Erol R., and Isabel V. Sawhill. 1988. "Defining and Measuring the Underclass." *Journal of Policy Analysis and Management* 7: 316–25.

Rieder, Jonathan. 1985. *Canarsie: The Jews and Italians of Brooklyn Against Liberalism.* Cambridge: Harvard University Press.

———. 1990. "Trouble in Store." *New Republic.* July 2.

Rigg, Cynthia, and Matt Richtel. 1990. "Korean Grocers Wilt as Competition Grows." *Crain's New York Business.* May 21.

Robinson, Reginald Leamon. 1993. " 'The Other Against Itself': Deconstructing the Violent Discourse Between Korean and African Americans." *Southern California Law Review* 67 (1): 15–115.

Roediger, David. 1991. *The Wages of Whiteness: Race and the Making of the American Working Class.* London: Verso.

Rogers, David. 1968. *110 Livingston Street: Politics and Bureaucracy in the New York School System.* New York: Random House.

———. 1990. "Community Control and Decentralization." In *Urban Politics, New York Style,* edited by Jewel Bellush and Dick Netzer. Armonk, N.Y.: M. E. Sharpe.

Rose, Peter I. 1981. "Blacks and Jews: The Strained Alliance." *Annals of the American Academy of Political and Social Science* 454: 55–69.

Rosenberg, Terry J. 1992. *Poverty in New York City, 1991: A Research Bulletin.* New York: Community Service Society.

Rossi, Peter H., ed. 1973. *Ghetto Revolts,* 2d ed. New Brunswick, N.J.: Transaction.

Rudé, George. 1980. *Ideology and Popular Protest.* New York: Pantheon.

Runcie, John. 1986. "Marcus Garvey and the Harlem Renaissance." *Afro-Americans in New York Life and History* 10 (2): 7–28.

Rupp, Leila, and Verta Taylor. 1987. *Survival in the Doldrums: The American Women's Rights Movement, 1945 to the 1960s.* New York: Oxford University Press.

Rustin, Bayard. 1965. "From Protest to Politics: The Future of the Civil Rights Movement." *Commentary* 39 (2): 25–31.

———. 1966. " 'Black Power' and Coalition Politics." *Commentary* 42 (3): 35–40.

———. 1970. "The Failure of Black Separatism." *Harper's.* January.

Safa, Helen I. 1983. "Caribbean Migration to the United States: Cultural Identity and the

Process of Assimilation." In *Different People: Studies in Ethnicity and Education*, edited by Edgar B. Giumbert. Atlanta: Center for Cross-Cultural Education.

Said, Edward W. 1981. *Covering Islam: How the Media and the Experts Determine How We See the Rest of the World*. New York: Pantheon.

Sa-I-Gu. 1993. Produced by Christine Choy, Elaine Kim, and Dai Sil Kim-Gibson. Written and directed by Dai Sil Kim-Gibson. Codirected by Christine Choy. 39 min. San Francisco: CrossCurrent Media. Videocassette.

Salisbury, Robert H. 1969. "An Exchange Theory of Interest Groups." *Midwestern Journal of Political Science* 13: 1–32.

Sandmeyer, Elmer C. 1939. *The Anti-Chinese Movement in California*. Urbana: University of Illinois Press.

Sassen, Saskia. 1988. *The Mobility of Labor and Capital: A Study in International Investment and Labor Flow*. Cambridge: Cambridge University Press.

Savitch, H. V. 1990. "The Federal Impact on City Politics." In *Urban Politics, New York Style*, edited by Jewel Bellush and Dick Netzer. Armonk, N.Y.: M. E. Sharpe.

Saxton, Alexander. 1971. *The Indispensable Enemy: Labor and the Anti-Chinese Movement in California*. Berkeley: University of California Press.

Schudson, Michael. 1989. "The Sociology of News Production." *Media, Culture and Society* 11: 263–82.

Schuman, Howard, et al. 1985. *Racial Attitudes in America*. Cambridge: Harvard University Press.

Scott, James C. 1985. *Weapons of the Weak: Everyday Forms of Peasant Resistance*. New Haven: Yale University Press.

———. 1990. *Domination and the Arts of Resistance: Hidden Transcripts*. New Haven: Yale University Press.

Sellers, Cleveland. 1973. *The River of No Return: The Autobiography of a Black Militant and the Life and Death of SNCC*. New York: William Morrow.

Sexton, Donald E., Jr. 1973. *Groceries in the Ghetto*. Lexington, Mass.: D. C. Heath and Company.

Shankman, Arnold. 1977. " 'Asiatic Ogre' or 'Desirable Citizen'? The Image of Japanese Americans in the Afro-American Press, 1867–1933." *Pacific Historical Review* 46 (4): 567–87.

———. 1978. "Black on Yellow: Afro-Americans View Chinese Americans, 1850–1935." *Phylon* 39 (1): 1–17.

Shefter, Martin. 1985. *Political Crisis/Fiscal Crisis: The Collapse and Revival of New York City*. New York: Basic.

Sigelman, Lee, and Susan Welch. 1991. *Black Americans' Views of Racial Inequality: The Dream Deferred*. New York: Cambridge University Press.

Sinden, Peter G. 1980. "Anti-Semitism and the Black Power Movement" *Ethnicity* 7: 34–46.

Skocpol, Theda. 1991. "Targeting Within Universalism: Politically Viable Policies to Combat Poverty in the United States." In *The Urban Underclass*, edited by Christopher Jencks and Paul E. Peterson. Washington, D.C.: The Brookings Institution.

Skolnick, Jerome. 1969. *The Politics of Protest: Violent Aspects of Protest and Confrontation*. National Commission on the Causes and Prevention of Violence Staff Study Series, vol. 3. Washington, D.C.: U.S. Government Printing Office.

Sleeper, Jim. 1990. *The Closest of Strangers: Liberalism and the Politics of Race in New York.* New York: W. W. Norton & Co.

Smelser, Neil J. 1962. *Theory of Collective Behavior.* New York: Free Press.

Smith, Michael Peter. 1988. *City, State, and Market: The Political Economy of Urban Society.* Oxford: Basil Blackwell.

Smith, Robert C. 1981. "Black Power and the Transformation from Protest to Politics." *Political Science Quarterly* 96 (3): 431–43.

Smith, Rogers M. 1997. *Civic Ideals: Conflicting Visions of Citizenship in U.S. History.* New Haven: Yale University Press.

Sniderman, Paul M., and Thomas Piazza. 1993. *The Scar of Race.* Cambridge: Belknap Press of Harvard University Press.

Snow, David A., Louis A. Zurcher, and Sheldon Eckland-Olson. 1980. "Social Networks and Social Movements: A Microstructural Approach to Differential Recruitment." *American Sociological Review* 45: 787–801.

Snow, David A., et al. 1986. "Frame Alignment Processes, Micromobilization, and Movement Participation." *American Sociological Review* 51: 464–81.

Snow, David A., and Robert D. Benford. 1988. "Ideology, Frame Resonance, and Participant Mobilization." *International Social Movement Research* 1: 197–217.

——. 1992. "Master Frames and Cycles of Protest." In *Frontiers in Social Movement Theory,* edited by Aldon D. Morris and Carol McClurg Mueller. New Haven: Yale University Press.

Sobel, B. Z., and May L. Sobel. 1966. "Negroes and Jews: American Minority Groups in Conflict." *Judaism* 15 (1): 3–22.

Sowell, Thomas. 1981. *Ethnic America: A History.* New York: Basic.

Spaights, Ernest, and Derek Kenner. 1983. "Black-Jewish Conflict: A Black Perspective." *Social Development Issues* 7 (2): 22–30.

Spear, Allan H. 1967. *Black Chicago: The Making of a Negro Ghetto, 1890–1920.* Chicago: University of Chicago Press.

Spoehr, Luther W. 1973. "Sambo and the Heathen Chinee: Californians' Racial Stereotypes in the Late 1870s." *Pacific Historical Review* 42 (2): 185–204.

Squires, Gregory. 1998. "The Role of Financial Institutions in Creating, Perpetuating, and Dismantling Racial Segregation in Urban Housing Markets." Paper presented at the Conference on Social Science Knowledge on Race, Racism, and Race Relations, McLean, Virginia, April 26–28.

Stafford, Susan Buchanan. 1987. "The Haitians: The Cultural Meaning of Race and Ethnicity." In *New Immigrants In New York,* edited by Nancy Foner. New York: Columbia University Press.

Steinberg, Marc. 1995. "The Roar of the Crowd: Repertoires of Discourse and Collective Action Among the Spitalfields Silk Weavers in Nineteenth-Century London." In *Repertoires and Cycle of Collective Action,* edited by Mark Traugott. Durham, N.C.: Duke University Press.

Steinberg, Stephen. 1981. *The Ethnic Myth: Race, Ethnicity, and Class in America.* New York: Atheneum.

——. 1989. "The Underclass: A Case of Color Blindness." *New Politics* 5 (2): 42–60.

——. 1991. "Shifting the Focus of Blame." *New Politics* 3 (3): 96–100.

Stepick, Alex. 1997. *Pride Against Prejudice: Haitians in the United States*. Boston: Allyn & Bacon.

Stone, Chuck. 1968. *Black Political Power in America*, rev. ed. New York: Dell.

Sturdivant, Frederick D., ed. 1969. *The Ghetto Marketplace*. New York: Free Press.

Suzuki, Bob H. 1989. "Asian Americans as the 'Model Minority': Outdoing Whites? Or Media Hype?" *Change* November / December: 13–19.

Swain, Carol. 1993. *Black Faces, Black Interests: The Representation of African Americans in Congress*. Cambridge: Harvard University Press.

Swidler, Ann. 1986. "Culture in Action: Symbols and Strategies." *American Sociological Review* 51: 273–86.

———. 1995. "Cultural Power and Social Movements." In *Social Movements and Culture*, edited by Hank Johnston and Bert Klandermans. Minneapolis: University of Minnesota Press.

Tabb, William K. 1970. *The Political Economy of the Black Ghetto*. New York: W. W. Norton & Co.

———. 1988. "What Happened to Black Economic Development." *Review of Black Political Economy* 17 (2): 65–88.

Takagi, Dana Y. 1992. *The Retreat From Race: Asian-American Admissions and Racial Politics*. New Brunswick, N.J.: Rutgers University Press.

Tarrow, Sidney. 1992. "Mentalities, Political Cultures, and Collective Action Frames: Constructing Meanings Through Action." In *Frontiers in Social Movement Theory*, edited by Aldon D. Morris and Carol McClurg Mueller. New Haven: Yale University Press.

———. 1994. *Power in Movement: Social Movements, Collective Action and Politics*. New York: Cambridge University Press.

Tate, Katherine. 1993. *From Protest to Politics: The New Black Voters in American Elections*. New York: Russell Sage Foundation.

Taylor, Patrick. 1989. *The Narrative of Liberation: Perspectives on Afro-Caribbean Literature, Popular Culture, and Politics*. Ithaca: Cornell University Press.

Taylor, Verta. 1989. "Social Movement Continuity: The Women's Movement in Abeyance." *American Sociological Review* 54: 761–75.

The Council of the City of New York. Committee on General Welfare. 1990. *An Analysis of the Report of the Mayor's Committee Investigating the Protest Against Two Korean-Owned Groceries on Church Avenue in Brooklyn*. New York.

Thompson, E. P. 1963. *The Making of the English Working Class*. New York: Vintage.

———. 1978. *The Poverty of Theory and Other Essays*. New York: Monthly Review.

Thompson, J. Phillip. 1990. "David Dinkins' Victory in New York City: The Decline of the Democratic Party and the Strengthening of Black Politics." *PS: Political Science and Politics* 23 (2): 145–48.

Tilly, Charles, et al. 1975. *The Rebellious Century, 1830–1930*. Cambridge: Harvard University Press.

Tilly, Charles. 1978. *From Mobilization to Revolution*. New York: Random House.

———. 1995. "Contentious Repertoires in Great Britain, 1758–1834." In *Repertoires and Cycles of Collective Action*, edited by Mark Traugott. Durham, N.C.: Duke University Press.

Tolbert, Emory J. 1980. *The UNIA and Black Los Angeles: Ideology and Community in the American Garvey Movement*. Los Angeles: UCLA Center for Afro-American Studies.

Touraine, Alain. 1981. *The Voice and the Eye: An Analysis of Social Movements.* New York: Cambridge University Press.

———. 1983. *Solidarity.* Cambridge: Cambridge University Press.

———. 1985. "An Introduction to the Study of Social Movements." *Social Research* 52: 749–87.

Troyna, B. 1987. "Reporting Racism: The 'British Way of Life' Observed." In *Race in Britain,* edited by C. Husband. London: Hutchinson.

Tuchman, Gaye. 1978. *Making News: A Study in the Construction of Reality.* New York: Free Press.

Turner, Ralph H., and Lewis M. Killian. 1957. *Collective Behavior.* Englewood Cliffs, N.J.: Prentice-Hall.

Turner, Ralph H. 1969. "The Public Perception of Protest." *American Sociological Review* 34 (6): 815–31.

Ueda, Reed. 1989. "The Coolie and the Model Minority: Reconstructing Asian American History." *Journal of Interdisciplinary History* 20 (1): 117–24.

Uhlaner, Carole J., et al. 1989. "Political Participation of Ethnic Minorities in the 1980's." *Political Behavior* 11 (3): 195–231.

U.S. Commission on Civil Rights. 1992. *Civil Rights Issues Facing Asian Americans in the 1990s.* Washington, D.C.: U.S. Government Printing Office.

Uyematsu, Amy. 1971. "The Emergence of Yellow Power in America." In *Roots: An Asian American Reader,* edited by Amy Tachiki et al. Los Angeles: UCLA Asian American Studies Center.

Valance, Nikos. 1991a. *Disinvestment City: Lending by Manufacturers Hanover Trust Corporation in New York and Texas Commerce Bank in Texas: An Analysis of Denial of Credit to Minorities.* New York: Unpublished report for Association of Community Organizations for Reform Now.

Valance, Nikos. 1991b. *Disinvestment City: The Sequel: Blacks and Other Minorities Need Not Apply.* New York: Unpublished report for Association of Community Organizations for Reform Now.

Valentine, Charles A. 1968. *Culture and Poverty: Critique and Counter-Proposals.* Chicago: University of Chicago Press.

Van Deburg, William L. 1992. *New Day in Babylon: The Black Power Movement and American Culture, 1965–1975.* Chicago: University of Chicago Press.

van den Berghe, Pierre L. 1967. *Race and Racism: A Comparative Perspective.* New York: Wiley.

van Dijk, Teun. 1991. *Racism and the Press.* London: Routledge.

———. 1993. *Elite Discourse and Racism.* Newbury Park, Calif.: Sage.

Vietorisz, Thomas, and Bennett Harrison. 1970. *The Economic Development of Harlem.* New York: Praeger.

Villemez, Wayne J., and John J. Beggs. 1984. "Black Capitalism and Black Inequality: Some Sociological Considerations." *Social Forces* 63 (1): 117–44.

Vincent, Theodore G., ed. 1973. *Voices of a Black Nation: Political Journalism in the Harlem Renaissance.* Trenton: Africa World.

Viteritti, Joseph P. 1990. "The New Charter: Will It Make a Difference?" In *Urban Politics, New York Style,* edited by Jewel Bellush and Dick Netzer. Armonk, N.Y.: M. E. Sharpe.

Vorspan, Albert. 1969. "Blacks and Jews." In *Black Anti-Semitism and Jewish Racism,* edited by Nat Hentoff. New York: Baron.

Wade, Richard C. 1990. "The Withering Away of the Party System." In *Urban Politics, New York Style,* edited by Jewel Bellush and Dick Netzer. Armonk, N.Y.: M. E. Sharpe.

Waldinger, Roger. 1986–1987. "Changing Ladders and Musical Chairs: Ethnicity and Opportunity in Post-Industrial New York." *Politics and Society* 14 (4): 369–401.

——. 1989a. "Structural Opportunity or Ethnic Advantage? Immigrant Business Development in New York." *International Migration Review* 23 (1): 48–72.

——. 1989b. "Race and Ethnicity." In *Setting Municipal Priorities 1990,* edited by Charles Brecher and Raymond D. Harlan. New York: New York University Press.

——. 1996. *Still the Promised City? African-Americans and New Immigrants in Postindustrial New York.* Cambridge: Harvard University Press.

——. Forthcoming. "The Economic Theory of Ethnic Conflict: A Critique and Reformulation." In *Immigrant Businesses on the Urban Economic Fringe: A Case for Interdisciplinary Research,* edited by Jan Rath. London: Macmillan.

Walker, Laura. 1991. "Liberalism and Racial Politics in New York." *Reconstruction* 1 (3): 77–82.

Walters, Ronald W. 1973. "African American Nationalism." *Black World* 22 (12): 9–27.

Walton, Hanes, Jr. 1972. *Black Politics: A Theoretical and Structural Analysis.* Philadelphia: J. B. Lippincott.

Waskow, Arthur I. 1966. *From Race Riot to Sit-In, 1919 and the 1960s.* New York: Anchor.

Wei, William. 1993. *The Asian American Movement.* Philadelphia: Temple University Press.

Weir, Lorna. 1993. "Limitations of New Social Movement Analysis." *Studies in Political Economy* 40: 73–102.

Wellman, David. 1993. *Portraits of White Racism,* 2d ed. New York: Cambridge University Press.

West, Cornell. 1993. *Race Matters.* Boston: Beacon.

Wilson, Basil. 1991. *David Dinkins and the Goliaths of New York City: The 1989 Mayoral Campaign.* Albany: SUNY African American Institute.

Wilson, James Q. 1961. "The Strategy of Protest: Problems of Negro Civic Action." *Journal of Conflict Resolution* 5 (3): 291–303.

Wilson, William Julius. 1980. *The Declining Significance of Race: Blacks and Changing American Institutions,* 2d ed. Chicago: University of Chicago Press.

——. 1987. *The Truly Disadvantaged: The Inner City, the Underclass, and Public Policy.* Chicago: University of Chicago Press.

——. 1991. "Public Policy Research and the Truly Disadvantaged." In *The Urban Underclass,* edited by Christopher Jencks and Paul E. Peterson. Washington, D.C.: The Brookings Institution.

Winant, Howard. 1994. *Racial Conditions: Politics, Theory, Comparisons.* Minneapolis: University of Minnesota Press.

Wohlstetter, Albert, and Roberta. 1969. " 'Third Worlds' Abroad and at Home." *Public Interest* 14: 88–107.

Woldemikael, Tekle Mariam. 1989. *Becoming Black American: Haitians and American Institutions in Evanston, Illinois.* New York: AMS.

Woliver, Laura. 1990. "A Measure of Justice: Police Conduct and Black Civil Rights." *Western Political Quarterly* 43 (2): 415–36.

Wong, Eugene F. 1985. "Asian American Middleman Minority Theory: The Framework of an American Myth." *Journal of Ethnic Studies* 13 (1): 51–88.

Wright, Lawrence. 1994. "One Drop of Blood." *New Yorker.* July 25.

Yi, Jeongduk. 1993. "Social Order and Contest in Meanings and Power: Black Boycotts Against Korean Shopkeepers in Poor New York City Neighborhoods." Ph.D. diss., City University of New York.

Yoon, In-Jin. 1997. *On My Own: Korean Businesses and Race Relations in America.* Chicago: University of Chicago Press.

Young, Phillip K. Y. 1983. "Family Labor, Sacrifice and Competition: Korean Greengrocers in New York City." *Amerasia* 10 (2): 53–71.

Young, Stacey. 1997. *Changing the World: Discourse, Politics, and the Feminist Movement.* New York: Routledge.

Young, Whitney M., Jr. 1965. "The Urban League and Its Strategy." *Annals of the American Academy of Political and Social Science* 357: 102–07.

Yu, Eui-Young, ed. 1994. *Black-Korean Encounter: Toward Understanding and Alliance.* Los Angeles: CSU Institute for Asian American and Pacific Asian Studies.

Yu, J. 1980. *The Korean Merchants in the Black Community: Their Relations and Conflicts with Strategies for Conflict Resolution and Prevention.* Elkins Park, Penn.: Philip Jaisohn Memorial Foundation.

Zald, Mayer N. 1987. "The Future of Social Movements." In *Social Movements in an Organizational Society,* edited by Mayer N. Zald and John D. McCarthy. New Brunswick, N.J.: Transaction.

——, and Bert Useem. 1987. "Movement and Countermovement Interaction: Mobilization, Tactics, and State Involvement." In *Social Movements in an Organizational Society,* edited by Mayer N. Zald and John D. McCarthy. New Brunswick, N.J.: Transaction.

——. 1996. "Culture, Ideology, and Strategic Framing." In *Comparative Perspectives on Social Movements,* edited by Doug McAdam et al. New York: Cambridge University Press.

Zenner, Walter P. 1980. "Middleman Minority Theories: A Critical Review." In *Sourcebook on the New Immigration: Implications for the United States and the International Community,* edited by Roy Simon Bryce-Laporte. New Brunswick, N.J.: Transaction.

——. 1991. *Minorities in the Middle: A Cross-Cultural Analysis.* Albany: SUNY Press.

Zéphir, Flore. 1996. *Haitian Immigrants in Black America: A Sociological and Sociolinguistic Portrait.* Westport, Conn.: Bergin & Garvey.

INDEX